Preface

IN 1945 THE American and British armies captured the archives of the German Foreign Office which had been evacuated from Berlin. Use of the archives for intelligence purposes began immediately. Later, it became evident that the documents concerning the aims and methods of German foreign policy should be published for the enlightenment of world opinion, including German opinion.

In June 1946 the Department of State and the British Foreign Office agreed to sponsor jointly the publication of approximately twenty volumes of documents illustrative of German foreign policy from 1918 to 1945. The French Government subsequently became a party to this agreement. The documents were to be printed in the original German, and the more important were also to be printed in English translation. It was agreed that the selection and editing were to be performed on the basis of the highest scholarly objectivity and that, to secure an authoritative and scholarly documentary record of German foreign policy, the services of private scholars should be enlisted, as well as the services of scholars in government service. Each Government reserved the right to publish separately any portion of the documents.

The Department of State has decided to publish separately the most significant documents bearing on German-Soviet relations during 1939–1941. This collection has been made by the Washington editors of the documents, Raymond James Sontag and James Stuart Beddie, assisted by Jean Brownell Dulaney.

Editors' Foreword

THE EDITORS have selected for publication at this time all documents essential to an understanding of the political relations between Nazi Germany and the Soviet Union from the first efforts to reach an agreement in the spring of 1939 to the outbreak of war in June 1941. The larger publication sponsored by the American, British, and French Governments will include additional details, as well as documents which throw light incidentally on Russo-German relations, but which are concerned with other subjects. The lengthy agreements defining frontiers, and the bulky details of economic relations, have been left to the larger publication. Documents summarizing economic negotiations have, however, been included. Each document has been printed in full, without omissions or alterations.

The translations, except for a few prepared by the editors, were made by the Central Translating Division of the Department of State, and revised by the editors.

The editors have had complete independence in their work and final responsibility for the selection of relevant documents.

RAYMOND JAMES SONTAG
JAMES STUART BEDDIE

NAZI-SOVIET
RELATIONS

1939-1941

Documents from the Archives of
The German Foreign Office

Edited by
RAYMOND JAMES SONTAG
and
JAMES STUART BEDDIE

GREENWOOD PRESS, PUBLISHERS
WESTPORT, CONNECTICUT

Library of Congress Cataloging in Publication Data

Germany. Auswärtiges Amt.
  Nazi-Soviet relations, 1939-1941.

  Reprint of the 1948 ed. published by the U. S. Dept.
of State, Washington, which was issued as no. 3023 of
its Publication.
  1. World War, 1939-1945—Diplomatic history—
Sources. 2. Germany—Foreign relations—Russia.
3. Russia—Foreign relations—Germany. 4. Russo-German
Treaty, 1939. I. Sontag, Raymond James, 1897-1972.
II. Beddie, James Stuart. III. Title. IV. Series:
United States. Dept. of State. Publication ; 3023.
D751.G46 1976   940.53'24'43   75-35371
ISBN 0-8371-8612-9

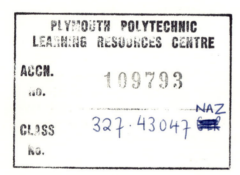
Originally published in 1948 by United States Government
Printing Office, for the Department of State, Washington

Reprinted in 1976 by Greenwood Press,
a division of Williamhouse-Regency Inc.

Library of Congress Catalog Card Number 75-35371

ISBN 0-8371-8612-9

Printed in the United States of America

CONTENTS

LIST OF PRINCIPAL PERSONS

ALFIERI, Dino, Italian Ambassador in Germany

ASTAKHOV, Georgei, Counselor of Embassy of the Soviet Embassy in Germany

BECK, Josef, Polish Minister of Foreign Affairs

BLÜCHER, Dr. Wipert, German Minister in Finland

CIANO, Count Galeazzo, Italian Minister of Foreign Affairs

CRIPPS, Sir Stafford, British Ambassador in the Soviet Union

DEKANOSOV, Vladimir G., Deputy People's Commissar for Foreign Affairs of the Soviet Union, later Soviet Ambassador in Germany

GAUS, Dr. Friedrich Wilhelm, Under State Secretary, Head of the Legal Division of the German Foreign Office

GÖRING, Hermann, Reichsmarshal, Reich Air Minister and Commander-in-Chief of the Air Force

GRUNDHERR, Dr. von, Minister, Head of the Baltic and Scandinavian Section of the Political Division of the German Foreign Office

HENCKE, Andor, Under State Secretary in the German Foreign Office

HEWEL, Walter, Representative of the Reich Foreign Minister on the staff of the Führer

HILGER, Gustav, Counselor of Legation, later Counselor of Embassy in the German Embassy in the Soviet Union

HITLER, Adolf, Führer of the German Reich and Supreme Commander of the Armed Forces

JODL, Major General Alfred, Chief of Operations Staff (*Wehrmachtführungsstab*) of the German High Command

KEITEL, Marshal Wilhelm, Chief of the High Command of the Armed Forces (*OKW*)

KOLLONTAY, Alexandra, Soviet Minister in Sweden

KÖSTRING, Lieut. General Ernst, Military Attaché of the German Embassy in the Soviet Union

LITVINOV, Maxim, Soviet Commissar for Foreign Affairs to May 3, 1939

MACKENSEN, Hans Georg von, German Ambassador in Italy

MATSUOKA, Yosuke, Japanese Foreign Minister

MEISSNER, Dr. Otto, Minister of State and Head of the Presidential Chancellery (*Praesidialkanzlei*)

MEREKALOV, Alexei, Soviet Ambassador in Germany

MIKOYAN, Anastas I., Soviet Commissar for Foreign Trade; Deputy Chairman of the Council of People's Commissars

MOLOTOV, Vyacheslav M., Chairman, later Deputy Chairman of the Council of People's Commissars of the Soviet Union; Commissar for Foreign Affairs from May 3, 1939

MUSSOLINI, Benito, Head of the Italian Government

OSHIMA, Hiroshi, Japanese Ambassador in Germany

OTT, General Eugen, German Ambassador in Japan

PAPEN, Franz von, German Ambassador in Turkey

POTEMKIN, Vladimir, Soviet Deputy Commissar for Foreign Affairs

RAEDER, Grand Admiral Erich, Commander-in-Chief of the German Navy

RIBBENTROP, Joachim von, Reich Foreign Minister

RITTER, Dr. Karl, Ambassador on special assignment in the German Foreign Office, in charge of economic warfare questions

ROSSO, Augusto, Italian Ambassador in the Soviet Union

SCHLIEP, Dr., Counselor of Legation, Head of the Eastern European Section of the Political Division of the German Foreign Office.

SCHMIDT, Dr. Paul Otto Gustav, Minister, Chief of the Bureau of the Reich Foreign Minister, interpreter in diplomatic negotiations

SCHNURRE, Dr. Karl, Counselor of Legation, later Minister, Head of the Eastern European and Baltic Section of the Commercial Policy Division of the German Foreign Office

SCHULENBURG, Friedrich Werner, Count von der, German Ambassador in the Soviet Union

SCHWERIN-KROSIGK, Lutz, Count von, Reich Finance Minister

SHKVARTSEV, Alexander, Soviet Ambassador in Germany

SKIRPA, Kazys, Lithuanian Minister in Germany

SOBOLEV, Arkady A., General Secretary of the Soviet Commissariat for Foreign Affairs

STALIN, Josef, Chairman of the Council of People's Commissars of the Soviet Union

STEINHARDT, Laurence A., United States Ambassador in the Soviet Union

STRANG, Sir William, Head of British Mission to the Soviet Union

TIPPELSKIRCH, Werner von, Counselor of Embassy, later Minister in the German Embassy in the Soviet Union

VISHINSKY, Andrei, Deputy Commissar for Foreign Affairs of the Soviet Union

WARLIMONT, General Walter, Deputy Chief of the Operations Staff (*Wehrmachtführungsstab*) of the German High Command (*OKW*)

WEIZSÄCKER, Ernst, Baron von, State Secretary in the German Foreign Office

WIEHL, Emil Karl Josef, Ministerialdirektor, Head of the Commercial Policy Division of the German Foreign Office

WOERMANN, Dr. Ernst, Under State Secretary, Head of the Political Division of the German Foreign Office

WUORIMAA, Aarne, Finnish Minister in Germany

ANALYTICAL LIST OF DOCUMENTS

I. Tentative Efforts to Improve German-Soviet Relations, April 17–
August 14, 1939

I. Tentative Efforts to Improve German-Soviet Relations, April 17–
August 14, 1939—Continued

II. AGREEMENT ACHIEVED, AUGUST 14–AUGUST 23, 1939—Continued

III. The Pact Executed and Amended, August 23–September 28, 1939—Continued

III. The Pact Executed and Amended, August 23–September 28, 1939—
Continued

III. THE PACT EXECUTED AND AMENDED, AUGUST 23–SEPTEMBER 28, 1939—
Continued

IV. GERMAN-SOVIET COOPERATION, OCTOBER 2, 1939–MAY 29, 1940—Continued

IV. GERMAN-SOVIET COOPERATION, OCTOBER 2, 1939–MAY 29, 1940—Continued

V. Friction in the Baltic and the Balkans, June 4–September 21, 1940—
Continued

VI. The U.S.S.R. and the Three Power Pact, September 25–November 26, 1940—Continued

VII. Soviet Resistance to the German Advance in the Balkans, December
18, 1940–March 13, 1941—Continued

VIII. THE SOVIET TREATIES WITH JUGOSLAVIA AND JAPAN, MARCH 25–APRIL 13,
1941—Continued

IX. The Failure of Efforts to Preserve Peace, April 15–June 22, 1941

IX. The Failure of Efforts to Preserve Peace, April 15–June 22, 1941—Continued

IX. The Failure of Efforts to Preserve Peace, April 15–June 22, 1941—Continued

I. TENTATIVE EFFORTS TO IMPROVE GERMAN-SOVIET RELATIONS, APRIL 17–AUGUST 14, 1939

Frames 231609–231610, serial 485

Memorandum by the State Secretary in the German Foreign Office (Weizsäcker)

St. S. Nr. 339   BERLIN, April 17, 1939.

The Russian Ambassador visited me today—for the first time since he took up his post here [1]—for a conversation on practical matters. He dwelt at length on a subject which he said was of particular interest to him: namely, the fulfillment of certain contracts for war matériel by the Skoda Works. Although the items involved are manifestly rather insignificant, the Ambassador regarded the fulfillment of the contracts as a test, to determine whether, in accordance with a recent statement by Director Wiehl [2] to him, we were really willing to cultivate and expand our economic relations with Russia. The matter of these supply contracts is being looked into elsewhere.

Toward the end of the discussion, I casually mentioned to the Ambassador that even granted goodwill on our part, a favorable atmosphere for the delivery of war materials to Soviet Russia was not exactly being created at present by reports of a Russian-British-French air pact and the like. Herr Merekalov seized on these words to take up political matters. He inquired as to the opinion here regarding the present situation in Central Europe. When I told him that as far as I knew Germany was the only country not participating in the present saber-rattling in Europe, he asked me about our relations with Poland and about the alleged military clashes on the German-Polish frontier. After I had denied the latter and made some rather restrained comments on German-Polish relations, the Russian asked me frankly [*unverblümt*] what I thought of German-Russian relations.

I replied to Herr Merekalov that, as everybody knew, we had always had the desire for mutually satisfactory commercial relations with Russia. It had appeared to me that the Russian press lately was not fully participating in the anti-German tone of the American and some

---

[1] Ambassador Merekalov had presented his credentials on June 5, 1938.
[2] Head of the Commercial Policy Division of the German Foreign Office.

1

of the English papers. As to the German press, Herr Merekalov could form his own opinion, since he surely followed it very closely.

The Ambassador thereupon stated approximately as follows:

Russian policy had always moved in a straight line. Ideological differences of opinion had hardly influenced the Russian-Italian relationship, and they did not have to prove a stumbling block with regard to Germany either. Soviet Russia had not exploited the present friction between Germany and the Western democracies against us, nor did she desire to do so. There exists for Russia no reason why she should not live with us on a normal footing. And from normal, the relations might become better and better.

With this remark, to which the Russian had led the conversation, Herr Merekalov ended the interview. He intends to go to Moscow in the next few days for a visit.

WEIZSÄCKER

Frame 111301, serial 103

The German Chargé in the Soviet Union (Tippelskirch) to the German Foreign Office

Telegram

No. 61 of May 4   Moscow, May 4, 1939—8 : 45 p. m.
                                   Received May 4, 1939—10 p. m.

Appointment of Molotov as Foreign Commissar simultaneously retaining his position as Chairman of the Council of People's Commissars is published as ukase of the Presidium of the Supreme Soviet of May 3 by Soviet press with great fanfare. Dismissal of Litvinov appears on last page as small notice under "Chronicle." Sudden change has caused greatest surprise here, since Litvinov was in the midst of negotiations with the English delegation, at the May Day Parade still appeared on the reviewing stand right next to Stalin, and there was no recent concrete evidence of shakiness in his position. Soviet press contains no comments. Foreign Commissariat is giving press representatives no explanations.

Since Litvinov had received the English Ambassador as late as May 2 and had been named in press of yesterday as guest of honor at the parade, his dismissal appears to be result of spontaneous decision by Stalin. The decision apparently is connected with the fact that differences of opinion arose in the Kremlin on Litvinov's negotiations. Reason for differences of opinion presumably lies in deep mistrust that Stalin harbors toward the entire surrounding capitalist world. At last Party Congress Stalin urged caution lest Soviet Union be drawn into conflicts. Molotov (no Jew) is held to be "most intimate friend and closest collaborator" of Stalin. His appointment is apparently to guarantee that the foreign policy will be continued strictly in accordance with Stalin's ideas.

TIPPELSKIRCH

Frame 211496, serial 388

Foreign Office Memorandum

To W IV 1493

This afternoon I asked the Soviet Chargé, Counselor of Embassy Astakhov, to come to see me and informed him that we had agreed, as requested by his Ambassador on April 17, to carry out the Soviet supply contracts with the Skoda Works. Appropriate instructions had already been given. I asked him to inform his Government of this.

Counselor of Embassy Astakhov was visibly gratified at this declaration and stressed the fact that for the Soviet Government the material side of the question was not of as great importance as the question of principle. He inquired whether we would not soon resume the negotiations which had been broken off in February. To this I replied that I could not yet give him any answer to that, as the examination of the numerous problems which the last Russian answer had raised was not yet completed.

Then Astakhov touched upon the dismissal of Litvinov and tried without asking direct questions to learn whether this event would cause a change in our position toward the Soviet Union. He stressed very much the great importance of the personality of Molotov, who was by no means a specialist in foreign policy, but who would have all the greater importance for the future Soviet foreign policy.

SCHNURRE

BERLIN, May 5, 1939.

Frame 211486, serial 388

Foreign Office Memorandum

MINUTE

The Counselor of the Russian Embassy, Astakhov, called on me this afternoon in order to introduce to me the Tass representative,

Filipov, who had just arrived. He began with the statement that he was happy that Herr Filipov could start his work under new conditions which were completely different from the past. The recently practiced reserve of the German press toward Soviet Russia had already attracted the attention of the foreign press. I for my part remarked that at the present time one could not talk about a corresponding Russian reserve toward Germany and pointed out the latest broadcasts of the Moscow Radio. To this Herr Astakhov remarked that Moscow apparently still was rather suspicious because, of course, they did not yet know how this reserve was to be interpreted, which was, after all, possibly only a short-lived tactical maneuver. At any rate, the Soviet Russians would be only too happy if such fears were unjustified.

Asked about the significance of the change in the direction of foreign affairs in Moscow, Herr Astakhov declared that previously it had, after all, not been a question of a personal policy of Litvinov, but of compliance with general principles. Therefore, for the time being one could not speak of a reorientation of policy, particularly since Soviet Russian policy depended on that of the others and not least on that of Germany.

BRAUN V. STUMM

BERLIN, May 9, 1939.

Frames 211504-211505, serial 388

Foreign Office Memorandum

To W IV 1870/39

MEMORANDUM

The Soviet Chargé, Counselor of Embassy Astakhov, called on me today in order to talk to me about the legal status of the Soviet Trade Mission in Prague, established there on the basis of the Soviet-Czechoslovak Trade Agreement of 1935. The Soviet Union wants to leave the Trade Mission in Prague as a section of the Soviet Trade Mission in Berlin, and requests that it be given temporarily the same legal status that it had under the Soviet-Czechoslovak Trade Agreement. Herr Astakhov invoked the German declaration, according to which the present Czechoslovak trade agreements would continue to be applied to the Protectorate of Bohemia and Moravia until something new had replaced them.

I received this request and promised an early answer. I told him as my personal opinion that there would hardly be any objections to the Soviet request.

During the subsequent conversation Astakhov again referred in great detail to the development of German-Soviet relations, as he had already done two weeks ago. He remarked that the German press for some weeks looked entirely different. The attacks hitherto directed against the Soviet Union were missing, reports were objective; in an industrial newspaper of the Rhineland he had even seen some photographs of Soviet installations. Of course, the Soviets could not judge whether this was only a temporary break that was used for tactical reasons. However, it was hoped that a permanent state of affairs would result from it. Astakhov stated in detail that there were no conflicts in foreign policy between Germany and Soviet Russia, and that therefore there was no reason for any enmity between the two countries. It was true that in the Soviet Union there was a distinct feeling of being menaced by Germany. It would undoubtedly be possible to eliminate this feeling of being menaced and the distrust in Moscow. During this conversation, he also again mentioned the Treaty of Rapallo. In reply to my incidental question, he commented on the Anglo-Soviet negotiations to the effect that under the present circumstances the result desired by England would hardly be achieved.

To substantiate his opinion concerning the possibility of a change in German-Soviet relations, Astakhov repeatedly referred to Italy and stressed that the Duce, even after the creation of the Axis, had implied that there were no obstacles to a normal development of the political and economic relations between the Soviet Union and Italy.

In my replies I was reserved and induced Astakhov, by means of incidental remarks only, to further elaborate his viewpoint.

SCHNURRE

BERLIN, May 17, 1939.

Frames 111353–111355, serial 103

Memorandum by the German Ambassador in the Soviet Union
(Schulenburg)

Tgb. Nr. A/1023   Moscow, May 20, 1939.

This afternoon at 4:00, I was received by the Chairman of the Council of People's Commissars and Commissar for Foreign Affairs Molotov. The interview took place in the Commissariat for Foreign Affairs. It lasted over an hour and was carried on in most friendly fashion. Herr Molotov, who speaks only Russian, had requested that no translator be brought along since he himself would provide an excellent interpreter. The latter, a rather young man, translated very correctly but slowly from the French. That explains in part the long duration of the conference.

I opened the conversation by saying to Herr Molotov that the last proposals of Herr Mikoyan in our economic negotiations had presented several difficulties which could not be immediately removed. We now believed that a way had been found to come to an understanding and we intended in the very near future to send Geheimrat Dr. Schnurre to Moscow to discuss with Herr Mikoyan whether an agreement could be reached on the basis of our proposals. I asked whether Herr Mikoyan was prepared to confer with Herr Schnurre.

Herr Molotov replied that the course of our last economic negotiations had given the Soviet Government the impression that we had not been in earnest in the matter and we had only played at negotiating for political reasons. At first it had been reported that a German delegation was coming for economic negotiations to Moscow (I suggested that this report did not emanate from us but from the Polish and French press), and later it was to the effect that Herr Schnurre was coming alone. Herr Schnurre did not come, but Herr Hilger [3] and I had conducted the negotiations and then these negotiations also had faded out. The Soviet Government could only agree to a resumption of the negotiations if the necessary "political bases" for them had been constructed [*wenn hierfür die notwendige "politische Grundlage" geschaffen sein werde.*].

I told Herr Molotov that we had never regarded the economic discussions as a game, but we had always conducted them entirely in earnest. We always had had and still have the sincerest intention to come to an agreement, and Berlin was of the opinion, if I understood it correctly, that a successful conclusion of the economic discussions would also help the political atmosphere. It had been technical reasons only that had been responsible for Herr Schnurre's absence and for the delay of the negotiations. The present economic conditions in Germany made it very difficult to fulfill the wishes of Herr Mikoyan. I asked Herr Molotov what he meant by the construction of political bases. I had had the impression that the German-Soviet atmosphere had improved during the last year or so, and I was astonished that economic negotiations should now be impossible while previously negotiations of the same sort had repeatedly taken place under more

[3] Of the staff of the German Embassy in Moscow.

unfavorable conditions and had been brought to a conclusion. Herr Molotov then declared that the way in which better political bases could be built was something that both Governments would have to think about. All of my determined efforts to bring Herr Molotov to make his wishes more definite and more concrete were in vain. Herr Molotov had apparently determined to say just so much and not a word more. He is known for this somewhat stubborn manner. I thereupon concluded the conversation and stated that I would inform my Government. Herr Molotov then bade me farewell in a very friendly fashion.

Immediately at the conclusion of my visit to Herr Molotov, I visited Herr Potemkin. I related to him the course of my conversation with the Chairman of the Council of People's Commissars, and I added that I had unfortunately not been able to find out from the conversation what Herr Molotov actually wanted. He certainly must have had something in mind. I asked Herr Potemkin to find out whether he could not possibly let me know what direction Herr Molotov's line of thought was taking. I gave the impression that I did not know at all what I should suggest to my Government. Nothing could be changed in the main lines of German policy. Thus, in my opinion, we would persevere in our East Asia policy. I could, however, add that this policy was in no way directed against the Soviet Union.

COUNT VON DER SCHULENBURG

Frame 111328, serial 103

The State Secretary in the German Foreign Office (Weizsäcker) to the German Ambassador in the Soviet Union (Schulenburg)

Telegram

No. 94   BERLIN, May 21, 1939.

Reference your telegram 73.[4] For Ambassador personally.

On basis of results so far of your discussions with Molotov, we must now sit tight [*ganz stillzuhalten*] and wait to see if the Russians will speak more openly.

I request that you act accordingly until otherwise instructed, but to wire from time to time any useful reports and news reaching you as well as your appraisal of the situation.

WEIZSÄCKER

---

[4] Not printed; it summarized interview between Schulenburg and Molotov described in preceding document.

Frames 111346–111347, serial 103

The German Ambassador in the Soviet Union (Schulenburg) to the State Secretary in the German Foreign Office (Weizsäcker)

Tgb. Nr. A/1023   Moscow, May 22, 1939.

DEAR HERR VON WEIZSÄCKER: I have the honor to transmit to you as an enclosure a copy of the memorandum [5] which gives the content and course of my interview with Herr Molotov on May 20. I have also included the memorandum with my report.

The Reich Minister directed me to maintain extreme caution in my conference with Molotov. As a result I contented myself with saying as little as possible and took this attitude all the more because the attitude of Herr Molotov seemed to me quite suspicious [*recht verdächtig*]. It cannot be understood otherwise than that the resumption of our economic negotiations does not satisfy him as a political gesture, and that he apparently wants to obtain from us more extensive proposals of a political nature. We must be extremely cautious in this field as long as it is not certain that possible proposals from our side will not be used by the Kremlin only to exert pressure on England and France. On the other hand, if we want to accomplish something here, it is unavoidable that we sooner or later take some action.

It is extraordinarily difficult here to learn anything at all about the course of the English-French-Soviet negotiations. My British colleague, who apparently is the only one who is active in that connection here (he was being announced to Herr Potemkin when I was visiting the latter), preserves an iron silence. Even neutral diplomats have not been able to learn anything.

My French colleague has been away for some time. The Counselor of Embassy and Chargé in the last few days asked us for a transit visa, so that it seems that he also is going to leave Moscow soon. If the reports are correct that France will now take over the negotiations in the matter of the French-British-Soviet "alliance," these negotiations may well take place not here but in Paris.

My Italian colleague is of the opinion that the Soviet Union will surrender her freedom of negotiation only if England and France give her a full treaty of alliance.

It is often stated here (I do not know whether it is correct) that one of the principal reasons for the hesitation of England in accepting the Soviet proposals for a military alliance is the question of Japan. London is afraid of driving the Japanese into our arms if she guar-

---

[5] *Ante,* p. 5.

antees the defense of all Soviet frontiers.   If Japan should come into our arms voluntarily, this consideration for England should be eliminated.

With best greetings and Heil Hitler, I am, Herr von Weizsäcker, yours very respectfully,

SCHULENBURG

Frames 178396–178397, serial 276

The State Secretary in the German Foreign Office (Weizsäcker) to the German Ambassador in the Soviet Union (Schulenburg)

BERLIN, May 27, 1939.

DEAR COUNT SCHULENBURG: We answered your letter of the 22d in our telegram of yesterday,[6] which will probably surprise you less than Herr Hilger, who was at hand at the birth of a very different sort of instruction.   I feel that I still owe you a word of explanation.   We are of the opinion here that the English-Russian combination certainly will not be easy to prevent.   However, there may even today be a rather wide field of negotiation into which we may be able to inject ourselves with an impeding and disturbing effect by use of a more unmistakable sort of language.   The possibility of success is considered here to be quite limited, so that one must weigh whether a very open statement in Moscow, instead of being beneficial, might not rather be harmful and perhaps produce a peal of Tartar laughter.   In weighing these points of view, it had also to be considered that one link in the whole chain, namely, a gradual conciliation between Moscow and Tokyo, is regarded by the Japanese as distinctly problematical.   Rome also was very hesitant, so that eventually the disadvantages of the proposed far-reaching step were regarded as the determining factor.   In short, we will remain within the instructions which we have sent to you, and we now want to see how deeply Moscow on the one hand and Paris–London on the other are willing to pledge themselves to each other.

Your reports and judgments of the situation are naturally most welcome here at all times.

Our inquiries about the return here of the Soviet Russian Ambassador, Merekalov, are only of significance in relation to the future moves at the Kremlin.

Heartiest greetings and best wishes.

Heil Hitler!

Always yours faithfully,   WEIZSÄCKER

---

[6] Telegram not printed.

P. S.   Berlin, May 30, 1939.

To my lines above I must add that now, with the consent of the Führer, a distinctly limited exchange of views with the Russians will take place by means of a conference which I am to hold today with the Russian Chargé. You will, of course, be officially informed of developments. I need, therefore, not go more deeply into the matter here.   W.

Frames 111372–111374, serial 103

Foreign Office Memorandum [7]

MAY 29, 1939.

1. We are faced with the fact that our Ambassador in Moscow had a talk with Herr Molotov about the resumption of German-Soviet commercial negotiations and that on this occasion Herr Molotov made them subject to the clarification of political relations between Germany and Soviet Russia. Of course we ask ourselves whether Herr Molotov wanted to express thereby a desire that a talk get under way concerning the political relations between us, or whether he wanted this considered simply as a form of rejection.

2. You yourself as well as their Ambassador occasionally have indicated possibilities of some day discussing the political relations between Germany and the Soviet Union, and we ask ourselves whether this is in harmony with Molotov's views or whether we are dealing here with different points of view of their Embassy here and their Foreign Commissariat.

3. If they should have the desire to have a political conversation with us, I personally can imagine this as entirely possible. I would consider as a condition that the aggressive promotion of the idea of world revolution no longer be an element in the present Soviet foreign policy. [Marginal notation: "mutually not to interfere in domestic politics in any way, for . . ."] If this condition is met—as certain signs might indicate—I could imagine that such a conversation could lead to useful results in the direction of a progressive normalization of German-Soviet Russian relations. [Marginal notation: "Ukraine."]

4. It is admittedly very doubtful whether the state of affairs in Europe just at the moment promises success from such talks, since the Soviet Government is engaged in negotiations with England, which indicate that Moscow is more or less determined to enter actively

---

[7] This and the following document are apparently a series of proposals submitted by Ribbentrop to Hitler.

into the English policy of encirclement. However, it is, of course, up to your Government [marginal note: "ice-cold"] to judge whether at this stage in the Anglo-Soviet negotiations, it still sees room for such a conversation with Germany.

[Penciled notation: "spare myself the reproach of not having spoken up."] [8]

Frames 111368–111371, serial 103

Foreign Office Memorandum

SECRET

I suggest that the request of the Soviet Embassy in Berlin for permission for the further maintenance of the Soviet Russian commercial agency in Prague as a branch of the Russian commercial agency in Berlin be used as the occasion for the following statement, to be made by Herr von Weizsäcker to the Russian representative in Berlin.

1. The question of the continued maintenance of the Russian commercial agency in Prague is one of principle. For that reason the Minister believed that in this matter he could not make a decision on his own responsibility and presented the matter to the Führer.

2. The German Reich Government would like to know whether the Soviet Government wishes to consider the maintenance of its commercial agency in Prague on a permanent basis or whether it has only a limited period in mind. What, in the latter case, would be the time limit?

3. It is not easy for the German Reich Government, under the present circumstances, to consent at all to the maintenance of this Russian commercial agency, even as a branch of the Berlin office. To its last suggestion particularly, of taking up direct commercial negotiations with Moscow, it received an answer in Moscow from which it believes it must infer that the Soviet Government is at present very little interested in resuming and strengthening German-Russian commercial relations. There is, in addition, the development of the foreign policy of the Soviet Union, which also calls for caution on the part of the German Reich Government with respect to the examination and granting of special Soviet Russian wishes, such as in this case of the Prague commercial agency. For the Reich Government has no doubt that Russia seems to be inclined actively to support the British policy of encirclement directed against Germany. The Reich Government, therefore, for its part, too, in its own understandable interest, considers a clarification of this development as the necessary condition for the granting of special concessions. But above all, as stressed in

---

[8] The penciled notations appear to be notes by State Secretary von Weizsäcker for his conversation with the Russian Chargé on May 30, *post*, p. 12.

point 2, it would be important to know for how long, under those circumstances, the Soviet Government requests permission for the continuance of its commercial agency in Prague.

Frames 111362-111367, serial 103

Memorandum by the State Secretary in the German Foreign Office (Weizsäcker)

STRICTLY SECRET   BERLIN, May 30, 1939.
St. S. Nr. 455

The Soviet Russian Chargé called on me this morning at my request. I designated as our subject of conversation the Soviet Russian request to continue accrediting their trade mission in Prague as a branch office of the trade mission in Berlin. In my subsequent remarks, which the Chargé interrupted by occasional objections, I adhered strictly to the instructions given to me.

First, I told the Chargé that the request of the Russian Government involved a matter of principle, and that for this reason the Foreign Minister had dealt with it. Herr von Ribbentrop had presented the matter to the Führer. At this point the attention of the Chargé was aroused, and he made sure by asking me again whether the Führer had really dealt with the matter.

I then continued that we would like to know whether the trade mission in Prague was to be retained permanently or only temporarily, and for what length of time. To this the Chargé immediately replied that he personally could only state that there was still much work to be done in order to complete current business in the Protectorate, but that his Government had probably been thinking of a permanent status.

In accordance with instructions I then went on to state that it would not be easy for us to give our consent to the retention of the trade mission in Prague, because we, i. e., Ambassador Count Schulenburg, had recently received from Herr Molotov a not very encouraging reply in the matter of our economic relations. The Chargé indicated that he was informed of the contents of the talk, and pending more detailed instructions interpreted it to the effect that in Moscow they wanted to avoid a repetition of what happened last January, i. e., they did not want to make preparations again for the trip of a German trade negotiator to Moscow only to receive a cancellation at the last moment, amidst the ridicule of the foreign press. Actually, Herr Molotov had stated that politics and economy could not be entirely separated in our relations; a certain connection between the two did actually exist. Apparently Potemkin in his communication to the Chargé here expressed the matter this way: that the contemplated trade negotiations could not be treated lightly.

After we had exchanged a few more words to clarify the incident of last January, I told the Chargé that I agreed with him that economics and politics could not be entirely separated from each other. It was for this very reason that I was having the conversation with him, because the British efforts to draw Russia into her sphere— efforts of which we were informed—indicated a political orientation in Moscow of which we would have to take account, even in considering less important problems, such as the Soviet Russian trade mission in Prague. I returned therefore to the question raised at the beginning of our conversation—namely, what length of time the Soviet Government would propose for the business of its trade mission in Prague.

The Chargé concluded from this part of the conversation that he would have to inquire again in Moscow as to what intentions they actually had for the trade mission in Prague and, furthermore, what Foreign Commissar Molotov actually meant to tell Count Schulenburg. The Chargé was willing to say on his own account that Herr Molotov had, to be sure, talked with the customary Russian distrust, but not with the intention of barring further German-Russian discussions.

After the discussion had reached this point I reminded the Chargé of certain conversations which he himself had conducted in the Office and above all of the statements of his Ambassador, now absent from Berlin, who told me in the middle of April of the possibility of a normalization and even further improvement of German-Russian political relations. From this point the conversation proceeded spontaneously and I changed over to a purely conversational tone and put aside paper and pencil.

I here reminded the Chargé of the remarks of his Ambassador about the more reserved language of the press on both sides in the last few months. I mentioned that to my knowledge the topic of Soviet Russia had receded into the background in official German speeches of recent months—which the Chargé confirmed but held that it could be interpreted in different ways. Finally I told the Chargé that the development of our relations with Poland, which was known to him, had actually made our hitherto restricted policy in the East freer.

After some concurring remarks by the Chargé, I told him that I personally thought the German position toward Soviet Russia was as follows: Germany was not narrow-minded, but she was not officious either. Among our German political merchandise, however, *one* item did not exist, namely a special liking for Communism. We had dealt with Communists in short order and we would continue to do so; moreover, we did not expect any special liking for National Socialism in Moscow either. At this point the Chargé interrupted with explanations as to how Russian relations with Italy and particularly Turkey, as well as other countries could be normal or even very good, although in those countries Communism was not favored at all. He strongly emphasized the possibility of a very clear distinction between maxims of domestic policy on the one hand and orientation of foreign policy on the other hand.

I then continued with my figure of speech and stated that among our political merchandise there was also a pretty good selection for Russia, ranging from normalization of our relations such as the Russian Ambassador had suggested to me, to unrelenting hostility. Normalization was indeed obstructed by a lot of rubble and I was convinced that many people would even like to pile it higher. The Chargé probably knew that Herr Beck, the Polish Foreign Minister, was also not entirely without his share in this. One could conduct interesting talks with Herr Beck, but he appeared to me to have become a little old, because he sometimes suffered from a regrettable weakness of memory. Thus, for instance, Beck's interpretation of the German policy toward the Ukraine was refuted by the German conduct in the case of the Carpathian Ukraine. However, I did not want to go into these things in detail; I thought that Germany had proved that she could cope with Communism at home; nor did she have any fear in foreign policy. I did not know whether there still was any room at all for a possible gradual normalization of relations between Soviet Russia and Germany, now that Moscow had perhaps already listened to the enticements of London. At any rate, however, since the Chargé and his Ambassador had talked so frankly in the Foreign Ministry, I would like to spare myself the reproach that we on our part had held back and had concealed our position. We did not ask anything from Moscow, we did not desire anything from Moscow, but neither did we want to be told by Moscow at a later date that we had erected between us an impenetrable wall of silence.

The Chargé, who had followed the talk attentively and had contributed to it a number of remarks not mentioned here, stated in conclusion that the ideological barrier between Moscow and Berlin was in reality erected by us. Before our treaty with Poland we had rejected a Russian offer of alliance and until recently there had been little comprehension here of the Russian thesis that foreign and domestic policy did not have to interfere with each other. He believed that his Government had not wavered in this viewpoint and was still faithful to it today. In conclusion the Chargé stated that he would report home about our talk, the second part of which he designated, for his part, as private, and he would request instructions from his Government as to what its real aims were concerning the trade mission in Prague, as well as whether he, the Chargé, had correctly interpreted the Molotov talk as in no way negative [*keineswegs zurückweisendes*].

I did not, of course, ask the Chargé about the state of the Anglo-Russian negotiations; nor did he mention anything about them. However, it cannot be contested that in his remarks today about our political relations he used basically the same language as hitherto and as his Ambassador did in the middle of last April. The Molotov-Schulenburg episode appears to me, therefore, to have been the product of sensitivity and distrust rather than a premeditated rejection.

WEIZSÄCKER

Frames 111375-111378, serial 103

The State Secretary in the German Foreign Office (Weizsäcker) to the German Ambassador in the Soviet Union (Schulenburg)

Telegram

MOST URGENT   BERLIN, May 30, 1939.

No. 101. For the Ambassador.
        For information.

Contrary to the policy previously planned, we have now decided to undertake definite negotiations with the Soviet Union. Accordingly, in the absence of the Ambassador I asked the Chargé, Astakhov, to see me today. The Soviet request for further continuance of their trade mission at Prague as a branch of the trade mission at Berlin provided the starting point of our conversation. Since the Russian request presents a question of policy the Reich Foreign Minister had also been considering it and he had taken the matter up with the Führer. To my inquiry as to whether the maintenance of the trade mission at Prague involved a permanent situation or a continuance over a limited period, the Chargé remarked that in his personal view it seemed most likely that the Soviet Government was thinking of a permanent arrangement. I replied that it would not be an easy matter for us to grant permission for continuance of the trade mission in Prague, since Ambassador Count Schulenburg had just received from Molotov a not very encouraging pronouncement on the subject of the general state of our relations. The Chargé, in the absence of more definite instructions, interpreted the conversation between Count Schulenburg and Molotov, of which he had knowledge, as meaning that at Moscow they wished to avoid a repetition of the course of events of last January. In Molotov's view political and economic matters could not be completely separated in our relationship. Between the two as a matter of fact, there was a definite connection.

After I had cleared up to some extent the events of January, I said to the Chargé that in our opinion also political and economic matters in Russo-German relations could not be entirely separated and I was conferring with him particularly because British efforts to draw Russia into their orbit pointed to a political orientation on the part of Moscow of which we would have to take notice even in relatively minor matters such as that of the trade mission in Prague. I would therefore have to renew my query regarding the length of time the Soviet Union desired the trade mission at Prague. The Chargé at this stage of the conversation stated that he must ask Moscow what the intentions there were regarding the trade mission at Prague and what Foreign Commissar Molotov had intended to say to Count Schulenburg. In his view Molotov had, it was true, spoken with the suspicion customary with the Russians, but not with the intention of putting a check on further Russo-German discussion.

In this connection I recalled to the Chargé certain conversations which he himself had carried on at the Foreign Office and especially statements made to me by the Soviet Ambassador about the middle of April about the possibility of normalization and even further improvement of Russo-German political relations, and at this point I also referred to the more moderate tone of the public statements on both sides for several months past and above all to the fact that the development of our relations with Poland had made our policy in the East, which had previously been hampered, more free. Following indications of agreement on the part of the Chargé, I said that in my personal opinion Germany was not narrow-minded as respects Soviet Russia, but also not importunate. Communism would continue to be rejected by us, while we, on the other hand, expected no affection for National Socialism from Moscow. The Chargé emphasized strongly in that connection the possibility of a very clear separation between principles governing internal policy on the one hand and the attitude adopted in foreign policy on the other. I continued that Russia, in addition to that normalization of our relationship at which the Russian Ambassador had hinted, could choose any course up to unyielding antagonism, even though many people, as, for instance, the Polish Foreign Minister, were interested in hindering such normalization. Beck's interpretation of Germany's Ukranian policy could, however, be best refuted by Germany's conduct in respect to the Carpatho-Ukraine. Whether there was still room for a gradual normalization, after Moscow had, perhaps already, given ear to the enticements of London, I did not know. However, after the Chargé and the Ambassador had made unequivocal statements at the Foreign Office, we wanted to escape the charge that we had kept silent about our own position. We were asking and we wanted nothing from Moscow; however, we did not want Moscow to be able to say to us later that we had erected an impassable wall of silence between us.

The Chargé replied that he believed that his Government was still of the opinion that foreign policy and internal policy need not disturb each other. He would report the conversation and request instructions from his Government both as to its intentions about the trade mission in Prague and as to whether he had correctly interpreted the statements of Molotov as being in no sense a rejection.

I got the impression from the conversation that the statements of Molotov should not be considered an intentional refusal.

Instructions for further treatment of the subject are being held in reserve.

WEIZSÄCKER

Frames 111379–111380, serial 103

The State Secretary in the German Foreign Office (Weizsäcker) to the German Ambassador in the Soviet Union (Schulenburg)

Telegram

VERY URGENT   BERLIN, May 30, 1939.
No. 102

With reference to telegram of today No. 101.

In the light of talk of today with Soviet Chargé here, about which other telegraphic instructions are under way, there are no objections here if Hilger gets in touch with Mikoyan of his own accord and without referring to an order. The fact that Hilger has worked for two and one-half weeks in Berlin with competent authorities on creation of a basis for commercial negotiations with Soviet Union ought to be sufficient occasion to initiate such a talk on his part. However, Hilger would have to confine himself in possible conversation to talking generally of his work here, without repeating the offer to resume negotiations. On the other hand, in view of Soviet sensitivity because of the recall of Schnurre some time ago, he may try to remove doubts of the seriousness of our intentions at that time and at present of expanding economic relations with the Soviet Union. If in this connection the Soviet negotiators touch upon political questions, Hilger is only to point out that political questions were the subject of direct conversation between the State Secretary and the Soviet Chargé and that the political authorities were probably about to clarify the situation further.

If during this talk the Soviets show willingness to resume economic negotiations Hilger could promise to get in touch with Berlin at once.

WEIZSÄCKER

Frames 111398–111401, serial 103

The German Ambassador in the Soviet Union (Schulenburg) to the State Secretary in the German Foreign Office (Weizsäcker) [9]

Moscow, June 5, 1939.

MY DEAR HERR VON WEIZSÄCKER: May I thank you very much for your kind and very interesting letter of the 27th of last month.

It is obvious that Japan would not like to see even the smallest agreement between us and the Soviet Union. The less our pressure becomes upon the western boundary of Russia, the stronger the might of the Soviet Union will make itself felt in Eastern Asia. The Italians really ought to welcome a German-Russian arrangement; they themselves have always avoided clashing with Moscow, and the Reich could take a stronger stand toward France if Poland were kept in check by the Soviet Union, thus relieving our eastern boundary. If the Italians nevertheless are "pretty reserved," the reason may be that they are not pleased to see the importance of the Reich within the Axis increase through an improvement in German-Soviet relations and the resulting automatic increase in our power.

It appears to me that they have gained the impression in Berlin that Herr Molotov had rejected a German-Soviet arrangement during the discussion with me. I have read through my telegram once

---

[9] Marginal notation: "F" [sent to the Führer].

again and compared it with my letter to you and my memorandum. I cannot discover what has given rise to this opinion in Berlin.[10] In reality, the fact is that Herr Molotov almost invited political discussions. Our proposal of conducting only economic negotiations appeared insufficient to him. Of course, there was and is the danger that the Soviet Government will utilize German proposals for pressure on the English and French. Herr Molotov in his speech at once utilized tactically our offer to begin economic negotiations. Caution on our part was and is therefore necessary, but it appears clear to me that no door has been shut and that the way is open for further negotiations.

We have heard and read with the very greatest interest of your conversation with Herr Astakhov. Incidentally, several days after having mailed my last letter to you I had occasion to talk again with Herr Potemkin about Soviet-German relations. I told him that I had racked my brains as to what positive steps could be taken to realize the suggestions of Herr Molotov. There were no points of friction, no controversial issues, between Germany and the Soviet Union. We had no border incidents to eliminate and no dispute to settle. We were asking nothing from the Soviet Union and the Soviet Union nothing from us, apparently. I asked Herr Potemkin, with whom— in private—I can talk much more freely, whether he could now tell me anything about the ideas of Herr Molotov. Herr Potemkin answered this in the negative; unfortunately, he could not add anything to the statements of Herr Molotov, who had spoken for the Soviet Government.[11]

I am curious whether your conversation with Astakhov will help the matter. Herr von Tippelskirch in my opinion was justified in calling attention to the fact that, through our nonaggression treaties with the Baltic countries, Russia has received from us, free of charge, increased security and thereby a German political down payment.

I would like to call attention to the fact that Herr Molotov mentioned in his speech three conditions, which must be met under any circumstances in order to achieve the English-French-Soviet alliance. In none of the three points is it stated that the demands of the Soviet Union refer exclusively to Europe. The Far East is not named, to be sure, but it is not excluded, either. As far as I know, however, Great Britain wants to assume new obligations only in Europe. From this a

---

[10] This sentence underlined and with marginal comment in Ribbentrop's handwriting: "?? Erl [edigt]"—[Taken care of].
[11] This sentence underlined and in margin " !! ".

new controversy may result, if the guarantee of the Baltic countries is achieved. The Soviet Russians are full of distrust toward us, but they do not much trust the democratic powers, either. Distrust is aroused very easily here and, once aroused, can be removed only with great difficulty.

It is significant that Molotov, in speaking of relations with England, did not mention the invitations which the British Government has extended to Mikoyan and recently to Voroshilov, too, following the visit of Mr. Hudson in Moscow.

I learn from a generally reliable source that Herr Potemkin was sent to Ankara in such a hurry in order to prevent Turkey from signing with the English. Herr Potemkin prevented the signature of the treaty, but not the "declaration." The Soviet Government is reported not to be opposed in principle to an English-Turkish agreement, but is said to consider it important that Turkey should not dash ahead, but should act at the same time and in the same manner as the Soviet Union.

The most recent border incidents on the Mongolian–Manchurian frontier seem to have been quite serious. According to Japanese reports, the "Mongols" on May 28 employed one hundred airplanes, forty-two of which the Japanese claim to have shot down. They claim that seventeen airplanes had been shot down previously. I believe that the Soviets are responsible for these serious incidents. They represent aid to China; they are to prevent the Japanese from withdrawing their very strong troop contingents from Manchuria to China.

With most cordial regards and Heil Hitler, I remain, my dear Herr von Weizsäcker,

Yours most respectfully,   SCHULENBURG

Frames 178376–178378, serial 276

Foreign Office Memorandum

BERLIN, June 15, 1939.

The Bulgarian minister called on me today and told me confidentially the following: The Soviet Russian Chargé, with whom he had no intimate relations, called on him yesterday without any apparent reason and stayed with him two hours. The long conversation, of which it could not be ascertained whether it had reflected the personal opinions of Herr Astakhov or the opinions of the Soviet Government, could be summarized approximately as follows:

The Soviet Union faced the present world situation with hesitation.

She was vacillating between three possibilities, namely the conclusion of the pact with England and France, a further dilatory treatment of the pact negotiations, and a *rapprochement* with Germany. This last possibility, with which ideological considerations would not have to become involved, was closest to the desires of the Soviet Union. In addition, there were other points, for instance that the Soviet Union did not recognize the Rumanian possession of Bessarabia. The fear of a German attack, however, either via the Baltic countries or via Rumania was an obstacle. In this connection the Chargé had also referred to *Mein Kampf*. If Germany would declare that she would not attack the Soviet Union or that she would conclude a nonaggression pact with her, the Soviet Union would probably refrain from concluding a treaty with England. However, the Soviet Union did not know what Germany really wanted, aside from certain very vague allusions. Several circumstances also spoke for the second possibility, namely to continue to conduct the pact negotiations with England in a dilatory manner. In this case the Soviet Union would continue to have a free hand in any conflict which might break out.

Herr Draganoff then stated that he had declared to the Soviet Russian Chargé that Germany, in his opinion, could have no aggressive aims against the Soviet Union, and he pointed out that the situation had also changed with respect to other countries, since *Mein Kampf* had been written. He reproached Russia with the fact that she had helped Rumania to the Dobruja, for which the Chargé tried to lay the blame exclusively on the Tsarist Government.

At the end Herr Draganoff repeated again that he had no indications why Herr Astakhov had given him this information. He was pondering the possibility that this was probably done with the intention of having Herr Draganoff report it to us.

WOERMANN

Frames 111436–111440, serial 103

The German Chargé in the Soviet Union (Tippelskirch) to the German Foreign Office

D/261   SECRET   Moscow, June 18, 1939.
W. 950/39g

Reference report of June 17, 1939, by a different channel.
Subject: Conversation with Commissar for Foreign Trade Mikoyan on June 17, 1939.

Enclosed I am sending a memorandum of Counselor of Legation Hilger on his conversation with Commissar for Foreign Trade Mikoyan on June 17, 1939. The fact that Mikoyan received Herr Hilger immediately after his arrival, after an appointment had been made on the day before, shows that Mikoyan is anxious not to lose contact. That Mikoyan would immediately accept the German proposal could hardly be expected considering the mentality of the Soviet Government, which at present is riding a high horse, and its known methods of negotiation. The continually repeated statement of Mikoyan that he suspects a political game behind our offer of negotiation may not be due only to tactical motives but may partly reflect his true opinion. Mikoyan seems to believe that we had deliberately chosen the present time for economic negotiations. This becomes clear from his remark that we expected an advantage from a resumption of the economic negotiations just now.

It is a remarkable nuance that Mikoyan in his answer uses the same formula as the communiqué published on June 16 on the first conversation of Molotov with the British and French Ambassadors and Strang. In this as well as in the other case the result is called "not entirely favorable."

v. TIPPELSKIRCH

(Enclosure)

SECRET

MEMORANDUM

Subject: Conversation with Mikoyan on June 17, 1939.

After the Embassy had made an appointment the People's Commissar Mikoyan received me today immediately after my return from Berlin.

I explained to Mikoyan the purpose of my trip and pointed out the unfavorable impression which his last communication of June 8 had left with us. At the same time I asked him to consider the fact of my trip to Berlin and the answer of the German Government which I had brought along as an additional proof of the seriousness of our intentions with respect to the expansion and strengthening of German-Soviet economic relations. Thereupon I read to Herr Mikoyan the text of the German answer that had been given to me in Berlin (cf. enclosure). The People's Commissar listened with rapt attention, while Babarin, newly appointed Deputy Commercial Representative in Berlin, who was present at the conversation, busily wrote down every word. The People's Commissar appeared to be visibly impressed with the German answer. Nevertheless, he declared after a short pause that the German answer had disappointed him, since it did not meet his conditions.

On the basis of the instructions received in Berlin on this subject, I then commented on the contents of the German answer in great detail. I stressed particularly the great German concession which was expressed in sending Counselor of Legation Schnurre and in accepting the last Soviet proposal as a basis for negotiations. I reminded the People's Commissar that during the negotiations in February he did not describe the last Soviet proposal as his last word, but as the basis of further negotiations. I further reminded him of his statement in the conversation of June 8, in which he had declared that the Soviet Government would see in the despatch of Herr Schnurre proof of the fact that the German Government was also serious in the matter of "policy" [*der* "*Politik*"].

Mikoyan replied that my two last statements corresponded entirely with the facts and that I had repeated his statements correctly. Nevertheless, he still did not believe he had assurance that it was for us not a question of continuing a political game in which the Germans had an interest just at the present moment and from which they expected advantages to them.

To this I replied sharply that I had often enough rejected his statements regarding a political game allegedly played by us and that they would not become more convincing by continuous repetition. I could not understand at all what risk for the Soviet Union the People's Commissar saw in the whole matter, since the Soviet Government was not delegating a special emissary to Berlin, but the German Government was sending Herr Schnurre to Moscow, and, in fact, in agreement with the request expressed by the Soviet Government in January of this year.

Herr Mikoyan replied that this statement by me was also correct, since the Soviet Government at that time had expressed the specific desire to conduct the negotiations in Moscow.

Thereupon I stated to the People's Commissar that I was completely in the dark about what he really wanted from us, after all, and what answer he had expected from the German Government.

Mikoyan replied that he had expected concrete statements as to which points of his last proposal we would and which we would not accept.

I told the People's Commissar that this was clearly apparent in the German answer and my oral comments of today. Therefore I would like to repeat for the third time that, after the existing obstacles had been removed on our part, we definitely expected agreement from the Soviet Government to our wishes and an increase in the Soviet offer of raw materials. All other less important points would have to be left to the negotiations suggested by us. This offer from us represented the maximum concession. If on this basis we did not soon arrive at concrete negotiations, the responsibility would fall alone upon the Soviet Government.

Thereupon, the People's Commissar declared that he unfortunately could not change his opinion that the German answer was "not entirely favorable." Nevertheless, he would present it to his Government and inform me of the result.

HILGER

Moscow, June 17, 1939.

[Subenclosure]

SECRET

. The German Government is willing to send Counselor of Legation Schnurre to Moscow with authority to negotiate expansion and strengthening of economic relations between the Reich and Soviet Russia and, if a common basis is found, to come to an agreement. From the fact of sending a German plenipotentiary as negotiator we request the Soviet Government to conclude that the German Government expects and desires a positive conclusion on a widened basis. We would have to refuse acceptance in advance of the Soviet counterproposal of February 1939, however, since this counterproposal itself is to be the basis of the negotiations. The Soviet Government, however, should note that in the meanwhile we have endeavored to remove obstacles which in February still appeared to us as insurmountable. However, we expect that the Soviet Government, too, will reexamine Soviet raw material deliveries in the light of German desires in order to establish a balance of give-and-take under the future treaty.

Frame 23208, serial 34

The German Ambassador in the Soviet Union (Schulenburg) to the German Foreign Office

Telegram

No. 113 of June 27   Moscow, June 27, 1939—5 : 42 p. m.
                                   Received June 27, 1939—8 : 30 p. m.

Reference your telegram of the 26th No. 132 [12]

As I see it, Mikoyan's tactics can be interpreted as follows: Mikoyan does not want to see the talks with us broken off, but wishes to keep

[12] Not printed.

the negotiations firmly in hand, in order to control their progress at any time. Obviously it would not fit very well into the framework of the Soviet Union's general policy, if a stir should be created by a resumption of the trade negotiations, and above all by repeated journeys of a special plenipotentiary to Moscow. The Soviet Government apparently believes that by resuming the trade negotiations at this particular moment we intend to influence the attitude of England and Poland, and thereby expect to gain certain political advantages. They fear that after gaining these advantages we would again let the negotiations lapse.

In order to dispel this distrust, there are in my opinion the following possibilities:

That I be directed to propose to Mikoyan the dispatch of a qualified special delegate with all necessary powers to Berlin, in order to continue and possibly conclude the negotiations there. In view of Mikoyan's tactics, this course seems to me to have a far better prospect of success. If Mikoyan should decline this proposal, the possibility would remain of entrusting me with the further conduct of the trade negotiations in Moscow.

I propose to supplement these considerations after I have had an opportunity to speak with Molotov.

SCHULENBURG

Frame 111454, serial 103

Foreign Office Memorandum

TO THE OFFICE OF THE MINISTER

In connection with the telegram of Count Schulenburg concerning the Hilger–Mikoyan conversation,[18] the Führer has decided the following:

The Russians are to be informed that we have concluded from their attitude that they make the continuation of further talks dependent upon the acceptance of the bases of our economic discussions, as they were fixed for January. Since this basis was not acceptable to us, we would not be interested in a resumption of the economic discussions with Russia at the present time.

The Führer agreed that this answer be delayed for a few days.

I notified the Reich Foreign Minister of this by telephone, and I am

---

[18] *Supra.*

sending this note only as a guide for a conference of the competent official with the Minister.

HEWEL

BERCHTESGADEN, June 29, 1939.

Respectfully submitted herewith to
State Secretary von Weizsäcker.
June 29, 1939.

Frames 111452–111453, serial 103

*The German Ambassador in the Soviet Union (Schulenburg) to the
German Foreign Office*

Telegram

URGENT   Moscow, June 29, 1939—2:40 a. m.
SECRET   Received June 29, 1939—7:20 p. m.

No. 115 of June 28

This afternoon I had a conversation with Molotov, who received me immediately after I had been announced. The conversation lasted over an hour and proceeded in a friendly manner.

I described to Molotov the impressions which I had gained from talk with influential personalities in Berlin, particularly with the Reich Foreign Minister. I pointed out that we would welcome a normalization of the relations between Germany and Soviet Russia, as the State Secretary had stated to the Soviet Chargé in Berlin. For this we had furnished a number of proofs, such as reserve in the German press, conclusion of the nonaggression treaties with the Baltic countries and desire for resumption of economic negotiations. From all this it was evident that Germany did not have any bad intentions toward the Soviet Union, particularly since the Berlin Treaty [14] was still in force. We, on the German side, would continue to take advantage of any opportunity to prove our goodwill. However, we had had no answer from the Soviet Union to the question of what Molotov meant in his last conversation with me by "creation of a new basis of our relationship" ["*Schaffung einer Neuregelung der Basis*"]. We also objected to the attitude of the Soviet press.

Molotov replied that he received my statements with satisfaction. The foreign policy of the Soviet Government was, in accordance with the pronouncements of its leaders, aimed at the cultivation of good relations with all countries, and this of course applied—provided there was reciprocity—to Germany too. He was gratified that in the

---

[14] Treaty of friendship and neutrality between Germany and the Soviet Union, signed at Berlin April 24, 1926.

opinion of the German Government the Berlin Treaty was still in force, particularly since the Soviet Government had had doubt about that. As to the question of the treaty negotiations for nonaggression pacts with the Baltic countries, Molotov remarked that Germany had concluded them in her own interest, and not out of love for the Soviet Union. He had to doubt the permanence of such treaties after the experience which Poland had had; to which I replied that Poland had herself caused the termination of the treaty by joining a combination hostile to us, which was irreconcilable with friendly relations to us.

Concerning the question of resuming economic negotiations Molotov referred to the last conversation between Mikoyan and Hilger. Molotov showed himself informed, approved the attitude of Mikoyan, and suggested that we give Mikoyan the desired information. After settlement of this question the trip to Moscow contemplated by Schnurre would perhaps prove useful.

My impression is that the Soviet Government is greatly interested in knowing our political views and in maintaining contact with us. Although a strong distrust was evident in everything that Molotov said, nevertheless he described normalization of relations with Germany as desirable and possible. Progress is to be seen also in the fact that Molotov, in connection with the resumption of economic negotiations, this time did not speak of prior creation of a political basis, but confined himself to Mikoyan's demand.

I request telegraphic instructions whether and in what form compliance should be given to Mikoyan's requests, presented also by Molotov.

(Cf. telegraphic reports No. 111 and 113 of the 25th and the 27th of this month.)[15]

SCHULENBURG

Frame 111464, serial 103

The State Secretary in the German Foreign Office (Weizsäcker) to the German Ambassador in the Soviet Union (Schulenburg)

Telegram

No. 134   BERLIN, June 30, 1939.

Reference your telegram 115.[16]

Reich Foreign Minister took note of your telegraphic report on conversation with Molotov. He is of the opinion that in the politi-

---

[15] Neither printed.
[16] *Supra.*

cal field enough had been said until further instruction and that for the moment the talks should not be taken up again by us.

Concerning the possible economic negotiations with the Russian Government, the deliberations here have not yet been concluded. In this matter, too, request that for time being nothing further be initiated, but that instructions be awaited.

WEIZSÄCKER

Frames 111466–111469, serial 103

The German Ambassador in the Soviet Union (Schulenburg) to the German Foreign Office

Telegram

VERY URGENT   Moscow, July 3, 1939—8:40 p. m.
No. 121 of July 3   Received July 4, 1939—1:20 a. m.

Reference telegram of July 2 No. 139.[17]

In accordance with instructions, I add to my telegram No. 115 of June 28 the following:

Molotov received me in the Kremlin, after I had announced my arrival three hours before. Correct translation was secured through Hilger. Molotov's translator failed to appear.

I opened the discussion with the statement that on the basis of the talks in Berlin, particularly with the Reich Foreign Minister, I had the impression that we would welcome a normalization of relations with the Soviet Union. The State Secretary had very clearly acquainted Herr Astakhov with our position. Indicative of this position was the following: correct tone of the German press toward the Soviet Union, conclusion of nonaggression treaties with the Baltic countries and our desire for resumption of economic negotiations.

Molotov listened attentively and stated that he received this communication with satisfaction. I continued that since the conversation of the State Secretary with Astakhov we had waited for a Soviet statement as to what Molotov had meant in his conversation with me on May 20 by the words "creation of a political basis for the resumption of economic negotiations"; I would also have to point out to him that the attitude of the Soviet press in all questions concerning Germany still gave cause for serious criticism. Herr Astakhov had been told that Herr Molotov wanted to answer me personally. Among other

---

[17] Not printed.

things I had come in order to inquire whether he had anything to tell me.

In his answer Molotov did not go into the question as to the meaning of the concept "political basis," but he declared that the Soviet Government in accordance with the enunciations of its leaders desired good relations with all countries and therefore—provided there was reciprocity—would also welcome a normalization of relations with Germany. It was not the fault of the Soviet Government if these relations had become bad. He could not accept the criticism of the Soviet press, since he was not aware of any hostile attitude of the press toward Germany.

I replied that much could be said about these questions; that I had not, however, come to talk of the past, but of the future.

Thereupon, Molotov asked how we visualized further developments and what changes had occurred lately in the relations between Germany and the Soviet Union. As to the nonaggression treaties, Germany had concluded them in the first place in her own interest, and they concerned only Germany and the countries participating, but not the Soviet Union. Furthermore, he would have to doubt the permanence of such treaties after the experiences which Poland had had.

I replied that our nonaggression treaties provided the Baltic countries with additional security, in which the Soviet Union was very much interested. Poland had herself provoked the termination of the treaty with us by behaving irresponsibly and joining a combination hostile to us, which was irreconcilable with friendly relations with us. To this Molotov stated that in his opinion the treaty concluded by Poland with England was a purely defensive instrument.

I disagreed and pointed out that the word "defensive" in this connection was of only academic significance. Then I returned to Molotov's question as to how we visualized further developments and said that, in my opinion, the main task in the future would be that both countries avoid everything that would lead to a further deterioration of relations and do everything that might result in their improvement. Germany had no ill intentions against the Soviet Union, and one of the proofs for that was the Berlin Treaty, which we had extended some time ago.

Thereupon Molotov asked, "Are you convinced that the Berlin Treaty is really still in force and has not been abrogated by later treaties concluded by Germany?" I replied the following: "I know of no such treaties and have no reason to doubt the validity of the Berlin Treaty."

At the end I asked Molotov what he had to say to the question of the resumption of economic negotiations.

Molotov replied that he knew the contents of the last conversation between Mikoyan and Hilger. He approved Mikoyan's (group missing) and suggested that we give Mikoyan the desired information.

I sought to convince Molotov that it would not be in the interest of speeding up the economic negotiations if details were discussed between Mikoyan and Hilger or me, since we continuously had to request instructions from Berlin. Schnurre, on the other hand, had all the necessary authority, knowledge, and experience and would be able to conclude the negotiations quickly to mutual satisfaction.

Thereupon Molotov indicated that cancellation of Schnurre's trip in February had annoyed the Soviet Union. They would leave it to Mikoyan, who had mastery of the subject matter, to ask for what he considered right. When we had given the information desired by Mikoyan, a trip by Schnurre to Moscow might perhaps prove useful.

The conversation closed in friendly spirit and with my repeated request that Molotov influence the attitude of the Soviet press.

SCHULENBURG

Frames 178431–178434, serial 276

The Counselor of Embassy of the German Embassy in the Soviet Union (Tippelskirch) to the German Ambassador in the Soviet Union (Schulenburg)

BERLIN, July 12, 1939.

MY DEAR MR. AMBASSADOR: Herr Lamla,[18] whom I asked to remember me to you, has probably already told you a few things. However, I still would like to report on my impressions here. The Reich Foreign Minister was busy with the Bulgarian state visit and was not able to see me. Otherwise, however, with the exception of Gaus and Selchow, who were on vacation, I have talked to all personalities concerned. The State Secretary was interested to hear an opinion as to what result the English-French-Soviet pact negotiations would have. He said that he could not imagine that the Soviet Union after having entered the negotiations would let them pass without result and sink back into isolation. He was also interested in your conversations with Molotov and remarked that in his opinion our side had done enough

---

[18] Of the staff of the German Embassy in Moscow.

politically for the moment. Then we discussed the instructions concerning the answer to Mikoyan, and I expressed myself as in favor of giving this information. (The instructions were submitted to the Führer by the Reich Foreign Minister and were dispatched after details had been added by the State Secretary.) The State Secretary believed that we might try to make some progress in the field of *economics*, but slowly and step by step. The State Secretary apparently did not want to go further into the subject of the "Berlin Treaty;" he asked about the result of the discussion with Molotov on this point. I referred to your second telegram and said that you had only touched upon the topic. My vacation appeared to him a little bit long!! I shall therefore be back at the beginning of August.

Herr Schnurre was not in a very good mood. He stressed repeatedly that without any *positive* reaction by Molotov it would be difficult to make any progress. He showed me an order of the Führer he had received by telephone on June 30 according to which further activities in Moscow were to be stopped in view of the conduct of the Russians. Thereupon, Schnurre drafted a memorandum and the order. I told him that the Embassy and particularly you, yourself, had done everything possible, but we could not drag Molotov and Mikoyan through the Brandenburger Tor.

Unfortunately, I stayed with Woermann only a short time, because the State Secretary called for me. He considered it as important that the Soviets, through Astakhov, had taken the initiative for the *rapprochement*. I did not deny that, but I called attention to the Fournier despatch published by the *Temps* about the negative statement of the Soviet Embassy here, which had escaped him. Incidentally, he made an interesting remark about the Berlin Treaty which makes it appear advisable not to touch upon the topic again without instructions. More details orally! I have talked with Schliep about the Komsomol people and caused him to have further steps taken now for the removal [*die Abbeförderung*].

Of course, we conferred with everyone else concerned, including Meyer-Heydenhagen. I have also roused Herr Schwendemann against the Komsomol people. Then I discussed with Braun Stumm (since Dr. Schmidt was not available) everything concerning the press in the sense of your letter to Seibert which, incidentally, Schmidt still had, and it fell on fertile ground.

In the Personnel Division I talked with Herren Kriebel, Schroeder, Dienstmann, Dittmann. In accordance with your instructions I expressed myself as against either one of us being reassigned.

According to my impressions the problem of the Soviet Union is still of the greatest interest here. The opinions, however, fluctuate and are undecided. The formation of a definite political opinion has not yet materialized.

Tonight I am going to Badgastein, Hotel Kaiserhof.

With most cordial regards I remain, my dear Ambassador, yours most respectfully, Heil Hitler.

W. VON TIPPELSKIRCH

Frame 111485, serial 103

The German Ambassador in the Soviet Union (Schulenburg) to the German Foreign Office

Telegram

URGENT   Moscow, July 22, 1939—1: 07 p. m.
No. 136 of July 22   Received July 22, 1939—1: 35 p. m.

Entire Soviet press today publishes following report under headline "In the Foreign Trade Commissariat":

"Soviet-German negotiations on commerce and credit have recently been resumed. Negotiations are being conducted by Babarin, the Deputy Commercial Representative in Berlin, for the Foreign Trade Commissariat, and by Schnurre for the Germans."

SCHULENBURG

Frames 69530–69536, serial 127

Foreign Office Memorandum

SECRET   BERLIN, July 27, 1939.
1216g

MEMORANDUM

In accordance with my instructions I invited the Soviet Chargé, Astakhov, and Babarin, the chief of the Soviet trade mission here, to Ewest for dinner last night. The Russians stayed until about half past twelve. The Russians started the talk about the political and economic problems which interest us in a very lively and interested manner so that an informal and thorough discussion of the individual topics mentioned by the Reich Foreign Minister was possible. The following parts of the conversation should be stressed:

1. Referring to remarks by Astakhov about close collaboration and community of interests in foreign policy which formerly existed between Germany and Russia, I explained that such collaboration

appeared attainable to me now, if the Soviet Government considered it desirable. I could visualize three stages:

Stage One: The reestablishment of collaboration in economic affairs through the credit and commercial treaty which is to be concluded.

Stage Two: The normalization and improvement of political relations. This included, among other things, respect for the interests of the other party in the press and in public opinion, and respect for the scientific and cultural activities of the other country. The official participation by Astakhov in German Art Day at Munich, or the invitation of German delegates to the Agricultural Exhibition in Moscow, as suggested by him to the State Secretary, could, for instance, be included under this heading.

Stage Three would be the reestablishment of good political relations, either a return to what had been in existence before (Berlin Treaty [19]) or a new arrangement which took account of the vital political interests of both parties. This stage three appeared to me within reach, because controversial problems of foreign policy, which would exclude such a relationship between the two countries, did not, in my opinion, exist in the whole area from the Baltic Sea to the Black Sea and the Far East. In addition, despite all the differences in *Weltanschauung*, there was *one* thing in common in the ideology of Germany, Italy, and the Soviet Union: opposition to the capitalist democracies. Neither we nor Italy had anything in common with the capitalism of the West. Therefore, it would appear to us quite paradoxical if the Soviet Union, as a Socialist state, were to side with the Western democracies.

2. With the strong agreement of Babarin, Astakhov designated the way of *rapprochement* with Germany as the one that corresponded with the vital interests of the two countries. However, he emphasized that the tempo must probably be very slow and gradual. The Soviet Union had been forced to feel itself most seriously menaced by the National Socialist foreign policy. We had appropriately called our present political situation encirclement. That was exactly how, after the events of September of last year, the political situation had appeared to the Soviet Union. Astakhov mentioned the Anti-Comintern Pact and our relations to Japan, and Munich and the free hand in Eastern Europe that we gained there, the political consequences of which were bound to be directed against the Soviet Union. Our assumption that the Baltic countries and Finland, as well as Rumania, were in our sphere of interest completed for the Soviet Government the feeling of being menaced. Moscow could not quite believe in a

[19] Treaty of friendship and neutrality between Germany and the Soviet Union, signed at Berlin April 24, 1926.

shift of German policy with respect to the Soviet Union. A change could only be expected gradually.

3. In my reply I pointed out that German policy in the East had taken an entirely different course in the meantime. On our part there could be no question of menacing the Soviet Union; our aims were in an entirely different direction. Molotov, himself, in his last speech had called the Anti-Comintern Pact camouflage for an alliance aimed against the Western democracies. He was acquainted with the Danzig question, and the related Polish question. I saw in these anything but a clash of interests between Germany and the Soviet Union. That we would respect the integrity of the Baltic countries and of Finland had become sufficiently clear through our nonaggression pacts and our nonaggression offers. Our relationship to Japan was that of a well-founded friendship, which was not, however, aimed against Russia. German policy was aimed against England. That was the decisive factor. As I had stated previously, I could imagine a far-reaching compromise of mutual interests with due consideration for the problems which were vital to Russia. However, this possibility was barred the moment the Soviet Union, by signing a treaty, sided with England against Germany. The Soviet Union would then have made its choice, and then would only be able to share the German opposition with England. Only for this reason would I have any objection to his view that the tempo of a possible understanding between Germany and the Soviet Union had to be slow. The time was opportune now, but would not be after the conclusion of a pact with London. This would have to be considered in Moscow. What could England offer Russia? At best, participation in a European war and the hostility of Germany, but not a single desirable end for Russia. What could we offer, on the other hand? Neutrality and staying out of a possible European conflict and, if Moscow wished, a German-Russian understanding on mutual interests which, just as in former times, would work out to the advantage of both countries.

4. During the subsequent discussion Astakhov came back again to the question of the Baltic countries and asked whether, besides economic penetration, we had more far-reaching political aims there. He also took up the Rumanian question seriously. As to Poland, he stated that Danzig would return to the Reich in one way or another and that the Corridor question would have to be solved somehow in favor of the Reich. He asked whether the territories which once belonged to Austria were not also tending toward Germany, particularly the Galician and Ukrainian territories. After describing our

commercial relations to the Baltic countries, I confined myself to the statement that no German-Russian clash of interests would result from all these questions. Moreover, the settlement of the Ukrainian question had shown that we did not aim at anything there that would endanger Soviet interests.

5. There was a rather extensive discussion about the question of why National Socialism had sought the enmity of the Soviet Union in the field of foreign policy. In Moscow, they had never been able to understand this. They had always had full understanding for the domestic opposition to Communism. I took advantage of this opportunity to explain in detail our opinion concerning the change in Russian Bolshevism during recent years. The antagonism of National Socialism resulted naturally from the fight against the Communist Party of Germany which depended upon Moscow and was only a tool of the Comintern. The fight against the German Communist Party had long been over. Communism had been eradicated in Germany. The importance of the Comintern had been overshadowed by the Politbureau, where an entirely different policy was being followed now than at the time when the Comintern dominated. The amalgamation of Bolshevism with the national history of Russia, which expressed itself in the glorification of great Russian men and deeds (celebration of the battle of Poltava, Peter the Great, the battle on Lake Peipus, Alexander Nevski), had really changed the international face of Bolshevism, as we see it, particularly since Stalin had postponed world revolution indefinitely. In this state of affairs we saw possibilities today which we had not seen earlier, provided that no attempt was made to spread Communist propaganda in any form in Germany.

6. At the end Astakhov stressed how valuable this conversation had been to him. He would report it to Moscow, and he hoped that it would have visible results in subsequent developments there. The question of the commerce and credit treaty was discussed in detail.

7. After the statements of the Russians I had the impression that Moscow had not yet decided what they want to do. The Russians were silent about the status and chances of the English pact negotiations. Considering all this, it looks as if Moscow, for the time being, is following a policy of delay and postponement toward us as well as England in order to defer decisions the importance of which they understand completely. Therefore the receptive attitude of the Russians after the various talks, particularly the attitude of Molotov; therefore the delay in the protracted economic negotiations, in which the Russians absolutely reserve the tempo to themselves; therefore

most likely also the retention of Ambassador Merekalov in Moscow. As a further handicap, there is the excessive distrust, not only toward us but toward England as well. From our point of view it may be considered a noteworthy success that Moscow, after months of negotiation with England, still remains uncertain as to what she ought to do eventually.

SCHNURRE

Frames 69528-69529, serial 127

The German Foreign Office to the German Ambassador in the Soviet Union (Schulenburg)

SECRET   BERLIN, July 29, 1939.

W 1216g

On the evening of the 26th of this month Schnurre had a detailed discussion with Astakhov and Babarin, the content of which is reported in the enclosed memorandum.[20] Astakhov's answer indicates that a detailed report from him is already available in Moscow. At the end Astakhov asked whether we would maintain similar opinions if a prominent Soviet representative were to discuss these questions with a prominent German representative. Schnurre answered this question essentially in the affirmative.

It would be important for us to know whether the statements made to Astakhov and Babarin have found any response in Moscow. If you see the opportunity of arranging a new talk with Molotov, I request that you sound him out in this sense and that, should the occasion arise, you use the line of thought of the memorandum. If it should develop that Molotov abandons the reserve thus far maintained by him, you can advance another step in your presentation and state somewhat more precisely what was expressed generally in the memorandum. This concerns particularly the Polish question. In *any* development of the Polish question, either in a peaceful manner as we desire it or in any other way that is forced upon us, we would be prepared to safeguard all Soviet interests and to reach an understanding with the Moscow Government. If the talk proceeds positively in the Baltic question too, the idea could be advanced that we will adjust our stand with regard to the Baltic in such a manner as to respect the vital Soviet interests in the Baltic.

Draft signed by VON WEIZSÄCKER

---

[20] *Supra.*

Frame 260369, serial 695

The State Secretary in the German Foreign Office (Weizsäcker) to the German Ambassador in the Soviet Union (Schulenburg)

VERY URGENT   BERLIN, August 3, 1939—1:47 p. m.
SECRET   Received Moscow, August 3, 1939—6:00 p. m.
No. 164 of August 3

For the Ambassador for his information.

Reference telegraphic instruction of today.[21] In accordance with the political situation and in the interest of speed, we are anxious, without prejudice to your conversation with Molotov scheduled for today, to continue in Berlin the clarification of terms for the adjustment of German-Soviet interests. To this end, Schnurre will receive Astakhov today and will tell him that we would be ready for more concrete discussions if that is also the desire of the Soviet Government. We would propose in this case that Astakhov obtain instructions from Moscow. We would then be prepared to speak quite concretely concerning problems of possible interest to the Soviet Union.

WEIZSÄCKER

Frames 69519–69521, serial 127

The Reich Foreign Minister to the German Ambassador in the Soviet Union (Schulenburg)

Telegram

VERY URGENT   BERLIN, August 3, 1939—3:47 p. m.
                          Received Moscow, August 4, 1939—4:30 a. m.
No. 166 of August 3

For the Ambassador personally!

Last evening I received the Russian Chargé, who had previously called at the Office on other matters. I intended to continue with him the conversations with which you are familiar, that had previously been conducted with Astakhov by members of the Foreign Office with my permission. I alluded to the trade agreement discussions, which are at present progressing satisfactorily, and designated such a trade agreement as a good step on the way toward a normalization of German-Russian relationships, if this was desired. It was well known that the tone of our press with regard to Russia had for over half a year been a very different one. I considered that, insofar as the desire

---

[21] No. 166, *infra*.

existed on the Russian side, a remolding of our relations was possible, on two conditions:

a) noninterference in the internal affairs of the other country (Herr Astakhov believes he can promise this forthwith) ;
b) abandonment of a policy directed against our vital interests. To this, Astakhov was unable to give any clear-cut answer, but he thought his Government had the desire to pursue a policy of mutual understanding with Germany.

I continued that our policy was a direct and long-range one; we were in no hurry. We were favorably disposed toward Moscow; it was therefore a question of what direction the rulers there wanted to take. If Moscow took a [negative] [22] attitude, we would know where we stood and how to act. If the reverse were the case, there was no problem from the Baltic to the Black Sea that could not be solved between the two of us. I said that there was room for the two of us on the Baltic and that Russian interests by no means needed to clash with ours there. As far as Poland was concerned, we were watching further developments attentively and dispassionately. In case of provocation on the part of Poland, we would settle matters with Poland in the space of a week. For this contingency, I dropped a gentle hint at coming to an agreement with Russia on the fate of Poland. I described German-Japanese relations as good and friendly; this relationship was a lasting one. As to Russian-Japanese relations, however, I had my own ideas (by which I meant a long-range *modus vivendi* between the two countries).

I conducted whole conversation in an even tone and in conclusion again made it clear to the Chargé that in international politics we pursued no such tactics as the democratic powers. We were accustomed to building on solid ground, did not need to pay heed to vacillating public opinion, and did not desire any sensations. If conversations such as ours were not handled with the discretion they deserved, they would have to be discontinued. We were making no fuss about it; the choice lay, as mentioned, with Moscow. If they were interested there in our ideas, why then Herr Molotov could shortly pick up the thread again with Count Schulenburg (this superseded by telegram No. 164 [23]).

Conclusion of the conversation.

---

[22] This word, missing in the telegram as received in the Moscow Embassy, has been supplied from the German Foreign Office file copy.
[23] *Ante*, p. 37.

Note for Count Schulenburg:
I conducted the conversation without showing any haste. The Chargé, who seemed interested, tried several times to pin the conversation down to more concrete terms, whereupon I gave him to understand that I would be prepared to make it more concrete as soon as the Soviet Government officially communicated its fundamental desire for a new relationship. Should Astakhov be instructed in this sense, we for our part would be interested in an early definite settlement. This exclusively for your personal information.

RIBBENTROP

Frames 69522-69527, serial 127

The German Ambassador in the Soviet Union (Schulenburg) to the German Foreign Office

Telegram

No. 158 of August 3   Moscow, August 4, 1939—12:20 a. m.

Re instruction W 1216g of July 29, and telegraphic directive of July 31.[24]

In a conference of 1¼ hours today, Molotov abandoned his usual reserve and appeared unusually open. I referred to my last conversation with M. and said that in the meantime economic negotiations had been resumed in Berlin and were apparently proceeding in a promising manner. We were consequently expecting an early conclusion. An exchange of ideas had further taken place between Schnurre and Soviet representatives in Berlin, as to the contents of which M. was surely informed. M. confirmed the fact that "by and large" he was posted in the matter. Referring to Astakhov's question as to whether Schnurre's statements would, if the occasion arose, be backed up by a qualified German personage, I declared that I was authorized to confirm explicitly the train of thought developed by Schnurre. I then explained how, on the basis of the three steps mentioned by Schnurre, we contemplated the normalization and improvement of our relations with the Soviet Union. In continuation I stated that from the Baltic to the Black Sea, in our opinion, no opposition of interests existed between Germany and the Soviet Union, that the Anti-Comintern Pact was not directed against the Soviet Union, that by concluding nonaggression pacts with the Baltic countries we

---

[24] Latter not printed.

had proven our decision to respect their integrity, and that our well-known demands on Poland meant no impairment of Soviet interests. We therefore believed that adjustment of interests was entirely possible and were asking the opinion of the Soviet Government in this matter.

M. answered point by point at some length. He stated that the Soviet Government had always desired the conclusion of an economic agreement and if a like desire existed on the German side, he considered the prospects for realization of an economic agreement as entirely favorable. So far as the attitude of the Soviet press was concerned, he considered our reproaches—with some exceptions—unjustified. But he took the stand that the press of both countries must desist from anything that might tend to exacerbate their relations. He considered the gradual resumption of cultural relations necessary and expedient and believed that a gratifying start had already been made toward improvement.

Going on to the question of political relations, M. declared that the Soviet Government also desired normalization and improvement of mutual relations. It was not its fault that relations had so deteriorated. The reason for this he saw, firstly, in the conclusion of the Anti-Comintern Pact and in everything that had been said and done in this connection. To my objection that the Anti-Comintern Pact was not directed against the Soviet Union and had been designated by M. himself on May 31st as an alliance against the Western democracies, M. said that the Anti-Comintern Pact had nevertheless encouraged the aggressive attitude of Japan toward the Soviet Union. In the second place, Germany had supported Japan, and thirdly, the German Government had repeatedly shown that it would not participate in any international conferences in which the Soviet Union participated. M. cited the meeting in Munich as an example.

I answered M. in detail, stressing that it was not a matter of discussing the past but of finding new ways.

M. replied that the Soviet Government was prepared to participate in the quest for such ways; yet he must insist on asking how my statements of today are to be reconciled with the three points mentioned by him. Proofs of a changed attitude of the German Government were for the present still lacking.

I thereupon again stressed the absence of opposition of interests in foreign policy and mentioned German readiness so to orient our behavior with regard to the Baltic States, if occasion arose, as to safeguard vital Soviet Baltic interests.

At the mention of the Baltic States, M. was interested in learning what States we meant by the term and whether Lithuania was one of them.

On the Polish question I stated that we persevered in our well-known demands on Poland but strove for a peaceful solution. If on the other hand a different solution were forced on us, we were prepared to protect all Soviet interests and come to an understanding with the Soviet Government on this matter.

M. showed evident interest but said that a peaceful solution depended first of all on us.

I vigorously contradicted this and pointed out that the British guarantee had unfortunately brought it about that the decision lay with the Polish authorities.

I then repudiated Molotov's assertion that Germany alone was to blame for deterioration in German-Soviet relations. I reminded him of the fateful consequences of the conclusion of the treaty of 1935 with France and added that the possible new participation by the Soviet Union in a combination hostile to Germany might play a similar role. M. replied that the present course taken by the Soviet Union aimed at purely defensive ends and at the strengthening of a defensive front against aggression. In contrast to this, Germany had supported and promoted the aggressive attitude of Japan by the Anti-Comintern Pact and in the military alliance with Italy was pursuing offensive as well as defensive aims.

In conclusion M. assured me that he would apprise his Government of my statements and repeated that the Soviet Government also desired normalization and improvement of relations.

From M.'s whole attitude it was evident that the Soviet Government was in fact more prepared for improvement in German-Soviet relations, but that the old mistrust of Germany persists. My over-all impression is that the Soviet Government is at present determined to sign with England and France if they fulfill all Soviet wishes. Negotiations, to be sure, might still last a long time, especially since mistrust of England is also great. I believe that my statements made an impression on M.; it will nevertheless take considerable effort on our part to cause the Soviet Government to swing about.

SCHULENBURG

Frames 178513–178517, serial 276

*The German Ambassador in the Soviet Union (Schulenburg) to
Counselor of Legation Schliep of the German Foreign Office*

Moscow, August 7, 1939.

DEAR COUNSELOR OF LEGATION SCHLIEP: Sincerest thanks for your
letter of the 2d of this month [25] and its interesting enclosure.

As a matter of fact, I have in the meantime received the telegraphic
instruction to take part in Party Day. On September 1, I am to travel
in the new grey uniform from Berlin to Nuernberg with the other
gentlemen of the Foreign Office. That means that I must be in Berlin
on August 27 at the latest. A final fitting and the purchase of a
number of accessories are unavoidable.

You know from our telegram that the political negotiations of the
British and the French have been interrupted for the time being.
Mr. Strang left by air this morning for London, where a great quantity of work had allegedly accumulated for him. At the end of the
week, the British and French officers will come. The British military
men here regard the prospects of the pending military negotiations
also with considerable scepticism. Among the members of the British
Military Mission is the former Air Attaché in Moscow, Collier. Collier is a very sober and quiet man and knows Soviet conditions well.
At the time of the intervention, he was in Archangel. The fact that
he is being sent is welcomed by the British here, since he will not be
taken in by the Russians and knows their methods of negotiation.

Concerning the political negotiations up to now, we hear that
throughout Herr Molotov sat like a bump on a log.* He hardly ever
opened his mouth, and if he did it was to utter only the brief remark:
"Your statements do not appear to me entirely satisfactory. I shall
notify my Government." The British and the French Ambassadors
are both said to be completely exhausted and glad that they now have
a breathing spell ahead of them. The Frenchman said to one of my
informants, "Thank God that that fellow † will not participate in the
military negotiations!"

Regarding my conversations with Molotov, you are, of course, informed. I believe that we put a few good fleas in the ears of the
Soviets, anyhow. At every word and at every step, one can see the
great distrust toward us. That this is so, we have known for a long

---

[25] Not printed.
* He has been very different toward Hilger and me of late; very communicative
and amiable. [Marginal note in the original]
† Molotov. [Footnote in the original]

time. The unfortunate part of it is, that the mistrust of such people is very easily kindled and can only be allayed slowly and with difficulty.

I recently wrote you of rumors concerning the fist-fight between the Turkish Ambassador Apaydin (who left here very suddenly) and his military attaché. At that time I didn't believe these rumors, but they seem to be correct. I hear now on good authority that the fracas even took place before witnesses. At first the military attaché was also recalled, but then this disciplinary measure was withdrawn, apparently so that the rumors concerning the fight which were circulating here would not receive new support.

My old acquaintance, Minister Idman, who at present is in charge of the Finnish Legation, told me that when he called on Molotov the latter expressed himself as very dissatisfied over the hostile attitude of the Finnish press toward Russia. Idman said he replied that the Finnish press is free to write what it wishes and if it prints anti-Russian articles the Soviet Union had certainly given occasion for them.

The Danish Minister here recently made his first call on Molotov. The Minister President brought up the question of the German-Danish Nonaggression Treaty. He had taken note of, but had made no comment on, the Minister's statement that Denmark was much reassured by the conclusion of the pact.

In conversation with Molotov, the Ministers of Latvia and Estonia here also characterized the German Nonaggression Treaties as guarantees of peace, and remarked that the conclusion of the treaties had been entirely natural, since Latvia and Estonia had similar non-aggression treaties with the Soviet Union. Molotov, however, had taken the position that these treaties indicated an inclination toward Germany, and he could not be moved from this position.

The Estonian Chargé here, in talking about the attitude of the Soviets toward Baltic questions, spoke of the possibility that Germany might guarantee the independence of Latvia and Estonia, as it had done with Belgium. I am of the opinion that the Soviets no longer want such a guarantee to be given by us.

General Köstring, who has gone to Berlin for a few days, will look you up and give you the news from here. I hope he has already done it. We are very curious to know what news he will bring us from Berlin. Just as eagerly we await the arrival of Herr von Tippelskirch on next Friday.

I hope the three Germans will arrive soon who are to visit the agricultural exhibition here at the invitation of the Soviet Government. The exhibition is really very much worth seeing (amazingly grandiose). Should not the Soviet Government be invited to the Eastern Fair at Königsberg? Obviously it is too late for the Soviet Union to participate and to send exhibits to the fair; however, in return for the invitation to the agricultural exhibition, a couple of Soviet representatives could at least be invited to visit the fair.

Here the rather terrific heat continues. I like it better than the usual rain and mud.

With warmest regards to your wife and with greetings to you, and with Heil Hitler! I remain, dear Herr Schliep,

Sincerely yours,   COUNT VON DER SCHULENBURG

Frames 23237–23241, serial 34

Foreign Office Memorandum

To W 1301/39g

MEMORANDUM

Soviet Chargé Astakhov called on me today at 11 a. m. for a conversation lasting an hour. First the journey of the German participants in the agricultural exhibition at Moscow was discussed (cf. separate memorandum [26]). I then asked Astakhov whether he had any news from Moscow regarding the questions which had been discussed between us. Astakhov replied in the affirmative and stated as follows:

The question informally discussed between us, as to whether a political thought should be inserted in the preamble to the credit agreement, had also been examined in Moscow. It was held more appropriate not to connect the trade and credit agreement with language of a political nature. This would be anticipating the future. I replied to Herr Astakhov that this was our view, too. Astakhov then mentioned that he had *once again* received an express instruction from Moscow to emphasize that the Soviet Government desired an improvement in relations with Germany. The declaration he had made to me the last time was thereby strengthened. I took advantage of this in the ensuing conversation to tell Astakhov the following:

We had noted with satisfaction that the Soviet Government was anxious to continue the conversation regarding the improvement of Soviet-German relations. We had wished that Molotov would let

---

[26] Not printed.

us know his basic attitude in regard to the status of Soviet interests in order to facilitate further conversations and had believed that it was premature for us to discuss concrete problems so long as we did not know exactly the interests of the Soviets.   But, in any event, one question was quite ripe, namely Poland.   The Polish delusion of grandeur, shielded by England, drove Poland constantly to new provocations.   We were still hoping that Poland would somehow come to reason, so that a peaceful solution could be found.   Failing this, it was possible that, against our will and against our desires, a solution by force of arms would have to take place.   If, as we had now done on various occasions, we had declared ourselves willing to enter upon a large-scale adjustment of mutual interests with Moscow, it was important for us to know the position of the Soviet Government on the question of Poland.   In Moscow, after political negotiations had brought no result, military negotiations were now being conducted with England and France.   We scarcely believe that, contrary to the direction in which her interests clearly lay, the Soviet Union will align herself with England and make herself, as had England, a guarantor of megalomaniac Polish aspirations.   It would, of course, mean a poor start for the German-Soviet conversations, if, however, as a result of the military negotiations in Moscow, a sort of military alliance were contemplated against us, with the Soviet Union participating.   These were therefore questions that were of interest to us at this stage of our conversations, and upon them depended, after all, the prospects of achieving a German-Soviet understanding: in the first place, then, the attitude of the Soviet Union on the Polish question, and, in the second place, the objectives that Moscow was pursuing in the military discussions with England and France.   I could again assure Herr Astakhov, as I had already done on various occasions, that, even in the event of a solution by force of arms, German interests in Poland were quite limited.   They did not at all need to collide with Soviet interests of any kind, but we had to know those interests.   If the motive behind the negotiations conducted by Moscow with England was the feeling of being threatened by Germany in the event of a German-Polish conflict, we for our part were prepared to give the Soviet Union every assurance desired, which would surely carry more weight than support by England, which could never become effective in Eastern Europe.

Astakhov was keenly interested, but naturally had no instructions of any kind from Moscow to discuss the subject of Poland or the subject of the negotiations in Moscow.   In the course of the conversation, however, he went quite extensively into both subjects on his own accord. The negotiations with England had begun at a time when there had still been no sign of a disposition on the part of Germany to come to an understanding. The negotiations had been entered upon without much enthusiasm, but they had to conduct them because they had to protect themselves against the German threat and had to accept assistance wherever it was offered. To be sure, the situation had changed since the conversations with Germany had started. But one could not now simply break off something which had been begun after mature consideration. The outcome of the negotiations was uncertain in his opinion, and it was quite possible that his Government likewise considered the question as completely open. Our conversation of today, just as those which previously took place, would surely tend in that direction. On the question of Poland, he said that he doubted whether he would receive a concrete reply from Moscow on this enormous problem. At this stage of the conversations it was somewhat like putting the cart before the horse to want to bring the question of Poland up now for final discussion. Astakhov sought to learn whether any German decisions in the Polish question could be expected in the next few days and what Germany's aims in respect to Poland were. I avoided a reply to this question and at any rate did not show such urgency in the matter. Astakhov will report and then revert to these questions. Astakhov was unable to answer an informal question regarding the possible return of his Ambassador. On the contrary, he asked me whether we had not heard anything from Moscow regarding Herr Merekalov. He emphasized, however, that it made no difference in our talks who was acting as the official representative of the Soviet Government in Berlin.

SCHNURRE

BERLIN, August 10, 1939.

Frames 228752–228755, serial 472

The German Ambassador in the Soviet Union (Schulenburg) to the State Secretary in the German Foreign Office (Weizsäcker)

Moscow, August 14, 1939.

MY VERY ESTEEMED HERR VON WEIZSÄCKER!

May I thank you most heartily for your gracious letter of the 7th instant.[27]

I am still of the opinion that any hasty measure in the matter of

---

[27] Not printed.

our relations with the Soviet Union should be avoided; it will almost always be harmful. So I consider it entirely right that our treatment of the Soviet Embassy in Berlin be relaxed only slowly.

The following were the main points in my last conversation with Herr Molotov: the statements about the Baltic States satisfied him to a certain extent, but he wanted to know whether we also included Lithuania among the Baltic States. My statements on the Polish question evidently impressed him, too; he followed my words with the greatest attentiveness. His comment on this point is perhaps worth noting: "Compliance with the desire of the Germans that, in the Polish matter, no 'solution' be *forced* on the Reich, depends, above all, on Germany itself." Herr Molotov apparently meant thereby that—whatever might happen—the fault would be ours. Finally—and this seems to me the most important point—Herr Molotov demanded that we cease to support Japanese "aggression." In this connection, it is perhaps not uninteresting to note that a member of the American Embassy here, which for the most part is very well informed, stated to one of our aides that we could at any moment upset the British-French negotiations, if we abandoned our support of Japan, sent our military mission back to China and delivered arms to the Chinese. I am afraid that these American ideas are very optimistic, however, and not readily workable, but the Reich Foreign Minister, after all, had some ideas of his own on this point. Something of this sort would, perhaps, have to take place if we are to make any progress.

The British and French military missions have been in Moscow for three days now. The Soviets made no great fanfare over their arrival. Only a very few conferences of the military men have taken place so far, and of their subject matter and outcome nothing is yet known. I assume that the negotiations will last a long time.

With reference to the foregoing, I should like to mention the following: I received instructions to participate in the Nuernberg Party Day, and am supposed to leave Berlin for Nuernberg on September 1 with the other gentlemen of the foreign service. I must also have the new grey uniform made for me for this purpose. Although all preparations have been made, I shall nevertheless have to make a three-day stop in Berlin in order to make the final arrangements and purchases. This means that I shall have to leave here on August 26th, at the latest. The instructions I have received from the Foreign Office are circular instructions, such as apparently every one of us has received. Would it not, as things stand, be better and more necessary for me not to go to Nuernberg this time, but to remain here? I am unable, of course, to judge of these matters with certainty, but I wanted, at least, to address an inquiry to you in the matter. As matters now stand, I consider it very proper that our political conversations with the Soviet Union be carried on in Berlin. In view of conditions here, however, it seems certain to me that from time to time in order to expedite matters I shall have to speak with Herr Molotov, the highest personage that can be reached. Surely I am the person who can best and most easily carry on conversations with Herr Molotov. This remarkable man and difficult character has now grown accustomed to me and has, in conversations with me, in great measure abandoned his otherwise always evident reserve. Any new man would have to start from scratch. But, as I stated, I am unable to judge whether this viewpoint should prevail or whether participation in the Nuernberg Party Day should have priority. I would therefore be very grateful to you if you would have a short telegram sent me on this subject.

With very best regards and a Heil Hitler! I am, my dear Herr von Weizsäcker,

Your ever very devoted   F. W. SCHULENBURG

Frames 69514–69515, serial 127

The German Foreign Office to the German Ambassador in the Soviet Union (Schulenburg)

Telegram

No. 171 of August 14   BERLIN, August 14, 1939—1: 52 p. m.
                    Received Moscow, August 14, 1939—5 p. m.

For the Ambassador for his information.

Astakhov called on me on Saturday in order to communicate to me the following:

He had received instructions from Molotov to state here that the Soviets were interested in a discussion of the individual groups of questions that had heretofore been taken up. A. designated as such questions, among others, besides the pending economic negotiations, questions of the press, cultural collaboration, the Polish question, the matter of the old German-Soviet political agreements. Such a discussion, however, could be undertaken only *by degrees* or, as we had expressed it, by stages. The Soviet Government proposed Moscow as the place for these discussions, since it was much easier for the Soviet Government to continue the conversations there. In this conversation,

A. left the matter open as to whom we would propose to conduct the conference, the Ambassador or another personage, to be sent out.

To my question as to what priority the Soviets assigned the question of Poland, A. replied that he had received no special instructions regarding sequence, but that the chief stress of his instructions lay in the phrase " by degrees."

These communications of A.'s were probably the amplified instructions to the Chargé of which you notified us.

Subject to further instructions.

Schnurre

II. AGREEMENT ACHIEVED, AUGUST 14–AUGUST 23, 1939

Frames 69510–69513, serial 127

The Reich Foreign Minister to the German Ambassador in the Soviet Union (Schulenburg)

Telegram

MOST URGENT   BERLIN, August 14, 1939—10:53 p. m.
                                        Received Moscow, August 15, 1939—4:40 a. m.

No. 175 of August 14

For the Ambassador personally.

I request that you call upon Herr Molotov personally and communicate to him the following:

1) The ideological contradictions between National Socialist Germany and the Soviet Union were in past years the sole reason why Germany and the U.S.S.R. stood opposed to each other in two separate and hostile camps. The developments of the recent period seem to show that differing world outlooks do not prohibit a reasonable relationship between the two states, and the restoration of cooperation of a new and friendly type. The period of opposition in foreign policy can be brought to an end once and for all and the way lies open for a new sort of future for both countries.

2) There exist no real conflicts of interest between Germany and the U.S.S.R. The living spaces of Germany and the U.S.S.R. touch each other, but in their natural requirements they do not conflict. Thus there is lacking all cause for an aggressive attitude on the part of one country against the other. Germany has no aggressive intentions against the U.S.S.R. The Reich Government is of the opinion that there is no question between the Baltic and the Black Seas which cannot be settled to the complete satisfaction of both countries. Among these are such questions as: the Baltic Sea, the Baltic area, Poland, Southeastern questions, etc. In such matters political cooperation between the two countries can have only a beneficial effect. The same applies to German and Soviet economy, which can be expanded in any direction.

3) There is no doubt that German-Soviet policy today has come to an historic turning point. The decisions with respect to policy to be made in the immediate future in Berlin and Moscow will be of deci-

sive importance for the aspect of relationships between the German people and the peoples of the U.S.S.R. for generations. On those decisions will depend whether the two peoples will some day again and without any compelling reason take up arms against each other or whether they pass again into a friendly relationship. It has gone well with both countries previously when they were friends and badly when they were enemies.

4) It is true that Germany and the U.S.S.R., as a result of years of hostility in their respective world outlooks, today look at each other in a distrustful fashion. A great deal of rubbish which has accumulated will have to be cleared away. It must be said, however, that even during this period the natural sympathy of the Germans for the Russians never disappeared. The policy of both states can be built anew on that basis.

5) The Reich Government and the Soviet Government must, judging from all experience, count it as certain that the capitalistic Western democracies are the unforgiving enemies of both National Socialist Germany and of the U.S.S.R. They are today trying again, by the conclusion of a military alliance, to drive the U.S.S.R. into the war against Germany. In 1914 this policy had disastrous results for Russia. It is the compelling interest of both countries to avoid for all future time the destruction of Germany and of the U.S.S.R., which would profit only the Western democracies.

6) The crisis which has been produced in German-Polish relations by English policy, as well as English agitation for war and the attempts at an alliance which are bound up with that policy, make a speedy clarification of German-Russian relations desirable. Otherwise these matters, without any German initiative, might take a turn which would deprive both Governments of the possibility of restoring German-Soviet friendship and possibly of clearing up jointly the territorial questions of Eastern Europe. The leadership in both countries should, therefore, not allow the situation to drift, but should take action at the proper time. It would be fatal if, through mutual lack of knowledge of views and intentions, our peoples should be finally driven asunder.

As we have been informed, the Soviet Government also has the desire for a clarification of German-Russian relations. Since, however, according to previous experience this clarification can be achieved only slowly through the usual diplomatic channels, Reich Foreign Minister von Ribbentrop is prepared to make a short visit to Moscow in order, in the name of the Führer, to set forth the Führer's views to

Herr Stalin.   Only through such a direct discussion, in the view of Herr von Ribbentrop, can a change be brought about, and it should not be impossible thereby to lay the foundations for a definite improvement in German-Russian relations.

ANNEX: I request that you do not give Herr Molotov these instructions in writing, but that you read them to him.   I consider it important that they reach Herr Stalin in as exact a form as possible and I authorize you at the same time to request from Herr Molotov on my behalf an audience with Herr Stalin so that you may be able to make this important communication directly to him also.   In addition to a conference with Molotov, an extended conference with Stalin would be a condition for my making the trip.

RIBBENTROP

Frames 254836–254837, serial 644

The German Ambassador in the Soviet Union (Schulenburg) to the German Foreign Office

Telegram

VERY URGENT   Moscow, August 16, 1939—2: 30 a. m.
SECRET
No. 175 of August 15

Reference your telegram No. 175 of August 14.

Molotov received with greatest interest the information I had been authorized to convey, designated it as extremely important, and declared that he would report it to his Government at once and give me an answer shortly.   He could already state that the Soviet Government warmly welcomed German intentions of improving relations with the Soviet Union and in view of my communication of today now believed in the sincerity of these intentions.

In the matter of the Reich Foreign Minister coming here, he wanted to state tentatively, as his own opinion, that such a trip required adequate preparation in order that the exchange of opinions might lead to results.

In this connection, he was interested in the question of how the German Government was disposed to the idea of concluding a non-aggression pact with the Soviet Union, and further, whether the German Government was prepared to influence Japan for the purpose of improvement in Soviet-Japanese relations and settlement of border conflicts and whether a possible joint guarantee of the Baltic States was contemplated by Germany.

With regard to sought-for expansion of commercial intercourse, M. admitted that negotiations were progressing successfully in Berlin and approaching a favorable conclusion.

M. repeated that if my communication of today included the idea of a nonaggression pact or something similar, this question must be discussed in concrete terms, in order that, in the event the Reich Foreign Minister comes here, it will not be a matter of an exchange of opinion but that concrete decisions will be made.

M. recognized that speed was necessary in order not to be confronted with accomplished facts, but stressed the fact that adequate preparation of the problems mentioned by him was indispensable.

A detailed memorandum [28] on the course of the conversation will follow Thursday by special courier via plane.

SCHULENBURG

Frames 69503-69509, serial 127

Memorandum by the German Ambassador in the Soviet Union (Schulenburg)

SECRET

I began the interview with Molotov on August 15 about 8 : 00 p. m. by stating that according to information which had reached us the Soviet Government was interested in continuing the political conversations, but that it preferred that they be carried on in Moscow.

Molotov replied that this was correct.

Then I read to Herr Molotov the contents of the instruction which had been sent to me and the German text was immediately translated into Russian, paragraph by paragraph. I also informed Molotov about the content of the annex to the instruction which I had received. Molotov took under consideration my communication that on the instructions of the Reich Foreign Minister I was to ask for an audience with Herr Stalin, as well as my statement that in addition to the conference with Molotov, an extended conference with Stalin was a condition for the proposed visit of the Reich Foreign Minister. With regard to the desire of the Reich Foreign Minister that the content of the instruction should reach Herr Stalin in as exact a form as possible, Molotov made a gesture of assent.

Molotov listened to the reading of the instruction with close [*gespannter*] attention, and he directed his secretary to make as extensive and exact notes as possible.

---

[28] See the following document.

Molotov then declared that in view of the importance of my communication he could not give me an answer at once but he must first render a report to his Government. He could state at once, however, that the Soviet Government warmly [*lebhaft*] welcomed the intention expressed on the German side to bring about an improvement in relations with the Soviet Union. Prior to the further communication which he would make to me shortly, after securing instructions from his Government, he wanted, at the moment, to express the following views of his own with regard to the proposals of the 'German Government.

A trip by the Reich Foreign Minister to Moscow would require extensive preparation if the intended exchange of views was to produce any result. In this connection, he asked me for information as to whether the following was in accordance with the facts.

The Soviet Government at the end of June of this year had received a telegraphic report from its Chargé in Rome about a conference between the latter and the Italian Foreign Minister, Ciano. In this conversation Ciano had said that there was a German plan under way which had as its goal a decisive improvement in German-Soviet relations. In that connection Ciano had referred to the following items in the plan:

1) Germany would not be disinclined to exercise influence on Japan for the purpose of an improvement of her relations with the Soviet Union and the elimination of the boundary disputes.

2) Further, the possibility was envisaged of concluding a non-aggression pact with the Soviet Union and making a joint guarantee of the Baltic States.

3) Germany was prepared to make an economic treaty with the Soviet Union on a broad basis.

The contents of the foregoing points had aroused great interest on the part of the Soviet Government and he, Molotov, would very much like to know how much of the plan which Ciano had outlined in the form just mentioned to the Soviet Chargé was true.

I replied that the statements of Ciano apparently rested on a report of the Italian Ambassador here, Rosso, of which we had already heard. The content of this report rested principally on Rosso's deductions.

To a question interjected by Molotov as to whether Rosso was inventing his information, I replied that that was only partly correct. We wanted, as Molotov knew, an improvement in German-Soviet relations and naturally had considered how such an improvement could be brought about. The result of these deliberations was contained in my communications which were known to Molotov and in the statements of the Reich Foreign Minister and of Herr Schnurre to Herr Astakhov.

Molotov replied that the question as to whether Rosso had informed his Government correctly did not interest him further. The Soviet Government at the present moment was interested above all in knowing whether plans such as those which were contained in Rosso's report, or something similar, actually did exist and whether the German Government was still following such a line of thought. He, Molotov, after hearing of the report from Rome had seen nothing improbable about it. The Soviet Government all through recent years had been under the impression that the German Government had no desire to bring about an improvement in relations with the Soviet Union. Now the situation had changed. From the conferences which had taken place in the last few weeks, the Soviet Government had gotten the impression that the German Government was really in earnest in its intentions to bring about a change in relations with the Soviet Union. He regarded the statement which had been made today as decisive and as one in which this wish was especially completely and clearly expressed. As regards the Soviet Government, it had always had a favorable attitude with regard to the question of good relations with Germany and was happy that this was now the case on the German side also. Whether the details as contained in Rosso's report were actually what the Germans had in mind was not of such overwhelming importance. He, Molotov, had the impression that there must be a great deal of truth in them, since these ideas paralleled those advanced from the German side for some months. In this connection he stated with satisfaction that the economic discussions in Berlin were continuing and apparently promised good results.

I remarked that the course of the economic negotiations was satisfactory to us as well, and I asked how he envisaged the further method of procedure in the political conversations.

Molotov repeated that he was interested above everything else in an answer to the question of whether on the German side there was the desire to make more concrete the points which had been outlined in Rosso's report. So, for example, the Soviet Government would like to know whether Germany saw any real possibility of influencing Japan in the direction of a better relationship with the Soviet Union. "Also, how did things stand with the idea of the conclusion of a nonaggression pact? Was the German Government sympathetically inclined to the idea or would the matter have to be gone into more deeply?" were Molotov's exact words.

I replied that, as regards the relationship to Japan, the Reich Foreign Minister had already said to Herr Astakhov that he had his own views on this matter. Thus it might be assumed that the Reich Foreign Minister was prepared to interest himself in this matter also, since his influence upon the Japanese Government was certainly not slight.

Molotov said that all this interested him very much and, at this point, he interjected that Ciano had told the Soviet Chargé that he would strongly support the ideas in the Rosso report. He continued that it was very important for the Soviet Government in connection with the intended trip of the Reich Foreign Minister to Moscow to obtain an answer to the question of whether the German Government was prepared to conclude a nonaggression pact or something similar with the Soviet Union. On an earlier occasion there had been mention of the possibility of "a resurrection and revival of earlier treaties."

I confirmed to Herr Molotov that we really were considering a new order of things [eine Neuordnung der Dinge] either in connection with what had gone before or perhaps on an entirely new foundation. I then asked him whether I might conclude that the questions which had been put by him would constitute the substance of the conferences with the Reich Foreign Minister in Moscow and that he had only communicated them to me so that I might prepare the Reich Foreign Minister for these questions.

Molotov replied that he would still have to make a further reply to me with regard to the question of the visit here by the Reich Foreign Minister. It seemed to him, however, that for such a journey a previous clarification and preparation of definite questions would be necessary, so that it would not be just conversations which were carried on in Moscow, but that decisions could be made as well. He heartily subscribed to my statement that a prompt clarification was desirable. He also had the opinion that haste was desirable, so that the march of events would not confront us with accomplished facts. He must, therefore, repeat that if the German Government was favorably inclined to the idea of the conclusion of a nonaggression pact, and if my statement of today included this or a similar idea, more concrete discussion of these questions should take place at once. He requested me to inform my Government in this sense.

COUNT VON DER SCHULENBURG

Moscow, August 16, 1939.

Frames 178545–178547, serial 276

The German Ambassador in the Soviet Union (Schulenburg) to the State Secretary in the German Foreign Office (Weizsäcker)

Moscow, August 16, 1939.

MY ESTEEMED STATE SECRETARY: With regard to my conversation of yesterday with Herr Molotov, I should like in all haste to stress especially the following:

Herr Molotov was quite unusually compliant and candid. I received the impression that the proposal of the visit of the Reich Minister was very flattering personally to Herr Molotov and that he considers it an actual proof of our good intentions. (I recall that—according to newspaper dispatches—Moscow requested that England and France send a Cabinet Minister here, and that, instead, only Herr Strang came, because London and Paris had been angry that Herr Voroshilov had not been permitted to accept the invitation to the British maneuvers, which is, in fact, quite another matter, since high Soviet Russians have heretofore never traveled abroad.)

In Herr Molotov's statements yesterday, the surprising moderation in his demands on us also seems to be worthy of note. He did not once use the words "Anti-Comintern Pact," and no longer demanded of us, as he did in the last conversation, "suppression" of support of Japanese aggression. He limited himself to the wish that we might bring about a Soviet-Japanese settlement.

More significant is his quite clearly expressed wish to conclude a nonaggression pact with us.

Despite all efforts, we did not succeed in ascertaining entirely clearly what Herr Molotov desired in the matter of the Baltic States. It appears that he *mentioned* the question of a joint guarantee of the Baltic States as only one point in Herr Rosso's report, but did not expressly make the demand that we give such a guarantee. Such a joint guarantee seems to me at variance with the behavior of the Soviet Government in the British-French negotiations.

It actually looks at the moment as if we would achieve the desired results in the negotiations here.

With cordial greetings and a Heil Hitler! I am, Herr State Secretary,

Your ever devoted   COUNT VON DER SCHULENBURG

Frames 69501–69502, serial 127

The Reich Foreign Minister to the German Ambassador in the Soviet Union (Schulenburg)

Telegram

URGENT   BERLIN, August 16, 1939—4:15 p. m.
                              Received Moscow, August 17, 1939—1 a. m.

No. 179 of August 16

For the Ambassador personally.

I request that you again call upon Herr Molotov with the statement that you have to communicate to him, in addition to yesterday's message for Herr Stalin, a supplementary instruction just received from Berlin, which relates to the questions raised by Herr Molotov. Please then state to Herr Molotov the following:

1) The points brought up by Herr Molotov are in accordance with German desires. That is, Germany is ready [*bereit*] to conclude a nonaggression pact with the Soviet Union and, if the Soviet Government so desires, one which would be irrevocable [*unkündbar*] for a term of twenty-five years. Further, Germany is ready to guarantee the Baltic States jointly with the Soviet Union. Finally, it is thoroughly in accord with the German position, and Germany is ready, to exercise influence for an improvement and consolidation of Russian-Japanese relations.

2) The Führer is of the opinion that, in view of the present situation, and of the possibility of the occurrence any day of serious incidents (please at this point explain to Herr Molotov that Germany is determined not to endure Polish provocation indefinitely), a basic and rapid clarification of German-Russian relations and the mutual adjustment of the pressing questions are desirable. For these reasons the Reich Foreign Minister declares that he is prepared to come by plane to Moscow at any time after Friday, August 18, to deal on the basis of full powers from the Führer with the entire complex of German-Russian questions and, if the occasion arises [*gegebenenfalls*], to sign the appropriate treaties.

ANNEX: I request that you read these instructions to Herr Molotov and ask for the reaction of the Russian Government and Herr Stalin. Entirely confidentially, it is added for your guidance that it would be of very special interest to us if my Moscow trip could take place at the end of this week or the beginning of next week.

RIBBENTROP

Frames 69496–69500, serial 127

The German Ambassador in the Soviet Union (Schulenburg) to the German Foreign Office

Telegram

VERY URGENT   Moscow, August 18, 1939—5:30 a. m.

SECRET

No. 182 of August 17

Reference your telegram 179 of August 16.

After I had read to Molotov the supplementary instructions, Molotov declared, without going into their content more closely, that he could give me today the answer of the Soviet Government to my communication of August 15. Stalin was following the conversations with great interest, he was being informed about all their details, and he was in complete agreement with Molotov.

Here Molotov read the answer of the Soviet Government, which in the text given to me is as follows:

"The Soviet Government has taken cognizance of the statement of the German Government transmitted by Count Schulenburg on August 15 concerning its desire for a real improvement in the political relations between Germany and the U.S.S.R.

"In view of the official statements of individual representatives of the German Government which have not infrequently had an unfriendly and even hostile character with reference to the U.S.S.R., the Soviet Government up till very recently has had the impression that the German Government was working for an excuse for a clash with the U.S.S.R., was preparing itself for such a clash, and was basing the necessity of its constantly increasing armament on the inevitability of such a clash. Not to mention the fact that the German Government by means of the so-called 'Anti-Comintern Pact' was attempting to build up a unified front of a group of states against the U.S.S.R., and was attempting with especial persistence to draw Japan in.

"It is understandable that such a policy on the part of the German Government compelled the U.S.S.R. to take serious steps in the preparation of a defense against possible aggression on the part of Germany against the U.S.S.R. and also to participate in the organization of a defensive front of a group of states against such an aggression.

"If, however, the German Government now undertakes a change from the old policy in the direction of a sincere improvement in political relations with the U.S.S.R., the Soviet Government can look upon such a change only with pleasure and is on its own part prepared to alter its policy in the direction of an appreciable [ernsthaften] improvement in relations with Germany.

"If there be added to this the fact that the Soviet Government has never had any sort of aggressive intentions toward Germany and will not have such, and that now as previously the Soviet Government considers a peaceful solution of the questions at issue in the field of relations between Germany and the U.S.S.R. as entirely possible, and that the principle of a peaceful existence of various political systems side by side represents a long established principle of the foreign policy of the U.S.S.R., one comes to the conclusion that for the establishment of new and improved political relations between the two countries, there are now at hand not only a real basis, but the actual prerequisites for undertaking serious and practical steps in that direction.

"The Government of the U.S.S.R. is of the opinion that the first step toward such an improvement in relations between the U.S.S.R. and Germany could be the conclusion of a trade and credit agreement.

"The Government of the U.S.S.R. is of the opinion that the second step, to be taken shortly thereafter, could be the conclusion of a non-aggression pact or the reaffirmation of the neutrality pact of 1926, with the simultaneous conclusion of a special protocol which would define the interests of the signatory parties in this or that question of foreign policy and which would form an integral part of the pact."

Next Molotov supplied the following supplementary information:

1) Economic agreements must be concluded first. What has been begun must be carried through to the end.

2) Then there may follow after a short interval, according to German choice, the conclusion of a nonaggression pact or the reaffirmation of the neutrality treaty of 1926. In either case there must follow the conclusion of a protocol in which, among other things, the German statements of August 15 would be included.

3) With regard to the proposed trip of the Reich Foreign Minister to Moscow, he declared that the Soviet Government was very gratified by this proposal, since the dispatch of such a distinguished public figure and statesman emphasized the earnestness of the intentions of the German Government. This stood in noteworthy contrast to England, who, in the person of Strang, had sent only an official of the second class to Moscow. A journey by the Reich Foreign Minister, however, required thorough preparation. The Soviet Government did not like the publicity that such a journey would cause. They preferred that practical work be accomplished without so much ceremony. To my remark that it was precisely by the journey of the Reich Foreign Minister that the practical goal could be speedily reached, Molotov countered that the Soviet Government nevertheless preferred the other way in which the first step had already been taken.

To my question as to how the Soviet Government reacted to my communication of today, Molotov declared that today's favorable German reply had not been known to the Soviet Government when its answer was prepared and it would still have to be examined, but that today's Soviet answer already contained all the essentials.   He suggested that on the German side we take up at once the preparation of a draft for the nonaggression pact or for the reaffirmation of the neutrality treaty, as the case might be, as well as for the protocol; the same would be done on the Soviet side.

I stated that I would report these proposals to my Government. With regard to the protocol, it would be desirable to have more exact information about the wishes of the Soviet Government.

The conversation was concluded with Molotov's expressing the desire to be supplied as soon as possible with our drafts.

SCHULENBURG

Frames 69492–69495, serial 127

The Reich Foreign Minister to the German Ambassador in the Soviet Union (Schulenburg)

Telegram

VERY URGENT   BERLIN, August 18, 1939—10:48 p. m.
                                    Received Moscow, August 19, 1939—5:45 a. m.
No. 185 of August 18

For the Ambassador personally.

Reference your telegram No. 182.[29]

Please arrange immediately another conversation with Herr Molotov and do everything possible to see that this conversation takes place without any delay.   At this conference, I would ask you to speak with Herr Molotov in the following sense:

The Reich Government, to its great satisfaction, has learned from his last statement the favorable attitude of the Soviet Government with regard to the remolding of German-Russian relations.   We, too, under normal circumstances, would naturally be ready to pursue a re-alignment of German-Russian relations further through diplomatic channels and to carry it out in the customary way.   But the present unusual situation made it necessary, in the opinion of the Führer, to employ a different method which would lead to quick results.   German-Polish relations were becoming more acute from day to day.   We had to take into account that incidents might occur any day that would make the outbreak of hostilities unavoidable.   To judge from the whole attitude of the Polish Government, the developments in this

[29] *Supra.*

respect by no means rested with us. The Führer considers it necessary that we be not taken by surprise by the outbreak of a German-Polish conflict while we are striving for a clarification of German-Russian relations. He therefore considers a previous clarification necessary, if only to be able to consider Russian interests in case of such a conflict, which would, of course, be difficult without such a clarification.

The statement made by Herr Molotov refers to your first communication of August 15th. My supplementary instruction had gone beyond this and stated clearly that we were in complete agreement with the idea of a nonaggression pact, a guarantee of the Baltic States, and German pressure on Japan. All factual elements for immediate commencement of direct verbal negotiations and for a final accord were therefore present.

Furthermore, you may mention that the first stage mentioned by Herr Molotov, namely, the conclusion of negotiations for a new German-Russian economic agreement, has today been completed, so that we should now attack the second stage.[30]

We were, therefore, now asking for an immediate reaction to the proposal made in the supplementary instruction regarding my immediate departure for Moscow. Please add in this connection that I would come with full powers from the Führer, authorizing me to settle fully and conclusively the total complex of problems.

As far as the nonaggression pact especially is concerned, it seems to us so simple as to require no long preparation. We have in mind here the following three points,[31] which I would ask you to read to Herr M., but not to hand to him.

ARTICLE 1. The German Reich and the U.S.S.R. will in no event resort to war or to any other use of force with respect to each other. .

ARTICLE 2. This agreement shall enter into force immediately upon signature and shall be valid and undenounceable thereafter for a term of twenty-five years.

Please state in this connection that I am in a position, with regard to this proposal, to arrange details in verbal discussions at Moscow

---

[30] For a summary of the German-Soviet Trade Agreement of August 19, 1939, see the memorandum by Schnurre of August 29, 1939, *post*, p. 83.

[31] In a telegram of August 19, 1939, 1:44 p. m. (Moscow, No. 185, not printed here) Ambassador Schulenburg called attention to the fact that the following draft of a nonaggression treaty contained only two articles.

and, if occasion arises, to comply with Russian wishes. I am also in a position to sign a special protocol regulating the interests of both parties in questions of foreign policy of one kind or another; for instance, the settlement of spheres of interest in the Baltic area, the problem of the Baltic States, etc. Such a settlement, too, which seems to us of considerable importance, is only possible, however, at an oral discussion.

Please emphasize in this connection, that German foreign policy has today reached a historic turning point. This time please conduct conversation, except for above articles of agreement, not in the form of a reading of these instructions, but by pressing emphatically, in the sense of the foregoing statements, for a rapid realization of my trip and by opposing appropriately any possible new Russian objections. In this connection you must keep in mind the decisive fact that an early outbreak of open German-Polish conflict is probable and that we therefore have the greatest interest in having my visit to Moscow take place immediately.

RIBBENTROP

Frames 69490–69491, serial 127

The German Ambassador in the Soviet Union (Schulenburg) to the German Foreign Office

Telegram

VERY URGENT   Moscow, August 19, 1939—5 : 50 p. m.
No. 187 of August 19

Reference your telegram No. 185 of August 18.

The Soviet Government agrees to the Reich Foreign Minister's coming to Moscow one week after proclamation of the signing of the economic agreement. Molotov stated that if the conclusion of the economic agreement is proclaimed tomorrow, the Reich Foreign Minister might arrive in Moscow on August 26 or 27.

Molotov delivered to me a draft of a nonaggression pact.

A detailed account of the two conversations I had with Molotov today, as well as the text of the Soviet draft, follows by wire at once.

SCHULENBURG

Frames 69481–69483, serial 127

The German Ambassador in the Soviet Union (Schulenburg) to the German Foreign Office

Telegram

VERY URGENT   Moscow, August 19, 1939.
SECRET

No. 189 of August 19

Supplementing my telegram No. 187 of August 19.

In my first conversation of today with Molotov—which began at 2 o'clock and lasted an hour—after having made the communications I had been charged with, I repeatedly tried to convince M. of the fact that a visit of the Reich Foreign Minister to Moscow was the only way of achieving the speed that was urgently called for because of the political situation. M. acknowledged the positive importance of the proposed trip, stressed the fact that the Soviet Government understood and esteemed the underlying purpose, but persisted in his opinion that for the present it was not possible even approximately to fix the time of the journey since it required thorough preparation. This applied both to the nonaggression pact and to the contents of the protocol to be concluded simultaneously. The German draft of the nonaggression pact was by no means exhaustive. The Soviet Government desired that one of the many nonaggression pacts that the Soviet Government had concluded with other countries (for example with Poland, Latvia, Estonia, etc.) should serve as a model for the nonaggression pact with Germany. He left it to the German Government to choose from among them the one that seemed suitable. Further, the content of the protocol was a very serious question and the Soviet Government expected the German Government to state more specifically what points were to be covered in the protocol. The attitude of the Soviet Government toward treaties which it concludes was a very serious one; it respected the obligations which it undertook and expected the same of its treaty partners.

To the reasons I repeatedly and very emphatically advanced for the need for haste, M. rejoined that so far not even the first step—the closing of the economic agreements—had been taken. First of all, the economic agreement had to be signed and proclaimed and put into effect. Then would come the turn of the nonaggression pact and protocol.

M. remained apparently unaffected by my protests, so that the first conversation closed with a declaration on the part of M. that he had imparted to me the views of the Soviet Government and had nothing to add to them.

Hardly half an hour after the close of the conversation, M. sent me word, asking me to call on him again at the Kremlin at 4 : 30 p. m.

He apologized for putting me to the trouble and explained that he had reported to the Soviet Government and was authorized to hand me a draft of the nonaggression pact. As far as the Reich Foreign Minister's trip was concerned, the Soviet Government agreed to Herr von Ribbentrop's coming to Moscow about a week after proclamation of the signing of the economic agreement. Thus, if this proclamation takes place tomorrow, Herr von Ribbentrop might arrive in Moscow on August 26 or 27. M. did not give reasons for his sudden change of mind. I assume that Stalin intervened. My effort to get M. to accept an earlier date for the Reich Foreign Minister's trip was, unfortunately, unsuccessful.

The text of the nonaggression pact draft will follow by wire.

SCHULENBURG

Frames 69479–69480, serial 127

The German Ambassador in the Soviet Union (Schulenburg) to the German Foreign Office

Telegram

VERY URGENT   Moscow, August 19, 1939—11 : 30 p. m.
SECRET
No. 190 of August 19

Supplementing my telegram No. 189 of August 19.

The Soviet nonaggression pact draft reads as follows:

"The Government of the U.S.S.R. and the German Government, desirous of strengthening the cause of peace among the nations and proceeding from the fundamental provisions of the Neutrality Agreement that was concluded in April 1926 between the U.S.S.R. and Germany, have reached the following accord:

ARTICLE 1. Both High Contracting Parties obligate themselves to desist reciprocally from any act of violence and any aggressive action whatsoever toward each other, or from an attack on each other either individually or jointly with other powers.

ARTICLE 2. Should one of the High Contracting Parties become the object of an act of violence or attack by a third power, the other High Contracting Party shall in no manner whatever give its support to such acts of that power.

ARTICLE 3. Should disputes or conflicts arise between the High Contracting Parties with regard to questions of one kind of another, both parties obligate themselves to settle these disputes and conflicts exclusively by peaceful means through mutual consultation or if necessary through the creation of suitable arbitration commissions.

ARTICLE 4. The present Treaty shall be concluded for a period of five years with the proviso that insofar as one of the High Contracting Parties does not denounce it one year before the expiration of the term the validity of the Treaty shall automatically be extended for another five years.

ARTICLE 5. The present Treaty shall be ratified in as short a time as possible, whereupon the Treaty shall enter into force.

Postscript. The present Pact shall be valid only if a special protocol is signed simultaneously covering the points in which the High Contracting Parties are interested in the field of foreign policy. The protocol shall be an integral part of the Pact."

SCHULENBURG

Frames 254844–254846, serial 644

The Reich Foreign Minister to the German Ambassador in the Soviet Union (Schulenburg)

Telegram

VERY URGENT   BERLIN, August 20, 1939—4:35 p. m.
                           Received Moscow, August 21, 1939—12:45 a. m.
No. 189 of August 20

For the Ambassador personally.

The Führer authorizes you to present yourself to Molotov at once and hand him the following telegram from the Führer to Herr Stalin:

"Herr Stalin, Moscow. 1) I sincerely welcome the signing of the new German-Soviet Commercial Agreement as the first step in the reordering of German-Soviet relations.

2) The conclusion of a nonaggression pact with the Soviet Union means to me the establishment of a long-range German policy. Germany thereby resumes a political course that was beneficial to both states during by-gone centuries. The Government of the Reich is therefore resolved in such case to act entirely consistent with such a far-reaching change.

3) I accept the draft of the nonaggression pact that your Foreign Minister, Herr Molotov, delivered, but consider it urgently necessary to clarify the questions connected with it as soon as possible.

4) The supplementary protocol desired by the Government of the Soviet Union can, I am convinced, be substantially clarified in the shortest possible time if a responsible German statesman can come to Moscow himself to negotiate. Otherwise the Government of the

Reich is not clear as to how the supplementary protocol could be cleared up and settled in a short time.

5) The tension between Germany and Poland has become intolerable. Polish demeanor toward a great power is such that a crisis may arise any day. Germany is determined, at any rate, in the face of this presumption, from now on to look after the interests of the Reich with all the means at its disposal.

6) In my opinion, it is desirable, in view of the intentions of the two states to enter into a new relation to each other, not to lose any time. I therefore again propose that you receive my Foreign Minister on Tuesday, August 22, but at the latest on Wednesday, August 23. The Reich Foreign Minister has full powers to draw up and sign the nonaggression pact as well as the protocol. A longer stay by the Reich Foreign Minister in Moscow than one to two days at most is impossible in view of the international situation. I should be glad to receive your early answer. Adolf Hitler."

Please deliver to Herr Molotov the above telegram of the Führer to Stalin in writing, on a sheet of paper without letterhead.

RIBBENTROP

Frame 260314, serial 695

The Reich Foreign Minister to the German Ambassador in the Soviet Union (Schulenburg)

Telegram

No. 191 of August 21   BERLIN, August 21, 1939—10:15 a. m.
                    Received Moscow, August 21, 1939—2:30 p. m.

For the Ambassador.

Please do your best to see that the journey materializes. Date as in telegram.

RIBBENTROP

Frames 260312–260313, serial 695

The German Ambassador in the Soviet Union (Schulenburg) to the German Foreign Office

Telegram

VERY URGENT   Moscow, August 21, 1939—5:30 p. m.
SECRET

Telegram No. 197 of August 21

Reference your telegrams No. 189 of August 20 and No. 191 of August 21.

Strongly stressing the extraordinary importance of, and exceptional need for haste, I delivered to Herr Molotov at 3 p. m. the Führer's message to Stalin, with a translation. M. read the document through and was evidently deeply impressed. He stated that he would forward the message and advise me immediately as soon as a decision was reached.

I tried with all the means at my disposal to make it clear to M. that an immediate journey of the Reich Foreign Minister was absolutely necessary in the interest of both countries. I closed with the request that, under any circumstances, I be given an answer today.

I have just learned that M. wishes to see me again at 5 p. m.

SCHULENBURG

Frame 260307, serial 695

The German Ambassador in the Soviet Union (Schulenburg) to the German Foreign Office

Telegram

VERY URGENT   Moscow, August 21, 1939.
SECRET
No. 199 of August 21

Supplementing my telegram No. 197 of August 21.

Molotov delivered to me at 5 p. m. Stalin's answer, couched in very conciliatory form in reply to the Führer's message. Stalin advises that the Soviet Government agrees to the arrival of the Reich Foreign Minister on August 23.

Molotov declared that it was the desire of the Soviet Government that tomorrow morning at the latest a short factual communiqué on the contemplated conclusion of a nonaggression pact and "pending" arrival of the Reich Foreign Minister be published in Moscow. Molotov requested German assent to this by midnight. I advise consenting since the Soviet Government places itself on record through publication.

Text of Stalin's letter follows at once by wire.

SCHULENBURG

Frame 260306, serial 695

The German Ambassador in the Soviet Union (Schulenburg) to the German Foreign Office

Telegram

VERY URGENT   Moscow, August 21, 1939—7 : 30 p. m.

SECRET

No. 200 of August 21

Supplementing my telegram No. 199 of August 21.

Text of Stalin's reply:

"August 21, 1939. To the Chancellor of the German Reich, A. Hitler. I thank you for the letter. I hope that the German-Soviet nonaggression pact will mark a decided turn for the better in the political relations between our countries.

The people of our countries need peaceful relations with each other. The assent of the German Government to the conclusion of a non-aggression pact provides the foundation for eliminating the political tension and for the establishment of peace and collaboration between our countries.

The Soviet Government has authorized me to inform you that it agrees to Herr von Ribbentrop's arriving in Moscow on August 23. J. Stalin."

SCHULENBURG

Frames 0032–0033, serial F 11

Full Powers
To the Reich Foreign Minister, Herr Joachim von Ribbentrop

I hereby grant full power to negotiate, in the name of the German Reich, with authorized representatives of the Government of the Union of Soviet Socialist Republics, regarding a nonaggression treaty, as well as all related questions, and if occasion arises, to sign both the non-aggression treaty and other agreements resulting from the negotiations, with the proviso that this treaty and these agreements shall enter into force as soon as they are signed.

ADOLF HITLER
RIBBENTROP

OBERSALZBERG, August 22, 1939.

Frames 130968–130970, serial 155

Memorandum by the State Secretary in the German Foreign Office
(*Weizsäcker*)

St. S. Nr. 644   BERLIN, August 22, 1939.

After the Reich Foreign Minister late yesterday evening had briefly informed the Japanese Ambassador by telephone from the Berghof about the latest turn between Berlin and Moscow, I received Herr Oshima about midnight for a conference which lasted about one hour. The Japanese Ambassador as usual showed himself well disposed. At the same time, I discerned in him a certain uneasiness, which increased in the course of the conversation.

I first described to Oshima the natural course of events which had led us to today's conclusion of a nonaggression pact. When Oshima expressed his own concern, we finally came to an agreement as to how Oshima might convince his Government of the necessity and the advantage of the current proceedings.

The ideas of Oshima were, as was to be expected, along two lines:

1) If Russia were relieved of anxiety in Europe, she would strengthen her East Asiatic front and put new life into the Chinese war.

2) The jurists in Tokyo (and there were a great many of them) would debate the consistency of our present proceedings with certain earlier German-Japanese conversations.

Oshima added that there was no use in trying to interfere with accomplished facts. He did, however, look for a certain shock in Japan, and he would like to abate this by making a telegraphic report tonight.

My discussion was along lines somewhat as follows:

1) We were doing nothing which would put in question our friendly relationship with Japan. On the contrary, we would continue to maintain that, and we esteemed the personalities, like Oshima, who had acted and would act most vigorously to that end.

2) The present proceedings were not a cause for surprise inasmuch as the Reich Foreign Minister had informed the Ambassador some months previously that a normalization of German-Russian relations was worth attempting.

3) Such an arrangement would also put us in a position to take steps to bring about a period of quiet in Japanese-Russian relations and to insure its continuance for a considerable period of time. That Japan was at the moment not seeking a Japanese-Russian conflict was certain. I had even received from the Russian side the impression that a Moscow-Tokyo agreement would be welcomed there.

4) Since the Anti-Comintern discussions (which had been mentioned by Oshima) had been undertaken, the front of our enemies had been dislocated both by Japan and by Germany. It was clear as day that for Japan England had become Enemy No. 1, just as Germany also was threatened much less by Russian than by English policy. The agreement which was being reached with Moscow was serving the interests of both of us.

5) If Oshima referred to certain earlier German-Japanese conversations, we would not argue the point with him that we had sought tirelessly to improve German-Japanese relations. We had waited for half a year to hear some echo from Japan. The Japanese Government, therefore, had the priority and Oshima had certainly had the merit of having always recognized this, and of having urged that these negotiations be speeded up.

6) Our economic, and also certain political, discussions with Moscow had lasted for some time. The negotiations for a nonaggression pact were, however, of very recent origin. It was only in the last two or three days that the possibility of this had appeared. Polish arrogance might force us into war even in the course of this week. With only such a limited amount of time available, we had been absolutely compelled to act.

The Ambassador took note of these remarks and in conclusion he assured me of his unaltered intention to work further for German-Japanese friendship. Besides, he hoped to be able to have a brief conference yet today with the Reich Foreign Minister, if the latter passed through Berlin, in order to give his report to Tokyo still more weight. If it were necessary, Oshima would come to the airfield.

WEIZSÄCKER

Frame 254847, serial 644

The Reich Foreign Minister to the German Foreign Office

Telegram [32]

VERY URGENT   Moscow, August 23, 1939—8 : 05 p. m.

No. 204 of August 23

Please advise the Führer at once that the first three-hour conference with Stalin and Molotov has just ended. At the discussion— which, moreover, proceeded affirmatively in our sense—it transpired that the decisive point for the final result is the demand of the Russians that we recognize the ports of Libau and Windau as within their sphere of influence. I would be grateful for confirmation before 8 o'clock German time that the Führer is in agreement. The signing

---

[32] Other copies of this message and of the reply to it indicate that the messages were transmitted by telephone (frame 24017, serial 34, and frame 260299, serial 695).

of a secret protocol on delimitation of mutual spheres of influence in the whole eastern area is contemplated, for which I declared myself ready in principle.

RIBBENTROP

Frame 24018, serial 34

The German Foreign Office to the Reich Foreign Minister

Telegram [83]

No. 235   BERLIN, August 23, 1939.

Reference your telegram No. 204.
Answer is Yes.   Agreed.

KORDT

Frames 0019–0030, serial F 11

Memorandum of a Conversation Held on the Night of August 23d to 24th, Between the Reich Foreign Minister, on the One Hand, and Herr Stalin and the Chairman of the Council of People's Commissars Molotov, on the Other Hand

VERY SECRET!

STATE SECRET

The following problems were discussed:

1) Japan:

The REICH FOREIGN MINISTER stated that the German-Japanese friendship was in no wise directed against the Soviet Union. We were, rather, in a position, owing to our good relations with Japan, to make an effective contribution to an adjustment of the differences between the Soviet Union and Japan.   Should Herr Stalin and the Soviet Government desire it, the Reich Foreign Minister was prepared to work in this direction.   He would use his influence with the Japanese Government accordingly and keep in touch with the Soviet representative in Berlin in this matter.

HERR STALIN replied that the Soviet Union indeed desired an improvement in its relations with Japan, but that there were limits to its patience with regard to Japanese provocations.   If Japan desired war, it could have it.   The Soviet Union was not afraid of it and was prepared for it.   If Japan desired peace—so much the better!   Herr Stalin considered the assistance of Germany in bringing about an

---

[83] Another copy of this message (frame 260299, serial 695) indicates that it was transmitted by telephone and received at Moscow at 11 p. m. on August 23.

improvement in Soviet-Japanese relations as useful, but he did not want the Japanese to get the impression that the initiative in this direction had been taken by the Soviet Union.

The REICH FOREIGN MINISTER assented to this and stressed the fact that his cooperation would mean merely the continuation of talks that he had for months been holding with the Japanese Ambassador in Berlin in the sense of an improvement in Soviet-Japanese relations. Accordingly, there would be no new initiative on the German side in this matter.

2) Italy:

HERR STALIN inquired of the Reich Foreign Minister as to Italian aims. Did not Italy have aspirations beyond the annexation of Albania—perhaps for Greek territory? Small, mountainous, and thinly populated Albania was, in his estimation, of no particular use to Italy.

The REICH FOREIGN MINISTER replied that Albania was important to Italy for strategic reasons. Moreover, Mussolini was a strong man who could not be intimidated.

This he had demonstrated in the Abyssinian conflict, in which Italy had asserted its aims by its own strength against a hostile coalition. Even Germany was not yet in a position at that time to give Italy appreciable support.

Mussolini welcomed warmly the restoration of friendly relations between Germany and the Soviet Union. He had expressed himself as gratified with the conclusion of the Nonaggression Pact.

3) Turkey:

HERR STALIN asked the Reich Foreign Minister what Germany thought about Turkey.

The REICH FOREIGN MINISTER expressed himself as follows in this matter: he had months ago declared to the Turkish Government that Germany desired friendly relations with Turkey. The Reich Foreign Minister had himself done everything to achieve this goal. The answer had been that Turkey became one of the first countries to join the encirclement pact against Germany and had not even considered it necessary to notify the Reich Government of the fact.

HERREN STALIN and MOLOTOV hereupon observed that the Soviet Union had also had a similar experience with the vacillating policy of the Turks.

The REICH FOREIGN MINISTER mentioned further that England had spent five million pounds in Turkey in order to disseminate propaganda against Germany.

HERR STALIN said that according to his information the amount which England had spent in buying Turkish politicians was considerably more than five million pounds.

4) England:

HERREN STALIN and MOLOTOV commented adversely on the British Military Mission in Moscow, which had never told the Soviet Government what it really wanted.

The REICH FOREIGN MINISTER stated in this connection that England had always been trying and was still trying to disrupt the development of good relations between Germany and the Soviet Union. England was weak and wanted to let others fight for its presumptuous claim to world domination.

HERR STALIN eagerly concurred and observed as follows: the British Army was weak; the British Navy no longer deserved its previous reputation. England's air arm was being increased, to be sure, but there was a lack of pilots. If England dominates the world in spite of this, this was due to the stupidity of the other countries that always let themselves be bluffed. It was ridiculous, for example, that a few hundred British should dominate India.

The REICH FOREIGN MINISTER concurred and informed Herr Stalin confidentially that England had recently put out a new feeler which was connected with certain allusions to 1914. It was a matter of a typically English, stupid maneuver. The Reich Foreign Minister had proposed to the Führer to inform the British that every hostile British act, in case of a German-Polish conflict, would be answered by a bombing attack on London.

HERR STALIN remarked that the feeler was evidently Chamberlain's letter to the Führer, which Ambassador Henderson delivered on August 23 at the Obersalzberg. Stalin further expressed the opinion that England, despite its weakness, would wage war craftily and stubbornly.

5) France:

HERR STALIN expressed the opinion that France, nevertheless, had an army worthy of consideration.

The REICH FOREIGN MINISTER, on his part, pointed out to Herren Stalin and Molotov the numerical inferiority of France. While Germany had available an annual class of more than 300,000 soldiers, France could muster only 150,000 recruits annually. The West Wall was five times as strong as the Maginot Line. If France attempted to wage war with Germany, she would certainly be conquered.

6) Anti-Comintern Pact:

The REICH FOREIGN MINISTER observed that the Anti-Comintern Pact was basically directed not against the Soviet Union but against the Western democracies. He knew, and was able to infer from the tone of the Russian press, that the Soviet Government fully recognized this fact.

HERR STALIN interposed that the Anti-Comintern Pact had in fact frightened principally the City of London and the small British merchants.

The REICH FOREIGN MINISTER concurred and remarked jokingly that Herr Stalin was surely less frightened by the Anti-Comintern Pact than the City of London and the small British merchants. What the German people thought of this matter is evident from a joke which had originated with the Berliners, well known for their wit and humor, and which had been going the rounds for several months, namely, "Stalin will yet join the Anti-Comintern Pact."

7) Attitude of the German people to the German-Russian Nonaggression Pact:

The REICH FOREIGN MINISTER stated that he had been able to determine that all strata of the German people, and especially the simple people, most warmly welcomed the understanding with the Soviet Union. The people felt instinctively that between Germany and the Soviet Union no natural conflicts of interests existed, and that the development of good relations had hitherto been disturbed only by foreign intrigue, in particular on the part of England.

HERR STALIN replied that he readily believed this. The Germans desired peace and therefore welcomed friendly relations between the Reich and the Soviet Union.

The REICH FOREIGN MINISTER interrupted here to say that it was certainly true that the German people desired peace, but, on the other hand, indignation against Poland was so great that every single man was ready to fight. The German people would no longer put up with Polish provocation.

8) Toasts:

In the course of the conversation, HERR STALIN spontaneously proposed a toast to the Führer, as follows:

"I know how much the German nation loves its Führer; I should therefore like to drink to his health."

HERR MOLOTOV drank to the health of the Reich Foreign Minister and of the Ambassador, Count von der Schulenburg.

HERR MOLOTOV raised his glass to Stalin, remarking that it had been Stalin who—through his speech of March of this year, which had been well understood in Germany—had brought about the reversal in political relations.

HERREN MOLOTOV and STALIN drank repeatedly to the Nonaggression Pact, the new era of German-Russian relations, and to the German nation.

The REICH FOREIGN MINISTER in turn proposed a toast to Herr Stalin, toasts to the Soviet Government, and to a favorable development of relations between Germany and the Soviet Union.

9) When they took their leave, HERR STALIN addressed to the Reich Foreign Minister words to this effect:

The Soviet Government takes the new Pact very seriously. He could guarantee on his word of honor that the Soviet Union would not betray its partner.

HENCKE

Moscow, August 24, 1939.

Frames 0048–0050, serial F 11

AUGUST 23, 1939.

Treaty of Nonaggression Between Germany and the Union of Soviet Socialist Republics

The Government of the German Reich and
the Government of the Union of Soviet Socialist Republics
desirous of strengthening the cause of peace between Germany and the U.S.S.R., and proceeding from the fundamental provisions of the Neutrality Agreement concluded in April 1926 between Germany and the U.S.S.R., have reached the following agreement:

ARTICLE I

Both High Contracting Parties obligate themselves to desist from any act of violence, any aggressive action, and any attack on each other, either individually or jointly with other powers.

ARTICLE II

Should one of the High Contracting Parties become the object of belligerent action by a third power, the other High Contracting Party shall in no manner lend its support to this third power.

ARTICLE III

The Governments of the two High Contracting Parties shall in the future maintain continual contact with one another for the purpose of consultation in order to exchange information on problems affecting their common interests.

ARTICLE IV

Neither of the two High Contracting Parties shall participate in any grouping of powers whatsoever that is directly or indirectly aimed at the other party.

ARTICLE V

Should disputes or conflicts arise between the High Contracting Parties over problems of one kind or another, both parties shall settle these disputes or conflicts exclusively through friendly exchange of opinion or, if necessary, through the establishment of arbitration commissions.

ARTICLE VI

The present treaty is concluded for a period of ten years, with the proviso that, in so far as one of the High Contracting Parties does not denounce it one year prior to the expiration of this period, the validity of this treaty shall automatically be extended for another five years.

ARTICLE VII

The present treaty shall be ratified within the shortest possible time. The ratifications shall be exchanged in Berlin. The agreement shall enter into force as soon as it is signed.

Done in duplicate, in the German and Russian languages.

Moscow, August 23, 1939.

For the Government of the German Reich:	With full power of the Government of the U.S.S.R.:
v. RIBBENTROP	V. MOLOTOV

Frames 182-183, serial F 19

Secret Additional Protocol

On the occasion of the signature of the Nonaggression Pact between the German Reich and the Union of Socialist Soviet Republics the undersigned plenipotentiaries of each of the two parties discussed in strictly confidential conversations the question of the boundary of their respective spheres of influence in Eastern Europe. These conversations led to the following conclusions:

1. In the event of a territorial and political rearrangement in the areas belonging to the Baltic States (Finland, Estonia, Latvia, Lithuania), the northern boundary of Lithuania shall represent the boundary of the spheres of influence of Germany and the U.S.S.R. In this connection the interest of Lithuania in the Vilna area is recognized by each party.

2. In the event of a territorial and political rearrangement of the areas belonging to the Polish state the spheres of influence of Germany and the U.S.S.R. shall be bounded approximately by the line of the rivers Narew, Vistula, and San.

The question of whether the interests of both parties make desirable the maintenance of an independent Polish state and how such a state should be bounded can only be definitely determined in the course of further political developments.

In any event both Governments will resolve this question by means of a friendly agreement.

3. With regard to Southeastern Europe attention is called by the Soviet side to its interest in Bessarabia. The German side declares its complete political disinterestedness in these areas.[34]

4. This protocol shall be treated by both parties as strictly secret.

Moscow, August 23, 1939.

For the Government of the German Reich:	Plenipotentiary of the Government of the U.S.S.R.:
v. RIBBENTROP	V. MOLOTOV

---

[34] The German text of this article of the Protocol is as follows: "Hinsichtlich des Südostens Europas wird von sowjetischer Seite das Interesse an Bessarabien betont. Von deutscher Seite wird das völlige politische Desinteressement an diesen Gebieten erklärt."

For a statement by the Reich Foreign Minister concerning the discussion of these subjects at the time of the conclusion of the Nonaggression Pact, see Ribbentrop's memorandum for Hitler of June 24, 1940, *post*, p. 157.

III. THE PACT EXECUTED AND AMENDED, AUGUST 23–SEPTEMBER 28, 1939

Frames 221102–221103, serial 439

The Reich Finance Minister (Schwerin-Krosigk) to the Reich Foreign Minister

ROME, August 23, 1939.

MY DEAR HERR VON RIBBENTROP: First, my cordial and sincere congratulations on the great success attained with the Russian pact.

This morning at 10 o'clock I had a conversation with Count Ciano and in accordance with our agreement I herewith report the contents.

After the usual words of salutation Count Ciano immediately talked about foreign policy and stressed the importance of your trip to Russia. Nevertheless, in case of Germany's intervention in Poland, England and France would, in his opinion, immediately participate in the war. The Ambassadors of both powers had just confirmed this to him expressly and very seriously. This created a very serious situation. For actually the Axis was not yet sufficiently prepared, above all, economically. Only in three to four years—Count Ciano corrected himself and said with strong emphasis "in three years"—would it be ready for war. We would certainly have initial military successes; but the enemy would recover and would wage a war of attrition of long duration along economic lines. Upon my objection that the Führer was of a different opinion and did not believe in a war with England and France, Count Ciano replied that he was aware of that, but that he was afraid that the Führer would not be proved right this time. Upon my reply that it was completely intolerable for a great nation to look on passively any longer at the systematic [mis?]treatment of Germans by Poles, and that therefore a solution of the Polish problem was absolutely necessary and that the whole German people was of one mind on that score, Count Ciano replied that a great deal would depend upon the attitude of the Axis peoples. For it would be necessary to fight with utmost tenacity, since in case of a defeat we would have to count on a peace which would practically mean the end of the Axis Powers. Count Ciano concluded the conversation by stating that despite the great diplomatic success of the Russian pact he considered the situation as very serious.

My audience with the Duce will take place tomorrow at 7 p. m. On Friday morning I shall return to Berlin.

Heil Hitler

Sincerely yours,   COUNT SCHWERIN-KROSIGK

[In handwriting:]

MY DEAR HERR VON WEIZSÄCKER: In view of the absence of Herr von Ribbentrop, I am sending you directly a copy of my letter addressed to him.

SCHWERIN-KROSIGK

Frames 78822–78825, serial 147

Letter from Hitler to Mussolini, August 25, 1939

DUCE: For some time Germany and Russia have been engaged in an exchange of views about a new attitude on both sides in regard to their political relations.

The necessity of arriving at some conclusions of this sort was increased by:

(1) The general situation of world politics as it affected both of the Axis Powers.

(2) The necessity of securing a clear statement of position from the Japanese Cabinet. Japan would probably agree to an alliance against Russia, which would have only a *secondary* interest, under the prevailing circumstances, for Germany, and in my opinion, for Italy also. She would not, however, undertake such definite obligations against England, and this, from the standpoint not only of Germany, but also of Italy, was of decisive importance. The intention of the military to force the Japanese Government in a short time to take a similarly clear position with respect to England had been stated months ago, but had never been realized in practice.

(3) The relation of Germany to Poland, not through the blame of the Reich, but as a result of the activity of England, has become considerably more unsatisfactory since spring, and in the last few weeks the position has become simply unbearable. The reports about the persecution of the Germans in the border areas are not invented press reports but represent only a fraction of the terrible truth. The customs policy of Poland, resulting in the throttling of Danzig, has brought about a complete standstill in Danzig's entire economic life for the past several weeks and would, if it were continued for only a brief length of time, destroy the city.

These grounds led me to hasten the conclusion of the German-Russian conversations. I have not kept you informed in detail, Duce, since I did not have an idea of the possible extent of these conversations, or any assurance of the possibility of their success.

The readiness on the part of the Kremlin to arrive at a reorientation of its relations with Germany, which became apparent after the departure of Litvinov, has become ever stronger in the last few weeks and has made it possible for me, after successful preparation, to send my Foreign Minister to Moscow for the conclusion of a treaty which is the most extensive nonaggression pact in existence and whose text will be made public. The pact is unconditional and includes also the obligation for consultation about all questions affecting Russia and Germany. I may tell you, Duce, that through these arrangements the favorable attitude of Russia in case of any conflict is assured, and *that the possibility of the entry of Rumania into such a conflict no longer exists!*

Even Turkey under these circumstances can only envisage a revision of her previous position. But I repeat once more, *that Rumania is no longer in a situation to take part in a conflict against the Axis!* I believe I may say to you, Duce, that through the negotiations with Soviet Russia a completely new situation in world politics has been produced which must be regarded as the greatest possible gain for the Axis.

About the situation on the German-Polish frontier, I can only inform Your Excellency that we have been for weeks in a state of alarm, that as a result of the Polish mobilization German preparations have naturally also been increased, and that in case of an intolerable Polish action, I will act immediately. The assertion of the Polish Government that it is not responsible for these inhuman proceedings, for the numerous border incidents (last night alone there were twenty-one Polish border violations), and for the firing on the German airplanes, which had already received orders to travel to East Prussia over the sea in order to avoid incidents, shows only that the Polish Government has its excitable soldiery [*Soldateska*] no longer under control. Since yesterday Danzig has been blockaded by Polish troops, a situation which is unendurable. Under these circumstances no one can say what the next hour may bring. I can only assure you there is a limit beyond which I will not be pushed under any circumstances.

In conclusion I can assure you, Duce, that in a similar situation I would have complete understanding for Italy and that in any such case you can be sure of my attitude.

ADOLF HITLER

Frames 78820–78821, serial 147

Letter from Mussolini to Hitler, August 25, 1939 [35]

FÜHRER: I am replying to your letter which has just been delivered to me by Ambassador von Mackensen.

(1) Concerning the agreement with Russia, I approve of that completely. His Excellency Marshal Göring will tell you that in the discussion which I had with him last April I stated that a *rapprochement* between Germany and Russia was necessary to prevent encirclement by the democracies.

(2) I consider it desirable to try to avoid a break or any deterioration in relations with Japan, since that would result in Japan's return to a position close to the democratic powers.   With this in mind, I have telegraphed to Tokyo and it appears that after the first surprise of public opinion passed, a better psychological attitude prevails.

(3) The Moscow treaty blockades Rumania and can alter the position of Turkey, which accepted the English loan, but which has not yet signed the treaty of alliance.   A new attitude on the part of Turkey would upset all the strategic plans of the French and English in the Eastern Mediterranean.

(4) As regards Poland I have complete understanding for the German position and for the fact that such strained relations cannot continue permanently.

(5) As for the *practical* position of Italy, in case of a military collision, my point of view is as follows:

If Germany attacks Poland and the conflict remains localized, Italy will afford Germany every form of political and economic assistance which is requested.

If Germany attacks, and Poland's allies open a counterattack against Germany, I want to let you know in advance that it would be better if I did not take the *initiative* in military activities in view of the *present* situation of Italian war preparations, which we have repeatedly previously explained to you, Führer, and to Herr von Ribbentrop.

Our intervention can, therefore, take place at once if Germany delivers to us immediately the military supplies and the raw materials to resist the attack which the French and English especially would direct against us.

At our meetings the war was envisaged for after 1942 and at such time I would have been ready on land, on sea, and in the air according to the plans which had been arranged.

---

[35] Translated from German Foreign Office's translation of Italian original.

I am also of the opinion that the purely military preparations which have already been undertaken and the others which will be entered upon in Europe and Africa will serve to immobilize important French and British forces.

I consider it my implicit duty as a true friend to tell you the whole truth and inform you about the actual situation in advance. Not to do so might have unpleasant consequences for us all. This is my point of view and since within a short time I must summon the highest governmental bodies of the realm, I ask you to let me know yours as well.

MUSSOLINI

Frames 24058–24061, serial 34

Foreign Office Memorandum

STRICTLY CONFIDENTIAL

W IV 3296

MEMORANDUM

The German-Soviet Trade Agreement concluded on August 19 covers the following:

1. Germany grants the Soviet Union a merchandise credit of 200 million Reichsmarks. The financing will be done by the German Golddiskontbank. This method of financing includes a 100 percent guarantee by the Reich. It is a credit based on bills of exchange. The bills of exchange are to be drawn for each individual transaction and have an average currency of 7 years. The interest is 5 percent. Under a secret final protocol, one-half percent of this is refunded to the Russian special accounts in Berlin, whereby the actual interest rate is reduced to 4½ percent.

2. The credit will be used to finance Soviet orders in Germany. The Soviet Union will make use of it to order the industrial products listed in schedule A of the agreement. They consist of machinery and industrial installations. Machine tools up to the very largest dimensions form a considerable part of the deliveries. And armaments in the broader sense (such as optical supplies, armor plate and the like) will, subject to examination of every single item, be supplied in smaller proportion.

3. The credit will be liquidated by Soviet raw materials, which will be selected by agreement between the two Governments. The annual interest will likewise be paid from the proceeds of Soviet merchandise, that is, from the special accounts kept in Berlin.

4. In order that we might secure an immediate benefit from the credit agreement, it was made a condition from the beginning that the Soviet Union bind itself to the delivery, starting immediately, of certain raw materials as current business. It was possible so to arrange these raw-material commitments of the Russians that our wishes were largely met. The Russian commitments of raw materials are contained in schedule C. They amount to 180 million Reichsmarks: half to be delivered in each of the first and second years following the conclusion of the agreement. It is a question, in particular, of lumber, cotton, feed grain, oil cake, phosphate, platinum, raw furs, petroleum, and other goods which for us have a more or less gold value.

5. Since these Soviet deliveries made as current business are to be compensated by German counterdeliveries, certain German promises of delivery had to be made to the Russians. The German industrial products to be supplied in current business as counterdeliveries for Russian raw materials are listed in schedule B. This schedule totals 120 million Reichsmarks and comprises substantially the same categories of merchandise as schedule A.

6. From the welter of difficult questions of detail which arose during the negotiations, the following might also be mentioned: guaranteeing of the rate of exchange of the Reichsmark. The complicated arrangement arrived at appears in the confidential protocol signed on August 26 of this year. In order not to jeopardize the conclusion of the agreement on August 19 of this year, the question was laid aside and settled afterwards. The questions of the liquidation of the old credits, the shipping clause, an emergency clause for the event of inability to deliver of either party, the arbitration procedure, the price clause, etc., were settled satisfactorily despite the pressure of time.

7. The agreement, which has come into being after extraordinary difficulties, will undoubtedly give a decided impetus to German-Russian trade. We must try to build anew on this foundation and, above all, try to settle a number of questions which could not heretofore be settled, because of the low ebb which had been reached in our trade relations. The framework now set up represents a minimum. Since the political climate is favorable, it may well be expected that it will be exceeded considerably in both directions, both in imports and exports.

8. Under the agreement, the following movement of goods can be expected for the next few years:

Exports to the U. S. S. R.	*Imports from the U. S. S. R.*
200 million Reichsmarks credit deliveries, schedule "A".	180 mill. RM. raw material deliveries, schedule "C".
120 mill. RM. deliveries as current business, schedule "B"	200 mill. RM. repayment of 1935 credit
	approx. 100 mill. RM. capitalized interest from present and last credit
X mill. RM. unspecified deliveries on current business	X mill. RM. unspecified deliveries of Soviet goods under German-Soviet Trade Agreement of Dec. 19, 1938.

The movement of goods envisaged by the agreement might therefore reach a total of more than 1 billion Reichsmarks for the next few years, not including liquidation of the present 200 million credit by deliveries of Russian raw materials beginning in 1946.

9. Apart from the economic import of the treaty, its significance lies in the fact that the negotiations also served to renew political contacts with Russia and that the credit agreement was considered by both sides as the first decisive step in the reshaping of political relations.

SCHNURRE

BERLIN, August 29, 1939.

Frame 111568, serial 103

The German Ambassador in the Soviet Union (Schulenburg) to the German Foreign Office

Telegram

VERY URGENT   Moscow, September 2, 1939—5:49 p. m.
No. 254 of September 2   Received September 2, 1939—6:10 p. m.

With reference to your telegram No. 233 of the 30th and No. 241 of the 1st.[36]

To my probing as to whether Istanbul rumors were correct, in accordance with which Turkey was already negotiating with the

---
[36] Neither printed.

Soviet Union, Molotov replied that the Soviet Government was actually engaged in exchange of opinion and was in contact with Turkey.

After consultation with Stalin, Molotov informed me at a second conference at 3 p. m., that there was only a nonaggression pact between the Soviet Union and Turkey and relations were good in general; the Soviet Government was prepared to work for permanent neutrality of Turkey as desired by us. Our conception of the position of Turkey in the present conflict was shared by the Soviet Government.

Please make no use of the above statements of Molotov in dealing with the Turks.

SCHULENBURG

Frame 69855, serial 127

The Reich Foreign Minister to the German Ambassador in the Soviet Union (Schulenburg)

Telegram

No. 253 of September 3   BERLIN, September 3, 1939—6: 50 p. m.
                Received Moscow September 4, 1939—12: 30 a. m.

Very Urgent! Exclusively for Ambassador. Strictly secret! For Chief of Mission or his representative personally. Top secret. To be decoded by himself. Strictest secrecy!

We definitely expect to have beaten the Polish Army decisively in a few weeks. We would then keep the area that was established as German sphere of interest at Moscow under military occupation. We would naturally, however, for military reasons, also have to proceed further against such Polish military forces as are at that time located in the Polish area belonging to the Russian sphere of interest.

Please discuss this at once with Molotov and see if the Soviet Union does not consider it desirable for Russian forces to move at the proper time against Polish forces in the Russian sphere of interest and, for their part, to occupy this territory. In our estimation this would be not only a relief for us, but also, in the sense of the Moscow agreements, in the Soviet interest as well.

In this connection please determine whether we may discuss this matter with the officers who have just arrived here and what the Soviet Government intends their position to be.

RIBBENTROP

Frames 69848-69849, serial 127

The German Ambassador in the Soviet Union (Schulenburg) to the German Foreign Office

Telegram

VERY URGENT   Moscow, September 5, 1939—2:30 p. m.
STRICTLY SECRET
No. 264 of September 5

Reference my telegram No. 261 of September 4.[37]

Molotov asked me to call on him today at 12:30 and transmitted to me the following reply of the Soviet Government:

"We agree with you that at a suitable time it will be absolutely necessary for us to start concrete action. We are of the view, however, that this time has not yet come. It is possible that we are mistaken, but it seems to us that through excessive haste we might injure our cause and promote unity among our opponents. We understand that as the operations proceed, one of the parties or both parties might be forced temporarily to cross the line of demarcation between the spheres of interest of the two parties; but such cases must not prevent the strict execution of the plan adopted."

SCHULENBURG

Frame 111576, serial 103

The German Ambassador in the Soviet Union (Schulenburg) to the German Foreign Office

Telegram

No. 266 of September 5   Moscow, September 5, 1939—5:02 p. m.
                                 Received September 5, 1939—6 p. m.

Reference your telegram No. 262 of the 4th.[37]

Today at 12:30 p. m. I again asked Molotov to have the Soviet Government continue to work on Turkey with a view to permanent neutrality. I mentioned that rumors were current to the effect that England was putting pressure on Rumania to take active part and was holding out a prospect of aid from British and French troops. Since this aid might come by sea, it was in the interests of the Soviet Government to prevail upon Turkey to close the Dardanelles completely.

_____
[37] Not printed.

Molotov replied that the Soviet Government had considerable influence with Turkey and was exerting it in the sense desired by us. Molotov added that there was only the nonaggression pact between the Soviet Union and Turkey; conversations regarding the conclusion of a mutual assistance pact had, it is true, been carried on at one time but had borne no fruit.

He would have rumors about Rumania looked into through the Soviet Embassy in Bucharest.

SCHULENBURG

Frames 211568–211569, serial 388

The German Ambassador in the Soviet Union (Schulenburg) to the German Foreign Office

Telegram

Pol. V 8924   Moscow, September 6, 1939—5 : 46 p. m.
No. 279 of September 6   Received September 6, 1939—8 : 15 p. m.

Reference your telegram No. 267 of the 5th.[39]

Since anxiety over war, especially the fear of a German attack, has strongly influenced the attitude of the population here in the last few years, the conclusion of a nonaggression pact with Germany has been generally received with great relief and gratification. However, the sudden alteration in the policy of the Soviet Government, after years of propaganda directed expressly against German aggressors, is still not very well understood by the population. Especially the statements of official agitators to the effect that Germany is no longer an aggressor run up against considerable doubt. The Soviet Government is doing everything to change the attitude of the population here toward Germany. The press is as though it had been transformed. Attacks on the conduct of Germany have not only ceased completely, but the portrayal of events in the field of foreign politics is based to an outstanding degree on German reports and anti-German literature has been removed from the book trade, etc.

The beginning of the war between Germany and Poland has powerfully affected public opinion here, and aroused new fear in extensive groups that the Soviet Union may be drawn into the war. Mistrust sown for years against Germany, in spite of effective counterpropaganda which is being carried on in party and business gatherings, cannot be so quickly removed. The fear is expressed by the population

---

[39] Not printed.

that Germany, after she has defeated Poland, may turn against the Soviet Union.   The recollection of German strength in the World War is everywhere still lively.

In a judgment of conditions here the realization is of importance that the Soviet Government has always previously been able in a masterly fashion to influence the attitude of the population in the direction which it has desired, and it is not being sparing this time either of the necessary propaganda.   SCHULENBURG

Frame 211562, serial 388

The German Ambassador in the Soviet Union (Schulenburg) to the German Foreign Office

Telegram

VERY URGENT   Moscow, September 9, 1939—12 : 56 a. m.
No. 300 of September 8   Received September 9, 1939—5 a. m.

I have just received the following telephone message from Molotov :

"I have received your communication regarding the entry of German troops into Warsaw. Please convey my congratulations and greetings to the German Reich Government. Molotov."

SCHULENBURG

Frame 69816, serial 127

The Reich Foreign Minister to the German Ambassador in the Soviet Union (Schulenburg)

Telegram

URGENT   BERLIN, September 9, 1939—12 : 50 a. m.
STRICTLY SECRET   Received Moscow, September 9, 1939—12 : 10 p. m.
No. 300 of September 8

For the Ambassador personally.
Reference your telegram No. 261.[40]
We are of course in accord with the Soviet Government that the validity of agreements arrived at in Moscow is not affected by local extension of our military operations. We must and will defeat the Polish Army wherever we meet it. Nothing in the Moscow arrangements is thereby altered. Military operations are progressing even beyond our expectations. The Polish Army, from all indications, is

---

[40] Not printed.

more or less in a state of dissolution. Under these circumstances, I consider it urgent that you resume the conversation with Molotov regarding the military intentions of the Soviet Government. It may be that the summoning of the Russian Military Attaché to Moscow indicates that decisions are in preparation there. I would therefore ask you to speak to Molotov on the subject again in an appropriate manner and to wire result.

RIBBENTROP

Frame 69815, serial 127

The German Ambassador in the Soviet Union (Schulenburg) to the German Foreign Office

Telegram

VERY URGENT   Moscow, September 9, 1939—4 : 10 p. m.
STRICTLY SECRET
No. 308 of September 9

Reference your telegram No. 300 of September 8.

Molotov told me today at 3 p. m. that a Soviet military action would take place within the next few days. The summoning of the Military Attaché to Moscow was in fact connected with it. Numerous reservists would also be called.

SCHULENBURG

Frame 69814, serial 127

The German Ambassador in the Soviet Union (Schulenburg) to the German Foreign Office

Telegram

VERY URGENT   Moscow, September 9, 1939—8 : 40 p. m.
STRICTLY SECRET
No. 310 of September 9

Supplementing my telegram No. 308 of September 9.

The Red Army has admitted to Lieutenant General Köstring [41] that the Soviet Union will intervene. Moreover, external evidence is multiplying of imminent Soviet military action: calling a large number of reservists up to 45 years of age, in particular technicians and physicians, sudden disappearance of important foods, preparation of schoolrooms as hospitals, curtailment in issuance of gasoline, and the like.

SCHULENBURG

[41] Military Attaché of the German Embassy in the Soviet Union.

Frames 69811-69813, serial 127

The German Ambassador in the Soviet Union (Schulenburg) to the German Foreign Office

Telegram

VERY URGENT   Moscow, September 10, 1939—9 : 40 p. m.

STRICTLY SECRET

No. 317 of September 10

Supplementing my telegram No. 310 of September 9 and with reference to telephone conversation of today with the Reich Foreign Minister.

In today's conference at 4 p. m. Molotov modified his statement of yesterday by saying that the Soviet Government was taken completely by surprise by the unexpectedly rapid German military successes. In accordance with our first communication, the Red Army had counted on several weeks, which had now shrunk to a few days. The Soviet military authorities were therefore in a difficult situation, since, in view of conditions here, they required possibly two to three weeks more for their preparations. Over three million men were already mobilized.

I explained emphatically to Molotov how crucial speedy action of the Red Army was at this juncture.

Molotov repeated that everything possible was being done to expedite matters. I got the impression that Molotov promised more yesterday than the Red Army can live up to.

Then Molotov came to the political side of the matter and stated that the Soviet Government had intended to take the occasion of the further advance of German troops to declare that Poland was falling apart and that it was necessary for the Soviet Union, in consequence, to come to the aid of the Ukrainians and the White Russians "threatened" by Germany. This argument was to make the intervention of the Soviet Union plausible to the masses and at the same time avoid giving the Soviet Union the appearance of an aggressor.

This course was blocked for the Soviet Government by a DNB report yesterday to the effect that, in accordance with a statement by Colonel General Brauchitsch, military action was no longer necessary on the German eastern border. The report created the impression that a German-Polish armistice was imminent. If, however, Germany concluded an armistice, the Soviet Union could not start a "new war."

I stated that I was unacquainted with this report, which was not in accordance with the facts. I would make inquiries at once.

SCHULENBURG

Frame 69805, serial 127

The Reich Foreign Minister to the German Ambassador in the Soviet Union (Schulenburg)

Telegram

URGENT   BERLIN, September 13, 1939—5 : 50 p. m.
                              Received Moscow, September 14, 1939—1 : 10 a. m.
No. 336 of September 13

For the Ambassador personally.

As soon as the exact outcome is known in the great battle in Poland, now approaching its end, we shall be in a position to give the Red Army the information it asked for regarding the various parts of the Polish Army. But even now, I would ask you to inform Herr Molotov that his remark regarding Colonel General Brauchitsch's statement was based on a complete misunderstanding. This statement referred exclusively to the exercise of executive power in the old territory of the Reich as regulated before the beginning of the German action against Poland, and had nothing whatever to do with a limitation of our military operations toward the east on former Polish territory. There can be no question of imminent conclusion of an armistice with Poland.

RIBBENTROP

Frames 69806–69808, serial 127

The German Ambassador in the Soviet Union (Schulenburg) to the German Foreign Office

Telegram

VERY URGENT   Moscow, September 14, 1939—6 p. m.
STRICTLY SECRET
No. 350 of September 14

Reference your telegram No. 336 of September 13.

Molotov summoned me today at 4 p. m. and stated that the Red Army had reached a state of preparedness sooner than anticipated. Soviet action could therefore take place sooner than he had assumed at our last conversation (see my telegram No. 317 of September 10). For the political motivation of Soviet action (the collapse of Poland and protection of Russian "minorities") it was of the greatest importance not to take action until the governmental center of Poland, the city of Warsaw, had fallen. Molotov therefore asked that he be informed as nearly as possible as to when the capture of Warsaw could be counted on.

Please send instructions.

I would direct your attention to today's article in *Pravda*, carried by DNB, which will be followed by a similar article in *Izvestia* tomorrow. The articles serve [to prepare] the political motivation mentioned by Molotov for Soviet intervention.

SCHULENBURG

Frames 69788-69790, serial 127

The Reich Foreign Minister to the German Ambassador in the Soviet Union (Schulenburg)

Telegram

VERY URGENT   BERLIN, September 15, 1939—8 : 20 p. m.
STRICTLY SECRET   Received Moscow, September 16, 1939—7 : 15 a. m.
No. 360 of September 15

For the Ambassador personally.

I request that you communicate the following to Herr Molotov at once:

1) The destruction of the Polish Army is rapidly approaching its conclusion, as appears from the review of the military situation of September 14 which has already been communicated to you. We count on the occupation of Warsaw in the next few days.

2) We have already stated to the Soviet Government that we consider ourselves bound by the definition of spheres of influence agreed upon in Moscow, entirely apart from purely military operations, and the same applies of course to the future as well.

3) From the communication made to you by Molotov on September 14, we assume that the Soviet Government will take a hand militarily, and that it intends to begin its operation now. We welcome this. The Soviet Government thus relieves us of the necessity of annihilating the remainder of the Polish Army by pursuing it as far as the Russian boundary. Also the question is disposed of in case a Russian intervention did not take place, of whether in the area lying to the east of the German zone of influence a political vacuum might not occur. Since we on our part have no intention of undertaking any political or administrative activities in these areas, apart from what is made

necessary by military operations, without such an intervention on the part of the Soviet Government there might be the possibility of the construction of new states there.

4) For the political support of the advance of the Soviet Army we propose the publication of a joint communiqué of the following content:

"In view of the complete collapse of the previous form of government in Poland, the Reich Government and the Government of the U. S. S. R. consider it necessary to bring to an end the intolerable political and economic conditions existing in these territories. They regard it as their joint duty to restore peace and order in these areas which are naturally of interest to them and to bring about a new order by the creation of natural frontiers and viable economic organizations."

5) We assume in proposing such a communiqué that the Soviet Government has already given up the idea, expressed by Molotov in an earlier conversation with you, of taking the threat to the Ukrainian and White Russian populations by Germany as a gruond for Soviet action. The assignment of a motive of that sort would be out of the question in practice. It would be directly contrary to the true German intentions, which are confined exclusively to the realization of well-known German spheres of interest. It would also be in contradiction to the arrangements made in Moscow and, finally, would—in opposition to the desire for friendly relations expressed on both sides—expose the two States before the whole world as enemies.

6) Since the military operations must be concluded as soon as possible because of the advanced season of the year, we would be gratified if the Soviet Government would set a day and hour on which their army would begin their advance, so that we on our part might govern ourselves accordingly. For the purpose of the necessary coordination of military operations on either side, it is also necessary that a representative of each Government, as well as German and Russian officers on the spot in the area of operations, should have a meeting in order to take the necessary steps, for which meeting we propose to assemble at Bialystok by air.

I request an immediate reply by telegraph. The change in text agreed upon by Gaus with Hilger has already been taken care of.

RIBBENTROP

Frames 69777–69778, serial 127

The German Ambassador in the Soviet Union (Schulenburg) to the German Foreign Office

Telegram

VERY URGENT   Moscow, September 16, 1939.
STRICTLY SECRET
No. 371 of September 16

Reference your telegram No. 360 of September 15.

I saw Molotov at 6 o'clock today and carried out instructions. Molotov declared that military intervention by the Soviet Union was imminent—perhaps even tomorrow or the day after. Stalin was at present in consultation with the military leaders and he would this very night, in the presence of Molotov, give me the day and hour of the Soviet advance.

Molotov added that he would present my communication to his Government but he believed that a joint communiqué was no longer needed; the Soviet Government intended to motivate its procedure as follows: the Polish State had collapsed and no longer existed; therefore all agreements concluded with Poland were void; third powers might try to profit by the chaos which had arisen; the Soviet Union considered itself obligated to intervene to protect its Ukrainian and White Russian brothers and make it possible for these unfortunate people to work in peace.

The Soviet Government intended to publicize the above train of thought by the radio, press, etc., immediately after the Red Army had crossed the border, and at the same time communicate it in an official note to the Polish Ambassador here and to all the missions here.

Molotov conceded that the projected argument of the Soviet Government contained a note that was jarring to German sensibilities but asked that in view of the difficult situation of the Soviet Government we not let a trifle like this stand in our way. The Soviet Government unfortunately saw no possibility of any other motivation, since the Soviet Union had thus far not concerned itself about the plight of its minorities in Poland and had to justify abroad, in some way or other, its present intervention.

In conclusion, Molotov urgently asked for an explanation of what was to become of Vilna. The Soviet Government absolutely wanted to avoid a clash with Lithuania and would, therefore, like to know whether some agreement had been reached with Lithuania regarding the Vilna region, particularly as to who was to occupy the city.

SCHULENBURG

Frames 69772-69773, serial 127

The German Ambassador in the Soviet Union (Schulenburg) to the German Foreign Office

Telegram

VERY URGENT   Moscow, September 17, 1939.
SECRET
No. 372 of September 17

Reference my telegram No. 371 of September 16.

Stalin received me at 2 o'clock at night in the presence of Molotov and Voroshilov and declared that the Red Army would cross the Soviet border this morning at 6 o'clock along the whole line from Polozk to Kamenetz-Podolsk.

In order to avoid incidents, Stalin urgently requested that we see to it that German planes as of today do not fly east of the Bialystok-Brest-Litovsk-Lemberg Line. Soviet planes would begin today to bomb the district east of Lemberg.

I promised to do my best with regard to informing the German Air Force, but asked in view of the little time left that Soviet planes not approach the above-mentioned line too closely today.

The Soviet commission will arrive in Bialystok tomorrow or day after tomorrow at the latest.

Stalin read me a note that is to be handed to the Polish Ambassador tonight, to be sent in copy to all the missions in the course of the day and then published. The note contains a justification for the Soviet action. The draft read to me contained three points unacceptable to us. In answer to my objections, Stalin with the utmost readiness so altered the text that the note now seems satisfactory for us. Stalin stated that the issuance of a German-Soviet communiqué could not be considered before two or three days.

In future all military matters that come up are to be handled by Lieutenant General Köstring directly with Voroshilov.

SCHULENBURG

Frame 111596, serial 103

The German Ambassador in the Soviet Union (Schulenburg) to the German Foreign Office

Telegram

URGENT   Moscow, September 17, 1939—8 : 23 a. m.
No. 374 of September 17   Received September 17, 1939—8 : 45 a. m.

Reference your telegram of the 16th, No. 358.[42]

On the occasion of my visit of today, Stalin informed me that the Turkish Government had proposed to the Soviet Government the conclusion of an assistance pact that was to apply to the Straits and the Balkans. The Turkish Government desires a pact with a restrictive clause whereby Turkey in rendering aid to the Soviet Union would be obligated only to such actions as are not directed against England and France.

The Soviet Government is not greatly edified by the Turkish proposal, and is considering proposing a clause to the Turkish Government to the effect that the Soviet Union on its part would not be obligated to any action directed against Germany. Stalin requested our reaction to this idea, but made it clearly evident that he considered the conclusion of the assistance pact in suitable form as very advantageous, since Turkey would in that case surely remain neutral. Voroshilov, who was present, added that such a pact would be a "hook" by which Turkey could be pulled away from France. Request instructions.

SCHULENBURG

Frame 111597, serial 103

Memorandum by the State Secretary in the German Foreign Office (Weizsäcker)

BERLIN, September 18, 1939.

To the Office of the Reich Foreign Minister with the request to transmit the following to the train for the Reich Foreign Minister:

Reaction to telegram No. 374 from Moscow regarding Turko-Russian assistance pact:

The matter should be discussed openly with the Italians. If they agree, the Soviet Government could be told that we concur in the basic idea, but parity would be preserved only if the Soviet Government were not obligated to action against Germany, Italy, and Bulgaria.

WEIZSÄCKER

---

[42] Not printed.

Frame 23373, serial 34

The German Ambassador in the Soviet Union (Schulenburg) to the German Foreign Office

Telegram

VERY URGENT   Moscow, September 18, 1939—3:59 p. m.
STRICTLY SECRET   Received September 18, 1939—5:45 p. m.
No. 385 of September 18

In the course of the conversation which I had this evening with Stalin about the dispatch of a Soviet commission to Bialystok, as well as the publication of a joint communiqué, Stalin said, somewhat suddenly, that on the Soviet side there were certain doubts as to whether the German High Command at the appropriate time would stand by the Moscow agreement and would withdraw to the line that had been agreed upon (Pissa–Narew–Vistula–San). I replied with emphasis that of course Germany was firmly determined to fulfill the terms of the Moscow agreements precisely, and I referred to point 2 of the communication made by me to Molotov on September 16 in accordance with the instructions of the Reich Foreign Minister (see telegram No. 360 of September 15 from there). I declared that it would be suitable for the High Command to withdraw to the line which had been agreed upon since, in this way, troops could be made available for the western front. Stalin replied that he had no doubt at all of the good faith of the German Government. His concern was based on the well-known fact that all military men are loath to give up occupied territories. At this point the German Military Attaché here, Lieutenant General Köstring, interjected that the German armed forces would do just as the Führer ordered. In view of Stalin's well-known attitude of mistrust, I would be gratified if I were authorized to make a further declaration of such a nature as to remove his last doubts.

SCHULENBURG

Frames 69766–69770, serial 127

Memorandum by Counselor of Legation Hilger of the German Embassy in the Soviet Union

Re: Publication of joint Soviet-German communiqué.

On September 17 at 3 p. m., the draft of a joint German-Soviet communiqué was transmitted by telephone with instructions to obtain the consent of the Soviet Government to the publication of such a communiqué on September 18. The text of this draft is enclosed (enclosure 1).

On September 17 at 11:30 p. m., the Ambassador submitted the draft to Herr Molotov for approval. The latter stated that he would have to consult with Herr Stalin on the matter. Herr Stalin, who was called on the telephone by Herr Molotov, declared that in his opinion, too, a joint communiqué had to be issued, but that he could not entirely agree to the text proposed by us since it presented the facts all too frankly [*da es den Tatbestand mit allzu grosser Offenheit darlege*]. Thereupon Herr Stalin wrote out a new draft in his own hand and asked that the consent of the German Government be obtained to this new draft. (See enclosure 2.)

On September 18 at 12:30 a. m., I communicated to Under State Secretary Gaus the text of the Soviet draft. Herr Gaus stated that he could not of his own accord declare himself on the matter and had to ascertain the decision of the Reich Foreign Minister.

On September 18 at 12 o'clock noon, the Chief of the Office of the Minister, Herr Kordt, called up on the telephone and informed me as follows:

"We agree to Russian proposal concerning communiqué and shall publish the communiqué in this form Tuesday in the morning papers. Ribbentrop."

I immediately transmitted the above communication by telephone to Herr Molotov's secretary.

On September 18 at 2:05 p. m., Herr Kordt called up again and informed Counselor of Embassy von Tippelskirch as follows:

"The communiqué will be published by us in some of the evening papers. Please advise the offices concerned."

I immediately apprised Herr Molotov's secretary of the above-mentioned communication also.

Two hours later the text of the communiqué appeared on the teletype and was also broadcast over the German short-wave radio.

Moscow, September 18, 1939.
Herewith most respectfully submitted
to the Ambassador
to the Counselor of Embassy
HILGER

On September 18 at 7:15 p. m., Herr Gaus called up and asked whether the communiqué would be published today in the Russian evening papers. If not, it should be broadcast today over the Soviet radio. The Reich Foreign Minister was very anxious that this be done. I told Herr Gaus that today, because it was the Russian Sunday, no evening papers had appeared; that I would inform them further regarding the radio. At 8:00 p. m. I was able to let Herr Gaus know that the Soviet radio had broadcast the communiqué several times since 4:00 p. m.

HI[LGER]

SEPTEMBER 18.

(Enclosure 1)

Draft of a Joint German-Soviet Communiqué

In view of the internal incapacity of the Polish State and of the dissension of the populations living in its former territory, the Reich Government and the Government of the U. S. S. R. consider it necessary to bring to an end the intolerable political and economic conditions existing in these territories. They regard it as their joint duty to restore peace and order in these areas which are naturally of interest to them and to bring about a new order by the creation of natural frontiers and viable economic organizations.

(Enclosure 2)[43]

In order to avoid all kinds of unfounded rumors concerning the respective aims of the German and Soviet forces which are operating in Poland, the Government of the German Reich and the Government of the U. S. S. R. declare that the operations of these forces do not involve any aims which are contrary to the interests of Germany and of the Soviet Union, or to the spirit or the letter of the Nonaggression Pact concluded between Germany and the U. S. S. R. On the contrary, the aim of these forces is to restore peace and order in Poland, which had been destroyed by the collapse of the Polish State, and to help the Polish population to reconstruct the conditions of its political existence.

---

[43] A note in Schulenburg's hand reads: "Stalin draft. September 18, '39."

Frame 23374, serial 34

The Reich Foreign Minister to the German Ambassador in the Soviet Union (Schulenburg)

Telegram

BERLIN, September 19, 1939.
(Sent from Special Train September 19—4:37 p. m.)

For the Ambassador personally.
Reference your telegram No. 385.

I request that you tell Herr Stalin that you reported to Berlin about your conference with him, and that you are now expressly directed by me to inform him that the agreements which I made on the authorization of the Führer at Moscow will, of course, be kept, and that they are regarded by us as the foundation stone of the new friendly relations between Germany and the Soviet Union.

RIBBENTROP

Frame 111608, serial 103

The German Ambassador in the Soviet Union (Schulenburg) to the German Foreign Office

Telegram

STRICTLY SECRET   Moscow, September 20, 1939—2:23 a. m.
No. 395 of September 19   Received September 20, 1939—4:55 a. m.

Molotov stated to me today that the Soviet Government now considered the time ripe for it, jointly with the German Government, to establish definitively the structure of the Polish area. In this regard, Molotov hinted that the original inclination entertained by the Soviet Government and Stalin personally to permit the existence of a residual Poland had given way to the inclination to partition Poland along the Pissa–Narew–Vistula–San Line. The Soviet Government wishes to commence negotiations on this matter at once, and to conduct them in Moscow, since such negotiations must be conducted on the Soviet side by persons in the highest positions of authority, who cannot leave the Soviet Union. Request telegraphic instructions.

SCHULENBURG

Frames 69721–69722, serial 127

The Reich Foreign Minister to the German Ambassador in the Soviet Union (Schulenburg)

Telegram

STRICTLY SECRET   BERLIN, September 23, 1939—3 : 40 a. m.
                          Received Moscow September 23, 1939—11 : 05 a. m.
No. 417 of September 22

Reference your telegram No. 295 [*395?*].   For the Ambassador personally.

We, too, consider the time now ripe to establish by treaty jointly with the Soviet Government the definitive structure of the Polish area. The Russian idea of a border line along the well-known Four-Rivers Line coincides in general with the view of the Reich Government. It was my original intention to invite Herr Molotov to Germany in order to formulate this treaty. In view of your report that the leading personages there cannot leave the Soviet Union, we agree to negotiations in Moscow. Contrary to my original purpose of entrusting you with these negotiations, I have decided to fly to Moscow myself. This particularly because—in view of the full powers granted me by the Führer, thus making it possible to dispense with counterinquiries, etc.—negotiations can be brought to a speedier conclusion. In view of the general situation, my sojourn in Moscow will have to be limited to one or two days at the most. Please call on Herren Stalin and Molotov and wire me earliest proposed date.

RIBBENTROP

Frame 111625, serial 103

The German Ambassador in the Soviet Union (Schulenburg) to the German Foreign Office

Telegram

VERY URGENT   Moscow, September 25, 1939—10 : 58 p. m.
STRICTLY SECRET   Received September 26, 1939—12 : 30 a. m.
No. 442 of September 25

Stalin and Molotov asked me to come to the Kremlin at 8 p. m. today. Stalin stated the following: In the final settlement of the Polish question anything that in the future might create friction between Germany and the Soviet Union must be avoided. From this point of view, he considered it wrong to leave an independent Polish rump state. He proposed the following: From the territory to the east of the demarcation line, all the Province of Lublin and that portion of the Province of Warsaw which extends to the Bug should be added to our share. In return, we should waive our claim to Lithuania.

Stalin designated this suggestion as a subject for the forthcoming negotiations with the Reich Foreign Minister and added that, if we consented, the Soviet Union would immediately take up the solution of the problem of the Baltic countries in accordance with the Protocol of August 23, and expected in this matter the unstinting support of the German Government. Stalin expressly indicated Estonia, Latvia, and Lithuania, but did not mention Finland.

I replied to Stalin that I would report to my Government.

SCHULENBURG

Frame 111637, serial 103

The German Foreign Office to the German Embassy in the Soviet Union

Telegram

VERY URGENT   BERLIN, September 27, 1939.

No. 435

For Reich Foreign Minister in person!

Telegram from Tallinn No. 163 of the 26th for Army High Command, Attaché Section:

The Estonian Chief of Staff informed me of the Russian demand for an alliance. He stated that a naval base at Baltischport and an air base on the Estonian islands were demanded by Russia. The General Staff recommended acceptance of the demands as German aid was most unlikely, hence the situation could only become worse. On September 25 and 26, Russian aircraft carried out extensive flights over Estonian territory. The General Staff gave orders not to fire on aircraft in order not to prejudice the situation. Rössing.[44] Frohwein.[45]

BRÜCKLMEIER

---

[44] German Military Attaché in Estonia.
[45] German Minister in Estonia.

Frame 111638, serial 103

The German Foreign Office to the German Embassy in the Soviet Union

Telegram

VERY URGENT   BERLIN, September 27, 1939.
No. 436

For Reich Foreign Minister in person.
Telegram from Helsinki No. 245 of the 26th:

The Foreign Minister notified me of demands made by Russia on Estonia and observed that Finland was prepared to improve her relations with Russia, but would never accept such demands and would rather let it come to the worst.

I pointed to the difference between the position of Estonia and that of Finland and advised the Foreign Minister to seek the security of his country in good relations with Germany and Russia.

The Foreign Minister agreed and emphasized complete elimination of English influence from the Baltic area.   Blücher.[46]

                                                    BRÜCKLMEIER

Frames 111639-111640, serial 103

The German Foreign Office to the German Embassy in the Soviet Union

Telegram

VERY URGENT   BERLIN, September 27, 1939.
No. 437

For Reich Foreign Minister in person.
Telegram from Reval No. 164 of the 26th:

The Foreign Minister conveyed a request to inform the Reich Foreign Minister of the following, if possible before his departure for Moscow:

The Estonian Government, under the gravest threat of imminent attack, perforce is prepared to accept a military alliance with the Soviet Union.   Minister Selter with staff will fly to Moscow tomorrow, Wednesday, to negotiate.   Aim of negotiation: Framing of a treaty in such manner that the sovereignty and internal security of the country are preserved and the Estonian nonaggression pact kept intact. Hence they intended to propose, in connection with the mutual assistance obligation of the contracting parties, to except the existing nonaggression pacts with third countries.   It is further desired that naval and air bases should be made available only in case of war, when assistance obligation comes into play; in peace time as far as possible only preparation of the bases.   The Russians first demanded Reval as a naval base, but seem prepared to agree to Baltischport or a port on Ösel.   The Estonians wish if possible to grant air bases only on island.

---

[46] German Minister in Finland.

The general tendency is to meet the demands only as far as necessary to prevent an attack and maintain existing good relations with Germany.   Frohwein.

BRÜCKLMEIER

Frame 281527, serial 838

Timetable of Ribbentrop's Second Visit to Moscow [47]

September 27, 1939

Arrival at airport 6 p. m.

First meeting 10 p. m. to 1 a. m.

September 28, 1939

Meeting resumed 3 to 6: 30 p. m.

Dinner at Kremlin.

One act of ballet (Swan Lake) ; Stalin meanwhile negotiated with the Latvians.

Meeting resumed at midnight.

Signing at 5 a. m.

Afterwards reception for the delegation at Ambassador's till about 6: 30 a. m.

September 29, 1939

Departure by air 12: 40 p. m.

Frames 0332-0331, serial F 2

German-Soviet Boundary and Friendship Treaty

The Government of the German Reich and the Government of the U.S.S.R. consider it as exclusively their task, after the collapse of the former Polish state, to re-establish peace and order in these territories and to assure to the peoples living there a peaceful life in keeping with their national character.   To this end, they have agreed upon the following:

ARTICLE I.

The Government of the German Reich and the Government of the U.S.S.R. determine as the boundary of their respective national interests in the territory of the former Polish state the line marked on the attached map, which shall be described in more detail in a supplementary protocol.[48]

---

[47] Found in the papers of Under State Secretary Hencke.
[48] Not printed here.

ARTICLE II.

Both parties recognize the boundary of the respective national interests established in article I as definitive and shall reject any interference of third powers in this settlement.

ARTICLE III.

The necessary reorganization of public administration will be effected in the areas west of the line specified in article I by the Government of the German Reich, in the areas east of this line by the Government of the U.S.S.R.

ARTICLE IV.

The Government of the German Reich and the Government of the U.S.S.R. regard this settlement as a firm foundation for a progressive development of the friendly relations between their peoples.

ARTICLE V.

This treaty shall be ratified and the ratifications shall be exchanged in Berlin as soon as possible. The treaty becomes effective upon signature.

Done in duplicate, in the German and Russian languages.

Moscow, September 28, 1939.

For the Government   By authority of the
of the German Reich: Government of the U.S.S.R.:
   J. RIBBENTROP   W. MOLOTOW

Frame 0319, serial F 2

Confidential Protocol

The Government of the U.S.S.R. shall place no obstacles in the way of Reich nationals and other persons of German descent residing in the territories under its jurisdiction, if they desire to migrate to Germany or to the territories under German jurisdiction. It agrees that such removals shall be carried out by agents of the Government of the Reich in cooperation with the competent local authorities and that the property rights of the emigrants shall be protected.

A corresponding obligation is assumed by the Government of the German Reich in respect to the persons of Ukrainian or White Russian descent residing in the territories under its jurisdiction.

Moscow, September 28, 1939.

For the Government   By authority of the
of the German Reich: Government of the U.S.S.R.:
   J. RIBBENTROP   W. MOLOTOW

Frames 0326-0325, serial F 2

Secret Supplementary Protocol

The undersigned Plenipotentiaries declare the agreement of the Government of the German Reich and the Government of the U.S.S.R. upon the following:

The Secret Supplementary Protocol signed on August 23, 1939, shall be amended in item 1 to the effect that the territory of the Lithuanian state falls to the sphere of influence of the U.S.S.R., while, on the other hand, the province of Lublin and parts of the province of Warsaw fall to the sphere of influence of Germany (cf. the map attached to the Boundary and Friendship Treaty signed today). As soon as the Government of the U.S.S.R. shall take special measures on Lithuanian territory to protect its interests, the present German-Lithuanian border, for the purpose of a natural and simple boundary delineation, shall be rectified in such a way that the Lithuanian territory situated to the southwest of the line marked on the attached map should fall to Germany.

Further it is declared that the economic agreements now in force between Germany and Lithuania shall not be affected by the measures of the Soviet Union referred to above.

Moscow, September 28, 1939.

For the Government of the German Reich:	By authority of the Government of the U.S.S.R.:
J. RIBBENTROP	W. MOLOTOW

Frame 0329, serial F 2

Secret Supplementary Protocol

The undersigned plenipotentiaries, on concluding the German-Russian Boundary and Friendship Treaty, have declared their agreement upon the following:

Both parties will tolerate in their territories no Polish agitation which affects the territories of the other party. They will suppress in their territories all beginnings of such agitation and inform each other concerning suitable measures for this purpose.

Moscow, September 28, 1939.

For the Government of the German Reich:	By authority of the Government of the U.S.S.R.:
J. RIBBENTROP	W. MOLOTOW

Frame 0330, serial F 2

Declaration of the Government of the German Reich and the Government of the U.S.S.R. of September 28, 1939

After the Government of the German Reich and the Government of the U.S.S.R. have, by means of the treaty signed today, definitively settled the problems arising from the collapse of the Polish state and have thereby created a sure foundation for a lasting peace in Eastern Europe, they mutually express their conviction that it would serve the true interest of all peoples to put an end to the state of war existing at present between Germany on the one side and England and France on the other. Both Governments will therefore direct their common efforts, jointly with other friendly powers if occasion arises, toward attaining this goal as soon as possible.

Should, however, the efforts of the two Governments remain fruitless, this would demonstrate the fact that England and France are responsible for the continuation of the war, whereupon, in case of the continuation of the war, the Governments of Germany and of the U.S.S.R. shall engage in mutual consultations with regard to necessary measures.

Moscow, September 28, 1939.

<table>
<tr><td>For the Government
of the German Reich:
J. Ribbentrop</td><td>By authority of the
Government of the U.S.S.R.:
W. Molotow</td></tr>
</table>

Frames 211596–211597, serial 388

The Reich Foreign Minister to the Chairman of the Council of People's Commissars of the Soviet Union (Molotov)

Moscow, September 28, 1939.

Mr. Chairman: I have the honor to acknowledge receipt of your letter of today, in which you communicate to me the following:

"With reference to our conversations, I have the honor to confirm herewith that the Government of the U.S.S.R. is willing, on the basis and in the sense of the general political understanding reached by us, to promote by all means the trade relations and the exchange of goods between Germany and the U.S.S.R. To this end an economic program will be drawn up by both parties, under which the Soviet Union will supply raw materials to Germany, for which Germany, in turn, will make compensation through delivery of manufactured goods over an extended period. Both parties shall frame this economic program in such a manner that the German-Soviet exchange of goods will again reach the highest volume attained in the past.

Both Governments will at once issue the necessary directives for the implementation of the measures mentioned and arrange that the negotiations are begun and brought to a conclusion as soon as possible."

In the name and by authority of the Government of the German Reich I am in accord with this communication and inform you that the Government of the German Reich in turn will take the necessary steps for this purpose.

Accept, Mr. Chairman, the renewed assurance of my highest consideration.

VON RIBBENTROP

Frames 0322-0321, serial F 2

The Reich Foreign Minister to the Chairman of the Council of People's Commissars of the Soviet Union (Molotov)

CONFIDENTIAL   Moscow, September 28, 1939.

MR. CHAIRMAN: I have the honor to acknowledge receipt of your letter of today, wherein you communicate to me the following:

"Implementing my letter of today about the formulation of a common economic program, the Government of the U.S.S.R. will see to it that German transit traffic to and from Rumania by way of the Upper Silesia–Lemberg–Kolomea railroad line shall be facilitated in every respect. The two Governments will, in the framework of the proposed trade negotiations, make arrangements without delay for the operation of this transit traffic. The same will apply to the German transit traffic to and from Iran, to and from Afghanistan, as well as to and from the countries of the Far East.

"Furthermore, the Government of the U.S.S.R. declares that it is willing, in addition to the quantity of oil previously agreed upon or to be agreed upon hereafter, to supply a further quantity of oil commensurate with the annual production of the oil district of Drohobycz and Boryslav, with the proviso that one half of this quantity shall be supplied to Germany from the oil fields of the aforesaid oil district and the other half from other oil districts of the U.S.S.R. As compensation for these supplies of oil, the U.S.S.R. would accept German supplies of hard coal and steel piping."

I take note of this communication with satisfaction and concur in it in the name of the Government of the German Reich.

Accept, Mr. Chairman, the renewed assurance of my highest consideration.

VON RIBBENTROP

IV. GERMAN-SOVIET CO-OPERATION, OCTOBER 2, 1939–MAY 29, 1940

Frames 111659–111660, serial 103

The Reich Foreign Minister to the German Ambassador in the Soviet Union (Schulenburg)

Telegram

No. 475   BERLIN, October 2, 1939.

For the Ambassador.

Please inform Molotov at once that according to reports I have received the Turkish Government would hesitate to conclude an assistance pact with France and England, if the Soviet Union emphatically opposed it. In my opinion, as already stated several times, it would also be in the Russian interest, on account of the question of the Straits, to forestall a tie-up of Turkey with England and France. I was therefore particularly anxious for the Russian Government to proceed in that direction, in order to dissuade Turkey from the final conclusion of assistance pacts with the Western powers and to settle this at once in Moscow. No doubt, the best solution at the moment would be the return of Turkey to a policy of absolute neutrality while confirming existing Russian-Turkish agreements.

Prompt and final diversion of Turkey from the projected Anglo-French treaty, said to have been recently initialed, would also clearly be in keeping with the peace offensive agreed upon in Moscow, as thereby another country would withdraw from the Anglo-French camp.

RIBBENTROP

Frame 111660, serial 103

The Reich Foreign Minister to the German Ambassador in Turkey (Papen)

Telegram

No. 352   BERLIN, October 2, 1939.

Ambassador Schulenburg received the following instructions:
Insert text of [preceding telegram]. End of instruction.

110

I request that you, for your part, likewise do your best to forestall the final conclusion of the assistance pact between Turkey and the Western powers. In this matter you also might point to the strong Russian aversion to a unilateral commitment of Turkey and explain that the conclusion of the assistance pact under present war conditions would necessarily be viewed differently by Germany than before the outbreak of the war.

RIBBENTROP

Frame 233367, serial 495

Memorandum by the State Secretary in the German Foreign Office
(Weizsäcker)

St. S. Nr. 769   BERLIN, October 2, 1939.

The Finnish Minister today requested me to clarify the significance of the arrangement of spheres of influence between Germany and Russia; he was particularly interested in knowing what effect the Moscow agreements might have on Finland.

I reminded the Minister that a short time ago Finland, as is well known, had rejected our proposal to conclude a nonaggression pact. Perhaps this was now regretted in Helsinki. For the rest, now as then it is the wish of Germany to live with Finland on the best and most friendly terms and, particularly in the economic sphere, to effect as extensive an exchange of goods as possible. If Herr Wuorimaa felt uneasy about Finland because of the Estonian incident and Herr Munters'[49] trip to Moscow, announced today, I would have to tell him that I was not informed as to Moscow's policies vis-à-vis Finland. But I felt that worries over Finland at this time are not warranted.

The Minister then spoke of the Ciano visit. In this connection I remarked that after the completion of the Polish campaign we had undoubtedly arrived at an important juncture in the war. The announced convocation of the Reichstag pointed to a statement from the Government in which the idea would surely be expressed that we regarded as senseless any opening of real hostilities in the West. Of course, should the Western powers fail to seize the opportunity for peace, one would probably have to resign oneself to a bitter struggle.

WEIZSÄCKER

---

[49] Latvian Foreign Minister.

Frame 111663–111664, serial 103

The German Ambassador in the Soviet Union (Schulenburg) to the German Foreign Office

Telegram

VERY URGENT   Moscow, October 3, 1939—7 : 04 p. m.
STRICTLY SECRET   Received October 3, 1939—11 : 10 p. m.
No. 463 of October 3

Molotov summoned me to his office at 2 p. m. today, in order to communicate to me the following:

The Soviet Government would tell the Lithuanian Foreign Minister, who arrives today, that, within the framework of an amicable settlement of mutual relations (probably similar to the one with Estonia), the Soviet Government was willing to cede the city of Vilna and its environs to Lithuania, while at the same time the Soviet Government would indicate to Lithuania that it must cede the well-known portion of its territory to Germany. Molotov inquired what formal procedure we had in mind for carrying this out. His idea was the simultaneous signing of a Soviet-Lithuanian protocol on Vilna and a German-Lithuanian protocol on the Lithuanian area to be ceded to us.

I replied that this suggestion did not appeal to me. It seemed to me more logical that the Soviet Government should exchange Vilna for the strip to be ceded to us and then hand this strip over to us. Molotov did not seem quite in accord with my proposal but was willing to let me ask for the viewpoint of my Government and give him a reply by tomorrow noon.

Molotov's suggestion seems to me harmful, as in the eyes of the world it would make us appear as "robbers" of Lithuanian territory, while the Soviet Government figures as the donor. As I see it, only my suggestion enters into consideration at all. However, I would ask you to consider whether it might not be advisable for us, by a separate secret German-Soviet protocol, to forego the cession of the Lithuanian strip of territory until the Soviet Union actually incorporates Lithuania, an idea on which, I believe, the arrangement concerning Lithuania was originally based.

SCHULENBURG

Frame 111666, serial 103

The German Ambassador in the Soviet Union (Schulenburg) to the German Foreign Office

Telegram

URGENT   Moscow, October 3, 1939—8:08 p. m.
STRICTLY SECRET   Received October 3, 1939—11:10 p. m.
No. 464 of October 3

Reference your telegram of the 2d No. 475.

I informed Molotov in detail of the contents of your instruction. Molotov stated that the Soviet Government shared our trend of thought and was proceeding in that direction. However, it appeared that Turkey had already become rather closely involved with England and France. The Soviet Government would continue to try to rectify or "neutralize" matters in our sense.

The Afghan Ambassador, with whom I spoke today, claimed to know that the Soviet Government demanded of Turkey absolute neutrality and the closing of the Straits.

Molotov himself said that the negotiations were still under way.

When I mentioned the rumors that England and France intended to assault Greece and overrun Bulgaria in order to set up a Balkan front, Molotov asserted spontaneously that the Soviet Government would never tolerate pressure on Bulgaria.

SCHULENBURG

Frame 111665, serial 103

The Reich Foreign Minister to the German Ambassador in the Soviet Union (Schulenburg)

Telegram

STRICTLY SECRET   BERLIN, October 4, 1939.
No. 488

Reference your telegram No. 463.

I, too, do not consider the method Molotov suggested for the cession of the Lithuanian strip of territory as suitable. On the contrary, please ask Molotov not to discuss this cession of territory with the Lithuanians at present, but rather to have the Soviet Government assume the obligation *toward Germany* to leave this strip of territory unoccupied in the event of a posting of Soviet forces in Lithuania, which may possibly be contemplated, and furthermore to leave it to Germany to determine the date on which the cession of the territory should be formally effected. An understanding to this effect should be set forth in a secret exchange of letters between yourself and Molotov.

Reich Foreign Minister

[Notes:]

As directed by the Reich Foreign Minister, this telegram is being dispatched *at once* with his signature. Gaus, October 4.

I telephoned the contents of the telegram in veiled language at 11 a. m. to Count Schulenburg. He fully understood the instruction. G[aus], October 4.

Frames 254871-254872, serial 644

The German Ambassador in the Soviet Union (Schulenburg) to the German Foreign Office

Telegram

VERY URGENT   Moscow, October 5, 1939—12:30 a. m.
STRICTLY SECRET

No. 470 of October 4

Reference my telegram No. 463 of October 3.

Immediately after Under State Secretary Gaus' first telephone call I transmitted to Molotov this morning the request not to divulge to the Lithuanian Foreign Minister anything regarding the German-Soviet understanding concerning Lithuania. Molotov asked me to see him at 5 p. m. and told me, that, unfortunately, he had been obliged yesterday to inform the Lithuanian Foreign Minister of this understanding, since he could not, out of loyalty to us, act otherwise. The Lithuanian delegation had been extremely dismayed and sad; they had declared that the loss of this area in particular would be especially hard to bear, since many prominent leaders of the Lithuanian people came from that part of Lithuania. This morning at 8 a. m. the Lithuanian Foreign Minister had flown back to Kowno, intending to return to Moscow in one or two days.

I said that I would immediately notify my Government by telephone, whereupon I called Herr Gaus. An hour later Molotov informed me that Stalin *personally* requested the German Government *not* to insist *for the moment* upon the cession of the strip of Lithuanian territory.

SCHULENBURG

Frames 69687-69689, serial 127

The Reich Foreign Minister to the German Ambassador in the Soviet Union (Schulenburg)

Telegram

VERY URGENT   BERLIN, October 5, 1939—3 : 43 a. m.
STRICTLY SECRET   Received Moscow, October 5, 1939—11 : 55 a. m.
No. 497 of October 4

Referring to today's telephonic communication from the Ambassador.

Legation in Kowno is being instructed as follows:

1) Solely for your personal information, I am apprising you of the following: At the time of the signing of the German-Russian Nonaggression Pact on August 23, a strictly secret delimitation of the respective spheres of influence in Eastern Europe was also undertaken. In accordance therewith, Lithuania was to belong to the German sphere of influence, while in the territory of the former Polish state, the so-called Four-River Line, Pissa–Narew–Vistula–San, was to constitute the border. Even then I demanded that the district of Vilna go to Lithuania, to which the Soviet Government consented. At the negotiations concerning the Boundary and Friendship Treaty on September 28, the settlement was amended to the extent that Lithuania, including the Vilna area, was included in the Russian sphere of influence, for which in turn, in the Polish area, the province of Lublin and large portions of the province of Warsaw, including the pocket of territory of Suwalki, fell within the German sphere of influence. Since, by the inclusion of the Suwalki tract in the German sphere of influence, a difficulty in drawing the border line resulted, we agreed that in case the Soviets should take special measures in Lithuania, a small strip of territory in the southwest of Lithuania, accurately marked on the map, should fall to Germany.

2) Today Count von der Schulenburg reports that Molotov, contrary to our own intentions, notified the Lithuanian Foreign Minister last night of the confidential arrangement. Please now, on your part, inform the Lithuanian Government, orally and in strict confidence, of the matter, as follows:

As early as at the signing of the German-Soviet Nonaggression Pact of August 23, in order to avoid complications in Eastern Europe, conversations were held between ourselves and the Soviet Government concerning the delimitation of German and Soviet spheres of influence. In these conversations I had recommended restoring the Vilna district to Lithuania, to which the Soviet Government gave me its consent. In the negotiations concerning the Boundary and Friendship Treaty of September 28, as is apparent from the German-Soviet boundary demarcation which was published, the pocket of territory of Suwalki jutting out between Germany and Lithuania had fallen to Germany. As this created an intricate and impractical boundary, I had reserved for Germany a border correction in this area, whereby a small strip of Lithuanian territory would fall to Germany. The award of Vilna to Lithuania was maintained in these negotiations also. You are now authorized to make it known to the Lithuanian Government that the Reich Government does not consider the question of this border revision timely at this moment. We make the proviso, however, that the Lithuanian Government treat this matter as strictly confidential. End of instruction for Kowno.

I request you to inform Herr Molotov of our communication to the Lithuanian Government. Further, please request of him, as already indicated in the preceding telegram, that the border strip of Lithuanian territory involved be left free in the event of a possible posting of Soviet troops in Lithuania and also that it be left to Germany to determine the date of the implementing of the agreement concerning the cession to Germany of the territory involved. Both of these points at issue should be set forth in a secret exchange of letters between yourself and Molotov.

RIBBENTROP

Frames 235040–235041, serial 506

Memorandum by the State Secretary in the German Foreign Office (Weizsäcker)

SECRET   BERLIN, October 5, 1939.
St. S. Nr. 786

The Lithuanian Minister called on me this evening in order, as was expected, to inquire about German claims to a strip of land in southwestern Lithuania. Herr Skirpa, however, even when he entered, had a friendlier appearance than was to be expected. For Minister Zechlin [50] had in the meantime delivered information in Kowno as instructed, so that I did not need to go any further into the questions that Herr Skirpa put. I restricted myself to a brief mention of to-day's telegraphic instructions to Herr Zechlin.[51] Since Herr Skirpa

[50] German Minister in Lithuania.
[51] See *supra.*

expressed to me the satisfaction of his Government that we had withdrawn our claim, I stressed that the announcement of our need was "not at the moment pressing." (It is noteworthy that Herr Skirpa knew and traced exactly on the map of Poland that happened to be spread out before us the line agreed upon by us in our secret protocol with the Russians.)

The Minister then gave the further information that the Russians expected to get an assistance pact with Lithuania as well as permission to station Russian garrisons, at the same time agreeing in principle to the joining [*Anschluss*] of Vilna and environs to Lithuania. Herr Skirpa asked me if I had any ideas or suggestions to give in this regard. I stated that I was not informed and added that in connection with our negotiations in Moscow German interests had not been claimed beyond the Russo-German line in the east known to Herr Skirpa.

In conclusion the Minister asked to be given any possible suggestions. Herr Urbsys [52] was still remaining in Kowno today and tomorrow; he himself—Skirpa—was at the disposal of the Reich Foreign Minister at any time.

WEIZSÄCKER

Frames 111680–111681, serial 103

The Reich Foreign Minister to the German Ambassador in the Soviet Union (Schulenburg)

Telegram

VERY URGENT   BERLIN, October 7, 1939.
No. 518

I am receiving reliable reports from Istanbul to the effect that Russo-Turkish negotiations might yet lead to the signing of a mutual assistance pact. Hence I request you to call on Herr Molotov immediately and to emphasize strongly once more how much we would regret it if the Soviet Government were unable to dissuade Turkey from concluding a treaty with England and France or to induce her to adopt an unequivocal neutrality. In the event that the Soviet Government itself cannot avoid concluding a mutual assistance pact with Turkey, we would regard it as a foregone conclusion that she would make a reservation in the pact whereby the pact would not obligate the Soviet Government to any kind of assistance aimed directly or indirectly against Germany. Indeed, Stalin himself prom-

---

[52] Lithuanian Foreign Minister.

ised this. Without such a reservation, the Soviet Government, as has been previously stressed, would commit an outright breach of the Nonaggression Pact concluded with Germany. It would, moreover, not suffice to make this reservation only tacitly or confidentially. On the contrary, we must insist that it be formally stipulated in such a manner *that the public will notice it.* Otherwise a very undesirable impression would be created on the public, and such an act would be apt to shake the confidence of the German public in the effectiveness of the new German-Russian agreements.

Please take this opportunity to inform yourself on the other details concerning the status of the Russo-Turkish negotiations and to find out what is to be agreed upon between the two Governments in regard to the question of the Straits.

Report by wire.

Reich Foreign Minister

Note: I communicated the contents of this instruction to Count Schulenburg this afternoon by telephone. The transmission was very good. Count Schulenburg said he had just come from Molotov, who had told him that he had not talked with the Turkish delegation since Sunday. Hence our warning certainly arrived in time. I replied that Count Schulenburg should nevertheless lose no time, as it was a matter of decisive importance, and the reports received here pointed to a rather advanced stage in the negotiations. Accordingly, Count Schulenburg is to call on Molotov again tomorrow morning.

Frame 0318, serial F 2

The Chairman of the Council of People's Commissars of the Soviet Union (Molotov) to the German Ambassador in the Soviet Union (Schulenburg)

SECRET   Moscow, October 8, 1939.

MR. AMBASSADOR: I have the honor hereby to confirm that in connection with the secret supplementary protocol, concluded on September 29 [*28*], 1939, between the U.S.S.R. and Germany, concerning Lithuania, the following understanding exists between us:

1) The Lithuanian territory mentioned in the protocol and marked on the map attached to the protocol shall not be occupied in case forces of the Red Army should be stationed [in Lithuania];

2) It shall be left to Germany to determine the date for the implementing of the agreement concerning the cession to Germany of the above-mentioned Lithuanian territory.

Please accept, Mr. Ambassador, the expression of my highest consideration.

W. MOLOTOW

Frames 357061–357062, serial 1369

Foreign Office Memorandum

[October ?, 1939.]

OUTLINES FOR MY CONVERSATIONS IN MOSCOW

1) The credit and trade treaty of August 19 of this year is not to be tampered with from either side. However, for our benefit, we must attempt to obtain a more expeditious delivery of raw materials (180 million Reichsmarks).

2) My principal task in the negotiations will be to find out whether Russia, over and above the treaty of August 19, 1939, could and would compensate for the loss in imports by sea and to what extent this might be done. The military and civil agencies have handed me a schedule of requirements totaling 70 million marks of immediate additional supplies. (Enclosure 1.[53]) The requests which I shall present in Moscow will go far beyond this schedule, as the German war needs are several times as great as the proposal of the Departments for the negotiations. (See enclosure 2.[53]) But the relatively modest schedule of departmental requirements shows how low the actual capacity of Russia for supplying raw materials is estimated. The reasons are inadequacies of transportation, of organization, of production methods, etc.

3) The plan to be proposed to the Russians would be as follows:

Apart from the treaty of August 19, 1939, the Soviet Union shall supply us X millions worth of raw materials, both such as are produced in Russia and such as Russia buys for us from other neutrals. The German *quid pro quo* for these raw materials could not follow at once, but would have to take the form of a supply and investment program, to extend over a period of about five years. Within this time we would be prepared, in order to meet our obligations arising from Russian deliveries of raw material, to set up plants in Russia in accordance with a large-scale program to be agreed upon. (See enclosure 3.[53])

---

[53] Not printed.

4) Within the framework of purely economic negotiations, the difficulties actually existing in Russia cannot be overcome, especially as we demand of the Russians performance in advance. A positive achievement can really only be expected, if an appropriate directive is issued by the highest Russian authorities, in the spirit of the political attitude toward us. In that respect these negotiations will be a test of whether and how far Stalin is prepared to draw practical conclusions from the new political course. The raw materials deliveries requested by us can only be carried out, in view of the unsatisfactory domestic supply situation of Russia, at the expense of their own Russian consumption.

5) Depending on the result of my conversations, it will be necessary that the raw materials program be taken up again from the strictly political point of view by a qualified personage.

6) In the Moscow negotiations it should furthermore be ascertained to what extent our imports heretofore made from Iran, Afghanistan, Manchuria, and Japan, can be transmitted via Russia.

SCHNURRE

Frame 111684, serial 103

The German Ambassador in the Soviet Union (Schulenburg) to the German Foreign Office

Telegram

VERY URGENT   Moscow, October 9, 1939—12 : 30 a. m.
No. 493 of October 8   Received October 9, 1939—3 a. m.

Reference your telegram of the 7th No. 518.

Molotov stated this evening at 9 p. m. that since October 1 no meeting had [taken place] with the Turkish Foreign Minister and that the outcome of the negotiations cannot as yet be surmised. Molotov expressed the view that in all likelihood a mutual assistance pact with Turkey would not be concluded. But under any circumstances the interests of Germany and the special nature of German-Soviet relations would be upheld. Molotov explained that the Soviet Government was pursuing the aim of inducing Turkey to adopt full neutrality and to close the Dardanelles, as well as to aid in maintaining peace in the Balkans.

SCHULENBURG

Frame 233368, serial 495

Memorandum by the State Secretary in the German Foreign Office
(Weizsäcker)

St. S. Nr. 793   BERLIN, October 9, 1939.

The Finnish Minister had announced a visit today to the Reich Foreign Minister. On the latter's instructions I received Herr Wuorimaa this afternoon. He presented the following facts:

By virtue of the developments in the Baltic States, Russia had now penetrated so far into the Baltic that the balance of power there had been upset, and predominance threatened to pass to Russia. The lack of interest in this matter on the part of Germany had attracted attention in Finland, since there was reason there to assume that Russia intended to make demands on Finland identical with those made on the Baltic States.

The Finnish Government had requested of Wuorimaa that he find out whether Germany remains indifferent to Russia's forward thrust in this direction and, should that not prove to be the case, to learn what stand Germany intends to take.

The Minister added that, on her part, Finland had tried her best during the last few weeks to regulate her commercial relations with Germany and maintain them on a normal basis and to carry out the policy of neutrality desired by Germany also.

I answered the Minister in the sense of the enclosed instructions to Helsinki.[55] Wuorimaa asked me to call him if we had anything further to add.

From the words of the Minister it could be inferred that the Finnish Government was rather disturbed over the Russian demands and would not submit to oppression as did Estonia and Latvia.

As regards this attitude on the part of the Minister I merely said that I hoped and wished that Finland might settle matters with Russia in a peaceful manner.

WEIZSÄCKER

---

[55] *Infra.*

Frame 233369, serial 495

The State Secretary in the German Foreign Office (Weizsäcker) to the German Minister in Finland (Blücher)

Telegram

No. [326]   BERLIN, October 9, 1939.

In connection with telegraphic instruction No. 322.[56]

The Finnish Minister, who will call today at the Foreign Office, is to receive the following information:

Our relationship to the three Baltic States rests on the well-known nonaggression pacts; our relationship to Denmark likewise. Norway and Sweden have declined nonaggression pacts with us, since they do not feel endangered by us and since they have hitherto not concluded any nonaggression pacts at all. Finland, to be sure, has such a pact with Russia, but declined our offer nevertheless. We regretted this circumstance, but were and are of the opinion that our traditionally good and friendly relations with Finland do not require any special political agreements.

With this absence of problems in the German-Finnish relations it is very easy to understand why in his utterances of October 6th—concerned for the greater part with our neighbors—the Führer did not mention Finland at all, just as he did not mention many other greater and smaller states. From this it only follows that between us there are no points of difference. In Moscow, where in the negotiations of the Reich Foreign Minister, German-Russian relations were discussed in broad political outline and where a treaty of friendship came into being, the well-known definitive line of demarcation was fixed. West of this line lie the German interests, east of it we have registered no interests. We are therefore not informed as to what demands Russia intends to make on Finland. We presume, however, that these demands would not be too far-reaching. For this reason alone a German stand on the question becomes superfluous. But after the developments cited above we would hardly be in a position, in any case, to intervene in the Russian-Finnish conversations.

WEIZSÄCKER

[56] Not printed.

Frame 235081, serial 506

*Memorandum by the State Secretary in the German Foreign Office
(Weizsäcker)*

St. S. Nr. 795   BERLIN, October 9, 1939.

The Swedish Minister called on me today to tell me that a serious situation would arise in the Baltic region if Russia were to make demands on Finland which threatened the independence and autonomy of Finland. The Minister wished to inform me of the preceding with reference to the close relations between Sweden and Finland. It should not be forgotten that, in contrast to Estonia and Latvia, strong and vigorous forces were in power in Finland, who would not submit to Russian oppression.

I replied to the Minister that nothing was known to me about the probable Russian demands on Finland. To my knowledge the word Finland had not been mentioned in connection with the visit of the Reich Foreign Minister to Moscow. The situation was that we had not put forth any claims to any interests east of the well-known line. I should, however, assume that Russia would not set forth any wishes that were too far-reaching as against Finland and that, therefore, a peaceable solution could be found.

WEIZSÄCKER

Frame 214964, serial 407

*The German Minister in Finland (Blücher) to the German Foreign
Office*

Telegram

VERY URGENT   HELSINKI, October 10, 1939—9 : 30 p. m.
                                   Received October 10, 1939—12 midnight.

No. 287 of October 10

All indications are that if Russia will not confine its demands to islands in the Gulf of Finland, Finland will offer armed resistance. The consequences for our war economy would be grave. Not only food and timber exports, but also indispensable copper and molybdenum exports from Finland to Germany would cease. For this reason I suggest you intercede with Russian Government in the sense that it should not go beyond a demand for the islands.

BLÜCHER

Frame 233342, serial 495

Memorandum by the State Secretary in the German Foreign Office (Weizsäcker)

CONFIDENTIAL   BERLIN, October 12, 1939.
St. S. Nr. 800

The Bulgarian Minister, supplementing his recent conversation with the Reich Foreign Minister, informed me today of the following:

The suggestions recently made by Molotov to the Bulgarian Government concerning a Russian-Bulgarian agreement were not clear at first. Later it became evident that Molotov was thinking of a Russian-Bulgarian mutual assistance pact in the event of attack by a third power. This suggestion was rejected in Sofia.

To my question why Bulgaria did not accept it, Draganoff offered as his own conjecture the following: Up to now Bulgaria had never concluded any treaty of alliance of this kind, not even with Germany, to whom she has for long had close ties. Probably his Government did not, for this reason, wish to swerve from this principle nor, above all, conclude a mutual assistance pact with Russia first.

Draganoff then went on to say that the Bulgarian Government made the following counterproposal: Bulgaria was ready to conclude a treaty of nonaggression or friendship with Russia if Moscow would present concrete proposals of this kind. A reply to this has not as yet reached Sofia.

I thanked the Ambassador for the information and promised to transmit it to the Reich Foreign Minister.

                                                     WEIZSÄCKER

Frames 69672–69675, serial 127

The Reich Foreign Minister to the German Ambassador in the Soviet Union (Schulenburg)

Telegram

BERLIN, October 18, 1939—12:40 a. m.
Received Moscow, October 18, 1939—10:05 a. m.
No. 594 of October 17

For the Ambassador in person.

At an occasion soon to arise, I intend to speak in public about the foreign political situation and shall then, with reference to Chamberlain's last speech, deal with the future aims of England and the British propaganda of lies. In this connection I would also like to refute a lie recently circulated in quite specific form by the enemy press, alleging that during my stay in Moscow I had asked the Soviet Union for military assistance, but had met with an outright refusal. I propose to say on this subject approximately the following:

"In its grave disappointment at the recent development in the international situation, which has been strongly influenced by the establishment of friendly relations between Germany and the Soviet Union, British propaganda has left nothing untried to discredit and disturb this development and German-Russian relations. In its well-known manner, it stopped at nothing and has made use of the grossest and most absurd lies. Thus, for instance, it has circulated the statement that in the Moscow negotiations I had asked Herr Stalin for military assistance against Poland, France, and England. To this, Herr Stalin, however, is said to have given only the tart reply: 'Not a single soldier.' But what in reality was the course of these Moscow negotiations? Let me reveal it to you:

"I came to Moscow on August 23 for the purpose of negotiating and concluding, in the name of the Führer, a nonaggression pact with the Soviet Union. I commenced the negotiations with Stalin and Molotov with the statement that I had not come to Moscow, as the British and French delegates had come at the time, to ask the Soviet Union for armed assistance in case a war should be forced upon the German Government by England. The German Government was not in need of assistance for this contingency, but would, in this event, have sufficient military strength to take up the struggle alone against Poland and its Western foes and to carry it to a victorious conclusion. To this, Stalin, with his characteristic clarity and precision, replied spontaneously: 'Germany was taking a proud attitude by rejecting at the outset any armed assistance from the Soviets. The Soviet Union, however, was interested in having a strong Germany as a neighbor and in the case of an armed showdown between Germany and the Western democracies the interests of the Soviet Union and of Germany would certainly run parallel to each other. The Soviet Union would never stand for Germany's getting into a difficult position.' I thereupon thanked Stalin for his clear and precise statement and told him that I would report to the Führer on this broad-minded attitude of the Soviet Government. Thus, the German-Russian negotiations were opened and this exchange of views created from the outset a broad-minded and friendly climate, in which within 24 hours the Nonaggression Pact and, in the course of further developments, at the end of September, the Boundary and Friendship Treaty were concluded. Upon the political foundation, it was likewise decided immediately to inaugurate a comprehensive economic program, the implementation of which is now being discussed at Moscow. Germany has need of the raw materials of the Soviet Union and the Soviet Union has need of manufactured articles. There is no reason why the flourishing trade of the past between the two nations should not soon revive. On the contrary, I am firmly convinced that the former traditional friendship between Germany and Russia has now been restored, and that it will grow stronger and stronger and that the exchange of goods, which is complementary by nature, will result in an undreamed-of prosperity for both nations in the future. Upon the same political foundation, the German-Soviet declaration of September 28, 1939, has also been agreed upon, to the effect that both Governments would work toward the restoration of peace upon conclusion of the Polish campaign. In case these efforts should fail—as they have—the responsibility of England and France for the continuation of the war would be established and at the same time provision would be made for a consultation between the Government of the Reich and the Soviet Government, in this contingency, on the necessary measures to be taken. These consultations are now under way and are proceeding in the same friendly spirit as the Moscow negotiations, and on the firm basis of kindred interests. In this connection, we expect an early visit of Herr Molotov to Berlin. I believe that this brief account is sufficient to sink once and for all the whole raft of lies of the British Ministry of Lies and the other blundering propaganda centers of our enemies, about the present German-Russian negotiations and the future pattern of relations between the two greatest countries of Europe."

Please inform Herr Stalin as promptly as possible of the account of the Moscow negotiations as given above and wire me his approval.

RIBBENTROP

Frame 69660, serial 127

The German Ambassador in the Soviet Union (Schulenburg) to the German Foreign Office

Telegram

URGENT   Moscow, October 19, 1939.
No. 568 of October 19

Reference your telegram No. 594 of October 17.

Molotov today informed me that Stalin approved the account of the negotiations in Moscow that the Reich Foreign Minister contemplates making in his forthcoming speech. He only asked that instead of the sentences quoted as the statement of Stalin: "Germany was taking a proud attitude . . . " up to " . . . getting into a difficult position," the following version be adopted: "The attitude of Germany in declining military aid commands respect. However, a strong Germany is the absolute prerequisite for peace in Europe, whence it follows that the Soviet Union is interested in the existence of a strong Germany. Therefore the Soviet Union cannot give its approval to the Western powers creating conditions which would weaken Germany and place her in a difficult position. Therein lies the community of interests between Germany and the Soviet Union."

SCHULENBURG

Frame 111764, serial 103

Memorandum by the State Secretary in the German Foreign Office (Weizsäcker)

St. S. Nr. 864   BERLIN, November 1, 1939.

Field Marshal Göring, Grand Admiral Raeder and Colonel General Keitel, independently of each other, have told me that the Russian delegation in Berlin expected too much in the way of inspection and procurement of German materials of war. Colonel General Keitel told me it was the Führer's opinion that materials regularly issued to troops could be shown to the Russians; what might be sold, we had to decide ourselves. Things in the testing stage or otherwise secret should not be shown to the Russians.

WEIZSÄCKER

Frame 111828, serial 103

The State Secretary in the German Foreign Office (Weizsäcker) to German Missions Abroad [57]

Telegram

Pol. VI 2651   BERLIN, December 2, 1939.

In your conversations regarding the Finnish-Russian conflict please avoid any anti-Russian note.

According to whom you are addressing, the following arguments are to be employed: The inescapable course of events in the revision of the treaties following the last Great War. The natural requirement of Russia for increased security of Leningrad and the entrance to the Gulf of Finland. The foreign policy pursued by the Finnish Government has in the last few years stressed the idea of neutrality. It has relied on the Scandinavian states and has treated German-Russian opposition as axiomatic. As a result Finland has avoided any *rapprochement* with Germany and has even rejected the conclusion of a nonaggression pact with Germany as compromising, even though

---

[57] As indicated on an accompanying list; list not printed.

Finland has a nonaggression pact with Russia. Also in the League of Nations, Finland, in spite of the debt of gratitude which she owed to Germany for the latter's help in 1918, has never come out for German interests. Foreign Minister Holsti is typical of this point of view and particularly hostile to Germany. Extensive elements in Finland emphasize their economic and ideological orientation in the direction of democratic England. Correspondingly the attitude of most of the organs of the press is outspokenly unfriendly to us. The platonic sympathy of England has confirmed Finland in her previous attitude and has done the country no good.

WEIZSÄCKER

Frame 111834, serial 103

Memorandum by the State Secretary in the German Foreign Office (Weizsäcker)

St. S. Nr. 949   BERLIN, December 5, 1939.

Colonel General Keitel telephoned me today on the following matter: Lately there have been repeated wrangles on the boundary between Russia and the Government General, into which the army, too, was drawn. The expulsion of Jews into Russian territory, in particular, did not proceed as smoothly as had apparently been expected. In practice, the procedure was, for example, that at a quiet place in the woods, a thousand Jews were expelled across the Russian border; 15 kilometers away, they came back, with the Russian commander trying to force the German one to readmit the group. As it was a case involving foreign policy, the O. K. W. was not able to issue directives to the Governor General in the matter. Naval Captain Bürkner will get in touch with the desk officer at the Foreign Office. Colonel General Keitel asked me to arrange for a favorable outcome of this interview.

WEIZSÄCKER

Frame 111835, serial 103

Memorandum by the State Secretary in the German Foreign Office (Weizsäcker)

St. S. Nr. 950   BERLIN, December 5, 1939.

Colonel General Keitel called me on the telephone today to say that the Russian schedule of requests for deliveries of German products was growing more and more voluminous and unreasonable. The negotiations with the Russians would necessarily, therefore, become more and more difficult. The Russians, for example, wanted machine tools for the manufacture of munitions, while the O. K. W. could not spare such machine tools in the present state of the war under any circumstances. The same was true in respect to supplies of air and naval war matériel.

I confirmed to Colonel General Keitel that the Foreign Office, too, intended to put a curb on Russian demands. We had not yet quite made up our mind how to do it, whether in Moscow or here through the ·Russian Ambassador. The Reich Foreign Minister, too, had yet to be informed.

In conclusion, Colonel General Keitel said that he was willing, either through General Thomas or by his own participation, to bring about a meeting, if necessary.

WEIZSÄCKER

Frames 111836–111837, serial 103

The State Secretary in the German Foreign Office (Weizsäcker) to the German Ambassador in the Soviet Union (Schulenburg)

Telegram

No. 1003   BERLIN, December 6, 1939.

Supplement to Instruction Pol. VI 2651, Item II.

Supplementing telegraphic instruction of December 2,[59] the following additional instruction was issued today to all the important missions:

In conversations regarding the Finnish-Russian conflict, you are requested to make use of the following considerations:

Only a few weeks ago Finland was about to come to an understanding with Russia, which might have been achieved by a prudent Finnish policy. An appeal to the League of Nations by the Finnish Government is the least suitable way of solving the crisis.

There is no doubt that British influence on the Finnish Government—partly operating through Scandinavian capitals—induced the Finnish Government to reject Russian proposals and thereby brought on the present conflict. England's guilt in the Russo-Finnish conflict should be especially emphasized.

[59] *Ante*, p. 127.

Germany is not involved in these events. In conversations, sympathy is to be expressed for the Russian point of view. Please refrain from expressing any sympathy for the Finnish position.

End of telegraphic instruction.

WEIZSÄCKER

Frames 395-393, serial F 18

Memorandum by the Reich Foreign Minister

RAM NR. 60   BERLIN, December 11, 1939.

I. I asked the Russian Ambassador to see me today at 5 p.m.

At the beginning of our conversation, I indicated to Herr Shkvartsev the inappropriateness of the report given out by the Tass agency yesterday, dealing with alleged armament supplies by Germany to Finland. I stressed the fact that this report had been denied yesterday by German sources. All the more did I regret that this report, apparently launched from English sources via Sweden and only designed to create discord between Germany and the Soviet Union, has been taken up in so striking a fashion by the official Russian agency.

On the armaments business with Finland I made the following suggestions to him:

1) Germany had before the commencement of hostilities last summer contracted with Finland for the supply of certain anti-aircraft guns in exchange for nickel shipments from Finland. After the hostilities began, further shipments ceased.

2) The Italian Government had inquired in October whether Germany was willing to permit the transit of fifty aircraft to Finland. At that time the threat of military measures between Russia and Finland could not yet be foreseen. Therefore, the German Government had, to be sure, refused transit by air, but raised no objection to transit by rail. The Italian Government, however, did not refer to this matter again, and neither the Italians nor the Finns made requests for a transit permit for the planes.

3) Some time ago an application was made to ship certain war materials for Finland from Belgium through Germany. This application, too, had been rejected.

I was now asking the Russian Ambassador to inform his Government of the foregoing and to point out that with publications such as the Tass report mentioned, only England's game was being played. England was behind Finland and according to intelligence received, England was also responsible for the failure of the Russo-Finnish negotiations last November. I should be grateful if the Russian Government would cause the Tass agency, before releasing such reports in the future, first to get in touch either with the German Embassy in

Moscow or with Berlin, in order that such unpleasant incidents might be avoided.

The Russian Ambassador showed appreciation of my viewpoint and promised to report to his Government accordingly.

II. I then spoke to the Russian Ambassador about the extensive demands for military supplies put forward by the Russian trade delegation. I wanted to say beforehand, that I had given instructions to comply with the Russian requests in any conceivable way, within the limits of possibility. But it should not be forgotten that Germany was at war and that certain things were simply not possible. As I had since been told, a new basis had been found in the meantime, upon which the further negotiations can soon be concluded in Moscow, between the newly arrived Russian delegation and our negotiators. I asked the Russian Ambassador, however, to point out in Moscow, that from the German side everything humanly possible has been done and that beyond that one could not go.

The Russian Ambassador promised to report to Moscow in this sense and stressed the point that from the Russian side any military information obtained here by the Russian delegation would, of course, be kept secret.

I told the Russian Ambassador that we had complete confidence in the Russian promises, but it should be understood by the Russians that there was certain material that we could not supply during the war.

RIBBENTROP

Frames 213-208, serial F 18

Foreign Office Memorandum

STATE SECRET

W 1027/40 g. Rs.

MEMORANDUM ON THE GERMAN-SOVIET COMMERCIAL AGREEMENT SIGNED ON FEBRUARY 11, 1940

The Agreement is based on the correspondence—mentioned in the preamble—between the Reich Minister for Foreign Affairs and the Chairman of the Council of People's Commissars, Molotov, dated September 28, 1939.[60] The Agreement represents the first great step toward the economic program envisaged by both sides and is to be followed by others.

1. The Agreement covers a period of 27 months, i. e., the Soviet deliveries, which are to be made within 18 months, will be compen-

[60] *Ante,* pp. 108-109.

sated by German deliveries in turn within 27 months.   The most difficult point of the correspondence of September 28, 1939, namely, that
the Soviet raw material deliveries are to be compensated by German
industrial deliveries over a *longer period*, is thereby settled in accordance with our wishes.   This was not possible without a hard fight.
Only the personal message of the Reich Foreign Minister to Stalin
brought the final settlement.   The stipulation of 18 and 27 months
represents a compromise solution, since at stated intervals—namely,
every 6 months—the mutual deliveries of goods must be balanced
according to the fixed ratio.   If this balance does not exist, i. e., particularly if the German deliveries fall behind the ratio of the Soviet
deliveries fixed by the Agreement, the other side is entitled to suspend
its deliveries temporarily until the fixed ratio is reestablished.   This
stipulation is annoying, but could not be eliminated by us, as Stalin
himself had adopted it during the final talks.

2. The Soviet deliveries.   According to the Agreement, the Soviet
Union shall within the first 12 months deliver raw materials in the
amount of approximately 500 million Reichsmarks.

In addition, the Soviets will deliver raw materials, contemplated in
the Credit Agreement of August 19, 1939, for the same period, in the
amount of approximately 100 million Reichsmarks.

The most important raw materials are the following:

> 1,000,000 tons of grain for cattle, and of legumes, in the amount of
> 120 million Reichsmarks
> 900,000 tons of mineral oil in the amount of approximately 115
> million Reichsmarks
> 100,000 tons of cotton in the amount of approximately 90 million
> Reichsmarks
> 500,000 tons of phosphates
> 100,000 tons of chrome ores
> 500,000 tons of iron ore
> 300,000 tons of scrap iron and pig iron
> 2,400 kg. of platinum
> Manganese ore, metals, lumber, and numerous other raw materials.

To this must also be added the Soviet exports to the Protectorate,
which are not included in the Agreement, in the amount of about 50
million Reichsmarks so that the net deliveries of goods from the Soviet
Union during the first treaty year amount to a total of 650 million
Reichsmarks.

In addition, there are other important benefits.   On the basis of the
correspondence of September 28, 1939, the Soviet Union had granted
us the right of transit to and from Rumania, Iran, and Afghanistan

and the countries of the Far East, which is particularly important in view of the German soybean purchases from Manchukuo. The freight rates of the Trans-Siberian Railroad were reduced by 50 percent for soybeans. The transit freight charges are to be settled by a clearing system and amount to approximately 100 million Reichsmarks.

Adding certain other items (clearing share in purchase of raw materials by the Soviet Union in third countries), it may be assumed that during the first 12 months *Soviet deliveries and services* will amount to a total of about 800 million Reichsmarks.

3. Thus far, only part of the Soviet deliveries has been fixed for the second treaty year. During the first 6 months of the second treaty year the Soviet Union will deliver to Germany 230 million Reichsmarks worth of raw materials of the same kind as in the first treaty year. It is contemplated that negotiations will be resumed before the expiration of the first treaty year and the quantities for the exchange of goods for the second treaty year fixed and even increased beyond the volume of the first treaty year.

4. The German deliveries comprise industrial products, industrial processes and installations as well as war matériel. The Soviet deliveries of the first 12 months are to be compensated by us within 15 months. The Soviet deliveries of the first 6 months of the second treaty year (13th to 18th month) are to be compensated by us within 12 months (from the 16th to the 27th month).

5. Among the Soviet deliveries within the first 18 months are 11,000 tons of copper, 3,000 tons' of nickel, 950 tons of tin, 500 tons of molybdenum, 500 tons of wolfram, 40 tons of cobalt. These deliveries of metals are intended for the carrying out of the German deliveries to the Soviet Union. Since these metals are not *immediately* available in Germany and will not be delivered until the treaty is in force, it will be necessary to bridge the initial period by using metals from our own stocks for the German deliveries to the Soviet Union and to replace them from the incoming Soviet metal deliveries. Any different arrangement, such as the advance delivery of metals which we demanded at first, could not be achieved.

Furthermore, the Soviet Union declared her willingness to act as buyer of metals and raw materials in third countries. To what degree this promise can be realized in view of the intensified English countermeasures cannot be judged at the present time. Since Stalin himself has repeatedly promised *generous* help in this respect it may be expected that the Soviet Union will make every effort.

6. The negotiations were difficult and lengthy. There were material and psychological reasons for this. Undoubtedly, the Soviet Union promised far more deliveries than are defensible from a purely economic point of view, and she must make the deliveries to Germany partly at the expense of her own supply. On the other hand, it is understandable that the Soviet Government is anxious to receive as compensation those things which the Soviet Union lacks. Since the Soviet Union does not import any consumer goods whatsoever, their wishes concerned exclusively manufactured goods and war matériel. Thus, in numerous cases, Soviet bottlenecks coincide with German bottlenecks, such as machine tools for the manufacture of artillery ammunition. It was not easy to find a compromise between the interests of both sides. Psychologically the ever-present distrust of the Russians was of importance as well as the fear of any responsibility. And People's Commissar Mikoyan had to refer numerous questions to Stalin personally, since his authority was not sufficient.

Despite all these difficulties, during the long negotiations the desire of the Soviet Government to help Germany and to consolidate firmly the political understanding in economic matters, too, became more and more evident.

The Agreement means a wide open door to the East for us. The raw material purchases from the Soviet Union and from the countries bordering the Soviet Union can still be considerably increased. But it is essential to meet the German commitments to the extent required. In view of the great volume this will require a special effort. If we succeed in extending and expanding exports to the East in the required volume, the effects of the English blockade will be decisively weakened by the incoming raw materials.

BERLIN, February 26, 1940.

SCHNURRE

Frames 242-240, serial F 18

The Reich Foreign Minister to the German Ambassador in the Soviet Union (Schulenburg)

Telegram

STATE SECRET   BERLIN, March 28, 1940.
No. 543

For the Ambassador personally. Secret.

During my recent visit to Rome, where—as you know—I worked on the improvement of Italian-Russian relations among other things, I already contemplated carrying out the plan of a visit by Herr Molotov to Berlin. Although I did not mention this idea to anyone, the Anglo-French propaganda, correctly guessing my intentions, spoke of it with the hope of interfering with the plan and thereby with the further consolidation of our relations with Russia. I could have denied the Anglo-French report without any trouble, but refrained from doing so out of consideration for Molotov. Then, the Russian press for its part issued a denial.

Nevertheless, I have not given up the idea of a visit by Molotov to Berlin. On the contrary, I should like to retain it, and if it can be realized I should like to put it into effect in the near future. It goes without saying that the invitation is not to be confined to Herr Molotov; it would suit our own needs better, as well as our really ever-closer relations with Russia, if Herr Stalin himself came to Berlin. The Führer would not only be particularly happy to welcome Stalin in Berlin, but he would also see to it that he would get a reception commensurate with his position and importance, and he would extend to him all the honors that the occasion demanded.

An invitation both to Herr Molotov and to Herr Stalin has, as you know, already been issued orally by me in Moscow and was accepted by both of them in principle. In what manner the invitation should now be repeated, and its definite acceptance and realization attained, you yourself can judge best. During the conversation to be conducted you will have to word the invitation to Herr Molotov more definitely, whereas you will have to state the invitation to Herr Stalin in the name of the Führer in less definite terms. We must, of course, avoid receiving a clear-cut refusal from Stalin.

Before you take any action, I request that you comment on the subject immediately, reporting to me by wire your opinion as to the procedure to be followed by you and the prospects for its success.

RIBBENTROP

Frames 0466–0467, serial F 5

The German Ambassador in the Soviet Union (Schulenburg) to the German Foreign Office

Telegram

VERY URGENT   Moscow, March 30, 1940—11:40 p. m.
STRICTLY SECRET   Received March 31, 1940—8:15 a. m.
No. 599 of March 30

For the Reich Foreign Minister personally.
Reference your telegram of the 28th, No. 543.

I. I personally believe firmly—as I reported on the occasion of my inquiry of October 17, telegram No. 554 [61]—that Molotov, conscious of his obligation, will visit Berlin as soon as the time and circumstances appear propitious to the Soviet Government. After careful examination of all factors known to me I cannot, however, conceal the fact that I consider the chances slight for the acceptance of an invitation at the present time. My opinion is based on the following considerations:

1. All our observations, particularly the speech of Molotov on March 29, confirm that the Soviet Government is determined to cling to neutrality in the present war and to avoid as much as possible anything that might involve it in a conflict with the Western powers. This must have been one of the main reasons why the Soviet Government broke off the war against Finland, abandoning the People's Government.

2. The Soviet Government having this attitude, it probably fears that a demonstration of the relations between the Soviet Union and Germany such as a visit by Molotov or by Stalin himself to Berlin might, at present, involve the risk of severance of diplomatic relations or even of warlike developments with the Western powers.

3. Indicative of the situation is the Tass denial mentioned by you, which denies with rather striking plainness and firmness all rumors about an allegedly impending trip to Germany by Molotov.

4. It is a known fact that Molotov, who has never been abroad, has strong inhibitions against appearing in strange surroundings. This applies as much if not more to Stalin.

Therefore, only very favorable circumstances or extremely important Soviet advantages could induce Molotov or Stalin to make such a trip, in spite of disinclinations and "wariness;" furthermore, Molotov, who never flies, will need at least a week for the trip, and there is really no suitable substitute for him here.

II. Although the prospects for success therefore appear to be slight, I will, of course, do everything in my power in order to try to realize the plan, in case it is to be pursued any further. A suitable starting point for an informal conversation on that subject can be found without much trouble. The course of the conversation will reveal whether and how far I can go into the subject. As regards the invitation to Stalin, the possibility of a meeting in a border town would have to be left open from the very beginning.

SCHULENBURG

---

[61] Not printed.

Frame 0465, serial F 5

The German Foreign Office to the German Ambassador in the
Soviet Union (Schulenburg)

Telegram

RAM Nr. 13 g. Rs.   BERLIN, April 3, 1940.
STATE SECRET
No. 570

For the Ambassador personally.
Reference your telegram No. 599, of March 30.
The Reich Foreign Minister requests that nothing further be initiated for the time being.

SCHMIDT
Minister

Frames 203141-203142, serial 354

The Reich Foreign Minister to the German Ambassador in the Soviet
Union (Schulenburg)

BERLIN, April 7, 1940.
Received Moscow, April 9, 1940.

You receive herewith two copies of a memorandum [62] which will be presented by our envoys in Oslo and Copenhagen on April 9, at 5:20 a. m., German summer time, to the Governments concerned. Until the step which you are instructed to take below has been carried out, the strictest secrecy is to be maintained with regard to the memorandum and this instruction, and no mention thereof is to be made even to any other member of the Embassy.

On April 9, at 7 a. m., German summer time, you are requested to ask for an interview with Herr Molotov, and, during the course of the morning, to hand him a copy of the memorandum.

You will kindly emphasize orally that we had absolutely reliable reports regarding an imminent thrust of Anglo-French military forces against the Norwegian and Danish coasts and therefore had to act without delay. As outlined in the memorandum, it is a matter of security measures. Swedish and Finnish territory will in no way be affected by our action.

The Reich Government is of the opinion that our actions are also in the interest of the Soviet Union, for execution of the Anglo-French

---

[62] Not printed here.

plan which is known to us would have caused Scandinavia to become a theater of war, and that, in all probability, would have led to a reopening of the Finnish question.

Please report immediately by wire how your communication is received.

RIBBENTROP

Frame 203133, serial 354

The German Ambassador in the Soviet Union (Schulenburg) to the German Foreign Office

Telegram

VERY URGENT   Moscow, April 9, 1940.

SECRET

No. 653 of April 9

Reference your instruction of April 7 (delivered by Counselor of Legation von Saucken) and our telegram No. 648 of April 9.[63]

For the Reich Foreign Minister in person.

Instruction carried out with Molotov today at 10:30 a. m., European time. Molotov declared that the Soviet Government understood the measures which were forced upon Germany. The English had certainly gone much too far; they had disregarded completely the rights of neutral nations. In conclusion, Molotov said literally: "We wish Germany complete success in her defensive measures."

SCHULENBURG

Frames 210958-210960, serial 384

Memorandum by the German Ambassador in the Soviet Union (Schulenburg)

Tgb. Nr. A. 1833/40   Moscow, April 11, 1940.

MEMORANDUM

For some time we have observed in the Soviet Government a distinct shift which was unfavorable to us. In all fields we suddenly came up against obstacles which were, in many cases, completely unnecessary; even in little things like visas they started to create difficulties; the release of the *Volksdeutsche* imprisoned by the Poles, which was promised by treaty, could not be achieved; the deportation of the German citizens long imprisoned in Soviet jails suddenly stopped; the

_____
[63] Latter not printed.

Soviet Government suddenly withdrew its promises already given with regard to the "North Base" ["*Basis Nord*"] in which our Navy is interested, etc. These obstacles, which were apparent everywhere, reached their climax in the suspension of petroleum and grain shipments to us. On the 5th of this month I had a long talk with Herr Mikoyan, during which the attitude of the People's Commissar was very negative. I had to make the most strenuous efforts to get at least some concessions from him.

We asked ourselves in vain what the reason might be for the sudden change of attitude of the Soviet authorities. After all, nothing at all had "happened"! I suspect that the tremendous clamor of our enemies and their sharp attacks on neutrals—particularly on the Soviet Union—and on neutrality in general were not without effect upon the Soviet Government, so that it feared being forced by the Entente into a great war for which it is not prepared, and that for this reason it wanted to avoid anything that might have furnished a pretext to the English and French for reproaching the Soviet Union with unneutral behavior or partisanship for Germany. It appeared to me as though the sudden termination of the Finnish war had come about from similar considerations. Of course, these suspicions could not be proved. However the situation had become so critical that I decided to call on Herr Molotov in order to talk these matters over with him, and after this discussion to notify the Foreign Office. On the 8th of this month I therefore asked for permission to see Herr Molotov—i. e., *before* the Scandinavian events. Actually, the visit to Herr Molotov did not take place until the morning of the 9th—i. e., *after* our Scandinavian operations. During this talk it became apparent that the Soviet Government had again made a complete about-face. Suddenly the suspension of the petroleum and grain shipments was termed "excessive zeal of subordinate agencies" which would be immediately remedied. (Herr Mikoyan is Assistant Chairman of the Council of People's Commissars, i. e., the highest Soviet personality after Herr Molotov!) Herr Molotov was affability itself, willingly received all our complaints and promised relief. Of his own accord he touched upon a number of issues of interest to us and announced their settlement in a positive sense. I must honestly say that I was completely amazed at the change.

In my opinion there is only one explanation for this about-face: our Scandinavian operations must have relieved the Soviet Government enormously—removed a great burden of anxiety, so to speak. What their apprehension consisted of, can again not be determined with certainty. I suspect the following: The Soviet Government is always extraordinarily well informed. If the English and French intended to occupy Norway and Sweden it may be assumed with certainty that the Soviet Government knew of these plans and was apparently terrified by them. The Soviet Government saw the English and French appearing on the shores of the Baltic Sea, and they saw the Finnish question reopened, as Lord Halifax had announced; finally they dreaded most of all the danger of becoming involved in a war with two Great Powers. Apparently this fear was relieved by us. Only in this way can the completely changed attitude of Herr Molotov be understood. Today's long and conspicuous article in *Izvestia* on our Scandinavian campaign (already sent to you by wire) sounds like one big sigh of relief. But, at any rate—at least at the moment—"everything is in order" again here, and our affairs are going as they should.

SCHULENBURG

Frame 112110, serial 103

The German Ambassador in the Soviet Union (Schulenburg) to the German Foreign Office

Telegram

VERY URGENT   Moscow, April 13, 1940—10:31 p. m.
SECRET   Received April 14, 1940—5:20 a. m.
No. 687 of April 13

Molotov today asked me to see him and brought up the following:

Persistent rumors were being circulated everywhere that Germany would soon be forced to include Sweden in her Scandinavian operations, particularly in order to ship more troops to Norway. Molotov added that in his opinion Germany, and definitely the Soviet Union, were vitally [*lebhaft*] interested in preserving Swedish neutrality. He asked me how much truth there was in these rumors.

First, I referred to my statement to him on April 9, that our operations would not touch Sweden and Finland and added that I was not aware of the slightest indication that we had any designs on Swedish territory. Nevertheless, I would pass his inquiry on to Berlin.

In conclusion, Molotov declared that the Soviet Government was greatly interested in preserving Swedish neutrality, that its violation was frowned upon by the Soviet Government, and that it hoped the inclusion of Sweden in our operations would not take place, if this could at all be avoided. Request instructions by wire.

SCHULENBURG

Frame 112111, serial 10?

The Reich Foreign Minister to the German Ambassador in the Soviet Union (Schulenburg)

Telegram

IMMEDIATE   BERLIN, April 15, 1940.
SECRET
No. 636

Reference your telegram No. 687.

I request that you explain to Herr Molotov our attitude toward Sweden as follows:

We share completely the attitude of the Soviet Government that preservation of Sweden's neutrality corresponds both to German and to Soviet interests. As you already told him on transmitting our memorandum on April 9 and repeated during the conversation of April 13, it is not our intention to extend our military operations in the north to Swedish territory. On the contrary, we are determined to respect unconditionally the neutrality of Sweden, as long as Sweden in turn also observes strict neutrality and does not support the Western powers.

Reich Foreign Minister

Frames 203979-203980, serial 357

The Reich Foreign Minister to the German Ambassador in the Soviet Union (Schulenburg)

BERLIN, May 7, 1940.
Received Moscow, May 10, 1940.

Enclosed you will find two copies of two memoranda [64] which will be presented by our Legations in The Hague, Brussels, and Luxemburg to the Governments there on the day and hour to be indicated to you orally by the courier. [Interlinear penciled notation: May 10, 1940, 5:45 a. m., German summer time.] Until the *démarche* ordered below has been accomplished, the memoranda and these instructions are to be kept strictly secret and not mentioned even to any member of the Embassy.

I request that after receipt of these instructions you enter on the copies of the attached memoranda—on the last page, beneath the text—the date of the day *before* that on which you deliver the copies to the Government in Moscow, preferably with typewriter, or else in ink.

---

[64] Not printed here.

About 7 o'clock in the morning, German summer time, on the day mentioned to you by the courier, I request that you ask for an appointment with Molotov and then, in the course of the morning at the earliest hour convenient to him, hand him a copy of the memoranda. I request that you tell Herr Molotov that the Reich Government, in view of our friendly relations, is anxious to notify the Soviet Government of these operations in the West, which were forced upon Germany by the impending Anglo-French push on the Ruhr region by way of Belgium and Holland.

For the rest, I request that you use the viewpoints and arguments to be found in the memoranda themselves.

I request that you report by wire immediately concerning the reception accorded your mission.

RIBBENTROP

Frame 203978, serial 357

The German Ambassador in the Soviet Union (Schulenburg) to the German Foreign Office

Telegram

VERY URGENT   Moscow, May 10, 1940—6 p. m.
No. 874 of May 10

Reference instructions of May 7.

For the Reich Foreign Minister:

I called on Molotov; instruction carried out. Molotov appreciated the news and added that he understood that Germany had to protect herself against Anglo-French attack. He had no doubt of our success.

SCHULENBURG

Frames 210963–210964, serial 384

The German Ambassador in the Soviet Union (Schulenburg) to the German Foreign Office

Telegram

VERY URGENT   Moscow, May 29, 1940—7:10 p. m.
No. 1006 of May 29   Received May 29, 1940—10:10 p. m.

Reference your telegram of the 28th No. 877.[65]

The reported agreement of the Soviet Government to the sending of Cripps appears credible, since the Soviet Government has always

---

[65] Not printed.

taken the position that it was of interest to it to learn what the British Government had to tell them, and that economic agreements with England were in harmony with the neutral position of the Soviet Union. In addition, the Soviet Union is interested in obtaining rubber and tin from England in exchange for lumber.

There is no reason for apprehension concerning Cripps' mission, since there is no reason to doubt the loyal attitude of the Soviet Union toward us and since the unchanged direction of Soviet policy toward England precludes damage to Germany or vital German interests. There are no indications of any kind here for belief that the latest German successes caused alarm or fear of Germany in the Soviet Government. All the assertions of the foreign and especially enemy press to the contrary are desperate attempts to sow distrust between Germany and the Soviet Union, to start a diplomatic activity against Germany at any cost in view of the precarious situation of the Allies, and to exploit this as propaganda for their own people.

The selection of Cripps as British plenipotentiary appears unfortunate in view of the attitude in Moscow: the Soviet Government prefers to negotiate important matters with a prominent representative of the foreign government.

As I see it here a trip by Ritter [66] and (group garbled) at the present time would have to avoid looking like a race with Cripps. The advisability of the trip would also have to be considered from the point of view of whether we would (group missing) anything new to offer the Soviet Government.

SCHULENBURG

---

[66] Ambassador Ritter of the German Foreign Office staff.

V. FRICTION IN THE BALTIC AND THE BALKANS, JUNE 4–SEPTEMBER 21, 1940

Frame 112206, serial 103

The German Ambassador in the Soviet Union (Schulenburg) to the German Foreign Office

Telegram

VERY URGENT
No. 1063 of June 3

Moscow, June 4, 1940—12 : 25 a. m.
Received June 4, 1940—5 : 15 a. m.

Molotov informed me today that Ambassador von Mackensen had stated to the Soviet Chargé in Rome around May 25—in connection with the apparently imminent Italian entrance into the war—that all problems in the Balkans are to be solved without war, i. e., by mutual cooperation among Germany, the Soviet Union, and Italy.

Molotov requested information as to whether this statement by Mackensen actually reflected the opinion of the Reich Government and the Italian Government.

Telegraphic instruction is requested.

SCHULENBURG

Frame 112208, serial 103

The German Ambassador in the Soviet Union (Schulenburg) to the German Foreign Office

Telegram

VERY URGENT
No. 1079 of June 6

Moscow, June 6, 1940—3 : 55 p. m.
Received June 6, 1940—6 : 30 p. m.

Reference your telegram of June 5, No. 938.[67]

In the conference on June 3, Molotov only asked for information without showing any intention of wanting to bind the German or Italian Government on any point. On the other hand, he showed clearly that the Soviet Government would be very pleased if Herr von Mackensen's statement reflected not only his personal opinion but actually the interpretation of the German and Italian Governments. The question as to how possible cooperation among the three in the Balkans would work out practically was not broached by Herr Molotov.

SCHULENBURG

---

[67] Not printed.

Frames 334518–334519, serial 1228

The German Foreign Office to the Representative of the German Foreign Office With the Reich Protector of Bohemia and Moravia

IMMEDIATE   BERLIN, June 8, 1940.
CONFIDENTIAL (ALSO IN THE REICH)
Pol. V 1581g

Subject: Hetman Skoropadsky's contemplated visit with the Reich Protector.

Reference your report of May 27, 1940—5769/D.Pol.5.[68]

In view of German-Soviet relations, it appears advisable to avoid anything which would be likely to arouse the Soviet Government's distrust in the Ukranian question. Accordingly, the Foreign Office attaches importance to having the Ukrainian organizations in Greater Germany carry on no political activities. This also applies to former Hetman Skoropadsky and his movement. The importance of the Hetman Movement has declined lately, to be sure, in favor of the Ukrainian National Organization (U. N. O.), which was promoted by the competent German internal authorities,[69] but even now the Hetman still has numerous adherents at his disposition outside Germany, especially in the United States and Canada, where several thousand Ukrainians have pledged their oath of allegiance to him and recognize his family as the hereditary dynasty.

The Foreign Office and the Gestapo are continuously in contact with the Hetman, who has always maintained a loyal attitude toward Germany. To assure him and his family an income consistent with his position, a considerable allowance is paid to him regularly by the Foreign Office in addition to the monthly honorarium provided by the late Reich President Field Marshal von Hindenburg in 1928. Unfortunately relations with him have for some time been deteriorating, because the 73-year-old Hetman evidently considers it his main duty to attack and cast suspicion on the other Ukrainian groups, especially the above-mentioned U. N. O.[69]

By order:
V. RINTELEN

---

[68] Not printed.
[69] The words underlined were stricken out in the draft of the letter.

Frames 219495–219496, serial 432

Foreign Office Memorandum

BERLIN, June 11, 1940.

The Lithuanian Minister called on me today to inform me of the further progress of the discussions with the Soviet Union. After the Soviet Union had raised the question of the safety of the Soviet garrisons in Lithuania and had rejected the suggestion for a mixed commission to investigate the incidents, the Lithuanian Government had of its own accord taken a series of measures which it thought would satisfy the Soviet Union. It might perhaps be admitted that relations between the Soviet garrisons and the Lithuanian population had earlier been treated too casually. Restrictive and control measures had now been taken, and many arrests and house searches made, etc. It was known that no reply was received to the Lithuanian suggestion of sending the Foreign Minister to Moscow. It was, therefore, all the more surprising that not the Foreign Minister but Minister President Merkys was summoned to Moscow.

On June 7 Merkys had had his first conversation with Molotov. The latter had reproached him severely regarding the safety of the Soviet garrisons and in this connection presented a great many detailed incidents. Molotov had in particular maintained persistently that Butayeff, a member of the Red Army, who according to Lithuanian reports had committed suicide, had been shot by Lithuanians. He had expressed his dissatisfaction very plainly and stressed that the Lithuanian Ministry of the Interior was not equal to its task.

In a subsequent conversation on June 9, Molotov had brought up questions of foreign policy, which had increased Lithuanian fears regarding the course of the conversations. Molotov had maintained that a military alliance existed between the three Baltic States and as proof had referred to the frequent meetings of the chiefs of staff of the three countries and to other frequent conferences between Baltic personalities. Merkys had replied that there existed neither secret nor open agreements which could violate the letter or the spirit of the Agreement of October 10, 1939. There was the old political treaty between the Baltic States but no military alliance. Merkys had then himself expressed the wish to invite the Foreign Minister to the conversations. The latter had arrived in Moscow yesterday afternoon. Herr Skirpa had not yet received any more recent reports. From the standpoint of protocol, everything had taken place in very polite form.

The Lithuanian Government still did not know what the intentions of the Soviet Union might be. The Lithuanian Government was prepared to do even more for the safety of the garrisons than it had done so far. If the Soviet Union now made broader political or military demands, the Lithuanian Government could not take the responsibility for their acceptance. Thus far, the subject of Lithuania's relations with Germany had not been discussed during the foreign policy conversations. However, it was no doubt to be expected that the Soviet Union would raise questions in this respect, too. Here I interjected that there was nothing in German-Lithuanian relations which was not or should not be known by the Soviet Union.

Herr Skirpa asked whether we had not instructed our Ambassador in Moscow to make inquiries. I replied in the negative and avoided further discussion of the matter with the remark that our Ambassador would certainly make a report of his own accord.

WOERMANN

Frame 175538, serial 270

The State Secretary in the German Foreign Office (Weizsäcker) to the German Ambassador in the Soviet Union (Schulenburg)

Telegram

No. 1003 of June 13   BERLIN, June 14, 1940—8:45 p. m.
Received Moscow June 14, 1940—11:30 p. m.

For the Chief of Mission or his representative personally. Strictly secret. To be deciphered personally. To be treated as confidential.

From a strictly secret source with which you are acquainted it has come to our knowledge that the Soviet Minister in Stockholm, Frau Kollontay, recently stated to the Belgian Minister there that it was to the common interest of the European powers to place themselves in opposition to German imperialism. It had become evident that the German danger was far greater than had been believed.

The Reich Foreign Minister requests you, if opportunity arises, and without revealing the source, to discuss tactfully with Molotov the hostile attitude of Minister Kollontay toward Germany.

WEIZSÄCKER

Frame 112211, serial 103

The Reich Foreign Minister to the German Ambassador in the Soviet Union (Schulenburg)

Telegram

No. 1007 of June 16, 1940   Reich Foreign Minister's Special Train

Reference your telegrams 1063 [71] and 1094.[72]

Please reply orally to Herr Molotov's question as follows:

1. As Mackensen reported upon inquiry, he did not make such a definite statement as was reported by the Soviet Chargé in Rome to the Soviet Government. He had, instead, stated during the conversation with the Chargé that in his opinion Germany and Italy were agreed that the Balkans should remain quiet and that a settlement of the unsolved Balkan question could probably be brought about more easily and without the use of force after the war.

2. The Reich Government was gratified that the war had not spread to the Balkans. Germany was, in principle, not interested there territorially but only commercially. Our attitude toward the Soviet Union in this question was finally and irrevocably established by the definite Moscow Agreement.

3. Italy's attitude toward the Balkans was also made unequivocally clear by Mussolini's speech on June 10 to the effect that Italy had no intention of drawing the Balkans into a war.

RIBBENTROP

Frames 214876–214877, serial 407

The German Foreign Office to the Reich Foreign Minister

Teletype

No. . .   BERLIN, June 16, 1940.

To Baumschule [73] for Sonnleitner.

With reference to the despatches from Kaunas No. 96 and No. 97 of June 15 [74] forwarded by teletype.

The Lithuanian Minister called up at about 2 a. m. today and said that, in accordance with a telephone report from Eydtkuhnen, Presi-

---

[71] *Ante*, p. 144.
[72] Not printed.
[73] Code name for the field office of the Reich Foreign Minister.
[74] Neither printed.

dent Smetona, accompanied by an adjutant and members of his family, as well as General Rastaikis (who was rejected by the Soviets as Prime Minister) and his brother, Colonel Rastaikis, with their wives, had arrived in Eydtkuhnen. The Minister, moreover, reported that a number of other prominent Lithuanian personalities were probably staying at the German-Lithuanian border and that they desired to enter Germany. Some of them would be in danger, should they fall into the hands of the Russians. The Minister requested that the German border authorities be instructed to let these personalities enter Germany. The official on [night] duty replied that he could not initiate anything independently in this matter and suggested making the request again in the morning.

By order of Under State Secretary Woermann I request instructions as to how to treat the application of the Lithuanian Minister. The question arises in particular whether former Interior Minister Skucas and the former director of the State Security Department, Powelaitis, who were to be tried in accordance with point 1 of the Soviet ultimatum, can be allowed to enter. Powelaitis, regarding whom inquiry has already been made there by teletype, has loyally cooperated with German authorities in fighting Polish intrigues.

Division for Political Affairs, Night Duty Officer
WELCK

Frame 214887, serial 407

Foreign Office Memorandum

The High Command of the Armed Forces [OKW] (Colonel von Geldern) reports that it has received from the Counterintelligence Office in Königsberg, the following communication:

Tonight at 3 o'clock President Smetona with family and entourage crossed the "green frontier." He had given orders to the Lithuanian garrisons of Mariampol and Tauroggen to cross the frontier into Germany fully equipped and armed.

The High Command of the Armed Forces requests instructions as to what action to take if the Lithuanian troops, which apparently have not yet arrived, should wish to cross the border.

VON KESSEL

BERLIN, June 16, 1940.

Frame 214873, serial 407

The Reich Foreign Minister to the German Foreign Office

BERLIN, June 16, 1940.

Baumschule No. 56 of June 16, 11:15 a. m.

1. I have already given orders through the Gestapo to intern the Lithuanian President, Smetona, with family and other functionaries who have crossed the "green frontier." This will be done by the Gestapo.

2. If Lithuanian troop contingents ask permission to cross the German border, this request may be granted. The troops are to be disarmed and likewise to be interned.

3. It is reported that a Lithuanian Colonel offered to have his regiment cross the border. It is requested that the disarming and interning of any Lithuanian soldiers who might cross the border be done by the Armed Forces in collaboration with the Border Police. In agreement with the State Police please take the measures necessary so that the border posts concerned may be immediately informed.

It is again pointed out that border crossings are to be permitted only upon request of the Lithuanians and that we, for our part, must not do anything to encourage such requests.

This communication is to be transmitted at once by the fastest route, orally and in written form, to the High Command of the Armed Forces [OKW] with the request for further action.

RIBBENTROP

Minute

The transmittal to the High Command of the Armed Forces [OKW] was made immediately in accordance with instructions. At the same time, the High Command of the Armed Forces [OKW] was asked to see to it that in every case of a border crossing of Lithuanian troop contingents a report be made immediately to the Foreign Office.

V. D. HEYDEN RYNSCH

Frame 214886, serial 407

Foreign Office Memorandum

SECRET   BERLIN, June 16, 1940.
Pol. I M 8560g.

MEMORANDUM

The High Command of the Armed Forces, Foreign Branch [*OKW Ausland*], Major Krummacher, transmitted the following at 11:35 a.m.:

"Order of the Führer

1. If Lithuanian troops cross the East Prussian border, they are to be disarmed. A further decision as to what is to be done with them should be awaited.
2. At present some German units are returning to their garrisons in East Prussia. They have received instructions not to undertake any maneuvers and to avoid anything which might look as if this return were in any way connected with events in Lithuania.

This is for your information so that possible Soviet Russian inquiries may immediately be answered in this sense."

VON GROTE

Frame 214861, serial 407

The Reich Foreign Minister's Personal Staff to the German Foreign Office

Telegram

Baumschule No. 57 of June 16.

Teletype to Herr v. Grundherr [75] via Minister's Office.

The Reich Foreign Minister requests you to submit a report as soon as possible as to whether in the Baltic States a tendency to seek support from the Reich can be observed or whether an attempt was made to form a bloc. Please transmit your report by teletype.

SONNLEITNER

---

[75] Of the Political Division of the German Foreign Office, in charge of Baltic affairs.

Frames 214862-214864, serial 407

The German Foreign Office to the Reich Foreign Minister

Teletype

To Baumschule   BERLIN, June 17, 1940.

Reference telegram Baumschule No. 57 of June 16, 1940.

I. The cooperation between the Baltic States of Estonia, Latvia, and Lithuania is based on the Treaty of Mutual Understanding and Cooperation concluded for ten years by these three States on September 12, 1934. In addition, Latvia and Estonia signed a mutual defense pact on November 1, 1923. In practice, the political cooperation consisted mainly of semiannual conferences of Foreign Ministers and joint press conferences; on the other hand, there has often been an abundance of discord and rivalry within the Baltic Entente. Latvia and Estonia explicitly indicated their disinterestedness in the Memel and Vilna questions, which were important to Lithuania. The assertion, now made by Russia, that Lithuania had joined the Estonian-Latvian military pact, is, according to information available here, without any foundation. Because of the very similar economic structure of these countries, the economic cooperation between the three States, in spite of much effort during the last few years, made no appreciable progress. Since the conclusion of the Soviet Mutual Assistance Pact with the Baltic countries in September-October 1939 there has been no closer cooperation in an anti-Russian sense among the Baltic States. In view of the occupation of their countries by Soviet Russian troops, the three Baltic Governments were aware of the danger of such a policy.

II. For the same reason, there can be no question—during the last few months—of dependence in foreign policy on Germany by the Baltic States. The Lithuanian Government, to be sure, has probably not been quite certain until the last few days whether or not we were politically completely disinterested in Lithuania, so that in many circles, as for instance in the case of the Lithuanian Minister here, there was perhaps some hope that Germany would, in case of further Russian demands, put in a good word for Lithuania in Moscow, although there was never, of course, any occasion given on our part for such an assumption.

On the other hand, our economic relations with the Baltic States have been strengthened very much since the beginning of the war. Regarding the great importance of the Baltic States to the war economy of the Reich, please see the attached memorandum from Minister Schnurre.

GRUNDHERR

(Annex)

Foreign Office Memorandum

The economic importance of the three Baltic States for our supply of food and of raw materials essential for war has become quite considerable as a result of the commercial treaties concluded with these three States during the last year.   In the course of the last six months, we have furthermore concluded secret agreements with all three States whereby the entire export of these countries, except the small part going to Russia and another small portion which goes to neutral countries, will be sent to Germany.   That means for all three States about 70 percent of their total exports.   German imports from the three Baltic States will in the current year amount to a total of approximately 200 million Reichsmarks—comprising grain, hogs, butter, eggs, flax, lumber, seeds, and in the case of Estonia, petroleum.

The consolidation of Russian influence in these areas will seriously endanger these necessary imports.   For one thing, the Russians will do their utmost to keep the raw materials, and especially food, at home for their own use.   On the other hand, if part continues to go to Germany, they will make quite different demands in regard to deliveries of German products from those made in the past by the Baltic States, so that in effect the previous exchange of goods will break down.   We were able to make the deliveries desired by the Baltic States much more easily, and in many cases, under the stress of circumstances, we were able to put these States off till later.

In contrast, the economic interests of the Soviet Union in the three Baltic States are of minor importance.   The Soviet Union was able to secure only about 10 percent of the export trade of these countries for itself by means of the treaties it recently concluded.

SCHNURRE

BERLIN, June 17, 1940.

Frame 214849, serial 407

The State Secretary in the German Foreign Office (Weizsäcker) to All German Missions

Circular telegram

Pol. VI 1673   BERLIN, June 17, 1940.

For information and the orientation of your conversation.

The unresisted reinforcement of Russian troops in Lithuania, Latvia, and Estonia and the reorganization of the Governments of the Baltic States, sought by the Russian Government to bring about more reliable cooperation with the Soviet Union, are the concern of Russia and the Baltic States. Therefore, in view of our unaltered friendly relations with the Soviet Union, there is no reason for nervousness on our part, which some of the foreign press has tried to impute to us in only too transparent a manner.

Please refrain from making any statement during conversations which could be interpreted as partisan.

Please acknowledge receipt.

WEIZSÄCKER

Frame 112228, serial 103

The German Ambassador in the Soviet Union (Schulenburg) to the German Foreign Office

Telegram

VERY URGENT   Moscow, June 18, 1940—1:10 a. m.
No. 1167 of June 17   Received June 18, 1940—4 a. m.

Molotov summoned me this evening to his office and expressed the warmest congratulations of the Soviet Government on the splendid success of the German Armed Forces. Thereupon, Molotov informed me of the Soviet action against the Baltic States. He referred to the reasons published in the press and added that it had become necessary to put an end to all the intrigues by which England and France had tried to sow discord and mistrust between Germany and the Soviet Union in the Baltic States.

For the negotiations concerning the formation of the new Governments the Soviet Government had, in addition to the Soviet envoy accredited there, sent the following special emissaries:

To Lithuania: Deputy Commissar of Foreign Affairs Dekanosov; to Latvia: Vishinski, the representative of the Council of Ministers; to Estonia: Regional Party Leader of Leningrad Zhdanov.

In connection with the escape of Smetona and the possible crossing of the frontier by Lithuanian army units, Molotov stated that the Lithuanian border was evidently inadequately guarded. The Soviet Government would, therefore, if requested, assist the Lithuanian Government in guarding its borders.

SCHULENBURG

Frames 112240–112241, serial 103

The German Ambassador in the Soviet Union (Schulenburg) to the German Foreign Office

Telegram

VERY URGENT   Moscow, June 23, 1940—9 : 26 p. m.
No. 1205 of June 23   Received June 23, 1940—11 : 20 p. m.

Reference your telegram No. 1065 of the 22d and my telegram No. 1195 of the 21st.[76]

Molotov made the following statement to me today : The solution of the Bessarabian question brooked no further delay. The Soviet Government was still striving for a peaceful solution, but it was determined to use force, should the Rumanian Government decline a peaceful agreement. The Soviet claim likewise extended to Bucovina, which had a Ukrainian population.

As justification Molotov declared that, although a long time had elapsed since his declaration before the Supreme Soviet, Rumania had done nothing to bring about a solution of the Bessarabian problem. Therefore, something would have to be done.

I stated to Molotov that this decision of the Soviet Government had not been expected by me. I had been of the opinion that the Soviet Government would maintain its claims to Bessarabia—not contested by us—but would not itself take the initiative toward their realization. I feared that difficulties in the foreign relations of Rumania, which was at present supplying us with very large amounts of essential military and civilian raw materials, would lead to a serious encroachment on German interests. I told Molotov that I would report to my Government at once, and I requested him not to take any decisive steps before my Government had taken a stand concerning the intentions of the Soviet Government.

Molotov promised to inform the Soviet Government of my request but emphasized expressly that the matter was extremely urgent. Molotov added that the Soviet Government expected Germany not to hinder but to support the Soviets in their action. The Soviet Government on its part would do everything to safeguard German interests in Rumania.

[76] Neither printed.

Accordingly, I request immediate instruction by wire. I take the liberty of calling attention to the numerous *Volksdeutsche* residing in Bessarabia and Bucovina for whom provision of some sort will have to be made.

SCHULENBURG

Frames 112244–112245, serial 103

The German Ambassador in the Soviet Union (Schulenburg) to the German Foreign Office

Telegram

No. 1212 of June 24   Moscow, June 24, 1940—6:50 p. m.
                               Received June 25, 1940—1 a. m.

The following information was published by Tass in the Soviet press of June 23, and previously broadcast over the radio on June 22:

"In connection with the entry of Soviet troops in the Baltic countries, rumors have recently again been spread to the effect that 100 to 150 divisions have been concentrated at the Lithuanian-German border, that this concentration of Soviet troops was due to the Soviet Union's dissatisfaction with Germany's successes in the West, and that this revealed a deterioration in Soviet-German relations, and is designed to exert pressure on Germany. Lately, various versions of these rumors are being repeated almost daily in the American, Japanese, English, French, Turkish, and Swedish press.

Tass is authorized to state that all these rumors, the absurdity of which is obvious anyway, by no means correspond to the truth. In the Baltic countries there are actually neither 100 nor 150 divisions, but altogether no more than 18 to 20 divisions, and these divisions are not concentrated at the Lithuanian-German border but in the various districts of the three Baltic Republics, and their purpose is not to exert 'pressure' on Germany but to provide a guarantee for the execution of the mutual assistance pacts between the U.S.S.R. and these countries.

Responsible Soviet circles are of the opinion that the spreading of these absurd rumors aims particularly at clouding Soviet-German relations. These gentlemen, however, pass off their secret wishes as reality. Apparently, they are incapable of grasping the obvious fact that the good neighborly relations, resulting from the conclusion of the Nonaggression Pact between the U.S.S.R. and Germany, cannot be shaken by any rumors or petty poisonous propaganda, because these relations are not based on motives of opportunism but on the fundamental interests of the U.S.S.R. and Germany."

SCHULENBURG

Frame 112246, serial 103

The German Ambassador in the Soviet Union (Schulenburg) to the German Foreign Office

Telegram

No. 1213 of June 24   Moscow, June 24, 1940—6 : 49 p. m.
                                       Received June 24, 1940—8 : 45 p. m.

Reference my telegram No. 1212 of the 24th.

After the conclusion of our conversation of yesterday concerning Bessarabia (cf. telegram No. 1212 [*1205?*] of June 23d) Molotov, with obvious complacency, brought up the Tass communiqué of June 22, whereupon I expressed my appreciation.

I infer from the wording of the communiqué that Stalin himself is the author. The refutation of numerous rumors now circulating concerning differences between Germany and the Soviet Union and concerning troop concentrations in connection with Soviet operations in the Baltic region, and the unequivocal clarification of German-Soviet relations ought to be altogether to our advantage at this important juncture. However, the further aim of the communiqué, to emphasize German-Soviet solidarity as a preparation for the solution of the Bessarabian problem. is just as plain.

                                                   SCHULENBURG

Frames 179–181, serial F 19

Memorandum by the Reich Foreign Minister for Hitler

The Secret Supplementary Protocol of August 23, 1939, reads as follows:

[Here follows the text of the Secret Supplementary Protocol of August 23, 1939, printed on page 78.]

As far as I can remember, the following took place at that time:

At the time of the delimitation of the mutual spheres of interest in Eastern Europe, the Soviets stressed their interest in Bessarabia when the Southeast of Europe was mentioned. On this occasion I stated orally our disinterestedness in the Bessarabian question. However, in order not to put down explicitly *in written form* the recognition of the Russian claim to Bessarabia because of the possibility of indiscretions, with which we had to count in view of the then still very vague German-Russian relationship, I chose a formulation of a *general nature* for the Protocol. This was done in such a way that when the Southeastern European problems were discussed I declared very generally that Germany was *politically* disinterested in "these areas," i. e., in the Southeast of Europe. The economic interest of Germany in these Southeastern European territories was duly stressed by me. This was in accordance with the general instructions given by the Führer for Southeastern Europe and also, as I recall it, with a special directive of the Führer which I received before my departure for Moscow, in which the Führer authorized me to declare German disinterestedness in the territories of Southeastern Europe, even, if necessary, as far as Constantinople and the Straits. However, the latter were not discussed.

R[IBBENTROP]

BAUMSCHULE, June 24, 1940.

Frames 210475-210476, serial 380

The Reich Foreign Minister to the German Ambassador in the Soviet Union (Schulenburg)

Telegram

VERY URGENT   Transmitted by telephone on June 25, 1940—6 p. m.
No. 1074.of June 25

For the Ambassador personally.

Please call on Herr Molotov and state the following:

1. Germany is abiding by the Moscow agreements. She takes, therefore, no interest in the Bessarabian question. In this territory live approximately 100,000 *Volksdeutsche.* Germany is naturally interested in the fate of these *Volksdeutsche* and expects their future to be safeguarded. The Reich Government reserves the right to make certain proposals to the Soviet Government at the appropriate time concerning the question of resettling these *Volksdeutsche* in the same manner as the *Volksdeutsche* in Volhynia.

2. The claim of the Soviet Government to Bucovina is something new. Bucovina was formerly an Austrian crown province and is densely populated with Germans. Germany is also particularly interested in the fate of these *Volksdeutsche.*

3. In the rest of Rumania Germany has very important [*stärkste*] economic interests. These interests include oil fields as well as agricultural land. Germany is, therefore, as we have repeatedly informed the Soviet Government, extremely interested in preventing these areas from becoming a theater of war.

4. Although fully sympathetic toward the settling of the Bessarabian problem, the Reich Government is, therefore, of the opinion that . . .⁷⁷ of the Soviet Union . . .⁷⁷ of the Moscow agreements, everything should be done in order to reach a peaceful solution of the Bessarabian question with the Rumanian Government. For its part the Reich Government would be prepared, in the spirit of the Moscow agreements, to advise Rumania, if necessary, to reach an amicable settlement of the Bessarabian question satisfactory to Russia.

Please point out again clearly to Herr Molotov our great interest in Rumania's not becoming a theater of war. As matters stand, we are of the opinion that a peaceful settlement in accordance with Russian views is altogether possible, provided the problem is properly handled.

We should be grateful to the Soviet Government for a communication concerning its ideas as to further treatment of the matter.

RIBBENTROP

Frames 224890–224891, serial 459

The German Ambassador in the Soviet Union (Schulenburg) to the German Foreign Office

Telegram

VERY URGENT   Moscow, June 26, 1940—12:59 a. m.
No. 1233 of June 25   Received June 26, 1940—12:25 p. m.

Reference your telegram No. 1074 of the 25th.

For the Reich Minister personally.

Instruction carried out at 9 o'clock this evening at Molotov's office. Molotov expressed his thanks for the understanding attitude of the German Government and its readiness to support the Soviet Union in achieving its claims. Molotov stated that the Soviet Government also desired a peaceful solution, but repeatedly stressed the fact that the question was particularly urgent and could brook no further delay.

I pointed out to Molotov that Soviet renunciation of Bucovina, which never belonged even to Tsarist Russia, would substantially facilitate a peaceful solution. Molotov countered by saying that Bucovina is the last missing part of a unified Ukraine and that for this reason the Soviet Government must attach importance to solving this question simultaneously with the Bessarabian question. Nevertheless, I gained the impression that Molotov did not entirely dismiss the possibility of

---

⁷⁷ Omission indicated in the Moscow Embassy text of message.

Soviet renunciation of Bucovina in the course of the negotiations with Rumania.

Molotov stated that our wishes concerning the *Volksdeutsche* could certainly be met in a manner similar to the arrangement in Poland.

Molotov promised to consider most favorably our economic interests in Rumania.

In conclusion, Molotov stated that he would report the German point of view to his Government and inform me of its attitude as soon as possible. Molotov added that there had been no discussion of the matter in Moscow or in Bucharest, up to the present. He further mentioned that the Soviet Government simply wished to pursue its own interests and had no intention of encouraging other states (Hungary, Bulgaria) to make demands on Rumania.

SCHULENBURG

Frames 224892–224893, serial 459

The German Ambassador in the Soviet Union (Schulenburg) to the German Foreign Office

Telegram

VERY URGENT   Moscow, June 26, 1940—3 : 36 p. m.
STRICTLY SECRET   Received June 26, 1940—10 : 35 p. m.
No. 1235 of June 26

Reference my telegram No. 1195 of the 21st.[78]

Following the conversation which the Italian Ambassador, Rosso, had with Foreign Commissar Molotov on June 20, the latter summoned Rosso yesterday afternoon. Molotov explained that he had reported the Italian Government's views to his Government, which had approved them. The Soviet Government was of the opinion that Italian-Soviet relations should be re-established quickly and definitely and should be put on the same basis as those of Germany and the Soviet Government. Molotov stated in this connection that the Soviet Government and Germany were on excellent terms and that the relations between Germany and the Soviet Government were working out very well.

Molotov then declared that in his opinion the war would last until next winter, that there were some political questions, however, which had to be solved without delay, and that he could briefly characterize the Soviet Government's relations with various countries as follows: With Hungary the Soviet Government was maintaining good rela-

[78] Not printed.

tions.   Certain Hungarian requests were considered reasonable by the Soviet Government.

Bulgaria and the Soviet Union were good neighbors.   The Soviet-Bulgarian relations were strong and could be strengthened even more. The Bulgarian demands for Dobruja and for access to the Aegean Sea were considered justified by the Soviet Government, which had recognized them and had no objections to their realization.

The Soviet Union's attitude toward Rumania was known.   The Soviet Union would prefer to realize her claims to Bessarabia (Bucovina was not mentioned) without war, but, if that was impossible because of Rumanian intransigence, she was determined to resort to force.   Regarding other areas of Rumania, the Soviet Government would communicate with Germany.   The Soviet Government regards Turkey with deep suspicion.`   This was a result of Turkey's unfriendly attitude toward Russia and other countries, by which Molotov obviously meant Germany and Italy.   Soviet suspicion of Turkey was intensified by the Turkish attitude in regard to the Black Sea, where Turkey desired to play a dominant role, and the Straits, where Turkey wanted to exercise exclusive jurisdiction.   The Soviet Government was reducing a Turkish threat to Batum, against which it would have to protect itself toward the south and southeast, in which connection the German and Italian interests would be considered.

In the Mediterranean, the Soviet Government would recognize Italy's hegemony, provided that Italy would recognize the Soviet Government's hegemony in the Black Sea.

Ambassador Rosso wired Molotov's statements to his Government with the comment that he . . .* them very sensible and recommended that they be acted upon as soon as possible.

SCHULENBURG

Frames 210457-210458, serial 380

The German Ambassador in the Soviet Union (Schulenburg) to the German Foreign Office

Telegram

VERY URGENT   [Moscow, June 26, 1940.]
No. 1236 of June 26

Reference my telegram No. 1233 of June 25.
For the Reich Foreign Minister personally.

---

*Group missing, apparently "considered". [Footnote in the German text.]

Molotov summoned me this afternoon and declared that the Soviet Government, on the basis of his conversation with me yesterday, had decided to limit its demands to the northern part of Bucovina and the city of Czernowitz. According to Soviet opinion the boundary line should run from the southernmost point of the Soviet West Ukraine at Mt. Kniatiasa, east along the Suczava and then northeast to Hertza on the Pruth, whereby the Soviet Union would obtain direct railway connection from Bessarabia via Czernowitz to Lemberg. Molotov added that the Soviet Government expected German support of this Soviet demand.

To my statement that a peaceful solution might more easily be reached if the Soviet Government would return the Rumanian National Bank's gold reserve, which had been transferred for safekeeping to Moscow during World War I, Molotov declared that this was absolutely out of the question, since Rumania had exploited Bessarabia long enough.

Regarding further treatment of the matter Molotov has the following idea: The Soviet Government will submit its demand to the Rumanian Minister here within the next few days and expects the German Reich Government at the same time urgently to advise the Rumanian Government in Bucharest to comply with the Soviet demands, since war would otherwise be unavoidable. Molotov promised to inform me immediately as soon as he had spoken to the Rumanian Minister.

Regarding the Rumanian Government's attitude toward the new Soviet Minister, Molotov appeared to be annoyed and pointed out that the Minister had not yet been given any opportunity to present his credentials, although the customary time had expired.

SCHULENBURG

N. B.   General Köstring has been informed.

Frame 224898, serial 459

The German Ambassador in the Soviet Union (Schulenburg) to the German Foreign Office

Telegram

VERY URGENT   Moscow, June 27, 1940—1: 10 a. m.
No. 1241 of June 26   Received June 27, 1940—6: 30 a. m.

Reference my telegram No. 1236 of June 26.

Molotov just informed me by telephone that he had summoned the Rumanian Minister at 10 o'clock this evening, had informed him of the Soviet Government's demand regarding the cession of Bessarabia and the northern part of Bucovina, and had demanded a reply from the Rumanian Government not later than tomorrow, i. e., on July [*June*] 27.

SCHULENBURG

Frame 224903, serial 459

The Reich Foreign Minister to the German Foreign Office

TELEPHONE MESSAGE FROM SPECIAL TRAIN TO MINISTER SCHMIDT

SECRET   June 27, 1940—10: 30 a. m.

The following instruction is to be transmitted immediately by telephone in plain to Minister Fabricius in Bucharest:

"You are requested to call immediately on the Foreign Minister in Bucharest and inform him as follows:

"The Soviet Government has informed us that it has demanded the cession of Bessarabia and the northern part of Bucovina from the Rumanian Government. In order to avoid war between Rumania and the Soviet Union, we can only advise the Rumanian Government to yield to the Soviet Government's demand. Please report by wire."

End of the instruction to Bucharest.

RIBBENTROP

(Telephoned to Counselor of Legation Stelzer at 11: 00 a. m.)

Frames 112294–112297, serial 104

The German Ambassador in the Soviet Union (Schulenburg) to the State Secretary in the German Foreign Office (Weizsäcker)

Tgb. Nr. A/3192/40   Moscow, July 11, 1940.

The renewed diplomatic activity which the Soviet Union has displayed during the last few weeks has naturally become a main subject of discussion among the members of the Diplomatic Corps here. Some things are not yet completely clear, as for instance the question as to why the Soviet Union *just at this time* proceeded or allegedly will yet proceed against a number of countries. Most of my colleagues are of the opinion that the Soviets, who are always very well informed, know or at least assume the end of the war to be imminent.

Regarding the action taken against Rumania, it has aroused general surprise here that the Soviet Union has also demanded the northern part of Bucovina. There had never been any statement of Soviet claims to this region. As is known, the Soviet Government has justified its claim by the fact that Bucovina has a Ukrainian population. This only applies to the northern part of the country, and the Soviet Union has finally contented itself with this part. I cannot get rid of the impression that it was Ukrainian circles in the Kremlin who have advocated and put through the claim for cession of Northern Bucovina. On several occasions, as for instance during the negotiations regarding the German-Soviet border in Poland, a very strong Ukrainian influence in the Kremlin was evident. Herr Stalin told me personally at that time that he was prepared to make concessions north of the boundary line where it runs through White Russia, but this was impossible in the south where Ukrainians live. Consequently, the cession of the city of Sinyava, very much desired by us, was cancelled by the Soviet Government after it had first agreed to it. It has not yet been possible to determine where this strong Ukrainian influence originates. There is no especially influential Ukrainian known to be among the immediate entourage of the leaders in the Kremlin. A clue might be obtained from the fact that young Pavlov (now in the Soviet Embassy in Berlin), who is the special pet of Herren Stalin and Molotov, once was described to me by Stalin as "our little Ukrainian."

The entire political interest in Moscow is now focused on events in the Baltic States and what will happen in relation to Turkey and Iran.

Most people believe that the three Baltic States will be changed into entities completely dependent on Moscow, i. e., will be incorporated into the Soviet Union. The Legations of the three Baltic States here in Moscow expect to be completely dissolved and to disappear in a very short time. It is generally believed that the Soviet Government will demand the withdrawal of all foreign missions in Kaunas, Riga, and Reval. The excitement among Lithuanians, Latvians, and Estonians here is extremely great. However, actual developments will have to be awaited.

This, no doubt, applies likewise to Turkey and Iran. Both Ambassadors here assert that neither in Moscow nor in Ankara nor in Teheran have any demands been made up to the present. However, it is certain that the situation is serious. I may add that, at least in Iranian circles here, there is much resentment against us, because of the publication of the sixth White Book. They believe that the White Book has induced the Soviet Government to take action against Iran. However, the Iranian Ambassador here is too clever not to see that the documents in the White Book were only a pretext for the Soviet Government's conduct and that Moscow would simply have found another pretext if this one had not presented itself at the moment.

Finally an interesting detail:

The Turkish Ambassador here is telling his friends among the diplomats that he received a plain telegram—which he even produces—from Saracoglu on July 6, in which the latter denies his conversation with Massigli [79] and refers in this connection to telegraphic statements from him to that effect. In the same breath, the Turkish Ambassador declares significantly that it was very annoying that his conversation with American Ambassador Steinhardt [80] thus had also been revealed.

COUNT VON DER SCHULENBURG

[79] French Ambassador in Turkey.
[80] American Ambassador in the Soviet Union.

Frame 112311, serial 104

The German Ambassador in the Soviet Union (Schulenburg) to the German Foreign Office

Telegram

VERY URGENT   Moscow, July 13, 1940—7:04 p. m.
No. 1363 of July 13   Received July 13, 1940—9:10 p. m.

Reference your telegram of the 8th, No. 1164, and my telegram of the 12th, No. 1348.[81]

Molotov summoned me today and stated the following: Stalin had carefully re-examined the situation with respect to the strip of Lithuanian territory and has concluded that our claim to this strip of territory and the Soviet obligation to cede it are incontestable. Under the present circumstances, however, the cession of this strip of territory would be extremely inconvenient and difficult for the Soviet Government. Therefore, Stalin and he himself earnestly request the German Government to consider whether, in conformity with the extraordinarily friendly relations between Germany and the Soviet Union, a way cannot be found which would leave this strip of territory permanently with Lithuania. Molotov added that we could of course at any time move the population of German origin out of Lithuania, as well as out of this strip of territory. Molotov stressed again and again the difficulties which would at present result for the Soviet Union from the cession of this strip of territory, and he made his and Stalin's request seem very urgent by repeatedly expressing hope of a German concession. Request instructions by wire. Perhaps, the Soviet request can be used to put through our economic and financial demands with respect to the Baltic States.

SCHULENBURG

Frames 112312–112313, serial 104

The German Ambassador in the Soviet Union (Schulenburg) to the German Foreign Office

Telegram

VERY URGENT   Moscow, July 13, 1940—9:17 p. m.
SECRET   Received July 14, 1940—9:15 a. m.
No. 1364 of July 13

Molotov informed me today that Cripps, the British Ambassador here, had been received by Stalin a few days ago upon request of the

---

[81] Neither printed.

British Government. On instructions from Stalin, Molotov gave me a memorandum of this conversation.

Cripps inquired regarding the attitude of the Soviet Government toward the following questions:

1. The British Government was convinced that Germany was striving for hegemony in Europe and wanted to engulf all European countries. This was dangerous to the Soviet Union as well as England. Therefore both countries ought to agree on a common policy of self-protection against Germany and on the re-establishment of the European balance of power.

2. Irrespective of this, England would like to trade with the Soviet Union, provided that England's exports would not be resold to Germany.

3. The British Government was of the opinion that unification and leadership of the Balkan countries for the purpose of maintaining the *status quo* was rightly the task of the Soviet Union. Under present circumstances this important mission could be carried out only by the Soviet Union.

4. The British Government knew that the Soviet Union was dissatisfied with the regime in the Straits and in the Black Sea. Cripps was of the opinion that the interests of the Soviet Union in the Straits must be safeguarded.

Stalin's answers are given as follows:

1. The Soviet Government was, of course, very much interested in present events in Europe, but he (Stalin) did not see any danger of the hegemony of any one country in Europe and still less any danger that Europe might be engulfed by Germany. Stalin observed the policy of Germany, and knew several leading German statesmen well. He had not discovered any desire on their part to engulf European countries. Stalin was not of the opinion that German military successes menaced the Soviet Union and her friendly relations with Germany. These relations were not based on transient circumstances, but on the basic national interests of both countries.

The so-called European balance of power had hitherto oppressed not only Germany, but also the Soviet Union. Therefore, the Soviet Union would take all measures to prevent the re-establishment of the old balance of power in Europe.

2. The Soviet Union did not object to trading with England, but she contested the right of England or any other country to interfere with German-Soviet commercial relations. The Soviet Union would export to Germany, in accordance with treaty provisions, part of the

nonferrous metals she bought abroad, because Germany needed these metals for the manufacture of the war matériel she delivered to the Soviet Union. If England did not recognize these conditions, trade between England and the Soviet Union was impossible.

3. In Stalin's opinion no power had the right to an exclusive role in the consolidation and leadership of the Balkan countries. The Soviet Union did not claim such a mission either, although she was interested in Balkan affairs.

4. Regarding Turkey Stalin declared that the Soviet Union was in fact opposed to the exclusive jurisdiction of Turkey over the Straits and to Turkey's dictation of conditions in the Black Sea. The Turkish Government was aware of that.

SCHULENBURG

Frames 214783-214788, serial 407

Foreign Office Memorandum

BERLIN, July 22, 1940.

The Lithuanian Minister called on me today and stated the following:

In view of the important events in his country he considered it his duty not to let these events pass into history without taking action. He had summarized his attitude toward events in Lithuania in a letter to the Reich Foreign Minister. The presentation of this letter amounted to a unilateral act on his part, for which he alone assumed responsibility. He himself did not wish to cause any embarrassment to German policy by this act.

The matter arose in the following way: Some time ago, as a precaution, Foreign Minister Urbsys instructed all Lithuanian Ministers to take such a step in case of a transfer of sovereignty to the Soviet Union. On the basis of a communication between the Lithuanian Ministers he felt sure that a corresponding note would be presented today in all capitals in which Lithuania was represented. The Minister then handed me the enclosed letter, which contains "a most solemn and determined protest."

I told Herr Skirpa that for the time being I wanted to keep the document myself, and I assumed from his statements that he did not expect any comment on it. However, I could not tell him whether as the German Government we would be prepared to accept such a note at all, and we would therefore have to reserve the right to return it to him.

The Minister then stated that particularly in view of the known attitude of Germany he had omitted one point in the note, which the other Lithuanian Ministers would include in their notes to the governments to which they were accredited, namely, the request that the incorporation not be recognized.   The Minister asked whether he could not at least orally present this request here.   I rejected this, whereupon the Minister stated that the request was to be considered as not having been made.   Finally, the Minister said that he intended to make known his action by an announcement from the Berlin office of the Elte Agency, since this appeared to him necessary for the assertion of his personal attitude toward events.

I requested the Minister to refrain from this, and he promised to comply.

Transmitted to the Reich Foreign Minister through the State Secretary with the request for instructions whether the note should be retained here.   The Latvian and Estonian Ministers may be expected to present similar notes here.   The Latvian Minister had already made an appointment with me for 5:30 p. m. today.

WOERMANN

[Enclosure]

The Lithuanian Minister in Germany (Skirpa) to the Reich Foreign Minister

3991   BERLIN, July 21, 1940.

HERR REICH MINISTER: I have the honor, Excellency, to bring the following to your attention:

As is already known, on June 14, 1940, the Union of Soviet Socialist Republics presented an ultimatum to Lithuania under flimsy and unjustified pretexts, in which it was demanded:

1. that the constitutional government of Lithuania be forced to resign immediately;

2. that the Minister of the Interior and the Chief of the State Security Police be tried without preferring charges based on law, and

3. that free and unlimited entry of Soviet military forces into Lithuania be granted.

On the following day the Russian Red Army, after having attacked the Lithuanian frontier guards, crossed the Lithuanian border and occupied all of Lithuania.   Furthermore, a puppet government was forced upon us by a high Soviet official sent from Moscow for this purpose, and the entire administration was put under the control of the Government of the Soviet Socialist Republics.

In order to incorporate Lithuania fully into the Union of Soviet Socialist Republics, elections to the Seim (Parliament) were ordered on July 14, resulting in the greatest falsification of the will of the Lithuanian population.

In order to quell any expression of resistance, even before the elections all Lithuanian clubs and organizations were suppressed, the Lithuanian press was seized and its editors removed by force, and the more or less influential personalities in public life were arrested. People who previously were considered open enemies of the Lithuanian State were appointed to Government offices, particularly in the State Security Police.

The Communist Party was the only political organization which was allowed to function legally. And it then exerted the decisive influence on the scheduled elections. Only one list of candidates was permitted, namely, the one that was agreeable to the Communist Party.

In order to force the necessary participation in the elections anybody who did not wish to vote was threatened with being declared an enemy of the people, and personal attendance was strictly checked.

It was immediately obvious that the Seim, elected under such circumstances, was only a blind tool in the hands of the Communist Party and thereby of the Government of the Soviet Socialist Republics. Today, on July 21, 1940, the Seim adopted a resolution to establish the Soviet system within the country and to incorporate Lithuania into the Union of Soviet Socialist Republics of Russia.

All these measures of the Government of the U.S.S.R. amount to a flagrant violation of all treaties signed between the Republic of Lithuania and the U.S.S.R., in particular however:

1. of the Peace Treaty of July 12, 1920, by which the U.S.S.R. as successor of the former Russian Tsarist Empire recognized unconditionally the independence and autonomy of Lithuania, and by which she renounced forever all rights of sovereignty which Russia previously had over Lithuania (see article 1);

2. of the Nonaggression Pact of September 22, 1926, and of its renewals of May 6, 1931, and of April 4, 1934. In this Pact the U.S.S.R. obligates herself to respect the sovereignty of Lithuania as well as her territorial integrity and inviolability under all circumstances (see article 2) and to refrain from any use of force (article 3);

3. Of the Mutual Assistance Pact of October 10, 1939, in which the Government of the U.S.S.R. repeats a solemn assurance to Lithuania not to violate in any way the sovereignty of the Lithuanian State, as well as its internal order.

In view of all these circumstances I feel compelled as the Minister appointed by the constitutional agencies of the Republic of Lithuania and accredited to the German Reich to lodge the most solemn and determined protest against the oppression of my country and the deprivation of sovereignty and national independence of Lithuania by the Union of Soviet Socialist Republics, and to declare that because the above-mentioned resolution of the Seim was imposed by Russian occupation authorities it amounts to nothing but the most outrageous falsification of the expression of the will of the Lithuanian people and that it is in the sharpest conflict with the constitution and interests of the Lithuanian State, as well as the free right of self-determination of nations, and that, therefore, it cannot be recognized as valid in any way.

I avail myself of the opportunity to renew to Your Excellency the assurance of my highest consideration.

K. SKIRPA

Frames 214780–214781, serial 104

Foreign Office Memorandum

BERLIN, July 22, 1940.

The Latvian Minister called on me today and gave me the enclosed letter to the Reich Foreign Minister, in which he as Minister of the "legitimate Government of Latvia" protests against the incorporation of Latvia into the Union of Soviet Socialist Republics. In this connection .the Minister remarked that he would not think of creating any difficulties for Germany. None could, in his opinion, result from his entering this protest here.

I told Herr Kreewinsch that I would keep his letter personally for the time being. I would notify him later whether the letter could remain here or not.

In connection with the memorandum of the conversation with the Lithuanian Minister [82] there is transmitted herewith this report to the Reich Foreign Minister through the State Secretary, with the request for action.

WOERMANN

---

[82] *Ante,* p. 168.

[Enclosure]

The Latvian Minister in Germany (Kreewinsch) to the Reich Foreign Minister

BERLIN, July 22, 1940.

HERR REICH MINISTER: I have the honor to inform Your Excellency of the following:

The Parliament which convened on the 21st instant in Riga has proclaimed Latvia a Soviet Republic, and it has addressed to Moscow the request that Latvia be incorporated into the Union of Soviet Socialist Republics. This resolution lacks any legal basis, since Parliament itself owes its existence to elections which were held under the terror of Russian occupation and which could not in any way be considered a free expression of the popular will. Previous to this, the invasion of Latvia by Soviet troops was already a violation of all existing treaties between Latvia and the Soviet Union.

As Envoy Extraordinary and Minister Plenipotentiary of the legitimate Government of Latvia I consider it my duty respectfully to inform Your Excellency of my protest against the above-mentioned action.

Accept, Excellency, the renewed assurances of my highest consideration.

EDG. KREEWINSCH

Frame 214771, serial 407

Foreign Office Memorandum

BERLIN, July 24, 1940.

I returned today in a friendly manner the notes regarding the incorporation of their countries into the Soviet Union to the Lithuanian and Latvian Ministers and justified this by stating that we could accept from Ministers only notes which they presented here in the name of their Governments. At the same time, in accordance with instructions, I did not indicate that they were returned by order of the Reich Foreign Minister.

The Estonian Minister likewise wished to hand me a similar note today. I requested him to refrain from doing so, giving the appropriate reasons.

The Lithuanian Minister informed me that of his own accord he had sent the Lithuanian Government a telegram of protest against the resolution of incorporation into the Soviet Union, stating among other things that he did not consider this resolution binding on the Lithuanian people, the nation or himself.   The Lithuanian and Estonian Ambassadors told me that they had not sent a similar telegram and did not contemplate doing so.

Furthermore, I told the three Ministers that they and the other members of the Legation, including families, if they so desired, could remain in Germany.   The three Ministers expressed their very great appreciation for this and also requested me to thank the Reich Foreign Minister.

WOERMANN

Frame 112343, serial 104

The German Ambassador in the Soviet Union (Schulenburg) to the German Foreign Office

Telegram

VERY URGENT   Moscow, July 29, 1940—7 : 10 p. m.
No. 1500 of July 29   Received July 29, 1940—8 : 20 p. m.

Reference my telegram of the 16th, No. 1472.[83]

Molotov summoned me today and stated that the Soviet Government was very much interested in receiving information about the subject of the recent discussions of Germany and Italy with the Hungarian, Rumanian, Bulgarian, and Slovakian statesmen.   I replied that I did not have any information yet, but would request it.

Speedy instructions by wire are requested, particularly in view of the speech on foreign policy Molotov is expected to make on August 1.

SCHULENBURG

Frame 112344, serial 104

The State Secretary in the German Foreign Office (Weizsäcker) to the German Ambassador in the Soviet Union (Schulenburg)

Telegram

URGENT   BERLIN, July 30, 1940.
No. 1307

Reference your telegrams No. 1472 [83] and 1500.
For the Ambassador personally.
The Reich Foreign Minister requests that you inform Herr Molotov

---

[83] Not printed.

at the first opportunity of the latest state visits to Germany, to the following effect:

The visit of the Rumanian Prime Minister and Foreign Minister in Germany was occasioned by the fact that the King of Rumania and the Rumanian Government lately had repeatedly requested the Reich Government to express its attitude toward the Hungarian and Bulgarian desires for [territorial] revision. During the visit, the Rumanian statesmen were advised by us to meet revisionist claims on a fair and reasonable basis and to negotiate directly with the Hungarian and Bulgarian Governments for this purpose. The Rumanian statesmen now held out prospects of initiating such negotiations. During the Bulgarian visit we notified Bulgarian statesmen to that effect. End of the instructions by the Reich Foreign Minister.

In accordance with instructions I shall similarly inform Ambassador Shkvarzev.

A report by wire is requested.

WEIZSÄCKER

Frame 357760, serial 1379

The Reich Foreign Minister to the German Ambassador in the Soviet Union (Schulenburg)

Telegram

No. 1339 of August 2   BERLIN, August 2, 1940—4:24 p. m.
                   Received Moscow, August 2, 1940—8:45 p. m.

Reference your telegram of July 13, No. 1363.

You are requested to inform Herr Molotov that the Reich Government has taken cognizance of the wish of the Soviet Government that Germany leave to the Soviet Union that part of Lithuania allocated to Germany by the Moscow agreements. This would represent a rather considerable change in the Moscow Treaty to the disadvantage of Germany. Before the Reich Government can consider the matter in detail, therefore, I should be interested in hearing what *quid pro quo* the Soviet Government would propose.

RIBBENTROP

Frame 211004, serial 384

Memorandum by the Reich Foreign Minister on the Reception of the Soviet Ambassador, Herr Shkvarzev, on August 6, 1940

RM 21/40

I received the Soviet Ambassador, Herr Shkvarzev, today and strongly remonstrated with him regarding the article, published in Riga in the newspaper *Jaunakas Zinas* on the 5th instant, entitled "German Communists Against Dictate at Compiègne." I strongly emphasized that this was an outright inflammatory article against Germany. The attacks on the German Government contained in that article were not calculated to further good German-Russian relations, which after all were desired by both sides. The contents and implications of this article did not correspond to the letter or the spirit of the Moscow agreements. The article was also in diametrical opposition to the desire, recently expressed by the Führer and the day before yesterday by Molotov in Moscow, of further strengthening friendly German-Russian relations. I requested the Ambassador to inform his Government immediately of this talk and to notify it that the Reich Government considered it appropriate to suppress such articles in the future.

Herr Shkvarzev did not make any comment on the article itself, but promised to report the matter immediately to Herr Molotov. As basis for his report a copy of the German News Agency despatch of the 6th instant covering the article was handed to him.

R[IBBENTROP][85]

BERLIN, August 6, 1940.

———————

Frame 357784, serial 1879

The German Foreign Office to the German Embassy in the Soviet Union and the German Legation in Lithuania

CONFIDENTIAL   BERLIN, August 9, 1940.
W XII 5228

For personal information only.

The incorporation of Lithuania into the territory of the Soviet Union creates a completely new situation for the Memel Free Port Zone. The Free Port Zone represented an international obligation,

———————

[85] Signature supplied from another copy of this memorandum.

made to facilitate the return by little Lithuania of her most important port to Germany. For Russia, which has expanded and has at her disposal a great number of Baltic Sea ports, it has lost its real significance; its continued existence would lead to politically dangerous Russian privileges on German territory. If Russia should demand the continuance of the Free Port Zone in Memel, the position taken here will be that the promises given in the German-Lithuanian Treaty of March 22, 1939, are no longer applicable to a Lithuania which has been incorporated into the Soviet Union. The competent offices will initiate the necessary steps for terminating the present state of affairs.

The question of handling Russian traffic via the German port of Memel will especially be kept in mind.

By order:
SCHNURRE

Frame 112386, serial 104

The German Ambassador in the Soviet Union (Schulenburg) to the German Foreign Office

Telegram

VERY URGENT   Moscow, August 13, 1940—12:25 a. m.
SECRET   Received August 13, 1940—4:25 a. m.
No. 1638 of August 12

Reference my telegram of the 7th, No. 1590.[86]

Concerning the Lithuanian strip of territory Molotov today handed me a long memorandum stating that territorial compensation was unacceptable to the Soviet Union, but declaring readiness to pay 3,860,000 gold dollars within 2 years (i. e., half of the sum the U. S. A. paid to Russia for the cession of Alaska), either in gold or goods, as Germany may prefer, for the retention of the strip of territory by the Soviet Union.

The text of the memorandum will be sent Wednesday via courier by plane.

SCHULENBURG

---

[86] Not printed.

Frames 100–101, serial F 18

Memorandum by the Reich Foreign Minister

RM 22

Subject: Conversation with the Russian Ambassador.

The Russian Ambassador made an appointment with me today in order to give me the answer of the Russian Government to the complaint concerning the article in the Latvian newspaper *Janaukas Zinas.* He said that he had instructions from his Government to inform me that the appearance of the article was due to a misunderstanding. His Government had given instructions to Latvia, which now belonged to the Soviet Union, that in the future such articles were to be suppressed.

I answered the Russian that I took note of that. Such articles were not advantageous for the development of the good German-Russian relations which we desired. In the German press in turn we would not tolerate articles against Russian conditions either.

I then asked the Ambassador what truth there was to press reports of a stiffening in Russo-Finnish relations; whether they had reached a final understanding on the Aaland problem or whether there were otherwise any reasons for this stiffening. Herr Shkvarzev stated that he had no information on that point.

The Ambassador and his interpreter made a somewhat dejected impression during the talk.

R[IBBENTROP]

BERLIN, August 14, 1940.

Frames 112436–112437, serial 104

The German Ambassador in the Soviet Union (Schulenburg) to the German Foreign Office

Telegram

URGENT   Moscow, August 30, 1940—10:12 p. m.
No. 1799 of August 30   Received August 31, 1940—12:10 a. m.

Reference instruction W XII 5228 of August 9.

Last night Molotov asked me to see him and handed me a *note verbale*,[87] in which the attention of the German Government is called to activities of German authorities in the Memel Free Port Zone which

---

[87] Not printed.

violate rights and interests of the Lithuanian Soviet Republic. Disregarding the rights fixed in the German-Lithuanian Treaty of May 20 concerning the Memel Free Port Zone (which are quoted in detail in the *note verbale*) German authorities had ordered German troops to invade the territory of the Free Zone, had discontinued the activities of the Customs Office, and had declared that all Lithuanian goods in this zone were to be removed. The German authorities had thereby seriously affected the economic situation and commercial possibilities of Lithuania, which now forms part of the Soviet Union. The Soviet Government was of the opinion that the Lithuanian Soviet Republic was entitled to all the rights and privileges granted by the German-Lithuanian Treaty as well as by the letters exchanged between Schnurre and Norkaitis on May 20, 1939, and that their validity could not be terminated by a unilateral act.

Molotov added orally that just as the German Government takes for granted the fulfillment of the commercial treaties concluded between Germany and the Baltic countries, so also must the Soviet Government demand the observance of the German-Lithuanian Treaty with regard to the Memel Free Port Zone which was likewise a commercial treaty.

Please enable me as soon as possible to answer the *note verbale*, the text of which will follow by the next courier.

Minister Schnurre will give his opinion on this issue separately.

SCHULENBURG

Frames 357804-357807, serial 1379

The Reich Foreign Minister to the German Ambassador in the Soviet Union (Schulenburg)

Telegram

VERY URGENT   BERLIN, August 31, 1940—3 : 12 a. m.
No. 1565 of August 30   Received Moscow August 31, 1940—10 a. m.

Please call on Herr Molotov and inform him orally of the Vienna conversations and the German-Italian award in the Hungarian-Rumanian matter, approximately as follows:

As Molotov was previously informed, both the Rumanian and the Hungarian Governments some time ago solicited the advice of the Führer and the Duce on the solution of the problem of territorial revision. The Führer and the Duce urgently advised both parties, as well as the Bulgarian Government, to come to an understanding as promptly as possible by way of direct, bilateral negotiations.

While the Bulgaro-Rumanian negotiations led relatively soon to an agreement in principle, and we can now look forward to the early conclusion of a formal agreement, it recently became more and more obvious that the Hungarian-Rumanian negotiations were running into very great difficulties and that no progress was discernible in reconciling the viewpoints of the two parties. Lately relations between Hungary and Rumania deteriorated to such an extent that the possibility of military complications had to be seriously faced. In compliance with the repeated requests of both the Hungarian and the Rumanian Governments, the Government of the Reich and the Italian Government found it necessary in repeated personal consultations to influence both parties toward effecting a speedier understanding. For this purpose, the meeting in Vienna was agreed upon a few days ago on very short notice. Since the attitude of the Rumanians and of the Hungarians held out no prospect of an agreement by direct negotiation, and since both parties requested arbitration by Germany and Italy, the Government of the Reich and the Italian Government withdrew their previous objections to such arbitration and assumed the task of settlement by arbitration.

The Government of the Reich decided upon this course in agreement with the Italian Government, because it was evident that there was no further prospect of reaching a peaceful solution by any other means and because both Axis Powers have a fundamental interest in the maintenance of peace and order in those areas. This concern arises, as has always been understood between ourselves and the Soviet Government, primarily from the fact that Germany and Italy are very closely involved [*verknüpft*] with the Rumanian economy. So, for example, the extraction of Rumanian oil, its shipment to Germany, the uninterrupted importation of Rumanian grain into Germany, etc., are becoming of ever more vital significance for the Axis Powers. Hence an armed conflict in those areas, whatever its cause, could not have been tolerated by the Axis. After the Soviet Government had peacefully settled her controversy with Rumania, and the Rumanian-Bulgarian problem likewise approached a settlement, it was imperative that the last remaining territorial problem should not lead to an armed conflict. Because of the very complicated geographical and ethnological situation in Transylvania, the decision was not an easy one. However, we finally found a way out of the difficulties, which was based upon a just and impartial consideration of all the interests concerned. By their award, which was accepted by both parties without reservation, Germany and Italy have now secured the peace that was threatened in the

Danube region. But in order to forestall once and for all a repetition of differences which might easily arise in areas of such territorial and ethnological complexity, the Axis Powers have undertaken to guarantee the territory of Rumania, which has now been definitively pacified. Since the award necessarily involved the cession of a considerable portion of Rumanian territory, it was a natural need for the Rumanians henceforth to be able to regard their boundary with Hungary and their territory in general as definitively secured. Since the territorial demands made by the Soviet Government on Rumania have been settled by the cession of Bessarabia, since the Bulgarian demands are now in course of being met, and since Rumania, through the award, has obtained her definitive boundary with Hungary, there could remain from this standpoint no further objection to the granting of such a guarantee by the Axis Powers.

Please tell Herr Molotov on my behalf that in view of the friendly relations between our countries, I attach great importance to informing the Soviet Government of these events.

We assume that, from the points of view set forth above, the Soviet Government, too, will welcome the settlement achieved by the Axis and regard it as a valuable contribution toward securing the peace in the Danube region.

RIBBENTROP

Frame 112444, serial 104

The German Ambassador in the Soviet Union (Schulenburg) to the German Foreign Office

Telegram[*]

VERY URGENT   Moscow, September 1, 1940—2 : 08 a.m.
SECRET   Received September 1, 1940—4 : 40 a. m.
No. 1815 of August 31

Reference your telegram of the 30th, No. 1565.

For the Reich Foreign Minister.

Instruction carried out. Molotov, who was reserved, in contrast to his usual manner, expressed his thanks for the information and stated as follows:

The Soviet Government was already informed regarding the Vienna conversations by the press and the radio. He asked me to call the attention of the German Government to the fact that by its action it

---

[*] A marginal note reads: "Forwarded under No. 95 at 5 : 30 a. m., September 1, to the Special Train. Telegram Control Office, September 1."

had violated article 3 of the Nonaggression Pact, which provided for consultation. The Soviet Government had been confronted with accomplished facts by the German Government; this violated existing agreements and conflicted with assurances the Soviet Government had received from Germany regarding questions of common interest to both countries. The present case involved two of the Soviet Union's neighbors, where she naturally had interests.

I told Molotov that I could not take a stand with regard to his remarks and that I would immediately notify my Government. Personally, I supposed that there had been no time for consultation in the present case because of the urgency of the matter.

SCHULENBURG

Frames 357818–357821, serial 1379

The Reich Foreign Minister to the German Ambassador in the Soviet Union (Schulenburg)

Telegram

No. 1580 of September 3   BERLIN, September 3, 1940—6 : 20 a. m.
                      Received Moscow September 3, 1940—1 : 50 p. m.

Reference your telegram No. 1815.

Please call on Herr Molotov again and to his statement that Germany, by her conduct in Vienna, had violated the obligation to consult contained in article 3 of the Nonaggression Pact, reply in accordance with the following memorandum and afterwards hand him this memorandum as a summary of your instructions. If there is anything you wish to say regarding the instructions, please report to me before you call on Molotov.

TEXT OF THE MEMORANDUM:

In his last oral discussion with Ambassador Count von der Schulenburg, when the latter acquainted him with the conferences at Vienna, Chairman Molotov said that he had to call Germany's attention to the fact that by her conduct in Vienna she had violated article 3 of the German-Russian Nonaggression Pact of August 23, 1939, which provided for consultation. The Soviet Government had been confronted by Germany with accomplished facts, which violated existing agreements and conflicted with assurances the Soviet Government had received from Germany regarding questions of common interest to the two countries. The present case involved two of the Soviet Union's neighbors, in which she naturally had interests.

Conscious of her friendly relations with the Soviet Union, which have developed in a manner satisfactory to both parties, and have been intensified both in the economic and in the political field since the conclusion of the treaties of 1939, the Government of the Reich takes the following position on the construction placed by the Soviet Government on the German-Russian Nonaggression Pact:

In article 3 of the German-Russian Nonaggression Pact an obligation was agreed upon for reciprocal information and consultation on questions of interest to both parties. Likewise at Moscow, at the delimitation of the respective spheres of influence, an interest in Bessarabia was stressed on the part of Soviet Russia, while Germany declared herself disinterested in these areas. But that Germany is intensely concerned in the remaining Rumanian territories and the other problems of the Danube region, and is even vitally concerned there, in view of the close interpenetration of the German economy with Rumania, particularly in the questions of oil and grain, is generally known and has, moreover, been communicated to the Soviet Government on various occasions and been recognized by it in its entirety. On the other hand, after the settlement of the Bessarabian question a like interest in the rest of Rumanian territory on the part of the Soviet Union is not evident, and has not been expressed to the Government of the Reich, either at the Moscow settlement or later. The same is true of Hungary. Hence the existence of mutual interests within the meaning of the Nonaggression Pact of Moscow is out of the question here. Thus, even if Rumania and Hungary are neighboring countries, Germany has certainly not committed a violation of the obligation for mutual consultation.

The Government of the Reich, moreover, believes itself the more justified in this view, in that the Soviet Government itself, on the occasion of various political moves in the recent past, by no means considered the fact of contiguity to Germany of the territories affected by her acts as a reason for prior consultation with the Government of the Reich. In this connection, the Government of the Reich refers to Russian action in the Baltic States, especially Lithuania. In the latter case, besides the fact that Lithuania is adjacent to Germany, an obligation existed to surrender to Germany a certain area in the southwest of Lithuania in the event that the Soviet Union should take special measures on Lithuanian territory for the safeguarding of her interests. Nevertheless, the Soviet Union effected a military occupation of that area also, although as a result of the Russian measures it should have been treated forthwith as German territory. Only after representations by the Government of the Reich was this question reopened.

Further, one might add that at the occupation of Bessarabia and Northern Bucovina the Government of the Reich likewise received only very short notice from the Soviet Government, although in view of the many Germans living there, in this case also, Germany had a special interest, and although the Government of the Reich had already pointed out that for Germany it was a new issue [*ein Novum*]. Nevertheless, in view of its cordial relations with the Soviet Union and in its desire to see the Danube region remain at peace, the Government of the Reich took it upon itself to give the Rumanian Government, which had made the most importunate representations for assistance to the Government of the Reich, the stern advice to settle this question peacefully, which meant the cession of that territory to the Soviet Union.

In conclusion, the Government of the Reich would like further to observe, with reference to the statement that Germany had confronted the Soviet Union with accomplished facts, that while the moves of the Soviet Union were planned moves for the occupation of various territories in the neighborhood of Germany and were not previously announced to the Government of the Reich, the steps of the Reich Government in the case of Rumania and Hungary served the purpose of securing the peace in the Danube region, which was gravely threatened by the tension between the two countries, and this could only be accomplished by rapid diplomatic intervention. Moreover, the Government of the Reich is probably not mistaken in believing that by its campaign of pacification in the Danube area it has rendered a substantial service to all countries bordering on that area.

RIBBENTROP

Frames 357823-357824, serial 1879

The German Ambassador in the Soviet Union (Schulenburg) to the German Foreign Office

Telegram

VERY URGENT   Moscow, September 4, 1940—5 : 30 p. m.
No. 1841 of September 4

Reference your telegram No. 1580 of September 3.

I would appreciate authorization to supplement the ideas contained in the memorandum to be handed to Molotov in the sense that the

Soviet Government really set off the great complex of questions by its settlement of the Bessarabian matter with unexpected speed and that it had thereby forced us, in order to avoid military complications in the Balkans, to take quick decisions in the matter of the Rumanian-Hungarian dispute. The beginning of the next to the last paragraph of the memorandum might give the Soviet Government the chance to protest that, before its action in Bessarabia, it had given the German Government the opportunity to state its views and had waited for the latter.

Further I would suggest deleting, in the third paragraph of the memorandum, the words: " . . . and has not been expressed to the Government of the Reich, either at the Moscow settlement or later," because they could provide Molotov with the opportunity again to revert to the talk between Mackensen and the Soviet Chargé in Rome last May (see our telegrams No. 1063 of June 3, No. 1079 of June 6, No. 1094 of June 7,[89] and the telegraphic instruction No. 1007 of June 15 [16]) and to state that the Soviet Government had at the time repeatedly demonstrated its interest.

Furthermore, my interview with Molotov would be substantially facilitated if I were enabled at the same time to communicate to him the position of the German Government, for which Molotov has in the meantime pressed several times, in the matter of the strip of Lithuanian territory as well as in the question of the Free Port Zone of Memel (see our telegrams No. 1799 and 1800 of August 30).[90] The question of the Free Port Zone of Memel was taken up with Schnurre on September 2 by Mikoyan in a manner which leaves no doubt as to the resentment felt by the Soviet Government, and makes much more difficult the further pursuit of our interests in the Baltic States. (See telegram No. 1829 of September 3).[91]

Please wire instructions.

SCHULENBURG

---

[89] Telegram of June 7 not printed.
[90] Latter not printed.
[91] Not printed.

Frame 112457, serial 104

The German Foreign Office to the German Ambassador in the Soviet Union (Schulenburg)

Telegram

STATE SECRET   BERLIN, September 5, 1940.

No. 1604

The Navy intends to abandon the base on the Murman Coast, as such are now available in Norway. Please inform the Russians of this decision and, on behalf of the Government of the Reich, convey our thanks for valuable assistance. In addition to the official note, the Commander-in-Chief of the Navy intends also to express his gratitude in a personal letter to the Commander-in-Chief of the Soviet Navy. Therefore please wire when notification has been made.

WOERMANN

Frames 357827-357830, serial 1379

The Reich Foreign Minister to the German Ambassador in the Soviet Union (Schulenburg)

Telegram

VERY URGENT   BERLIN, September 6, 1940—4:35 a. m.
                                    Received Moscow, September 6, 1940—10 a. m.

No. 1609 of September 5

For the Ambassador personally.

Reference your telegram No. 1841.

To your suggestions I state the following for your information:

1) It is correct that the Hungarian and Bulgarian revisionist demands on Rumania were set in motion by the occupation of Bessarabia and Northern Bucovina. However, we cannot very well claim that it was the Russian action which made our diplomatic intervention so urgent that for this reason it was no longer possible for us to approach the Soviet Union. Besides, the necessity for swift diplomatic action is emphasized in the closing sentence of the memorandum. You will please insert therefore, in the first sentence of the next to the last paragraph of the memorandum, after the words "occupation of Bessarabia and Northern Bucovina," the qualifying clause: "which also gave the impulse for the launching of revisionist demands on Rumania."

2) That the Soviet Government, before the occupation of Bessarabia and Northern Bucovina, formally gave us an opportunity to express our views is not disputed in our memorandum, but it is stressed that it gave us only a very short period in which to do so. In this regard, therefore, a change in the memorandum is not necessary.

3) The words in the third paragraph of the memorandum, stating that a like interest in Rumania on the part of the Soviet Union was not expressed to the Government of the Reich, either at the Moscow settlement or later, please leave unchanged. If Herr Molotov should object that the Soviet Government had demonstrated its interest in Rumania during discussion of the conversation between Mackensen and the Soviet Chargé in Rome, the reply should be made that such an interest could not be inferred from his inquiry at that time, as he had then only inquired about the attitude of the Reich Government toward an alleged statement of Mackensen, which in fact he had not made in the sense imputed to him at all. Besides, I might tell you for your personal information that this passage in our memorandum is of particular importance because we are anxious at this opportunity to demonstrate once and for all to the Soviet Union that we have really vital importance [*Bedeutung*] and predominant interests in Rumania which led us to guarantee the Rumanian territory within its present borders. Please bear this in mind in connection with the orientation of your conversations now and in the future as well. If necessary, you could point out orally to Herr Molotov in this connection that after the settlement of the Bessarabian question the purely geographical contiguity of the Soviet Union to Rumania could not be invested with a significance comparable to the German interests in Rumania. The Soviet Union, in contrast to Germany, certainly has sufficient oil wells and grain production, so that her relationship to Rumania for this very reason could decidedly not be placed on a level with ours. But please do not of your own accord give occasion for a discussion in such detail.

4) I leave it to you whether or not you think it opportune to bring up on this occasion the question of the strip of Lithuanian territory. If you think it advisable, you may tell Herr Molotov that the Government of the Reich is prepared in principle, against adequate compensation, to forego the cession of the strip of Lithuanian territory which was agreed upon in Moscow. The compensation which the Soviet Union has offered is certainly not acceptable to us. At the

moment we are engaged in drawing up a proposal for adequate compensation and we shall soon approach the Soviet Government with this proposal.

5) On the other hand, I request you not to broach the question of the Free Port of Memel on this occasion. We must persist in our view that we cannot grant the Soviet Government a free port zone in Memel. But this question will have to be discussed separately with the Soviet Government.

Please report by wire on the course of your interview with Herr Molotov.

RIBBENTROP

Frame 112472, serial 104

The German Ambassador in the Soviet Union (Schulenburg) to the German Foreign Office

Telegram

VERY URGENT   Moscow, September 10, 1940—12 : 55 a. m.
                               Received September 10, 1940—4 : 30 a. m.
No. 1884 of September 9

Reference your telegram No. 1609 of the 5th.

For the Reich Minister personally.

Instruction carried out. Handed memorandum to Molotov this evening. Molotov read it through attentively and declared that the matter was so important for the Soviet Government that it would reply in writing. But he had to state now, that the position taken by the German Government could not alter the Soviet position. The Soviet Government persisted in its view that the conduct of the German Government in Vienna was not entirely in good faith [*nicht ganz loyal*], as [the German Government] could not have been in doubt that the Soviet Government was interested in Rumania and Hungary. The Soviet Government was, however, by no means disputing the fact that Germany had special interests in Rumania.

To justify his position, Molotov pointed out that the entire world press assumed as a matter of course that in the present case a consultation between Germany and the Soviet Union had certainly taken place.

SCHULENBURG

Frame 214737, serial 407

The German Ambassador in the Soviet Union (Schulenburg) to the German Foreign Office

Telegram

URGENT

Moscow, September 10, 1940—5:58 p. m.
Received September 11, 1940—8 p. m.

No. 1900 of September 11

Reference your telegram No. 1649 of the 10th.[92]

Molotov displayed great interest in, and had me repeat several times, the statement that "the Government of the Reich is prepared in principle, against adequate compensation, to forego the cession of the strip of Lithuanian territory which was agreed upon in Moscow." I had the impression that Molotov was satisfied. The statement that the compensation offered was certainly not acceptable to us and that we were engaged in drawing up a counter-proposal, Molotov noted with interest, without any further comment.

SCHULENBURG

Frames 0463–0464, serial F 5

The Reich Foreign Minister to the German Ambassador in the Soviet Union (Schulenburg)

Telegram

RAM 37 g. Rs.   BERLIN, September 16, 1940.
No. . .

For the Ambassador personally.

Please call on Herr Molotov on the afternoon of September 21, if by that time you are not otherwise instructed, and communicate to him verbally and casually, preferably while engaged on another errand, the following:

The continued penetration of English planes into Germany and into the territories occupied by Germany makes it necessary to strengthen the defenses at several points, and particularly in northern Norway. Part of this reinforcement is an antiaircraft artillery battalion, which, with its equipment, is to be stationed in northern Norway. Investigation of the transport facilities revealed that for this purpose the route by way of Finland would present the least difficulty. This

---

[92] Not printed.

antiaircraft battery will presumably be landed near Haparanda on September 22 and transported to Norway, part way by rail, and the rest by road.

The Finnish Government, appreciating the special circumstances, has granted the German request to permit this transport to take place.

We are anxious to inform the Soviet Government of this step in advance. Wire report that instruction has been carried out.

We assume—and request express confirmation—that the Soviet Government will keep this communication strictly secret.

RIBBENTROP

Frame 0464-serial F 5

The Reich Foreign Minister to the German Minister in Finland (Blücher)

Telegram

No. . .   BERLIN, September 16, 1940.

For the Minister personally.

Arrangements have been made by German and Finnish military authorities for the transport of an antiaircraft artillery battalion through Finland. I wired the Moscow Embassy in this matter as follows:

Insert [preceding document].

End of telegram to Moscow.

Please notify the Foreign Minister in Helsinki on the afternoon of September 21 of the step which is being taken in Moscow.

RIBBENTROP

Frames 112531-112538, serial 104

Memorandum by the German Ambassador in the Soviet Union (Schulenburg)

SEPTEMBER 21, 1940.

Subject: Interview with Molotov on Vienna conversations.

Before my departure for Berlin, Molotov received me at 5 p. m. on September 21, 1940. On this occasion he handed me an exhaustive memorandum [93] in reply to the German memorandum on the subject of

---

[93] For text, see enclosure to this document.

the Vienna conversations, which I had transmitted to him on September 9, 1940, on behalf of the Government of the Reich.[94]

In the course of the interview, Molotov explained verbally the contents of the memorandum, expressing essentially the same ideas as on September 9. (See memorandum of Hilger, Counselor of Embassy, of September 18, 1940.) [95]

When I pointed out that I could not recall that he—Molotov—had ever spoken of German support for the claims of the Soviet Government to Southern Bucovina and that I could merely remember the casual little phrase that the Soviet Government would "for the present" confine itself to Northern Bucovina, Molotov replied that apparently he had made this remark in an indefinite way at the time.

Then Molotov reverted—repeatedly—to the last paragraph of the memorandum, in which he emphasized that an amendment or annulment of article 3 of the Nonaggression Treaty might be discussed, if this article inconvenienced us in any way or had proved restrictive.

I replied that in my opinion the German Government had no intentions at all along these lines.

Herr Molotov further stated that the German action at Vienna had given the foreign press cause to speak of German-Russian disagreements and to assert that the guarantee of the Rumanian border was directed against the Soviet Union. It would have been easy to forestall such rumors by asking the Soviet Government in advance about its intentions. In this case, the Soviet Government would have given the unequivocal reply that it had no aggressive designs on Rumania.

In conclusion, Herr Molotov repeated his request that during my stay in Berlin I do everything to clarify the position of the Soviet Government on this question, which, of course, I promised to do.

COUNT VON DER SCHULENBURG

Moscow, September 21, 1940.

[Enclosure]

The People's Commissariat of Foreign Affairs of the Soviet Union to the German Embassy in the Soviet Union

In reply to German Ambassador Count von der Schulenburg's memorandum of September 9 of this year, the People's Commissariat for Foreign Affairs has the honor to state as follows:

---

[94] For text, see telegrams from the Reich Foreign Minister to the German Ambassador in the Soviet Union, Nos. 1580 of September 3 and 1609 of September 5, 1940, *ante*, pp. 181 and 185.

[95] Not printed. For the Ambassador's account of his presentation of the German memorandum, see his telegram No. 1884 of September 9, 1940, *ante*, p. 187.

1) In reply to the declaration of the People's Commissar for Foreign Affairs, V. M. Molotov, of August 31 of this year, to the effect that the Government of the German Reich had disregarded article 3 of the treaty of consultation, the Government of the German Reich states that Germany did not violate her obligation to consult. In justification of its position, the Government of the German Reich states that, after the solution of the Bessarabian question, the U.S.S.R. and Germany, from the standpoint of the Moscow Nonaggression Pact, no longer had any common interests with respect to Rumania and Hungary.

The Soviet Government is of the opinion that such a construction by the Government of the German Reich contravenes article 3 of the Treaty of August 23, 1939, by virtue of which the contracting parties obligate themselves in the future to "maintain continual contact with one another for the purpose of consultation in order to exchange information on problems affecting their common interests."

There is no doubt that the decisions reached at Vienna regarding the transfer of a considerable portion of Transylvania to Hungary and regarding the guarantee of the national territory of Rumania by Germany and Italy involve the very questions that affect the common interests of our countries and consequently make the consultation provided for in article 3 of the Treaty of August 23, 1939 obligatory. Definite information regarding the above-mentioned decisions at Vienna was not given by the Government of the German Reich to the Soviet Government until after the Vienna Award, which confronted the Soviet Government with an accomplished fact.

The Soviet Government must also point to the fact that the granting of the guarantee to Rumania in respect to her national territory gave justification for the assertion that this action of the Government of the German Reich was directed against the U.S.S.R. As is known, assertions of this kind actually received a wide circulation. If, however, the Government of the German Reich had approached the Government of the U.S.S.R. on this question in advance, every justification for the circulation of such assertions would have disappeared and the Government of the German Reich at the same time would have fully convinced itself that the U.S.S.R. does not intend to threaten the territorial integrity of Rumania. From this is evident the extraordinary importance of timely information and consultation on questions affecting the common interests of the U.S.S.R. and Germany.

The Soviet Government regrets to have to state that the view expressed in the reply of the Government of the German Reich of September 9 of this year is also at variance with the declaration made on June 23 of this year by Count von der Schulenburg on behalf of the Government of the German Reich. As is known, the Government of the German Reich in that case replied—to a specific inquiry of the Soviet Government—that the obligation to inform and consult arising from article 3 of the Treaty is applicable to the countries of southeastern Europe and the Balkans. It appears from the foregoing that the Government of the German Reich in June of this year recognized the obligation to consult on questions concerning such countries as Rumania and Hungary, particularly on such important questions as those dealt with at Vienna, which affect the interests of the U.S.S.R.

The Soviet Government, for its part, considers it as its duty to state that it reaffirms its declarations concerning the recognition of the special economic interests of Germany in Rumania, especially in the domain of oil and grain supplies. At the same time, however, it is compelled to declare that the inference which might be drawn from Count von der Schulenburg's memorandum of September 9 of this year is incorrect: that after the solution of the Bessarabian question the Soviet Government had recognized in its entirety the exclusive interest of Germany in the Rumanian question and also in other questions affecting the Danube basin. In reality, the Soviet Government has neither orally nor in writing recognized any such rights on the part of Germany.

2) To justify the omission of such a consultation with the Government of the U.S.S.R. in the Vienna decisions, the Government of the German Reich cites the fact that allegedly the Government of the U.S.S.R. did not consult with the Government of the German Reich, either, on its measures in the Baltic States, especially in Lithuania, and gave only short notice with regard to Bessarabia and Northern Bucovina.

The Soviet Government must, in the first place, point out that during the entire period of the validity of the Treaty of August 23, 1939 the Government of the German Reich did not once declare that the Soviet Government had violated its treaty obligations or had failed to consult with the Government of the German Reich on the above-mentioned questions. The Soviet Government is of the opinion that the best way to establish mutual understanding and to secure the complete and effective performance of the obligations imposed by the Treaty is by a timely declaration of claims that may arise, in case there actually are such claims. The Soviet Government must point out that during the whole year that the Treaty of August 23, 1939 has been in effect it had not received any such declarations or claims from the Government of the German Reich.

To turn to the substance of the above-mentioned matter, the Soviet Government believes it necessary to declare that the said statement of the Government of the German Reich is not in accord with the real situation. The Soviet Government not only informed the Government of the German Reich in advance regarding the measures it intended to take in the Baltic States, especially in Lithuania, but even received from the Government of the German Reich on June 17 of this year a communication stating that the measures taken by the Soviet Government in those countries were regarded by Germany as measures which concerned solely the Soviet Union and those countries. Such a declaration from the Government of the German Reich was entirely comprehensible to the Soviet Government, as Germany had as recently as August 1939 recognized the special interests of the Soviet Union in respect to the Baltic States, and the measures which the Soviet Union had taken regarding those states, especially Lithuania, in no way went beyond the scope of the Soviet-German Pact of August 23, 1939. In regard to a certain area in the Southeast of Lithuania, however, the Soviet Government in June of this year clearly confirmed the rights of Germany, and reserved its new proposals concerning this Lithuanian area for a special arrangement with the Government of the German Reich.

The same holds true as regards the question of Bessarabia and Bucovina, in regard to which the Soviet Government held a consultation with the Government of the German Reich, at which it met the viewpoint of the Government of the German Reich by substantially paring down its intentions with regard to Bucovina. At the same time it voiced the hope that the Government of the German Reich would give its support in the future, when the question of Southern Bucovina was reopened. This declaration of the Soviet Government met with no objection from the Government of the German Reich.

Its attitude on questions pertaining to Rumania was, moreover, communicated by the Soviet Government on June 25 of this year to the Italian Government through the Italian Ambassador, Herr Rosso, and it was convinced that the Government of the German Reich would be duly informed of this communication of the Soviet Government. In this communication, the Soviet Government, while emphasizing that it wished to obtain from Rumania merely what rightfully belonged to it, declared: "Regarding other territories of Rumania, the

U.S.S.R. is mindful of the interests of Italy and Germany and is prepared to come to an understanding with them on these questions."

On the basis of the foregoing explanations, the Soviet Government deems it necessary to declare that the measures it took in regard to the Baltic States and in Bessarabia were entirely in accord with the Soviet-German Treaty, while the new and lesser problems which were not anticipated in this Treaty are being solved and will be solved by the Soviet Government in consultation with the Government of the German Reich.

Hence the reference by the Government of the German Reich to the measures carried out by the Soviet Union in the Baltic region as an explanation of the failure to consult with the Soviet Government regarding the Vienna decision is not confirmed by the facts and therefore not justified.

3) In conclusion the Government of the German Reich points to the circumstance that in the solution of the Hungarian-Rumanian dispute on August 30 it had to proceed by swift diplomatic intervention.

Here the Soviet Government deems it necessary to recall that this question had been considered as early as the conferences in Salzburg between the Government of the German Reich and the Governments of Hungary and Rumania and that, consequently, the Government of the German Reich had sufficient time at its disposal to consult with the Soviet Government on this question.

The aforesaid circumstances, therefore, cannot serve as justification for the failure of the Government of the German Reich to comply with the obligation to consult, imposed by the Nonaggression Treaty, in the Rumanian question and in the Hungarian-Rumanian dispute.

The Soviet Government is firmly convinced that the precise and strict observance of this Treaty, particularly of article 3 of the Treaty, is also one of the most important conditions in the matter of the pacification of the Danube region, to which reference is made in the memorandum of September 9 of this year.

In conclusion, the Soviet Government deems it necessary to add to the foregoing considerations that, if article 3 of the Nonaggression Treaty involves certain inconveniences and restrictions from the standpoint of the Government of the German Reich, the Soviet Government is prepared to negotiate on the question of an amendment to or deletion of this article of the Treaty. The Soviet Government considers it desirable to have a special agreement to consider the time and manner of dealing with this question.

Moscow, September 21, 1940.

VI. THE U.S.S.R. AND THE THREE POWER PACT, SEPTEMBER 25–NOVEMBER 26, 1940

Frames 0452–0454, serial F 5

The Reich Foreign Minister to the German Embassy in the Soviet Union

Telegram

STRICTLY SECRET   BERLIN, September 25, 1940.
STATE SECRET

RAM. 33/40 g. Rs.

No. 1746

Strictly secret. Exclusively for the Chargé in person.

The following instruction is only to be carried out if on Thursday you receive from my Ministerial Office by telephone or telegraph the word "Execution."

Please call on Herr Molotov on Thursday, September 26, and tell him on my behalf that in view of the cordial relations existing between Germany and the Soviet Union I was desirous of informing him in advance, in strict confidence, of the following:

1) The warmongering agitation in America, which at this stage of the final defeat of England is seeking a last outlet in the extension and prolongation of the war, has led to negotiations between the two Axis powers on the one hand and Japan on the other, which will result, presumably in the next few days, in the signing of a military alliance between the three powers.

2) This alliance, consistent with its origin, is directed exclusively against American warmongers. To be sure, this is, as usual, not expressly stated in the treaty, but can be unmistakably inferred from its terms.

3) The treaty, of course, does not pursue any aggressive aims against America. Its exclusive purpose is rather to bring the elements pressing for America's entry into the war to their senses, by conclusively demonstrating to them that if they enter the present struggle, they will automatically have to deal with the three great powers as adversaries.

4) From the beginning of their negotiations, the three treaty powers have been in complete agreement that their alliance shall in no way affect the relationship each of them has with the Soviet Union. In order to dispel any doubt of this abroad as well, a special article was inserted in the treaty to the effect that the existing political relations [*Status*] between each of the three treaty powers and the Soviet Union shall not be affected by the treaty. This proviso means, therefore, that not only the treaties concluded by the three powers with the Soviet Union, particularly the German-Soviet treaties of the autumn of 1939, shall remain in full force and effect, but that this applies in general to the entire political relationship to the Soviet Union.

5) The pact would probably serve as a damper on the warmongers, especially in America, would operate against a further extension of the present war, and perhaps, in this sense would serve the restoration of world peace.

6) At this opportunity please also tell Herr Molotov that I had taken cognizance of the memorandum handed to Count Schulenburg on September 21 and that I intended shortly to address a personal letter to Herr Stalin in which I would reply to the memorandum in the spirit of German-Russian friendship, but beyond that would frankly and confidently set forth the German conception of the present political situation. I hoped that this letter would contribute anew to the strengthening of our friendly relations. Besides, the letter would contain an invitation to Berlin for Herr Molotov, whose return visit we were expecting after two visits to Moscow and with whom on this occasion I should like to discuss important questions relating to the establishment of common political aims for the future.

(*Reich Foreign Minister*)

RIBBENTROP

Frame 112539, serial 104

Foreign Office Memorandum

URGENT

W 4499g

It is necessary to obtain a decision from the Führer regarding the continuance of trade with the Soviet Union. The directives issued during the last few weeks by the Reich Marshal concerning the absolute priority of all armament contracts and the further increasing of these armament contracts make it impossible for German industry to execute, in addition to these contracts, the scheduled deliveries to Russia. In this state of affairs, it will be impossible to balance the considerable deficit already existing in German deliveries. On the contrary, a further great lag in German deliveries must be expected.

The Moscow negotiations on the balancing of the deliveries were broken off on the 12th of this month as the delegation had not sufficient authority to reply to the Soviet proposals. If satisfactory replies are not given Moscow soon, a *suspension of the Russian deliveries* to Germany is to be expected. This applies particularly to the Russian supplies of grain and oil. The continuance of the exchange of goods with the Soviet Union at the present level depends on whether the Russian transactions have a priority, as before, or at least a preferential parity with the armament contracts. This can only be decided by the Führer. The German economic authorities, especially the Reich Ministry for Economic Affairs, are finding themselves unable, because of the directives which have been issued, to deal with the question of foreign trade with Russia constructively.

Herewith to be submitted to the Reich Foreign Minister.

General Thomas informs me that the Reich Marshal expects my report on the Moscow negotiations soon. I request an opportunity to report in person first.

SCHNURRE

BERLIN, September 26, 1940.

Frames 0455-0457, serial F 5

The German Chargé in the Soviet Union (Tippelskirch) to the German Foreign Office

Telegram

VERY URGENT   Moscow, September 27, 1940—5 : 13 a. m.
STRICTLY SECRET   Received September 27, 1940—9 : 15 a. m.
STATE SECRET
No. 2041 of September 26

Reference your telegram of the 26th, No. 1746.[96]

For the Reich Foreign Minister in person.

Instruction carried out with Molotov tonight at 10 p. m. as directed. Molotov listened very attentively to the communication. At item 6) Molotov showed evident satisfaction and said that at the moment an

---

[96] Reference is to the Reich Foreign Minister's telegram No. 1746 of September 25, 1940, dispatched from Berlin on September 26, *ante*, p. 195.

indication of his attitude was not necessary, as the reply to the letter that the Reich Foreign Minister intended to send to Stalin would provide an opportunity for it.

Before Molotov went into the matter of the military alliance with Japan, he inquired—on the basis of a telegraphic report from the Soviet Embassy in Berlin—regarding a German-Finnish agreement, which, according to a Finnish communiqué, provided for the granting of passage for German troops through Finland to Norway, and which was referred to by Press Chief Schmidt at his press conference. At the same time Molotov mentioned a report from the Berlin Office of the United Press, which was broadcast over the radio, stating that German troops had landed in the Finnish port of Vasa. I said that I had no further information on the subject.

Thereafter Molotov stated as follows on the subject of the military alliance: He gratefully took note of the communication from the Reich Foreign Minister. The Soviet Embassy in Tokyo had a few days ago reported on a plan for such an agreement. The Soviet Government, was, of course, extremely interested in this question, because it involved a neighboring country to which the Soviet Union was linked by numerous interests. Hence it was understandable that the Soviet Government not only had a great interest, but also the desire to be informed in advance regarding the agreement and its contents. This desire the Soviet Government based on articles 3 and 4 of the Nonaggression Treaty. If the reverse were the case, the Soviet Government would also inform us in advance and communicate to us the contents of the treaty. The Soviet Government so construed article 4 that it was entitled to see the treaty between the Axis Powers and Japan and to receive information of any secret protocols and agreements as well, for which confidential treatment was promised in advance. He asked to be informed whether the German Government concurred in his interpretation of article 4 and reiterated his desire to be acquainted with the contents of the treaty before its signing, in order to be able to express his views on it. If, contrary to his expectation, the German Government did not agree with his interpretation of article 4, he asked that the position of the German Government be communicated to him.

As particularly significant in Molotov's utterances appear to me:

1) The great interest he showed in the treaty with Japan.

2) The constant harping on article 3 and especially article 4 of the Nonaggression Treaty, in which connection he quoted article 18 [sic] verbatim.

3) The insistence on seeing the text of the treaty, including the secret portions.

After Molotov had concluded his statements on the question of the military alliance, he reverted again to the German-Finnish agreement referred to at the beginning and declared that for the last three days the Soviet Government had received reports relative to the landing of German troops at Vasa, Uleaborg and Pori, without having been informed thereof by Germany.

The Soviet Government wished to receive the text of the agreement on the passage of troops through Finland, including its secret portions. This demand, too, was based on articles 3 and 4 of the Nonaggression Treaty. If we concurred in this interpretation of the articles mentioned, he asked to be informed as to the object of the agreement, against whom it was directed, and the purposes that were being served thereby. The agreement was being discussed in public, while the Soviet Government knew nothing about it.

I told Molotov that I would communicate his statements to my Government.

TIPPELSKIRCH

Frames 0458–0462, serial F 5

Foreign Office Memorandum

STATE SECRET
W 4520/40 g Rs.

1) In the period from August 24 to September 12 of this year, negotiations took place in Moscow at the request of the Russians, for the purpose of reviewing the status of the shipments from both sides under the Commercial Treaty of February 11, 1940. The negotiations revealed that German deliveries for the first half-year fell short of the commitment in the Treaty by roughly 73 million Reichsmarks. The Russians handed in proposals for the balancing of this deficit which amounted substantially to a shortening of the delivery periods. Negotiations were temporarily broken off on September 12, in order that we might reexamine the Soviet proposals in Berlin and work out German counterproposals for additional shipments to the Soviet Union. The Russians stated that, in accordance with the Treaty provisions, they would temporarily suspend their shipments, if neither their proposals nor our counterproposals led to the projected ratio of deliveries.

2) The German commitments for the coming half-year are:

    to February 11, 1941   RM. 233 million

    to May 11, 1941   RM. 311 million

    including the undelivered balance of 73 million Reichsmarks mentioned above.

This must be augmented by German shipments in return for Bessarabian grain and Bessarabian oil seed (RM. 40 million) and shipments in return for the German raw-material imports from the Baltic territories. The survey undertaken jointly with the Reich Ministry for Economic Affairs and the High Command of the Armed Forces revealed that if the armament program ordered by the Führer is carried out, neither a balancing of the existing deficit of 73 million Reichsmarks nor the delivery on schedule of the remainder of the German commitment is possible. In addition, there is the directive issued by the Reich Marshal to avoid shipments to Russia which would directly or indirectly strengthen Russia's war potential. If these decisions are upheld, the suspension of Russian shipments to Germany must shortly be expected.

3) This means that the large deliveries of raw materials, especially of *grain, petroleum,* cotton, precious and nonferrous metals, phosphate, will cease, at least for a time, and at the best will recommence later on a much smaller scale and with great sacrifices of German supplies. Particularly serious, in the opinion of the Reich Food Ministry, would be the effect on *grain supplies.* Russia has supplied us to date with almost one million tons of grain. Russia is the only country that has a good grain harvest and therefore might be in a position to continue with large shipments. The Reich Food Ministry points out that the national grain reserve will be used up in the current crop year, so that we would enter the next crop year without such a reserve.

4) The Reich Minister for Economic Affairs, the Reich Food Minister, and the High Command of the Armed Forces requested us to obtain from the Führer another decision regarding the continuation of trade with the Soviet Union. Raw material deliveries from Russia can only be kept at approximately their present level if the German shipments to the U. S. S. R. are prepared at the rate indicated under item 2 (RM. 233 million, RM. 311 million and 40 million Reichsmarks of Bessarabian grain, etc.), and, as formerly, receive a priority or at least a preferred parity rating as against the armament contracts. Since supplies of machinery, of rolling mill products and

coal are principally involved, such an arrangement can only be made at the expense of the armament contracts.

5) The Russians, presumably reacting to the changed German attitude, have cancelled all long-range projects in the Commercial Treaty of February 11, 1940. This means that they do not wish to receive long-term deliveries of processes, installations, and capital goods, but restrict themselves to goods which will benefit their economy, especially their military rearmament, within the next 8 to 10 months. Hence the impact on our own military requirements in the resulting narrower sphere of machinery and rolling mill products is much more severe than formerly.

6) The supplies from the Russians have heretofore been a very substantial prop to the Germany war economy. Since the new commercial treaties went into effect, Russia has supplied over 300 million Reichsmarks worth of raw materials, roughly 100 million Reichsmarks of which was grain. Russia has thus far received compensation only in the amount of about 150 million Reichsmarks. The striking disproportion between German and Russian deliveries is evident from the fact that in August, as against 65 million Reichsmarks of Russian deliveries, there were only 20 million Reichsmarks of German deliveries. Our sole economic connection with Iran, Afghanistan, Manchukuo, Japan and, beyond that, with South America, is the route across Russia, which is being used to an increasing extent for German raw material imports (soy-beans from Manchukuo).

BERLIN, September 28, 1940.   SCHNURRE

Submitted to the Reich Foreign Minister as directed.

                                    SCHNURRE [97]
BERLIN, September 28, 1940.

Frames 112554-112558, serial 104

The Reich Foreign Minister to the German Embassy in the Soviet Union

Telegram

RUSH   BERLIN, October 2, 1940.
No. 1787

Reference your telegram No. 1041 [*2041*].[98]

---

[97] An appended handwritten note reads as follows: "The contents of the Memorandum were read to the Reich Marshal, who agreed with the views of Minister Schnurre. Sch [?]30/9"
[98] *Ante*, p. 197.

Please call on Herr Molotov again and, in reply to his statement, tell him as follows:

I.

The German-Finnish agreement he mentioned involved a purely technical matter of military communications without political implications. Just as we reached an understanding with Sweden about similar transport through Swedish territory to the areas of Oslo, Trondheim, and Narvik, an understanding was reached with Finland about transit to the area of Kirkenes. The area of Kirkenes, which needed military protection against England because of the mines there, can be reached by us by land only through Finnish territory. The transport went by way of Uleaborg and Vasa, but not by way of Pori. In view of the purely technical communications aspect of the matter we naturally saw no reason expressly to notify the Soviet Government of it. The understanding with Finland was reached by an exchange of notes, which contains verbatim the following four points:

"1. The Finnish Government, upon request of the Government of the Reich, grants the through-transport of matériel with escort personnel from the northern ports of the Baltic Sea by way of Rovaniemi and the northern Arctic Ocean Road to Kirkenes in Northern Norway.

"2. The Government of the German Reich shall duly indicate to the Finnish Government the ports of debarkation selected, the number of the transport vessels, the dates of sailing and arrival, and the scheduled daily stages of the transports in Northern Finland.

"3. The Government of the German Reich shall notify the Finnish Government at least one day in advance of the arrival of the transport vessels.

"4. Ordnance shall be shipped apart from the troops in separate freight cars. A special agreement will be made regarding the number of officers and men for the guard details on the freight cars carrying ordnance."

Should Herr Molotov expressly ask for it, you are authorized to hand him the text of the foregoing four points in the form of a memorandum.

II.

In respect to the Three Power Pact between Germany, Italy and Japan, Herr Molotov will surely have seen from the contents of the Pact, which have meanwhile been published, as well as from the official statement made by the German Government in connection with it, that the question raised by him in regard to articles 3 and 4 of the German-Soviet Nonaggression Pact was pointless. The three partners were from the beginning in complete agreement that their accord should in no way affect the Soviet Union. Therefore the most comprehensive formula imaginable was selected in article 5 of the Pact, which made it clear that not only the treaties concluded with the Soviet Union, but also the entire political relationship to the Soviet Union was left entirely unchanged by the Pact. Therefore there can be no question of a coalition of powers which was directly or indirectly aligned against the Soviet Union in the sense of article 4 of the German-Soviet Nonaggression Pact. On the contrary, it was clearly stated in the declaration of the German Government that the parties to the Three Power Pact were looking toward further favorable developments in the relations already existing with the Soviet Union.

Since the whole relationship of Germany, and the relationship of Italy and Japan to the Soviet Union as well, was left out of the picture by an express stipulation in the Three Power Pact, it therefore did not affect common German-Soviet interests and thus did not come under the provision for consultations in article 3 of the German-Soviet Nonaggression Pact. Nevertheless, I considered it proper to inform Herr Molotov as soon as there was a definite prospect that the Pact would be signed. Actually, the last decisions in this connection were not made in Tokyo until September 27.

Moreover, you are explicitly authorized by me to tell Herr Molotov most emphatically that no agreements of any sort have been made with Japan other than the published text of the Treaty. There were no secret protocols nor any other secret agreements.

In a few days I expect to dispatch to Herr Stalin the letter which I promised.

(*Reich Foreign Minister*)
RIBBENTROP

Frames 112559-112560, serial 104

The German Chargé in the Soviet Union (Tippelskirch) to the German Foreign Office

Telegram

VERY URGENT   Moscow, October 4, 1940—10 : 40 p. m.
SECRET   Received October 5, 1940—6 : 30 a. m.
No. 2095 of October 4

Reference your telegram of the 2d, No. 1787.
For the Reich Minister personally.

Molotov received me today at 6 p. m., after he had at first asked me to call at 5; when I drove into the Kremlin I met the English Ambassador in his car.   Molotov apologized upon greeting me, for having had to change the time of the visit because of pressure of business.

To the communications I made in accordance with instructions, Molotov made the following remarks.

I. German-Finnish Agreements.

Under the German-Russian accord, Finland, as we knew, belonged to the sphere of influence of the Soviet Union.   The interest of the Soviet Union in the agreement was therefore understandable and for this reason the Soviet Union wanted to be duly informed.   The Soviet Government was anxious, if possible, to be given additional, more detailed information about the German-Finnish agreement, especially regarding the number of German troops involved and the duration of the agreement (whether meant for a single action or for a longer period?), and also whether all the German troops would go only to Kirkenes.

To my query as to whether the Soviet Government had not also been informed by the Finnish Government, Molotov replied in the negative and added that the Finnish Government had informed him "at about the time of the publication of the report", but it had not yet replied to the questions addressed to it.

I told Herr Molotov that I would communicate his wish to Berlin and remarked that, as far as I knew, it was not our intention to retain German troops in Finland and that, moreover, the agreement was conditional upon the threat to Kirkenes by England.

Upon his request, I left with Herr Molotov the text of the four points.

II. Three Power Pact.

Herr Molotov: The Soviet Government would have to examine the matter closely since my communications contained views of the German Government with regard to the interpretation of articles 3 and 4 of the German-Soviet Nonaggression pact.   He could, therefore, say nothing further on this at the moment.

TIPPELSKIRCH

Frames 112565–112566, serial 104

Foreign Office Memorandum [99]

W 4646/40g   OCTOBER 8, [1940]—7:30 p. m.

To the Office of the Reich Foreign Minister.

Please send the following by teletype to Fuschl:

In the matter of the granting of the Petsamo nickel concession the Finnish Government finds itself exposed to daily increasing pressure from the Soviet Government. The Finns are afraid that bad intentions lie concealed behind Molotov's persistence. If the Finnish Government yields to Russian pressure and by national emergency legislation cancels the present Canadian nickel concession and gives it to the Soviet Government, an unpleasant and unfavorable situation would arise for us: Our own nickel interests, which had been established in the negotiations with the Finnish Government, would be completely wiped out, as Russia will not respect the German-Finnish agreements. With the transfer of the nickel concession Soviet Russia will acquire exclusive territorial influence in this area as well and thereby border directly on the area of Kirkenes, which is protected by our troops. The military, and the Reich Marshal in particular, have voiced the hope that we shall not lose Petsamo. The deputy of the Reich Marshal, Lt. Col. Veltjens, has, among other things, obtained an option for the nickel concession, as compensation for the German supplies of arms.

Up to now the Foreign Office has been telling the Finns that Germany will confine herself to carrying out the German-Finnish nickel contracts and will not on her own initiative take up the question of the concession with the Russians. It will now be necessary to go beyond that and to strengthen the Finnish will to resist. They should be told we were in favor of their holding the question of the concession in abeyance and not definitely concluding the matter by the transfer to Russia. It is not necessary to comply with the wish of the Finns that we support their attitude in Moscow.

Minister Schnurre requests an opportunity to report personally on this situation and on the present status of the delivery of arms to Finland. The matter is urgent, since otherwise it must be expected that the Finns will give in.

---

[99] A notation reads "By teletype to Fuschl, No. 84." At Fuschl, near Salzburg, was a residence of the Reich Foreign Minister.

Frame 112568, serial 104

The Reich Foreign Minister to the German Embassy in the Soviet Union

Telegram

No. 1832   BERLIN, October 9, 1940.

Please call on Herr Molotov tomorrow, Thursday, and communicate to him the following. I request you, however, not to let this communication appear as the real reason for your call, but rather to use some other reason and merely to introduce the following as incidental to the discussion of the other subject.

Lately there have appeared in the English press various reports concerning the dispatch of fairly large German military units to Rumania. These reports are entirely tendentious. The truth of the matter is this: On the basis of the guarantee given it by the Axis Powers, the Rumanian Government some time ago made a request of us to make available to it, for the training of the Rumanian army, a German military mission with certain instruction units from the German army. In view of our interest in seeing that quiet and order are maintained in the Balkans, and in order to protect our oil and grain interests against any attempt on the part of England to disturb them, we declared ourselves willing to accede to the Rumanian request. As the Soviet Union is well aware, we have a vital interest in these territories, which we cannot leave exposed to the menace of the English, whose press continually plays with such ideas. In view of the friendly relations existing with the Soviet Government, we wished to inform her of this.

I have already informed Ambassador Shkvartsev in the same sense today.

RIBBENTROP

Frames 112577-112578, serial 104

The German Chargé in the Soviet Union (Tippelskirch) to the German Foreign Office

Telegram

VERY URGENT   Moscow, October 10, 1940—11:20 p. m.
No. 2142 of October 10   Received October 11, 1940—3:25 a. m.

Reference your telegram No. 1832 of October 9.

I called on Molotov today at 6:30 p. m. I used as the occasion of my visit the message that Hilger had given to People's Commissar

Mikoyan three days ago regarding the impending arrival of a German delegation for the purpose of resuming economic negotiations. I stressed the fact that in view of the importance of the question I was very anxious to inform him—Molotov—too, that the delegation led by Schnurre would be strengthened by influential personalities who were authorized to make independent decisions and that as a result of the preliminary work done in Berlin we had the impression that a basis for an understanding had been created.

Molotov appeared interested, inquired about the exact date of Schnurre's arrival and stated that we now had to await the results of the negotiations.

After that I brought the conversation around informally to the real purpose of my visit and gave Molotov the prescribed information, to which he listened with interest. After I had finished Molotov stated that if it were only a question of "instruction units" the numerical strength of the German troop units in Rumania could not be very large. To Molotov's question as to whether I knew the number of German troops sent to Rumania I replied in the negative, but I again stressed the vital German interest in those territories, which had to be protected against any danger from the English. Molotov did not wish to admit the existence of such danger, remarking with a smile that England now had other worries and ought to be glad to save her own life.

In conclusion, Molotov inquired regarding the information which he had recently requested in the Finnish matter, to which I replied that this information would presumably be brought back by the Ambassador, who would return in a few days.

TIPPELSKIRCH

Frames 0433–0451, serial F 5

Letter From the Reich Foreign Minister to Stalin

BERLIN, October 13, 1940.

MY DEAR HERR STALIN: Over a year ago, through your decision and the Führer's, the relations between Germany and Soviet Russia were reexamined and put on a completely new basis. I believe that the decision to reach an understanding between our two countries—which resulted from the realization that the *Lebensräume* of our peoples adjoin each other but need not necessarily overlap, and which led to a delimitation of mutual spheres of influence and to the German-Soviet Russian Nonaggression and Friendship Treaties—has proved advantageous to both sides. I am convinced that the consistent continuance of this policy of good neighborliness and a further strengthening of the political and economic collaboration will redound to the greater and greater benefit of the two great peoples in the future. Germany, at any rate, is prepared and determined to work to this end.

With such a goal, it seems to me, a direct contact between the responsible personalities of both countries becomes particularly important. I believe that such a personal contact through other than the customary diplomatic channels is indispensable from time to time in authoritarian regimes such as ours. Today I would, therefore, like to review briefly the events since my last visit to Moscow. Because of the historical importance of these events and in continuation of our exchange of ideas of last year, I would like to review for you the policy which Germany has pursued during this period.

After the conclusion of the Polish Campaign we became aware—and this was confirmed by many reports which were received during the winter—that England, faithful to her traditional policy, was building her whole war strategy on the hope of an extension of the war. The attempts made in 1939 to win over the Soviet Union to a military coalition against Germany had already pointed in this direction. They were frustrated by the German-Soviet Russian Agreement. Later on, the attitude of England and France in the Soviet Russian-Finnish conflict was similar.

In the spring of 1940, these concealed intentions became quite evident. With this began the active phase of the English policy of extending this war to other peoples of Europe. After the end of the Soviet Russian-Finnish War, Norway was selected as the first target. By the occupation of Narvik and other Norwegian bases, Germany's iron ore supplies were to be cut off and a new front established in Scandinavia. It was only due to the timely intervention of the German leadership in Berlin and to the quick blows of our troops—who chased the English and the French out of Norway—that all of Scandinavia did not become a theater of war.

Several weeks later this Anglo-French game was to be repeated in Holland and Belgium. And here, too, Germany was able at the eleventh hour to prevent the contemplated thrust of the Anglo-French armies against the Ruhr Region (of which we had been informed some time before) by decisive victories of our armies. Today, even in France, "England's continental sword," it has become apparent to most Frenchmen that their country in the last analysis had to bleed to death as a victim of this traditional "humanitarian" policy of England. As to the present English rulers, who declared war on Germany and who thereby plunged the British people into misfortune, even they themselves were finally no longer able to conceal their traditional British policy and their contempt for their own allies. On the contrary, when fate turned against them, all their hypocritical protestations ceased. With true English cynicism, they have treacherously forsaken their friends. In fact, in order to save themselves they slandered their erstwhile allies, and later on they even openly opposed them by force. Andalsnes, Dunkerque, Oran, Dakar, are names which—it appears to me—could sufficiently enlighten the world on the value of England's friendship. However, on this occasion we Germans, too, learned a lesson: that the English are not only unscrupulous politicians, but also bad soldiers. Our troops have routed them wherever they accepted battle. The German soldier was superior to them everywhere.

The Balkans were the next aim of the English policy of extending the war. According to reports which have reached us, all sorts of plans were repeatedly drawn up there this year, and in one instance their execution was already ordered. That those plans were not duly carried out was—as we know today—due exclusively to the almost unbelievable dilettantism and the astonishing discord among the political as well as the military leaders of England and France.

Germany's foes have endeavored to conceal from the world their measures for extending the war, and they have tried before the whole world to brand our exposure of these English methods of extending the war as a maneuver of German propaganda. In the meanwhile, fate would have it that documents of inestimable importance fell into the hands of the German armies advancing with lightning speed in the various theaters of war. As is well known, we succeeded in capturing the secret political files of the French General Staff, which were already prepared for shipment, and thereby obtained incontrovertible proof of the correctness of our reports regarding the intentions of our adversary and the conclusions we had drawn from them. A number of these documents, as you will remember, have already been published in the press, and an enormous amount of material is still being translated and examined. If needed, it is to be published in a White Book. With truly striking conclusiveness the background of the English war policy is here revealed. You will understand that we are gratified at being able to open the eyes of the world to the unprecedented incompetence as well as to the almost criminal recklessness with which the present English rulers, by their declaration of war on

Germany, plunged into misfortune not only their own people but also other peoples of Europe. But even beyond that, the documents at our disposal prove that the gentlemen from the Thames would not have shrunk from attacking completely disinterested nations, merely because they continued their natural trade with Germany despite British representations and even threats. Undoubtedly, the Soviet-Russian oil centers of Baku and the oil port of Batum would even this year have become the victim of British attacks, if the collapse of France and the expulsion of the British Army from Europe had not broken the British spirit of aggression and put an abrupt end to these activities.

Nevertheless, recognizing the complete absurdity of continuing this war, on July 19 the Führer again offered peace to England. After the refusal of this last offer Germany is now determined to prosecute the war against England and her Empire until the final defeat of Britain. This fight to the finish is now in progress and will only end when the foe is annihilated militarily or when a real understanding is assured through elimination of the forces responsible for the war. It does not matter when this takes place.

For one thing is sure: the war as such has been won by us anyway. It is only a question of how long it will be before England, under the impact of our operations, admits to complete collapse.

In this final phase of the war, to guard against any moves which England might yet make in her desperate situation, the Axis, as an obvious precaution, was forced to secure its military and strategic position in Europe as well as its political and diplomatic position in the world. In addition, it had to safeguard the requirements for maintaining our economic life. Immediately after the end of the campaign in the West, Germany and Italy started with this task, and now they have carried it out in its broad outlines. In this connection there may also be mentioned the—for Germany—unprecedented task of securing her Norwegian coastal positions all the way from the Skagerrak to Kirkenes. Germany has therefore entered into certain purely technical agreements with Sweden and Finland, of which I have already fully informed you through the German Embassy. They are exclusively for the purpose of facilitating supply of the coastal cities in the North (Narvik and Kirkenes)—which are difficult for us to reach by land—by shipping supplies via the territory of these countries.

The policy which we have recently pursued in the Rumanian-Hungarian controversy is similarly oriented. Our guarantee to Rumania is due exclusively to the necessity of protecting this Balkan region—which is especially important from the standpoint of the German supplies of oil and grain—against any disturbance by war, sabotage, etc., in the interior of this area, as well as against invasion attempts from the outside. The anti-German press tried at that time to place on the guarantee of the Axis Powers to Rumania constructions the purpose of which was all too apparent. The truth of the matter is that toward the end of August—as we know—the situation between Rumania and Hungary, fomented by English agents as the notorious agitators in the Balkans, had reached such a point that the outbreak of war was imminent and, in fact, air skirmishes had already occurred. It was obvious that the peace could be saved in the Balkans only through the most rapid diplomatic intervention. There was no time for any negotiations or consultations. Matters had already gone too far from a military standpoint. This accounts for the completely improvised meeting in Vienna and the award within 24 hours. It is, therefore, probably superfluous to emphasize that the tendency shown in the anti-German press at that time—to construe these German-Italian actions as aimed against the Soviet Union—was entirely unfounded and dictated solely by the intention to disrupt relations between the Axis and the Soviet Union.

The German Military Mission, too, sent a few days ago at the request of the Rumanians, together with the attached instruction units of the German Armed Forces, which again was taken as an occasion for flimsy speculations by our foes, serves both to train the Rumanian Army and to safeguard German interests, because the German economy and the economies of these territories are closely interdependent. If England, as some reports seem to indicate, really intended to undertake some action against the oil fields of Rumania, for instance, we have indeed already taken measures to give the appropriate answer to such British attempts at intervention from abroad or of sabotage from within. In view of the completely misleading and tendentious press reports, which have been increasing in number during the last few days, I informed your Ambassador, Herr Shkvarzev, a few days ago as to the true motives for our action and of the measures actually taken.

In connection with the sabotage attempts by the British, the question raised by your Government concerning reorganization of the regime on the Danube is of some importance. I may inform you that, in agreement with the Italian Government, we shall make proposals in the next few days which will take into account your wishes in the matter.

After these measures to safeguard the position of the Axis in Europe, the principal interest of the Reich Government and of the Italian Government during recent weeks was aimed at preventing the spread of the war beyond Europe into a world conflagration. For, as the hopes of the English of finding allies in Europe faded, the English Government intensified its efforts to support particularly those circles which in the democracies overseas aimed at an entry into the war against Germany and Italy and on the side of England. In contrast to this was the interest of those peoples which were animated in the same degree by the desire for a New Order in the world as against the congealed plutocratic democracies and which saw, just as we did, these interests threatened by a further extension of the European War into a world conflagration. This condition applied particularly to Japan. Some time ago, therefore, upon orders from the Führer, I sent an emissary to Tokyo to ascertain unofficially whether the common interests could be expressed in the form of a pact directed against the further extension of the war to other peoples. The exchange of ideas which followed very soon resulted in a complete and general consensus between Berlin, Rome, and Tokyo, on the fact that, in the interest of an early restoration of peace, any further spread of war should be prevented and that the best way to counteract the warmongering of an international clique would be by a military alliance of the Three Powers. Thus, despite all the British intrigues, the Berlin Treaty was concluded with surprising rapidity—as I was able to advise you through the Embassy as soon as the final agreement had been reached on the day before the signing. I believe that the conclusion of this Treaty will hasten the downfall of the present English rulers, who are alone in opposing the final restoration of peace, and that it will thereby serve the interests of all peoples.

As to the question of the attitude toward the Soviet Union of the three partners to this Alliance, I should like to state in advance that from the very beginning of the exchange of views all Three Powers held equally to the opinion that this Pact was not aimed in any way against the Soviet Union; that, on the contrary, the friendly relations between the Three Powers and their treaties with the Soviet Union should remain completely unaffected by this agreement. This attitude has, indeed, found its formal expression in the text of the Berlin Treaty. As to Germany, the conclusion of this Pact is the logical result of a conception of foreign policy—long adhered to by the Reich Government—in which both friendly German-Soviet cooperation and friendly German-Japanese cooperation have a place side by side and undisturbed. Beyond that, however, friendly relations between Germany and Soviet Russia as well as friendly relations between Soviet Russia and Japan, together with the friendship between the Axis Powers and Japan, are logical elements of a natural political coalition which, if intelligently managed, will work out to the best advantage of all the powers concerned. You will remember that at the time of my first visit to Moscow I discussed similar ideas with you quite frankly and that I offered our good offices for the adjustment of differences still existing at the time between the Soviet Russians and the Japanese. I have endeavored since then to work in this direction, and I would welcome it, if the trend toward reaching an understanding with the Soviet Union—which is becoming more and more clearly manifest in Japan, too—could lead to its logical goal.

In summing up, I should like to state that, in the opinion of the Führer, also, it appears to be the historical mission of the Four Powers—the Soviet Union, Italy, Japan, and Germany—to adopt a long-range policy and to direct the future development of their peoples into the right channels by delimitation of their interests on a worldwide scale.

In order further to clarify issues of such decisive importance for the future of our peoples and in order to discuss them in concrete form, we would welcome it if Herr Molotov would pay us a visit in Berlin soon. I should like to extend a most cordial invitation to him in the name of the Reich Government. After my two visits to Moscow, it would now be a particular pleasure for me personally to see Herr Molotov in Berlin. His visit would then give the Führer the opportunity to explain to Herr Molotov personally his views regarding the future molding of relations between our two countries. Upon his return, Herr Molotov will be able to report to you at length concerning the aims and intentions of the Führer. If then—as I believe I may expect—the opportunity should arise for further elaboration of a common policy in accordance with my foregoing statements, I should be happy to come to Moscow again personally in order to resume the exchange of ideas with you, my dear Herr Stalin, and to discuss—possibly together with representatives of Japan and Italy—the bases of a policy which could only be of *practical* advantage to all of us.

With best regards I remain
    Respectfully yours,   RIBBENTROP

Frame 0430, serial F 5

The German Ambassador in the Soviet Union (Schulenburg) to the German Foreign Office

Telegram

VERY URGENT   Moscow, October 18, 1940—12:08 a. m.
STATE SECRET   Received October 18, 1940—1:50 a. m.
No. 2200 of October 17

For the Reich Foreign Minister.

Today I handed Herr Molotov the letter intended for Herr Stalin and strongly urged him to accept the invitation to Berlin as soon as possible. Molotov stated again that he could not deny that he owed a visit to Berlin, but that he would have to reserve his answer until after he had studied the letter.

I then touched upon the complaints of the resettlement commissions in the Balkan countries and in Bessarabia. Molotov, of course, attempted to dispute the justice of the complaints, but in the end he promised to reexamine them.

SCHULENBURG

Frame 0429, serial F 5

The Reich Foreign Minister to the German Ambassador in the Soviet Union (Schulenburg)

Telegram

VERY URGENT   SONNENBURG, October 18, 1940.
STATE SECRET   Received Berlin October 18, 1940—3:30 p. m.
No. 1878   Transmitted to Moscow, 5:15 p. m.

For the Ambassador personally.

I request immediate information by wire as to why my letter to Stalin was not delivered to the Soviet Russian Government until October 17, and why, in keeping with the importance of its contents and the entire matter, the letter addressed to Stalin was not—as I had taken for granted—delivered by you to Herr Stalin at a personal audience.

RIBBENTROP

Frames 0427–0428, serial F 5

The German Ambassador in the Soviet Union (Schulenburg) to the German Foreign Office

Telegram

VERY URGENT	Moscow, October 19, 1940—3 : 20 p. m.
STATE SECRET	Received October 19, 1940—6 p. m.
No. 2209 of October 19	

Reference your telegram of the 18th, No. 1878.

For the Reich Foreign Minister.

I handed Molotov the letter intended for Stalin after careful examination of the factual and personal situation here. After I had informed Molotov, in accordance with instructions of some time ago, of your intention to address a letter to Stalin and of its probable contents, a proposal on my part to hand the letter directly to Stalin would have caused serious annoyance to Herr Molotov. It seemed to me imperative to avoid this, in view of the fact that Molotov is the closest confidant of Stalin and that we will have to deal with him on all great political issues in the future.

In addition, Stalin has recently shown a strong reserve in public, and I was therefore justified in assuming that he would avoid a personal meeting with me on some pretext or other. In this connection, I may recall the statement in the Soviet press of September 7, according to which Stalin had not seen me for more than 6 months. Insistence upon a reception by Stalin might easily have been construed on the Soviet side as a reaction to this published statement.

That the letter was not delivered until October 17 is explained by the fact that I did not arrive in Moscow until the evening of October 15, because the plane was late. Before the letter was handed over, we first had to translate it into Russian, since we know from experience that translations made by the Soviets are bad and full of inaccuracies. Considering the extraordinary political significance of the letter it was extremely important to transmit to Stalin a translation that was flawless as to form and content lest the letter convey an inaccurate impression. Because of the length and importance of the letter it was not possible, despite the most strenuous efforts, to translate it into Russian and to prepare a final copy in Russian in a shorter space of time.

SCHULENBURG

Frames 0431-0432, serial F 5

*The German Ambassador in the Soviet Union (Schulenburg) to the
German Foreign Office*

Telegram

VERY URGENT   Moscow, October 22, 1940—5 : 02 a. m.
No. 2236 of October 21   Received October 22, 1940—7 : 35 a. m.

Reference your telegram of October 20, No. 1890.[1]
For the Reich Foreign Minister personally.

Tonight Molotov handed me Stalin's sealed answer together with
a copy. The form and style of the letter leave no doubt that the letter
was composed by Stalin personally.

Literally translated, the letter reads as follows:

"MY DEAR HERR VON RIBBENTROP: I have received your letter. I
thank you sincerely for your confidence, as well as for the instructive
analysis of recent events which is contained in your letter.

I agree with you that a further improvement in the relations
between our countries is entirely possible on the permanent basis
of a long-range delimitation of mutual interests.

Herr Molotov admits that he is under obligation to pay you a return visit in Berlin. He hereby accepts your invitation.

It remains for us to agree on the date of arrival in Berlin. The
time from the 10th to the 12th of November is most convenient for
Herr Molotov. If it is also agreeable to the German Government,
the question may be considered as settled.

I welcome the desire expressed by you to come to Moscow again
in order to resume the exchange of ideas begun last year on questions
of interest to both our countries, and I hope that this wish will be
realized after Herr Molotov's trip to Berlin.

As to joint deliberation on some issues with Japanese and Italian
participation, I am of the opinion (without being opposed to this
idea in principle) that this question would have to be submitted to a
previous examination.

Most respectfully yours"

Molotov added orally that he planned to arrive in Berlin on the 10th,
11th or 12th of November. No decision has yet been reached concerning the duration of his stay. It was to be made dependent upon the
exigencies of the situation.

Hilger will arrive in Berlin Thursday morning, will bring along
Stalin's original letter and discuss further details of the visit there.

---

[1] Not printed.

Molotov requested that the whole affair be treated in strict confidence for the time being.

SCHULENBURG

Frame 112626, serial 104

The German Ambassador in the Soviet Union (Schulenburg) to the German Foreign Office

Telegram

URGENT   Moscow, November 2, 1940—2:30 a. m.
Received November 2, 1940—7:50 a. m.

No. 2313 of November 1

Reference my telegram No. 2310.[2]

For the State Secretary.

In today's discussion between Schnurre and Mikoyan, Mikoyan complained in a tone of obvious annoyance that we were not willing to undertake the delivery of war matériel desired by the Soviet Government, yet we were delivering war matériel to Finland and other countries.

This is the first time that our deliveries of arms to Finland have been mentioned by the Soviets.

SCHULENBURG

Frames 46290–46313, serial 66

Memorandum of the Conversation Between the Reich Foreign Minister and the Chairman of the Council of People's Commissars of the U.S.S.R. and People's Commissar for Foreign Affairs, V. M. Molotov, in the Presence of the Deputy People's Commissar for Foreign Affairs, Dekanosov, as Well as Counselor of Embassy Hilger and Herr Pavlov, Who Acted as Interpreters; Held in Berlin on November 12, 1940

RM 41/40

After some introductory words the Reich Foreign Minister stated that since the two visits which he had made to Moscow last year much had happened. Referring to the talks which he had had in Moscow with the Russian statesmen, and supplementing what he had recently written in the letter to Stalin, he now wanted to make a few more statements regarding the German view of the general situation and on Russo-German relations, without thereby anticipating the Führer,

[2] Not printed.

who would talk in detail with Herr Molotov in the afternoon and would give him his considered opinion regarding the political situation. After this discussion with the Führer, there would be further opportunities for talks with the Reich Foreign Minister, and it might be assumed that this German-Russian exchange of views would have a favorable effect upon the relations between the two countries.

Molotov replied that the contents of the letter to Stalin, which already contained a general review of events since last fall, were known to him, and he hoped that the analysis given in the letter would be supplemented by oral statements of the Führer with regard to the over-all situation and German-Russian relations.

The Reich Foreign Minister replied that in the letter to Stalin he had already expressed the firm conviction of Germany, which he wished to stress again on this occasion, that no power on earth could alter the fact that the beginning of the end had now arrived for the British Empire. England was beaten, and it was only a question of time when she would finally admit her defeat. It was possible that this would happen soon, because in England the situation was deteriorating daily. Germany would, of course, welcome an early conclusion of the conflict, since she did not wish under any circumstances to sacrifice human lives unnecessarily. If, however, the British did not make up their minds in the immediate future to admit their defeat, they would definitely ask for peace during the coming year. Germany was continuing her bombing attacks on England day and night. Her submarines would gradually be employed to the full extent and would inflict terrible losses on England. Germany was of the opinion that England could perhaps be forced by these attacks to give up the struggle. A certain uneasiness was already apparent in Great Britain, which seemed to indicate such a solution. If, however, England were not forced to her knees by the present mode of attack, Germany would, as soon as weather conditions permitted, resolutely proceed to a large-scale attack and thereby definitely crush England. This large-scale attack had thus far been prevented only by abnormal weather conditions.

On the other hand, England hoped for aid from the United States, whose support, however, was extremely questionable. Regarding possible military operations by land, the entry of the United States into the war was of no consequence at all for Germany. Germany and Italy would never again allow an Anglo-Saxon to land on the European Continent. The aid which England could get from the American fleet was also very uncertain. Thus, America would confine herself to sending war matériel, primarily planes, to the British. How much of this matériel would really arrive in England it was difficult to say. It might be assumed, however, that as a result of the measures taken by the German Navy, shipments from America would arrive in England only in very meagre quantities, so that in this respect, too, American support was more than doubtful. Under these circumstances, the question of whether America would enter the war or not was a matter of complete indifference to Germany.

As to the political situation, the Reich Foreign Minister remarked that now, after the conclusion of the French campaign, Germany was extraordinarily strong. The Führer would probably give Herr Molotov further information on this point. The course of the war had brought neither losses of personnel—as regrettable as the sacrifices might be for the families directly afflicted—nor material losses of any importance. Germany, therefore, had at her disposal an extraordinarily large number of divisions, and her air force was constantly growing stronger. The submarines and other naval units were continually being augmented. Under those circumstances, any attempt at a landing or at military operations on the European Continent by England or by England backed by America was doomed to complete failure at the start. This was no military problem at all. This the English had not yet understood, because apparently there was some degree of confusion in Great Britain and because the country was led by a political and military dilettante by the name of Churchill, who throughout his previous career had completely failed at all decisive moments and who would fail again this time.

Furthermore, the Axis completely dominated its part of Europe militarily and politically. Even France, which had lost the war and had to pay for it (of which the French, incidentally, were quite aware) had accepted the principle that France in the future would never again support England and de Gaulle, the quixotic conqueror of Africa. Because of the extraordinary strength of their position, the Axis Powers were not, therefore, considering how they might win the war, but rather how rapidly they could end the war which was already won.

As a result of this whole development, i. e., the natural desire of Germany and Italy to end the war as rapidly as possible, both countries had looked around for friends who pursued the same interest, that is, who were against any extension of the war and aimed at a speedy conclusion of the war. The Tripartite Pact between Germany,

Italy, and Japan had been the result of these efforts. The Reich Foreign Minister could state confidentially that a number of other countries had also declared their solidarity with the ideas of the Three Power Pact.

In this connection the Reich Foreign Minister emphasized that during the talks on the Three Power Pact, which were concluded very rapidly, as he had already stated in the letter to Stalin, one idea had been paramount in the minds of all three participants, namely, that the Pact should not in any way disturb the relationship of the Three Powers to Russia. This idea had been advanced by the Reich Foreign Minister and had been at once spontaneously approved by Italy and Japan. Japan, in particular—whose friendship for Germany, in view of the warmongering agitation in the United States, was of special importance in the interest of preventing a spread of the war—had given it her backing. Relations with Russia were clarified in article 5 of the Tripartite Pact of Berlin and had actually been the first subject settled.

The Reich Foreign Minister pointed out that from the very first moment of his Moscow visit he had made clear his view that in the basic foreign policy of the New Germany, friendship with Japan (as expressed in the Tripartite Pact) and friendship with Russia were not only absolutely consistent with each other but could be of positive value in the realization of this foreign policy so far as the desire for a speedy end to the war is concerned—a desire which was surely shared by Soviet Russia. Molotov would recall that the Reich Foreign Minister had stated in Moscow that Germany would very much welcome an improvement in relations between Russia and Japan. He (the Reich Foreign Minister) had taken with him to Germany Stalin's concurrence in the idea that it would also be in the Russian interest if Germany would exert her influence in Tokyo in favor of a Russo-Japanese *rapprochement*. The Reich Foreign Minister pointed out that he had consistently exerted this influence in Tokyo, and he believed that his work had to a certain degree already been effective. Not only since his Moscow visit, but even seven to eight years ago, he (the Reich Foreign Minister) in conversations with the Japanese had always advocated Russo-Japanese accord. He took the position that just as it had been possible to delimit the mutual spheres of interest between Soviet Russia and Germany, a delimitation of interests could also be achieved between Japan and Russia. With regard to her *Lebensraum* policy, Japan now was oriented not toward the East and North, but toward the South, and the Reich Foreign Minister believed that by his influence he had contributed something to this development. Another reason why Germany had striven for an understanding with Japan was the realization that England would some day go to war against the Reich. Therefore, in good season Germany had adopted an appropriate policy toward Japan.

The Führer now was of the opinion that it would be advantageous in any case if the attempt were made to establish the spheres of influence between Russia, Germany, Italy, and Japan along very broad lines. The Führer had considered this question long and thoroughly, and he had reached the following conclusion: By reason of the position which the four nations occupied in the world, a wise policy would normally direct the momentum of their *Lebensraum* expansion entirely southward. Japan had already turned toward the South, and she would have to work for centuries in order to consolidate her territorial gains in the South. Germany had defined her spheres of influence with Russia, and after the establishment of a new order in Western Europe she would also find her *Lebensraum* expansion to be in a southerly direction, i. e., in Central Africa in the region of the former German colonies. Similarly Italian expansion was to the south in the African portion of the Mediterranean, i. e., North and East Africa. He, the Foreign Minister, wondered whether Russia in the long run would not also turn to the South for the natural outlet to the open sea that was so important for Russia. These were, the Reich Foreign Minister stated in conclusion, the great concepts which during recent months had frequently been discussed between the Führer and himself and which were also to be presented to Molotov on the occasion of the Berlin visit.

To a question by Molotov as to which sea the Reich Foreign Minister had meant when he had just spoken of access to the sea, the latter replied that according to German opinion great changes would take place all over the world after the war. He recalled the fact that he had declared to Stalin in Moscow that England no longer had the right to dominate the world. England was pursuing an insane policy, for which she would some day have to pay the cost. Germany believed, therefore, that great changes would occur in the status of British imperial possessions. Thus far, both partners had benefited from the German-Russian Pact, Germany as well as Russia, which was able to carry out her rightful revisions in the West. The victory of Germany over Poland and France had contributed considerably to the successful achievement of these revisions. Both partners of the German-Russian Pact had together done some good business.

This was the most favorable basis for any pact. The question now was, whether they could not continue in the future also to do good business together and whether Soviet Russia could not derive corresponding advantages from the new order of things in the British Empire, i. e., whether in the long run the most advantageous access to the sea for Russia could not be found in the direction of the Persian Gulf and the Arabian Sea, and whether at the same time certain other aspirations of Russia in this part of Asia—in which Germany was completely disinterested—could not also be realized.

The Reich Foreign Minister further brought up the subject of Turkey. Thus far that country had outwardly had an alliance with France and England. France had been eliminated by her defeat, and England's value as an ally would become more and more questionable. Therefore, Turkey had been clever enough in recent months to reduce her ties with England to a level that amounted really to nothing more than the former neutrality. The question arose as to what interest Russia had in Turkey. In view of the imminent end of the war, which was in the interest of all countries, including Russia, he believed that Turkey should be induced to free herself more and more from the tie with England. He (the Reich Foreign Minister) did not want to pass final judgment on details, but he believed that with the adoption of a common platform by Russia, Germany, Italy, and Japan, Turkey ought gradually to be steered toward these countries. Thus far, he had not discussed these matters with the Turks in any concrete way. He had only stated in a confidential talk with the Turkish Ambassador that Germany would welcome it if Turkey, by pursuing in intensified degree her present political line, would arrive at absolute neutrality, and he had added that Germany did not make any claims whatsoever to Turkish territory.

The Reich Foreign Minister further declared that in this connection he understood completely Russia's dissatisfaction with the Straits Convention of Montreux. Germany was even more dissatisfied, for she had not been included in it at all. Personally he (the Reich Foreign Minister) was of the opinion that the Montreux Convention, like the Danube Commissions, must be scrapped and replaced by something new. This new agreement must be concluded between those powers that were particularly interested in the issue, primarily Russia, Turkey, Italy, and Germany. It was clear that Soviet Russia could not be satisfied with the present situation. Germany found the idea acceptable that in the Black Sea Soviet Russia and the adjacent countries should enjoy certain privileges over other countries of the

world. It was absurd that countries that were thousands of miles away
from the Black Sea should claim to have the same rights as the Black
Sea powers. The new Straits agreement with Turkey would, moreover,
have to secure certain special privileges to Russia, on the details of
which he could not yet comment at the moment, but which would
have to grant to the warships and merchant fleet of the Soviet Union
in principle freer access to the Mediterranean than heretofore. Russia was entitled to that. He (the Reich Foreign Minister) had
already discussed these matters with the Italians, and the arguments
which he had just indicated had received most sympathetic consideration in Italy. It appeared advisable to him that Russia, Germany,
and Italy should pursue a common policy toward Turkey in order to
induce that country without loss of face to free herself from her ties
with England, which could hardly be pleasing to the three countries.
Turkey would thereby not only become a factor in the coalition of
powers against the spread of war and for an early establishment of
peace, but she would also be prepared to scrap the Montreux Convention voluntarily and, in conjunction with these three countries, to
create a new Straits convention which would satisfy the just demands
of all and give Russia certain special privileges. In this matter they
might consider jointly whether it would not be possible to recognize
the territorial integrity of Turkey.

The Reich Foreign Minister summed up the matter by stating that
the following issues were involved—

1. To consider jointly how the countries of the Tripartite Pact
could reach an agreement of some kind with the Soviet Union, expressing the Soviet Union's solidarity with the aim of the Tripartite
Pact, namely the prevention of the spread of war and the early establishment of world peace.

Moreover, other common issues could be designated on which the
countries wished to collaborate and, finally, mutual respect for one
another's interests might be agreed upon. These were approximately
the guide lines for such a contemplated agreement. The details would
have to be discussed further. If these arguments appeared acceptable
to the Soviet Government, a joint declaration by the Soviet Government and the powers of the Tripartite Pact pledging the early
restoration of peace would in effect result.

2. Joint examinations as to whether in some way the interests of the
four countries could be clarified for the future on a very long-range
scale.

3. The issue of Turkey and the Straits question were also involved.

On all these points, it was to be kept in mind that the Reich Foreign Minister did not yet wish to make any concrete proposals; he had only presented a summary of the ideas which the Führer and he had in mind when the letter to Stalin was sent. If, however, these ideas appeared feasible to the Soviet Government, the Reich Foreign Minister would be quite ready to come to Moscow himself and discuss the matters personally with Stalin. He wondered whether the simultaneous presence of his Italian and Japanese colleagues, who, as far as he knew, were also prepared to come to Moscow, could be of advantage in the matter. Of course, the relationship of Russia to the Axis, as well as relations between Russia and Japan, would first have to be clarified through diplomatic channels.

At the end the Reich Foreign Minister added another remark regarding his recent conversation with the Chinese Ambassador. He had not been prompted from any direction to hold this conversation, but he had had indications that the Japanese would not have any objections to it. In line with the efforts to bring about a speedy end to the war, he had asked himself whether there was not the possibility of reconciling the differences between Chiang Kai-shek and Japan. He had not, by any means, offered Germany's mediation, but, in view of the long and friendly relations existing between Germany and China, had merely informed Marshal Chiang Kai-shek of the German view. Japan was about to recognize the Nanking Government; on the other hand, reports were current to the effect that Japan as well as China desired to seek a compromise. Whether these reports were based on fact could not be definitely ascertained. It would undoubtedly be well, however, if a compromise between the two countries could be found. For this reason he (the Reich Foreign Minister) had summoned the Chinese Ambassador in order to communicate to him the German position on this question, since he did not consider it impossible that something was being initiated between Japan and China of which he wished to inform Molotov during this exchange of ideas.

Molotov agreed with the remark concerning the advantages of a Sino-Japanese accord and replied to the statements of the Reich Foreign Minister by saying that they had been of great interest to him and that an exchange of ideas regarding the great problems concerning not only Germany and Soviet Russia but also other states as well might, indeed, be useful. He had well understood the statements of the Reich Foreign Minister regarding the great importance of the

Tripartite Pact. As the representative of a nonbelligerent country, however, he had to ask for a number of explanations in order to ascertain more clearly the meaning of the Pact. When the New Order in Europe and the Greater East Asian Sphere were discussed in the Treaty, the concept of a "Greater East Asian Sphere" was quite vague, at least for a person who had not participated in the preparation of the Pact. Therefore, it would be important for him to obtain a more accurate definition of this concept. Moreover, the participation of the Soviet Union in the actions envisaged by the Reich Foreign Minister must be discussed in detail, and that not only in Berlin, but also in Moscow.

The Reich Foreign Minister replied that the concept of the Greater East Asian Sphere had been new to him, too, and that it had not been defined to him in detail either. The formulation had been suggested in the last few days of the negotiations, which, as already mentioned, had proceeded very rapidly. He could state, however, that the concept of a "Greater East Asian Sphere" had nothing to do with the vital Russian spheres of influence. During the pact negotiations, as already mentioned, the first matter discussed was that nothing aimed directly or indirectly against Russia might be included in the Pact.

Molotov replied that precision was necessary in a delimitation of spheres of influence over a rather long period of time. Therefore, he had asked to be informed of the opinion of the authors of the Pact or, at least, of the opinion of the Reich Government on this point. Particular vigilance was needed in the delimitation of the spheres of influence between Germany and Russia. The establishment of these spheres of influence in the past year was only a partial solution, which had been rendered obsolete and meaningless by recent circumstances and events, with the exception of the Finnish question, which he would discuss in detail later. It would necessarily take some time to make a permanent settlement. In this connection, in the first place, Russia wanted to come to an understanding with Germany, and only then with Japan and Italy, after she had previously obtained precise information regarding the significance, the nature, and the aim of the Tripartite Pact.

At this point the conversation was interrupted in order to give the Russian delegates time for breakfast in a small circle before the conversation with the Führer began.

SCHMIDT
(*Minister*)

BERLIN, November 13, 1940.

Frames 0281–0259, serial F 3

Memorandum of the Conversation Between the Führer and the Chairman of the Council of People's Commissars and People's Commissar for Foreign Affairs, Molotov, in the Presence of the Reich Foreign Minister, the Deputy People's Commissar, Dekanosov, as Well as of Counselor of Embassy Hilger and Herr Pavlov, Who Acted as Interpreters, on November 12, 1940

STATE SECRET

Füh. 32/40 g. Rs.

After some words of welcome, the Führer stated that the idea that was uppermost in his mind in the conversations now taking place was this: In the life of peoples it was indeed difficult to lay down a course for development over a long period in the future and the outbreak of conflicts was often strongly influenced by personal factors; he believed, nevertheless, that an attempt had to be made to fix the development of nations, even for a long period of time, in so far as that was possible, so that friction would be avoided and the elements of conflict precluded as far as humanly possible.   This was particularly in order when two nations such as the German and Russian nations had at their helm men who possessed sufficient authority to commit their countries to a development in a definite direction. In the case of Russia and Germany, moreover, two very great nations were involved which need not by nature have any conflict of interests, if each nation understood that the other required certain vital necessities without the guarantee of which its existence was impossible. Besides this, both countries had systems of government which did not wage war for the sake of war, but which needed peace more than war in order to carry out their domestic tasks. With due regard for vital needs, particularly in the economic field, it should really be possible to achieve a settlement between them, which would lead to peaceful collaboration between the two countries beyond the life span of the present leaders.

After Molotov had expressed his entire agreement with these arguments, the Führer continued that it was obviously a difficult task to chart developments between peoples and countries over a long period. He believed, however, that it would be possible to elaborate clearly and precisely certain general points of view quite independently of personal motives and to orient the political and economic interests of peoples in such a manner as to give some guarantee that conflicts would be avoided even for rather long periods. The situation in which the conversation of today was taking place was characterized by the fact that Germany was at war, while Soviet Russia was not. Many of the measures taken by Germany had been influenced by the fact of her belligerency. Many of the steps that were necessary in the course of the war had developed from the conduct of the war itself and could not have been anticipated at the outbreak of war. By and large, not only Germany but also Russia had gained great advantages. On further consideration, the political collaboration during the one year of its existence had been of considerable value to both countries.

Molotov stated that this was quite correct.

The Führer declared further that probably neither of the two peoples had realized its wishes 100 percent. In political life, however, even a 20–25 percent realization of demands was worth a good deal. He believed that not every wish would be fulfilled in the future either, but that the two greatest peoples of Europe, if they went along together, would, in any case, gain more than if they worked against each other. If they stood together, some advantage would always accrue to both countries. If they worked against each other, however, third countries would be the sole gainers.

Molotov replied that the argument of the Führer was entirely correct and would be confirmed by history; that it was particularly applicable to the present situation, however.

The Führer then went on to say that proceeding from these ideas he had again quite soberly pondered the question of German-Russian collaboration, at a time when the military operations were in effect concluded.

The war had, moreover, led to complications which were not intended by Germany, but which had compelled her from time to time to react militarily to certain events. The Führer then outlined to Molotov the course of miltary operations up to the present, which had led to the fact that England no longer had an ally on the continent. He described in detail the military operations now being carried out against England, and he stressed the influence of atmospheric conditions on these operations. The English retaliatory measures were ridiculous, and the Russian gentlemen could convince themselves at first hand of the fiction of alleged destruction in Berlin. As soon as atmospheric conditions improved, Germany would be poised for the great and final blow against England. At the moment, then, it was her aim to try not only to make military preparations for this final struggle, but also to clarify the political issues which would be of importance during and after this showdown. He had, therefore, re-examined the relations with Russia, and not in a negative spirit, but with the intention of organizing them positively—if possible, for a long period of time. In so doing he had reached several conclusions:

1. Germany was not seeking to obtain military aid from Russia;

2. Because of the tremendous extension of the war, Germany had been forced, in order to oppose England, to penetrate into territories remote from her and in which she was not basically interested politically or economically;

3. There were nevertheless certain requirements, the full importance of which had become apparent only during the war, but which were absolutely vital to Germany. Among them were certain sources of raw materials which were considered by Germany as most vital and absolutely indispensable. Possibly Herr Molotov was of the opinion that in one case or another they had departed from the conception of the spheres of influence which had been agreed upon by Stalin and the Reich Foreign Minister. Such departures had already occurred in some cases in the course of Russian operations against Poland. In a number of cases, on calm consideration of the German and Russian interests, he (the Führer) had not been ready to make concessions, but he had realized that it was desirable to meet the needs of Russia half-way, as, for instance, in the case of Lithuania. From an economic point of view, Lithuania had, it is true, had a certain importance for us, but from a political point of view, we had understood the necessity of straightening out the situation in this whole field in order thereby to prevent in the future the spiritual revival of tendencies that were capable of causing tension between the two countries of Germany and Russia. In another case, namely, that of the South Tyrol, Germany had taken a similar position. However, in the course of the war, factors had arisen for Germany which could not have been anticipated at the outbreak of the war, but which had to be considered absolutely vital from the standpoint of military operations.

He (the Führer) now had pondered the question how, beyond all petty momentary considerations, further to clarify in bold outline the collaboration between Germany and Russia and what direction future German-Russian developments should take. In this matter the following viewpoints were of importance for Germany:

1. Need for Lebensraum [*Raumnot*]. During the war Germany had acquired such large areas that she would require one hundred years to utilize them fully.

2. Some colonial expansion in Central Africa was necessary.

3. Germany needed certain raw materials, the supply of which she would have to safeguard under all circumstances. And

4. She could not permit the establishment by hostile powers of air or naval bases in certain areas.

In no event, however, would the interests of Russia be affected. The Russian empire could develop without in the least prejudicing German interests. (Molotov said this was quite correct.) If both countries came to realize this fact, they could collaborate to their mutual advantage and could spare themselves difficulties, friction, and nervous tension. It was perfectly obvious that Germany and Russia would never become one world. Both countries would always exist separate from each other as two powerful elements of the world. Each of them could shape its future as it liked, if in so doing it considered the interests of the other. Germany herself had no interests in Asia other than general economic and commercial interests. In particular, she had no colonial interests there. She knew, furthermore, that the possible colonial territories in Asia would probably fall to Japan. If by any chance China, too, should be drawn into the orbit of the awakening [*erwachenden*] nations, any colonial aspirations would be doomed to disappointment from the start in view of the masses of people living there.

There were in Europe a number of points of contact [*Berührungsmomenten*] between Germany, Russia, and Italy. Each one of these three countries had an understandable desire for an outlet to the open sea. Germany wanted to get out of the North Sea, Italy wanted to remove the barrier of Gibraltar, and Russia was also striving toward the ocean. The question now was how much chance there was for these great countries really to obtain free access to the ocean without in turn coming into conflict with each other over the matter. This was also the viewpoint from which he looked upon the organization of European relations after the war. The leading statesmen of Europe must prevent this war from becoming the father of a new war. The issues to be settled had, therefore, to be settled in such a manner that, at least in the foreseeable future, no new conflict could arise.

In this spirit, he (the Führer) had talked with the French statesmen and believed that he had found among them some sympathy for a settlement which would lead to tolerable conditions for a rather long period and which would be of advantage to all concerned, if only to the extent that a new war did not again have to be feared immediately. Referring to the preamble of the Armistice Treaty with France, he had pointed out to Pétain and Laval that, as long as the war with England lasted, no step might be taken which would in any way be incompatible with the conditions for ending this war against Great Britain.

Elsewhere, too, there were problems such as these, but ones which arose only for the duration of the war. Thus, for instance, Germany had no political interests whatsoever in the Balkans and was active there at present exclusively under the compulsion of securing for herself certain raw materials. It was a matter of purely military interests, the safeguarding of which was not a pleasant task, since, for instance, a German military force had to be maintained in Rumania, hundreds of kilometers away from the supply centers.

For similar reasons the idea was intolerable to Germany that England might get a foothold in Greece in order to establish air and naval bases there. The Reich was compelled to prevent this under any circumstances.

The continuation of the war under such circumstances was of course not desirable. And that is why Germany had wanted to end the war after the conclusion of the Polish campaign. At that time England and France could have had peace without personal sacrifices; they had, however, preferred to continue the war. Of course, blood also creates rights, and it was inadmissible that certain countries should have declared and waged war without afterward paying the cost. He (the Führer) had made this clear to the French. At the present stage of developments, however, the question was which of the countries responsible for the war had to pay more. At any rate, Germany would have preferred to end the war last year and to have demobilized her army in order to resume her peacetime work, since from an economic point of view any war was bad business. Even the victor had to incur such expenses before, during, and after the war that he could have reached his goal much more cheaply in a peaceful development.

Molotov concurred in this idea, stating that in any case it was vastly more expensive to attain a goal by military measures than by peaceful means. The Führer pointed out further that under the present circumstances Germany had been forced by wartime developments to become active in areas in which she was politically disinterested but had at most economic interests. Self-preservation, however, absolutely dictated this course. Nevertheless, this activity of Germany—forced upon her in the areas in question—represented no obstacle to any pacification of the world which would later be undertaken, and which would bring to the nations working toward the same end that for which they hoped.

In addition, there was the problem of America. The United States was now pursuing an imperialistic policy. It was not fighting for England, but only trying to get the British Empire into its grasp. They were helping England, at best, in order to further their own rearmament and to reinforce their military power by acquiring bases. In the distant future it would be a question of establishing a great solidarity among those countries which might be involved in case of an extension of the sphere of influence of this Anglo-Saxon power, which had a more solid foundation, by far, than England. In this case, it was not a question of the immediate future; not in 1945, but in 1970 or 1980, at the earliest, would the freedom of other nations be seriously endangered by this Anglo-Saxon power. At any rate, the Continent of Europe had to adjust itself now to this development and had to act jointly against the Anglo-Saxons and against any of their attempts to acquire dangerous bases. Therefore, he had undertaken an exchange of ideas with France, Italy, and Spain, in order with these countries to set up in the whole of Europe and Africa some kind of Monroe Doctrine and to adopt a new joint colonial policy by which each of the powers concerned would claim for itself only as much colonial territory as it could really utilize. In other regions, where Russia was the power in the foremost position, the interests of the latter would, of course, have to come first. This would result in a great coalition of powers which, guided by sober appraisal of realities, would have to establish their respective spheres of interest and would assert themselves against the rest of the world correspondingly. It was surely a difficult task to organize such a coalition of countries; and yet, to conceive it was not as difficult as to carry it out.

The Führer then reverted to the German-Russian efforts. He understood thoroughly Russia's attempts to get ice-free ports with absolutely secure access to the open sea. Germany had enormously expanded her *Lebensraum* in her present eastern provinces. At least half of this area, however, must be regarded as an economic liability. Probably both Russia and Germany had not achieved everything they had set out to do. In any case, however, the successes had been great on both sides. If a liberal view were taken of the remaining issues and due regard were taken of the fact that Germany was still at war and had to concern herself with areas which, in and for themselves, were of no importance to her politically, substantial gains for both partners could be achieved in the future, too. In this connection the Führer again turned to the Balkans and repeated that Germany would at once oppose by military action any attempt by England to get a foothold in Salonika. She still retained unpleasant memories from the last war of the then Salonika Front.

To a question of Molotov's as to how Salonika constituted a danger, the Führer referred to the proximity of the Rumanian petroleum fields, which Germany wished to protect under all circumstances. As soon as peace prevailed, however, the German troops would immediately leave Rumania again.

In the further course of the conversation, the Führer asked Molotov how Russia planned to safeguard her interests in the Black Sea and in the Straits. Germany would also be prepared at any time to help effect an improvement for Russia in the régime of the Straits.

Molotov replied that the statements of the Führer had been of a general nature and that in general he could agree with his reasoning. He was also of the opinion that it would be in the interest of Germany and the Soviet Union if the two countries would collaborate and not fight each other. Upon his departure from Moscow, Stalin had given him exact instructions, and everything that he was about to say was identical with the views of Stalin. He concurred in the opinion of the Führer that both partners had derived substantial benefits from the German-Russian agreement. Germany had received a secure hinterland that, as was generally known, had been of great importance for the further course of events during the year of war. In Poland, too, Germany had gained considerable economic advantages. By the exchange of Lithuania for the Voivodeship of Lublin, all possible friction between Russia and Germany had been avoided. The German-Russian agreement of last year could therefore be regarded as fulfilled, except for one point, namely, Finland. The Finnish question was still unsolved, and he asked the Führer to tell him whether the German-Russian agreement, as far as it concerned Finland, was still in force. In the opinion of the Soviet Government, no changes had occurred here. Also, in the opinion of the Soviet Government, the German-Russian agreement of last year represented only a partial solution. In the meanwhile, other issues had arisen that also had to be solved.

Molotov then turned to the matter of the significance of the Tripartite Pact. What was the meaning of the New Order in Europe and in Asia, and what role would the U.S.S.R. be given in it? These issues must be discussed during the Berlin conversations and during the contemplated visit of the Reich Foreign Minister to Moscow, on which the Russians were definitely counting. Moreover, there were issues to be clarified regarding Russia's Balkan and Black Sea interests with respect to Bulgaria, Rumania, and Turkey. It would be easier for the Russian Government to give specific replies to the questions raised by the Führer, if it could obtain the explanations just requested. It would be interested in the New Order in Europe, and particularly in the tempo and the form of this New Order. It would also like to have an idea of the boundaries of the so-called Greater East Asian Sphere.

The Führer replied that the Tripartite Pact was intended to regulate conditions in Europe as to the natural interests of the European countries and, consequently, Germany was now approaching the Soviet Union in order that she might express herself regarding the areas of interest to her. In no case was a settlement to be made without Soviet Russian cooperation. This applied not only to Europe, but also to Asia, where Russia herself was to cooperate in the definition of the Greater East Asian Sphere and where she was to designate her claims there. Germany's task in this case was that of a mediator. Russia by no means was to be confronted with a *fait accompli*.

When the Führer undertook to try to establish the above-mentioned coalition of powers, it was not the German-Russian relationship which appeared to him to be the most difficult point, but the question of whether a collaboration between Germany, France, and Italy was possible. Only now that he believed this problem could be solved, and after a settlement in broad outlines had in effect been accepted by the three countries, had he thought it possible to contact Soviet Russia for the purpose of settling the questions of the Black Sea, the Balkans, and Turkey.

In conclusion, the Führer summed up by stating that the discussion, to a certain extent, represented the first concrete step toward a comprehensive collaboration, with due consideration for the problems of Western Europe, which were to be settled between Germany, Italy, and France, as well as for the issues of the East, which were essentially the concern of Russia and Japan, but in which Germany offered her good offices as mediator. It was a matter of opposing any attempt on the part of America to "make money on Europe." The United States had no business either in Europe, in Africa, or in Asia.

Molotov expressed his agreement with the statements of the Führer regarding the role of America and England. The participation of Russia in the Tripartite Pact appeared to him entirely acceptable in principle, provided that Russia was to cooperate as a partner and not be merely an object. In that case he saw no difficulties in the matter of participation of the Soviet Union in the common effort. But the aim and the significance of the Pact must first be more closely defined, particularly because of the delimitation of the Greater East Asian Sphere.

In view of a possible air raid alarm the talk was broken off at this point and postponed until the following day, the Führer promising Molotov that he would discuss with him in detail the various issues which had come up during the conversation.

SCHMIDT

BERLIN, November 16, 1940.

<hr/>

Frames 154–190, serial F 18

Memorandum of the Conversation Between the Führer and the Chairman of the Council of People's Commissars Molotov in the Presence of the Reich Foreign Minister and the Deputy People's Commissar for Foreign Affairs, Dekanosov, as Well as of Counselor of Embassy Hilger and Herr Pavlov, Who Acted as Interpreters, in Berlin on November 13, 1940

Füh. 33/40

The Führer referred to the remark of Molotov during yesterday's conversation, according to which the German-Russian agreement was fulfilled "with the exception of one point: namely, of Finland."

Molotov explained that this remark referred not only to the German-Russian agreement itself, but in particular to the Secret Protocols too.

The Führer replied that, in the Secret Protocol, zones of influence and spheres of interest had been designated and distributed between Germany and Russia. In so far as it had been a question of actually taking possession, Germany had lived up to the agreements, which was not quite the case on the Russian side. At any rate, Germany had not occupied any territory that was within the Russian sphere of influence.

Lithuania had already been mentioned yesterday. There could be no doubt that in this case the changes from the original German-Russian agreement were essentially due to Russian initiative. Whether the difficulties—to avoid which the Russians had offered their suggestion—would actually have resulted from the partition of Poland, could be left out of the discussion. In any case, the Voivodeship of Lublin was no compensation, economically, for Lithuania. However, the Germans had seen that in the course of events a situation had resulted which necessitated revision of the original agreement.

The same applied to Bucovina. Strictly speaking, in the original agreement Germany had declared herself disinterested only in Bessarabia. Nevertheless, she had realized, in this case too, that revision of the agreement was in certain respects advantageous for the other partner.

The situation regarding Finland was quite similar. Germany had no political interest there. This was known to the Russian Government. During the Russo-Finnish War Germany had meticulously fulfilled all her obligations in regard to absolutely benevolent neutrality.

Molotov interposed here that the Russian Government had had no cause for criticism with regard to the attitude of Germany during that conflict.

In this connection the Führer mentioned also that he had even detained ships in Bergen which were transporting arms and ammunition to Finland, for which Germany had actually had no authority. Germany had incurred the serious opposition of the rest of the world, and of Sweden in particular, by her attitude during the Russo-Finnish War. As a result, during the subsequent Norwegian campaign, itself involving considerable risks, she had to employ a large number of divisions for protection against Sweden, which she would not have needed otherwise.

The real situation was as follows: In accordance with the German-Russian agreements, Germany recognized that, politically, Finland was of primary interest to Russia and was in her zone of influence. However, Germany had to consider the following two points:

1. For the duration of the war she was very greatly interested in the deliveries of nickel and lumber from Finland, and

2. She did not desire any new conflict in the Baltic Sea which would further curtail her freedom of movement in one of the few merchant shipping regions which still remained to her. It was completely incorrect to assert that Finland was occupied by German troops. To be sure, troops were being transported to Kirkenes via Finland, of which fact Russia had been officially informed by Germany. Because of the length of the route, the trains had to stop two or three times in Finnish territory. However, as soon as the transit of the troop contingents to be transported had been completed, no additional troops would be sent through Finland. He (the Führer) pointed out that

both Germany and Russia would naturally be interested in not allowing the Baltic Sea to become a combat zone again. Since the Russo-Finnish War, the possibilities for military operations had shifted, because England had available long-range bombers and long-range destroyers. The English thereby had a chance to get a foothold on Finnish airports.

In addition, there was a purely psychological factor which was extremely onerous. The Finns had defended themselves bravely, and they had gained the sympathies of the world—particularly of Scandinavia. In Germany too, during the Russo-Finnish War, the people were somewhat annoyed at the position which, as a result of the agreements with Russia, Germany had to take and actually did take. Germany did not wish any new Finnish war because of the aforementioned considerations. However, the legitimate claims of Russia were not affected by that. Germany had proved this again and again by her attitude on various issues, among others, the issue of the fortification of the Aaland Islands. For the duration of the war, however, her economic interests in Finland were just as important as in Rumania. Germany expected consideration of these interests all the more, since she herself had also shown understanding of the Russian wishes in the issues of Lithuania and Bucovina at the time. At any rate, she had no political interest of any kind in Finland, and she fully accepted the fact that that country belonged to the Russian zone of influence.

In his reply Molotov pointed out that the agreement of 1939 had referred to a certain stage of the development which had been concluded by the end of the Polish War, while the second stage was brought to an end by the defeat of France, and that they were really in the third stage now. He recalled that by the original agreement, with its Secret Protocol, the common German-Russian boundary had been fixed and issues concerning the adjacent Baltic countries and Rumania, Finland, and Poland had been settled. For the rest, he agreed with the remarks of the Führer on the revisions made. However, if he drew up a balance sheet of the situation that resulted after the defeat of France, he would have to state that the German-Russian agreement had not been without influence upon the great German victories.

As to the question of the revision of the original agreement with regard to Lithuania and the Voivodeship of Lublin, Molotov pointed out that the Soviet Union would not have insisted on that revision if Germany had not wanted it. But he believed that the new solution had been in the interest of both parties.

At this point the Reich Foreign Minister interjected that, to be sure, Russia had not made this revision an absolute condition, but at any rate had urged it very strongly.

Molotov insisted that the Soviet Government would not have refused to leave matters as provided in the original agreement. At any rate, however, Germany, for its concession in Lithuania, had received compensation in Polish territory.

The Führer interjected here that in this exchange one could not, from the point of view of economics, speak of adequate compensation.

Molotov then mentioned the question of the strip of Lithuanian territory and emphasized that the Soviet Government had not received any clear answer yet from Germany on this question. However, it awaited a decision.

Regarding Bucovina, he admitted that this involved an additional territory, one not mentioned in the Secret Protocol. Russia had at first confined her demands to Northern Bucovina. Under the present circumstances, however, Germany must understand the Russian interest in Southern Bucovina. But Russia had not received an answer to her question regarding this subject either. Instead, Germany had guaranteed the entire territory of Rumania and completely disregarded, Russia's wishes with regard to Southern Bucovina.

The Führer replied that it would mean a considerable concession on the part of Germany, if even part of Bucovina were to be occupied by Russia. According to an oral agreement, the former Austrian territories were to fall within the German sphere of influence. Besides, the territories belonging to the Russian zone had been mentioned by name: Bessarabia, for example. There was, however, not a word regarding Bucovina in the agreements. Finally, the exact meaning of the expression "sphere of influence" was not further defined. At any rate, Germany had not violated the agreement in the least in this matter. To the objection of Molotov that the revisions with regard to the strip of Lithuanian territory and of Bucovina were not of very great importance in comparison with the revision which Germany had undertaken elsewhere by military force, the Führer replied that so-called "revision by force of arms" had not been the subject of the agreement at all.

Molotov, however, persisted in the opinion previously stated: that the revisions desired by Russia were insignificant.

The Führer replied that if German-Russian collaboration was to show positive results in the future, the Soviet Government would have to understand that Germany was engaged in a life and death struggle, which, at all events, she wanted to conclude successfully. For that, a number of prerequisites depending upon economic and military factors were required, which Germany wanted to secure for herself by all means. If the Soviet Union were in a similar position, Germany on her part would, and would have to, demonstrate a similar understanding for Russian needs. The conditions which Germany wanted to assure did not conflict with the agreements with Russia. The German wish to avoid a war with unforeseeable consequences in the Baltic Sea did not mean any violation of the German-Russian agreements according to which Finland belonged in the Russian sphere of influence. The guarantee given upon the wish and request of the Rumanian Government was no violation of the agreements concerning Bessarabia. The Soviet Union had to realize that in the framework of any broader collaboration of the two countries advantages of quite different scope were to be reached than the insignificant revisions which were now being discussed. Much greater successes could then be achieved, provided that Russia did not now seek successes in territories in which Germany was interested for the duration of the war. The future successes would be the greater, the more Germany and Russia succeeded in fighting back to back against the outside world, and would become the smaller, the more the two countries faced each other breast to breast. In the first case there was no power on earth which could oppose the two countries.

In his reply Molotov voiced his agreement with the last conclusions of the Führer. In this connection he stressed the viewpoint of the Soviet leaders, and of Stalin in particular, that it would be possible and expedient to strengthen and activate the relations between the two countries. However, in order to give those relations a permanent basis, issues would also have to be clarified which were of secondary importance, but which spoiled the atmosphere of German-Russian relations. Finland belonged among these issues. If Russia and Germany had a good understanding, this issue could be solved without war, but there must be neither German troops in Finland nor political demonstrations in that country against the Soviet-Russian Government.

The Führer replied that the second point could not be a matter for debate, since Germany had nothing whatsoever to do with these things. Incidentally, demonstrations could easily be staged, and it was very difficult to find out afterward who had been the real instigator. However, regarding the German troops, he could give the assurance that, if a general settlement were made, no German troops would appear in Finland any longer.

Molotov replied that by demonstrations he also understood the dispatch of Finnish delegations to Germany or receptions of prominent Finns in Germany. Moreover, the circumstance of the presence of German troops had led to an ambiguous attitude on the part of Finland. Thus, for instance, slogans were brought out that "nobody was a Finn who approved of the last Russo-Finnish Peace Treaty", and the like.

The Führer replied that Germany had always exerted only a moderating influence and that she had advised Finland and also Rumania, in particular, to accept the Russian demands.

Molotov replied that the Soviet Government considered it as its duty definitively to settle and clarify the Finnish question. No new agreements were needed for that. The old German-Russian agreement assigned Finland to the Russian sphere of influence.

In conclusion the Führer stated on this point that Germany did not desire any war in the Baltic Sea and that she urgently needed Finland as a supplier of nickel and lumber. Politically, she was not interested and, in contrast to Russia, had occupied no Finnish territory. Incidentally, the transit of German troops would be finished within the next few days. No further troop trains would then be sent. The decisive question for Germany was whether Russia had the intention of going to war against Finland.

Molotov answered this question somewhat evasively with the statement that everything would be all right if the Finnish Government would give up its ambiguous attitude toward the U.S.S.R., and if the agitation against Russia among the population (bringing out of slogans such as the ones previously mentioned) would cease.

To the Führer's objection that he feared that Sweden might intervene in a Russo-Finnish War the next time, Molotov replied that he could not say anything about Sweden, but he had to stress that Germany, as well as the Soviet Union, was interested in the neutrality of Sweden. Of course, both countries were also interested in peace in the Baltic, but the Soviet Union was entirely able to assure peace in that region.

The Führer replied that they would perhaps experience in a different part of Europe how even the best military intentions were greatly restricted by geographical factors. He could, therefore, imagine that in the case of a new conflict a sort of resistance cell would be formed in Sweden and Finland, which would furnish air bases to England or even America. This would force Germany to intervene. He (the Führer) would, however, do this only reluctantly. He had already mentioned yesterday that the necessity for intervention would perhaps also arise in Salonika, and the case of Salonika was entirely sufficient for him. He had no interest in being forced to become active in the North too. He repeated that entirely different results could be achieved in future collaboration between the two countries and that Russia would after all, on the basis of the peace, receive everything that in her opinion was due her. It would perhaps be only a matter of six months or a year's delay. Besides, the Finnish Government had just sent a note in which it gave assurance of the closest and friendliest cooperation with Russia.

Molotov replied that the deeds did not always correspond with the words, and he persisted in the opinion which he had previously expressed: that peace in the Baltic Sea region could be absolutely insured, if perfect understanding were attained between Germany and Russia in the Finnish matter. Under those circumstances he did not understand why Russia should postpone the realization of her wishes for six months or a year. After all, the German-Russian agreement contained no time limits, and the hands of none of the partners were tied in their spheres of influence.

With a reference to the changes made in the agreement at Russia's request, the Führer stated that there must not be any war in the Baltic. A Baltic conflict would be a heavy strain on German-Russian relations and on the great collaboration of the future. In his opinion, however, future collaboration was more important than the settlement of secondary issues at this very moment.

Molotov replied that it was not a matter of war in the Baltic, but of the question of Finland and its settlement within the framework of the agreement of last year. In reply to a question of the Führer, he declared that he imagined this settlement on the same scale as in Bessarabia and in the adjacent countries, and he requested the Führer to give his opinion on that.

When the Führer replied that he could only repeat that there must be no war with Finland, because such a conflict might have far-reaching repercussions, Molotov stated that a new factor had been introduced into the discussion by this position, which was not expressed in the treaty of last year.

The Führer replied that during the Russo-Finnish War, despite the danger that in connection with it Allied bases might be established in Scandinavia, Germany had meticulously kept her obligations toward Russia and had always advised Finland to give in.

In this connection the Reich Foreign Minister pointed out that Germany had even gone so far as to deny to the Finnish President the use of a German cable for a radio address to America.

Then the Führer went on to explain that just as Russia at the time had pointed out that a partition of Poland might lead to a strain on German-Russian relations, he now declared with the same frankness that a war in Finland would represent such a strain on German-Russian relations, and he asked the Russians to show exactly the same understanding in this instance as he had shown a year ago in the issue of Poland. Considering the genius of Russian diplomacy, ways and means could certainly be found to avoid such a war.

Molotov replied that he could not understand the German fear that a war might break out in the Baltic. Last year, when the international situation was worse for Germany than now, Germany had not raised this issue. Quite apart from the fact that Germany had occupied Denmark, Norway, Holland, and Belgium, she had completely defeated France and even believed that she had already conquered England. He (Molotov) did not see where under those circumstances the danger of war in the Baltic Sea should come from. He would have to request that Germany take the same stand as last year. If she did that unconditionally, there would certainly be no complications in connection with the Finnish issue. However, if she made reservations, a new situation would arise which would then have to be discussed.

In reply to the statements of Molotov regarding the absence of military danger in the Finnish question, the Führer stressed that he too had some understanding of military matters, and he considered it entirely possible that the United States would get a foothold in those regions in case of participation by Sweden in a possible war. He (the Führer) wanted to end the European War, and he could only repeat that in view of the uncertain attitude of Sweden a new war in the Baltic would mean a strain on German-Russian relations with unforeseeable consequences. Would Russia declare war on the United States, in case the latter should intervene in connection with the Finnish conflict?

When Molotov replied that this question was not of present interest, the Führer replied that it would be too late for a decision when it became so. When Molotov then declared that he did not see any indication of the outbreak of war in the Baltic, the Führer replied that in that case everything would be in order anyway and the whole discussion was really of a purely theoretical nature.

Summarizing, the Reich Foreign Minister pointed out that

(1) the Führer had declared that Finland remained in the sphere of influence of Russia and that Germany would not maintain any troops there;

(2) Germany had nothing to do with demonstrations of Finland against Russia, but was exerting her influence in the opposite direction, and

(3) the collaboration of the two countries was the decisive problem of long-range importance, which in the past had already resulted in great advantages for Russia, but which in the future would show advantages compared with which the matters that had just been discussed would appear entirely insignificant. There was actually no reason at all for making an issue of the Finnish question. Perhaps it was a misunderstanding only. Strategically, all of Russia's wishes had been satisfied by her peace treaty with Finland. Demonstrations in a conquered country were not at all unnatural, and if perhaps the transit of German troops had caused certain reactions in the Finnish population they would disappear with the end of those troop transits. Hence, if one considered matters realistically, there were no differences between Germany and Russia.

The Führer pointed out that both sides agreed in principle that Finland belonged to the Russian sphere of influence. Instead, therefore, of continuing a purely theoretical discussion, they should rather turn to more important problems.

After the conquest of England the British Empire would be apportioned as a gigantic world-wide estate in bankruptcy of 40 million square kilometers. In this bankrupt estate there would be for Russia access to the ice-free and really open ocean. Thus far, a minority of 45 million Englishmen had ruled 600 million inhabitants of the British Empire. He was about to crush this minority. Even the United States was actually doing nothing but picking out of this bankrupt estate a few items particularly suitable to the United States. Germany, of course, would like to avoid any conflict which would divert her from her struggle against the heart of the Empire, the British Isles. For that reason, he (the Führer) did not like Italy's war against Greece, as it diverted forces to the periphery instead of concentrating them against England at one point. The same would occur during a Baltic war. The conflict with England would be fought to the last ditch, and he had no doubt that the defeat of the British Isles would lead to the dissolution of the Empire. It was a chimera to believe that the Empire could possibly be ruled and held together from Canada. Under those circumstances there arose world-wide perspectives. During the next few weeks they would have to be settled in joint diplomatic negotiations with Russia, and Russia's participation in the solution of these problems would have to be arranged. All the countries which could possibly be interested in the bankrupt estate would have to stop all controversies among themselves and concern themselves exclusively with the partition of the British Empire. This applied to Germany, France, Italy, Russia, and Japan.

Molotov replied that he had followed the arguments of the Führer with interest and that he was in agreement with everything that he had understood. However, he could comment thereon less than the Führer, since the latter had surely thought more about these problems and formed more concrete opinions regarding them. The main thing was first to make up their minds regarding German-Russian collaboration, in which Italy and Japan could be included later on. In this connection nothing should be changed that had been started; rather, they should only contemplate a continuation of what had been begun.

The Führer mentioned here that the further efforts in the sense of the opening up of great prospects would not be easy and emphasized in this connection that Germany did not want to annex France, as the Russians appeared to assume. He wanted to create a world coalition of interested powers which would consist of Spain, France, Italy, Germany, Soviet Russia, and Japan and would to a certain degree represent a coalition—extending from North Africa to Eastern Asia—of all those who wanted to be satisfied out of the British bankrupt estate. To this end all internal controversies between the members of this coalition must be removed or at least neutralized. For this purpose the settlement of a whole series of questions was necessary. In the West, i. e. between Spain, France, Italy, and Germany, he believed he had now found a formula which satisfied everybody alike. It had not been easy to reconcile the views of Spain and France for instance, in regard to North Africa; however, recognizing the greater future possibilities, both countries finally had given in. After the West was thus settled, an agreement in the East must now be reached. In this case it was not a matter of relations between Soviet Russia and Turkey only, but also of the Greater Asian Sphere. The latter consisted not only of the Greater East Asian Sphere, but also of a purely Asiatic area oriented toward the south, that Germany even now recognized as Russia's sphere of influence. It was a matter of determining in bold outlines the boundaries for the future activity of peoples and of assigning to nations large areas where they could find an ample field of activity for fifty to a hundred years.

Molotov replied that the Führer had raised a number of questions which concerned not only Europe but, beyond that, other territories too. He wanted to discuss first a problem closer to Europe, that of Turkey. As a Black Sea power, the Soviet Union was tied up with a number of countries. In this connection there was still an unsettled question that was just now being discussed by the Danube Commission. Moreover, the Soviet Union had expressed its dissatisfaction to Rumania that the latter had accepted the guarantee of Germany and Italy without consultation with Russia. The Soviet Government had already explained its position twice, and it was of the opinion that the guarantee was aimed against the interests of Soviet Russia, "if one might express oneself so bluntly." Therefore, the question had arisen of revoking this guarantee. To this the Führer had declared that for a certain time it was necessary and its removal therefore impossible. This affected the interests of the Soviet Union as a Black Sea power.

Molotov then came to speak of the Straits, which, referring to the Crimean War and the events of the years 1918-19, he called England's historic gateway for attack on the Soviet Union. The situation was all the more menacing to Russia, as the British had now gained a foothold in Greece. For reasons of security the relations between Soviet Russia and other Black Sea powers were of great importance. In this connection Molotov asked the Führer what Germany would say if Russia gave Bulgaria, that is, the independent country located closest to the Straits, a guarantee under exactly the same conditions as Germany and Italy had given one to Rumania. Russia, however, intended to agree beforehand on this matter with Germany and, if possible, with Italy too.

To a question by Molotov regarding the German position on the question of the Straits, the Führer replied that the Reich Foreign Minister had already considered this point and that he had envisaged a revision of the Montreux Convention in favor of the Soviet Union.

The Reich Foreign Minister confirmed this and stated that the Italians also took a benevolent attitude on the question of this revision.

Molotov again brought up the guarantee to Bulgaria and gave the assurance that the Soviet Union did not intend to interfere in the internal order of the country under any circumstances. "Not a hairsbreadth" would they deviate from this.

Regarding Germany's and Italy's guarantee to Rumania, the Führer stated that this guarantee had been the only possibility of inducing Rumania to cede Bessarabia to Russia without a fight. Besides, because of her oil wells, Rumania represented an absolute German-Italian interest, and, lastly, the Rumanian Government itself had asked that Germany assume the air and ground protection of the oil region, since it did not feel entirely secure from attacks by the English. Referring to a threat of invasion by the English at Salonika, the Führer repeated in this connection that Germany would not tolerate such a landing, but he gave the assurance that at the end of the war all German soldiers would be withdrawn from Rumania.

In reply to Molotov's question regarding Germany's opinion on a Russian guarantee to Bulgaria, the Führer replied that if this guarantee was to be given under the same conditions as the German-Italian guarantee to Rumania, the question would first arise whether Bulgaria herself had asked for a guarantee. He (the Führer) did not know of any request by Bulgaria. Besides, he would, of course, have to inquire about the position of Italy before he himself could make any statement.

However, the decisive question was whether Russia saw a chance to gain sufficient security for her Black Sea interests through a revision of the Montreux Convention. He did not expect an immediate answer to this question, since he knew that Molotov would first have to discuss these matters with Stalin.

Molotov replied that Russia had only one aim in this respect. She wanted to be secure from an attack by way of the Straits and would like to settle this question with Turkey; a guarantee given to Bulgaria would alleviate the situation. As a Black Sea power Russia was entitled to such security and believed that she would be able to come to an understanding with Turkey in regard thereto.

The Führer replied that this would conform approximately with Germany's views, according to which only Russian warships might pass freely through the Dardanelles, while the Straits would be closed to all other warships.

Molotov added that Russia wanted to obtain a guarantee against an attack on the Black Sea via the Straits not only on paper but "in reality" and believed that she could reach an agreement with Turkey in regard thereto. In this connection he came back again to the question of the Russian guarantee to Bulgaria and repeated that the internal regime of the country would remain unaffected, whereas on the other hand Russia was prepared to guarantee Bulgaria an outlet to the Aegean Sea. He was again addressing to the Führer—as the one who was to decide on the entire German policy—the question as to what position Germany would take with regard to this Russian guarantee.

The Führer replied with a counter-question as to whether the Bulgarians had actually asked for a guarantee, and he again stated that he would have to ask the Duce for his opinion.

Molotov stressed that he was not asking the Führer for a final decision, but that he was asking only for a provisional expression of opinion.

The Führer replied that he could not under any circumstances take a position before he had talked with the Duce, since Germany was interested in the matter only secondarily. As a great Danubian power, she was interested only in the Danube River, but not in the passage into the Black Sea. For if she were perchance looking for sources of friction with Russia, she would not need the Straits for that.

The talk then turned again to the great plans for collaboration between the powers interested in the British Empire's bankrupt estate. The Führer pointed out that he was not, of course, absolutely sure whether these plans could be carried out. In case it was not possible, a great historical opportunity would be missed, at any rate. All these questions would perhaps have to be examined again in Moscow by the Foreign Ministers of Germany, Italy, and Japan together with Herr Molotov, after they had been appropriately prepared through diplomatic channels.

At this point in the conversation the Führer called attention to the late hour and stated that in view of the possibility of English air attacks it would be better to break off the talk now, since the main issues had probably been sufficiently discussed.

Summarizing, he stated that subsequently the possibilities of safeguarding Russia's interests as a Black Sea power would have to be examined further and that in general, Russia's further wishes with regard to her future position in the world would have to be considered.

In a closing remark Molotov stated that a number of important and new questions had been raised for Soviet Russia. The Soviet Union, as a powerful country, could not keep aloof from the great issues in Europe and Asia.

Finally he came to speak of Russo-Japanese relations, which had recently improved. He anticipated that the improvement would continue at a still faster pace and thanked the Reich Government for its efforts in this direction.

Concerning Sino-Japanese relations, it was certainly the task of Russia and Germany to attend to their settlement. But an honorable solution would have to be assured for China, all the more since Japan now stood a chance of getting "Indonesia."

SCHMIDT

BERLIN, November 15, 1940.

Frames 136-153, serial F 18

Memorandum of the Final Conversation Between Reich Foreign Minister von Ribbentrop and the Chairman of the Council of People's Commissars of the U.S.S.R. and People's Commissar for Foreign Affairs, Herr Molotov, on November 13, 1940

SECRET

RM 42/40

Duration of conversation: 9:45 p. m. until 12 midnight.

Because of the air raid alert that had been ordered, Reich Minister for Foreign Affairs von Ribbentrop and Herr Molotov went into the Reich Foreign Minister's air raid shelter after the supper at the Embassy of the U.S.S.R. at 9:40 p. m. on November 13, 1940, in order to conduct the final conversation.

The Reich Foreign Minister opened the conversation with the statement that he wanted to take the opportunity to supplement and give more specific form to what had been discussed thus far. He wanted to explain to Herr Molotov his conception of the possibility of establishing a joint policy of collaboration between Germany and the Soviet Union for the future and to enumerate the points which he had in mind in this connection. He had to stress explicitly, however, that this was merely a matter of ideas which were still rather rough, but which might perhaps be realized at some time in the future. By and large, it was a matter of achieving future collaboration between the countries of the Tripartite Pact—Germany, Italy, and Japan—and the Soviet Union, and he believed that first a way must be found to define in bold outlines the spheres of influence of these four countries and to reach an understanding on the problem of Turkey. From the very beginning it was clear in this connection that the problem of the delimitation of the spheres of influence concerned all four countries, whereas only the Soviet Union, Turkey, Italy, and Germany were interested in the settlement of the Straits question. He conceived the future developments as follows: Herr Molotov would discuss with Herr Stalin the issues raised in Berlin; then, by means of further conversations, an agreement could be reached between the Soviet Union and Germany; thereupon the Reich Foreign Minister would approach Italy and Japan in order to find out how their interests with respect to the delimitation of spheres of influence could be reduced to a common formula. He had already approached Italy as to Turkey. The further *modus procedendi* between Italy, the Soviet Union, and Germany would be to exert influence upon Turkey in the spirit of the wishes of the three countries. If they succeeded in reducing the interests of the four countries concerned to a common denominator—which, given good will, was entirely possible—it would undoubtedly work to the advantage of all concerned. The next step would consist in attempting to record both sets of issues in confidential documents. If the Soviet Union entertained a similar view, that is, would be willing to work against the extension, and for the early termination of the war (the Reich Foreign Minister believed that Herr Molotov had indicated his willingness in the previous discussions), he had in mind as the ultimate objective an agreement for collaboration between the countries of the Tripartite Pact and the Soviet Union. He had drafted the contents of this agreement in outline form and he would like to inform Herr Molotov of them today, stressing in advance that he had not discussed these issues so concretely either with Japan or with Italy. He considered it necessary that Germany and the Soviet Union settle the issues first. This was not by any means a matter of a German proposal, but—as already mentioned—one of still rather rough ideas, which would have to be deliberated by both parties and discussed between Molotov and Stalin. It would be advisable to pursue the matter further, particularly in diplomatic negotiations with Italy and Japan, only if the question had been settled as between Germany and the Soviet Union.

Then the Reich Foreign Minister informed Herr Molotov of the contents of the agreement outlined by him in the following words:

The Governments of the states of the Three Power Pact, Germany, Italy, and Japan, on the one side, and the Government of the U. S. S. R. on the other side, motivated by the desire to establish in their natural boundaries an order serving the welfare of all peoples concerned and to create a firm and enduring foundation for their common labors toward this goal, have agreed upon the following:

ARTICLE 1

In the Three Power Pact of September 27, 1940, Germany, Italy, and Japan agreed to oppose the extension of the war into a world conflict with all possible means and to collaborate toward an early restoration of world peace. They expressed their willingness to extend their collaboration to nations in other parts of the world which are inclined to direct their efforts along the same course as theirs. The Soviet Union declares that it concurs in these aims and is on its part determined to cooperate politically in this course with the Three Powers.

ARTICLE 2

Germany, Italy, Japan, and the Soviet Union undertake to respect each other's natural spheres of influence. In so far as these spheres of influence come into contact with each other, they will constantly consult each other in an amicable way with regard to the problems arising therefrom.

ARTICLE 3

Germany, Italy, Japan, and the Soviet Union undertake to join no combination of powers and to support no combination of powers which is directed against one of the Four Powers.

The Four Powers will assist each other in economic matters in every way and will supplement and extend the agreements existing among themselves.

The Reich Foreign Minister added that this agreement was intended for a period of ten years, with the provision that the Governments of the Four Powers, before the expiration of this term, were to reach an understanding regarding the matter of an extension of the agreement.

The agreement itself would be announced to the public. Beyond that, with reference to the above-mentioned agreement, a confidential (secret) agreement could be concluded—in a form still to be determined—establishing the focal points in the territorial aspirations of the Four Countries.

As to Germany, apart from the territorial revisions to be made in Europe at the conclusion of the peace, her territorial aspirations centered in the Central African region.

The territorial aspirations of Italy, apart from the European territorial revisions to be made at the conclusion of the peace, centered in North and Northeast Africa.

The aspirations of Japan would still have to be clarified through diplomatic channels. Here too, a delimitation could easily be found, possibly by fixing a line which would run south of the Japanese home islands and Manchukuo.

The focal points in the territorial aspirations of the Soviet Union would presumably be centered south of the territory of the Soviet Union in the direction of the Indian Ocean.

Such a confidential agreement could be supplemented by the statement that the Four Powers concerned, except for the settlement of individual issues, would respect each other's territorial aspirations and would not oppose their realization.

The above-mentioned agreements could be supplemented by a second secret protocol, to be concluded between Germany, Italy, and the Soviet Union. This second secret protocol could perhaps read that Germany, Italy, and the Soviet Union, on the occasion of the signing of the agreement between Germany, Italy, Japan, and the Soviet Union, were agreed that it was in their common interest to release Turkey from her previous ties and win her progressively to a political collaboration with them.

They declare that they would pursue this aim in close contact with each other, in accordance with a procedure to be established.

Germany, Italy, and the Soviet Union would jointly exert their influence to the end that the Straits Convention of Montreux, presently in force, would be replaced by another convention which would accord to the Soviet Union the unrestricted right of passage through the Straits for her warships at any time, whereas all other powers except the other Black Sea countries, but including Germany and Italy, would renounce in principle the right of passage through the Straits for their warships. Transit through the Straits for merchant ships would, of course, have to remain free in principle.

In this connection, the Reich Foreign Minister stated as follows:

The German Government would welcome it if the Soviet Union were prepared for such collaboration with Italy, Japan, and Germany. This matter was to be clarified in the near future by the German Ambassador in Moscow, Count von der Schulenburg, and the Soviet Ambassador in Berlin. In conformity with the statement contained in Herr Stalin's letter, that he was not adverse to a fundamental examination of the question, which had been confirmed by Herr Molotov during his stay in Berlin, a conference of the Foreign Ministers of Germany, Italy, and Japan for the purpose of signing such an agreement might be envisaged as the ultimate goal. He, the Reich Foreign Minister, was of course aware that such questions required careful examination; he did not, therefore, expect any answer from Herr Molotov today, but he was happy to have had the opportunity to inform Herr Molotov in this slightly more concrete form of the thoughts that had recently been motivating Germany. Furthermore, he wished to tell Herr Molotov the following:

As Herr Molotov knew, he (the Reich Foreign Minister) had always shown a particular interest in the relations between Japan and the Soviet Union. He would appreciate it if Herr Molotov could say what the state of these relations was at the present time. As far as the German Government was informed, Japan was anxious to conclude a nonaggression treaty. It was not his intention to interfere in matters which did not directly concern him, but he believed that it would be useful if this question were also discussed between him and Molotov. If a mediating influence on the part of Germany were desired, he would be glad to undertake this office. To be sure, he still clearly recalled Herr Stalin's remark, when Herr Stalin said that he knew the Asiatics better than Herr von Ribbentrop did. Nevertheless, he wished to mention that the willingness of the Japanese Government to come to a broad understanding with the Soviet Union was known to him. He also had the impression that if the nonaggression pact materialized the Japanese would be prepared to settle all other issues in a generous manner. He wished to stress explicitly that Japan had not asked the German Government to mediate. He, the Reich Foreign Minister, was, however, informed of the state of affairs, and he knew that, in case of the conclusion of a nonaggression pact, Japan would be willing to recognize the Russian spheres of influence in Outer Mongolia and Sinkiang, provided an understanding with China were reached. An agreement could also be reached on possible Soviet aspirations in the direction of British India, if an understanding were reached between the Soviet Union and the Tripartite Pact. The Japanese Government was disposed to meet the Soviet wishes half-way in regard to the oil and coal concessions on Sakhalin Island, but it would first have to overcome resistance at home. This would be easier for the Japanese Government if a nonaggression pact were first concluded with the Soviet Union. Thereafter, the possibility would undoubtedly arise for an understanding on all other points also.

The Reich Foreign Minister concluded by requesting Herr Molotov to inform him of his views on the issues presented by him.

Herr Molotov replied that, concerning Japan, he had the hope and conviction that they would now make more progress on the road to understanding than had previously been the case. Relations with Japan had always been fraught with difficulties and reverses. Nevertheless, there now seemed to be prospects of an understanding. The Japanese Government had suggested the conclusion of a nonaggression treaty to the Soviet Government—in fact, even before the change of government in Japan—in which connection the Soviet Government had put a number of questions to the Japanese Government. At present, the answer to these questions had not yet been received. Only when it arrived could negotiations be entered into—negotiations which could not be separated from the remaining complex of questions. The solution of the problem would therefore require some time.

As for Turkey, the Soviet Union assumed that they would have to reach an understanding with Turkey on the Straits question first of all. Germany and the Soviet Union were agreed that the Convention of Montreux was worthless. For the Soviet Union, as the most important Black Sea power, it was a matter of obtaining effective guarantees of her security. In the course of her history, Russia had often been attacked by way of the Straits. Consequently paper agreements would not suffice for the Soviet Union; rather, she would have to insist on effective guarantees of her security. Therefore, this question had to be examined and discussed more concretely. The questions which interested the Soviet Union in the Near East, concerned not only Turkey, but Bulgaria, for instance, about which he, Molotov, had spoken in detail in his previous conversation with the Führer. But the fate of Rumania and Hungary was also of interest to the Soviet Union and could not be immaterial to her under any circumstances. It would further interest the Soviet Government to learn what the Axis contemplated with regard to Yugoslavia and Greece, and, likewise, what Germany intended with regard to Poland. He recalled the fact that, regarding the future form of Poland, a Protocol existed between the Soviet Union and Germany for the implementation of which an exchange of opinion was necessary. He asked whether from the German viewpoint this Protocol was still in force. The Soviet Government was also interested in the question of Swedish neutrality, and he wanted to know whether the German Government still took the stand that the preservation of Swedish neutrality was in the interest of the Soviet Union and Germany. Besides, there existed the question of the passages out of the Baltic Sea (Store Belt, Lille Belt, Oeresund, Kattegat, Skagerrak). The Soviet Government believed that discussions must be held regarding this question similar to those now being conducted concerning the Danube Commissions. As to the Finnish question, it was sufficiently clarified during his previous conversations with the Führer. He would appreciate it if the Reich Foreign Minister would comment on the foregoing questions, because this would facilitate the clarification of all other questions which Herr von Ribbentrop had previously raised.

In his answer the Reich Foreign Minister stated that he had no comment to make on the Bulgarian question, other than what the Führer had already told Herr Molotov; that, first, it would have to be determined whether Bulgaria desired a guarantee at all from the Soviet Union, and that, moreover, the German Government could not take a stand on this question without previously consulting Italy. On all other questions he felt he had been "queried too closely" ["*überfragt*"], by Herr Molotov. As to the preservation of Sweden's neutrality, we were just as much interested in it as the Soviet Union. As to the passages out of the Baltic Sea, the Baltic Sea was at present an inland sea, where we were interested in the maintenance of the free movement of shipping. Outside of the Baltic Sea, however, there was war. The time was not yet ripe for discussing the new order of things in Poland. The Balkan issue had already been discussed extensively in the conversations. In the Balkans we had solely an economic interest, and we did not want England to disturb us there. The granting of the German guarantee to Rumania had apparently been misconstrued by Moscow. He wanted to repeat again, therefore, that at that time it was a matter of averting a clash between Hungary and Rumania through quick action. If he, the Reich Foreign Minister, had not intervened at that time, Hungary would have marched against Rumania. On the other hand, Rumania could not have been induced to cede so much territory, if the Rumanian Government had not been strengthened by the territorial guarantee. In all its decisions, the German Government was guided solely by the endeavor to preserve peace in the Balkans and to prevent England from gaining a foothold there and from interfering with supplies to Germany. Thus our action in the Balkans was motivated exclusively by the circumstances of our war against England. As soon as England conceded her defeat and asked for peace, German interests in the Balkans would be confined exclusively to the economic field, and German troops would be withdrawn from Rumania. Germany had—as the Führer had repeatedly declared—no territorial interests in the Balkans. He could only repeat again and again that the decisive question was whether the Soviet Union was prepared and in a position to cooperate with us in the great liquidation of the British Empire. On all other questions we would easily reach an understanding if we could succeed in extending our relations and in defining the spheres of influence. Where the spheres of influence lay had been stated repeatedly. It was therefore—as the Führer had so clearly put it—a matter of the interests of the Soviet Union and Germany requiring that the partners stand not breast to breast but back to back, in order to support each other in the achievement of their aspirations. He would appreciate it if Herr Molotov would comment on this matter. Compared to the great basic issues, all others were completely insignificant and would be settled automatically as soon as an over-all understanding was reached. In conclusion, he wished to remind Herr Molotov that the latter owed him an answer to the question of whether the Soviet Union was in principle sympathetic to the idea of obtaining an outlet to the Indian Ocean.

In his reply Molotov stated that the Germans were assuming that the war against England had already actually been won. If, therefore, as had been said in another connection, Germany was waging a life and death struggle against England, he could only construe this as meaning that Germany was fighting "for life" and England "for death." As to the question of collaboration, he quite approved of it, but he added that they had to come to a thorough understanding. This idea had also been expressed in Stalin's letter. A delimitation of the spheres of influence must also be sought. On this point, however, he (Molotov) could not take a definitive stand at this time, since he did not know the opinion of Stalin and of his other friends in Moscow in the matter. However, he had to state that all these great issues of tomorrow could not be separated from the issues of today and the fulfillment of existing agreements. The things that were started must first be completed before they proceeded to new tasks. The conversations which he—Molotov—had had in Berlin had undoubtedly been very useful, and he considered it appropriate that the questions raised should now be further dealt with through diplomatic channels by way of the ambassadors on either side.

Thereupon Herr Molotov cordially bade farewell to the Reich Foreign Minister, stressing that he did not regret the air raid alarm, because he owed to it such an exhaustive conversation with the Reich Foreign Minister.

HILGER

Moscow, November 18, 1940.

Frames 177500–177501, serial 273

The State Secretary in the German Foreign Office (Weizsäcker) to All German Diplomatic Missions and the Offices in Paris and Brussels

[Circular telegram]

Multex 425   BERLIN, November 15, 1940.

The conversations between the German and the Soviet-Russian Governments on the occasion of the presence of Molotov in Berlin were conducted on the basis of the treaties concluded last year and resulted in complete agreement regarding the firm determination of both countries to continue in the future the policy inaugurated by these treaties. Beyond that, they served the purpose of coordinating the policy of the Soviet Union with the policy of the Tripartite Pact. As already expressed in the final communiqué regarding the visit of Molotov, this exchange of views took place in an atmosphere of mutual confidence and resulted in agreement by both sides on all important questions of interest to Germany and the Soviet Union. This result clearly proves that all conjectures regarding alleged German-Russian conflicts are in the realm of fantasy and that all speculations of the foe as to a disturbance in the German-Russian relationship of trust and friendship are based on self-deception.

This is particularly stressed by the friendly visit of Molotov in Berlin. [This sentence added in Ribbentrop's handwriting.]

Same text to all missions.

Please acknowledge receipt.

WEIZSÄCKER

Frames 183883–183889, serial 292

Draft [3]

AGREEMENT BETWEEN THE STATES OF THE THREE POWER PACT, GERMANY, ITALY, AND JAPAN, ON THE ONE SIDE, AND THE SOVIET UNION ON THE OTHER SIDE

The Governments of the states of the Three Power Pact, Germany, Italy and Japan, on the one side,
                                       and
the Government of the U. S. S. R. on the other side,
motivated by the desire to establish in their natural spheres of influ-

---

[3] This draft was found in the secret files of the German Embassy in Moscow. It bears no date; apparently it formed the basis for Schulenburg's conversation with Molotov reported on November 26, 1940.

ence in Europe, Asia, and Africa a new order serving the welfare of all peoples concerned and to create a firm and enduring foundation for their common labors toward this goal, have agreed upon the following:

ARTICLE I

In the Three Power Pact of Berlin, of September 27, 1940, Germany, Italy, and Japan agreed to oppose the extension of the war into a world conflict with all possible means and to collaborate toward an early restoration of world peace. They expressed their willingness to extend their collaboration to nations in other parts of the world which are inclined to direct their efforts along the same course as theirs. The Soviet Union declares that it concurs in these aims of the Three Power Pact and is on its part determined to cooperate politically in this course with the Three Powers.

ARTICLE II

Germany, Italy, Japan, and the Soviet Union undertake to respect each other's natural spheres of influence. In so far as these spheres of interest come into contact with each other, they will constantly consult each other in an amicable way with regard to the problems arising therefrom.

Germany, Italy, and Japan declare on their part that they recognize the present extent of the possessions of the Soviet Union and will respect it.

ARTICLE III

Germany, Italy, Japan, and the Soviet Union undertake to join no combination of powers and to support no combination of powers which is directed against one of the Four Powers.

The Four Powers will assist each other in economic matters in every way and will supplement and extend the agreements existing among themselves.

ARTICLE IV

This agreement shall take effect upon signature and shall continue for a period of ten years. The Governments of the Four Powers shall consult each other in due time, before the expiration of that period, regarding the extension of the agreement.

Done in four originals, in the German, Italian, Japanese, and Russian languages.

Moscow,   1940.

Draft

SECRET PROTOCOL NO. 1

Upon the signing today of the Agreement concluded among them, the Representatives of Germany, Italy, Japan and the Soviet Union declare as follows:

1) Germany declares that, apart from the territorial revisions in Europe to be carried out at the conclusion of peace, her territorial aspirations center in the territories of Central Africa.

2) Italy declares that, apart from the territorial revisions in Europe to be carried out at the conclusion of peace, her territorial aspirations center in the territories of Northern and Northeastern Africa.

3) Japan declares that her territorial aspirations center in the area of Eastern Asia to the south of the Island Empire of Japan.

4) The Soviet Union declares that its territorial aspirations center south of the national territory of the Soviet Union in the direction of the Indian Ocean.

The Four Powers declare that, reserving the settlement of specific questions, they will mutually respect these territorial aspirations and will not oppose their achievement.

Moscow, on

Draft

SECRET PROTOCOL NO. 2 TO BE CONCLUDED AMONG GERMANY, ITALY, AND THE SOVIET UNION

On the occasion of the signing today of the Agreement among Germany, Italy, Japan, and the Soviet Union, the Representatives of Germany, Italy and the Soviet Union declare as follows:

1) Germany, Italy, and the Soviet Union agree in the view that it is in their common interest to detach Turkey from her existing international commitments and progressively to win her over to political collaboration with themselves. They declare that they will pursue this aim in close consultation, in accordance with a common line of action which is still to be determined.

2) Germany, Italy, and the Soviet Union declare their agreement to conclude, at a given time, a joint agreement with Turkey, wherein the Three Powers would recognize the extent of Turkey's possessions.

3) Germany, Italy, and the Soviet Union will work in common toward the replacement of the Montreux Straits Convention now in

force by another convention. By this convention the Soviet Union would be granted the right of unrestricted passage of its navy through the Straits at any time, whereas all other Powers except the other Black Sea countries, but including Germany and Italy, would in principle renounce the right of passage through the Straits for their naval vessels. The passage of commercial vessels through the Straits would, of course, have to remain free in principle.

Moscow,   1940.

Frames 112669–112670, serial 104

The German Ambassador in the Soviet Union (Schulenburg) to the German Foreign Office

Telegram

VERY URGENT   Moscow, November 26, 1940—5 : 34 a. m.
STRICTLY SECRET   Received November 26, 1940—8 : 50 a. m.
No. 2362 of November 25

For the Reich Minister in person.

Molotov asked me to call on him this evening and in the presence of Dekanosov stated the following:

The Soviet Government has studied the contents of the statements of the Reich Foreign Minister in the concluding conversation on November 13 and takes the following stand:

"The Soviet Government is prepared to accept the draft of the Four Power Pact which the Reich Foreign Minister outlined in the conversation of November 13, regarding political collaboration and reciprocal economic [support⁴] subject to the following conditions:

"1) Provided that the German troops are immediately withdrawn from Finland, which, under the compact of 1939, belongs to the Soviet Union's sphere of influence. At the same time the Soviet Union undertakes to ensure peaceful relations with Finland and to protect German economic interests in Finland (export of lumber and nickel).

"2) Provided that within the next few months the security of the Soviet Union in the Straits is assured by the conclusion of a mutual assistance pact between the Soviet Union and Bulgaria, which geographically is situated inside the security zone of the Black Sea boundaries of the Soviet Union, and by the establishment of a base for land and naval forces of the U.S.S.R. within range of the Bosporus and the Dardanelles by means of a long-term lease.

---

⁴ "*Unterstützung*" in Moscow Embassy draft; garbled in text as received in Berlin.

"3) Provided that the area south of Batum and Baku in the general direction of the Persian Gulf is recognized as the center of the aspirations of the Soviet Union.

"4) Provided that Japan [renounces [5]] her rights to concessions for coal and oil in Northern Sakhalin.

"In accordance with the foregoing, the draft of the protocol concerning the delimitation of the spheres of influence as outlined by the Reich Foreign Minister would have to be amended so as to stipulate the focal point of the aspirations of the Soviet Union south of Batum and Baku in the general direction of the Persian Gulf.

"Likewise, the draft of the protocol or agreement between Germany, Italy, and the Soviet Union with respect to Turkey should be amended so as to guarantee a base for light naval and land forces of the U.S.S.R. on [am] the Bosporus and the Dardanelles by means of a long-term lease, including—in case Turkey declares herself willing to join the Four Power Pact—a guarantee of the independence and of the territory of Turkey by the three countries named.

"This protocol should provide that in case Turkey refuses to join the Four Powers, Germany, Italy, and the Soviet Union agree to work out and to carry through the required military and diplomatic measures, and a separate agreement to this effect should be concluded.

"Furthermore there should be agreement upon:

"*a*) a third secret protocol between Germany and the Soviet Union concerning Finland (see Point 1 above).

"*b*) a fourth secret protocol between Japan and the Soviet Union concerning the renunciation by Japan of the oil and coal concession in Northern Sakhalin (in return for an adequate compensation).

"*c*) a fifth secret protocol between Germany, the Soviet Union, and Italy, recognizing that Bulgaria is geographically located inside the security zone of the Black Sea boundaries of the Soviet Union and that it is therefore a political necessity that a mutual assistance pact be concluded between the Soviet Union and Bulgaria, which in no way shall affect the internal regime of Bulgaria, her sovereignty or independence."

In conclusion Molotov stated that the Soviet proposal provided for five protocols instead of the two envisaged by the Reich Foreign Minister. He would appreciate a statement of the German view.[6]

SCHULENBURG

[5] "*Verzichtet*" in Moscow Embassy draft; omitted in text as received in Berlin.
[6] The next account of a discussion of the proposed treaty found in the German Foreign Office files appears in Ambassador Schulenburg's telegram to the Foreign Office No. 122 of January 17, 1941, *post*, p. 270.

VII. SOVIET RESISTANCE TO THE GERMAN ADVANCE IN THE BALKANS, DECEMBER 18, 1940–MARCH 13, 1941

Führer's Directive [7]

THE FÜHRER AND COMMANDER-IN-CHIEF
OF THE GERMAN ARMED FORCES

OKW/WFSt/Abt. L (I) Nr. 33 408/40 g K CHEFS.
MILITARY SECRET [*Geheime Kommandosache*]

TOP SECRET [*Chef Sache*]　　　　　　FÜHRER'S HEADQUARTERS,
BY OFFICER ONLY　　　　　　　　　　December 18, 1940

DIRECTIVE No. 21
OPERATION BARBAROSSA

The German Armed Forces must be prepared *to crush Soviet Russia in a quick campaign* (Operation Barbarossa) even before the conclusion of the war against England.

For this purpose the *Army* will have to employ all available units, with the reservation that the occupied territories must be secured against surprise attacks.

For the *Air Force* it will be a matter of releasing such strong forces for the eastern campaign in support of the Army that a quick completion of the ground operations may be expected and that damage to Eastern German territory by enemy air attacks will be as slight as possible. This concentration of the main effort in the East is limited by the requirement that the entire combat and armament area dominated by us must remain adequately protected against enemy air attacks and that the offensive operations against England, particularly her supply lines, must not be permitted to break down.

The main effort of the *Navy* will remain unequivocally directed against *England* even during an eastern campaign.

I shall order the *concentration* against Soviet Russia possibly eight weeks before the intended beginning of operations.

---

[7] This document is from the German Wehrmacht archives. It is the only document in this collection derived from a source other than the German Foreign Office archives.

Preparations requiring more time to start are to be started now—if this has not yet been done—and are to be completed by May 15, 1941.

It is to be considered of decisive importance, however, that the intention to attack is not discovered.

The preparations of the High Commands are to be made on the following basis:

I. *General Purpose:*

The mass of the Russian *Army* in Western Russia is to be destroyed in daring operations, by driving forward deep armored wedges, and the retreat of units capable of combat into the vastness of Russian territory is to be prevented.

In quick pursuit a line is then to be reached from which the Russian Air Force will no longer be able to attack German Reich territory. The ultimate objective of the operation is to establish a defense line against Asiatic Russia from a line running approximately from the Volga River to Archangel. Then, in case of necessity, the last industrial area left to Russia in the Urals can be eliminated by the Luftwaffe.

In the course of these operations the Russian *Baltic Sea Fleet* will quickly lose its bases and thus will no longer be able to fight.

Effective intervention by the Russian *Air Force* is to be prevented by powerful blows at the very beginning of the operation.

II. *Probable Allies and their Tasks:*

1. On the flanks of our operation we can count on the active participation of *Rumania* and *Finland* in the war against Soviet Russia.

The High Command will in due time concert and determine in what form the armed forces of the two countries will be placed under German command at the time of their intervention.

2. It will be the task of *Rumania*, together with the forces concentrating there, to pin down the enemy facing her and, in addition, to render auxiliary services in the rear area.

3. *Finland* will cover the concentration of the redeployed German *North Group* (parts of the XXI Group) coming from Norway and will operate jointly with it. Besides, Finland will be assigned the task of eliminating Hangö.

4. It may be expected that *Swedish* railroads and highways will be available for the concentration of the German North Group, from the start of operations at the latest.

III. *Direction of Operations:*

A. *Army* (hereby approving the plans presented to me):

In the zone of operations divided by the Pripet Marshes into a southern and northern sector, the main effort will be made *north* of this area. Two Army Groups will be provided here.

The southern group of these two Army Groups—the center of the entire front—will be given the task of annihilating the forces of the enemy in White Russia by advancing from the region around and north of Warsaw with especially strong armored and motorized units. The possibility of switching strong mobile units to the North must thereby be created in order, in cooperation with the Northern Army Group operating from East Prussia in the general direction of Leningrad, to annihilate the enemy forces fighting in the Baltic. Only after having accomplished this most important task, which must be followed by the occupation of Leningrad and Kronstadt, are the offensive operations aimed at the occupation of the important traffic and armament center of Moscow to be pursued.

Only a surprisingly fast collapse of Russian resistance could justify aiming at both objectives simultaneously.

The most important assignment of the XXI Group, even during the eastern operations, will still be the protection of Norway. The additional forces available are to be employed in the north (mountain corps), first to secure the Petsamo Region and its ore mines as well as the Arctic Ocean route, and then to advance jointly with Finnish forces against the Murmansk railroad and stop the supply of the Murmansk region by land.

Whether such an operation with *rather strong* German forces (two or three divisions) can be conducted from the area of and south of Rovaniemi depends upon Sweden's willingness to make the railroads available for such a concentration.

The main body of the Finnish Army will be assigned the task, in coordination with the advance of the German northern flank, of pinning down strong Russian forces by attacking west of or on both sides of Lake Ladoga and of seizing Hangö.

The Army Group employed south of the Pripet Marshes is to make its main effort in the area from Lublin in the general direction of Kiev, in order to penetrate quickly with strong armored units into the deep flank and rear of the Russian forces and then to roll them up along the Dnieper River.

The German-Rumanian groups on the right flank are assigned the task of:

(*a*) protecting Rumanian territory and thereby the southern flank of the entire operation.

(*b*) pinning down the opposing enemy forces while Army Group South is attacking on its northern flank and, according to the progressive development of the situation and in conjunction with the Air Force, preventing their orderly retreat across the Dniester during the pursuit,

[and,] *in the North*, of reaching Moscow quickly.

The capture of this city means a decisive success politically and economically and, beyond that, the elimination of the most important railway center.

B. *Air Force:*

Its task will be to paralyze and to eliminate as far as possible the intervention of the Russian Air Force as well as to support the Army at its main points of effort, particularly those of Army Group Center and, on the flank, those of Army Group South. The Russian railroads, in the order of their importance for the operations, will be cut or the most important near-by objectives (river crossings) seized by the bold employment of parachute and airborne troops.

In order to concentrate all forces against the enemy Air Force and to give immediate support to the Army the armament industry will not be attacked during the main operations. Only after the completion of the mobile operations may such attacks be considered—primarily against the Ural Region.

C. *Navy:*

The Navy's role against Soviet Russia is, while safeguarding our own coast, to prevent an escape of enemy naval units from the Baltic Sea. As the Russian Baltic Sea Fleet, once we have reached Leningrad, will be deprived of its last base and will then be in a hopeless situation, any larger naval operations are to be avoided before that time.

After the elimination of the Russian Fleet it will be a question of protecting all the traffic in the Baltic Sea, including the supply by sea of the northern flank of the Army (mine clearance!).

IV. All orders to be issued by the commanders-in-chief on the basis of this directive must clearly indicate that they are *precautionary measures* for the possibility that Russia should change her present attitude toward us. The number of officers to be assigned to the preparatory work at an early date is to be kept as small as possible;

additional personnel should be briefed as late as possible and only to the extent required for the activity of each individual. Otherwise, through the discovery of our preparations—the date of their execution has not even been fixed—there is danger that most serious political and military disadvantages may arise.

V. I expect reports from the commanders-in-chief concerning their further plans based on this directive.

The contemplated preparations of all branches of the Armed Forces, including their progress, are to be reported to me through the High Command [*OKW*].

ADOLF HITLER [8]

Frame 112785, serial 104

Memorandum by the State Secretary in the German Foreign Office (Weizsäcker)

St. S. Nr. 925   DECEMBER 31, 1940.

The Finnish Minister, whom I saw today on the occasion of the signing of a treaty, in connection with his New Year's wishes expressed hope for his country. He stated that in his homeland people were now reassured, because they thought they knew that in a future conflict with Russia they would not stand alone.

In my reply I used the formula that the Russian Government certainly realized that Germany did not desire any new unrest in the North.

WEIZSÄCKER

Frames 112944–112945, serial 104

The Reich Foreign Minister to the German Ambassador in the Soviet Union (Schulenburg), the German Ambassador in Turkey (Papen), the German Minister in Yugoslavia (Heeren), and the German Minister in Greece (Erbach-Schönberg)

Telegrams

STATE SECRET   BERLIN, January 7, 1941.
Pol I 1650 gRs
No. 36 to Moscow
No. 12 to Ankara
No. 11 to Belgrade
No. 81 to Athens

----

[8] The document also bears four sets of initials, apparently those of Keitel, Jodl, Warlimont, and one unidentified.

I. For confidential information of the Chief of the Mission and the Military, Naval, and Air Attachés only.

Since early in January the movement of strong German troop formations to Rumania has been going on via Hungary. The movement of troops is being carried on with the full concurrence of the Hungarian and Rumanian Governments. For the time being the troops will be quartered in the south of Rumania.

The troop movements result from the fact that the necessity must be seriously contemplated of ejecting the English completely from all of Greece. German troops have been provided in such strength that they can easily cope with any military task in the Danubian Region and with any eventualities from any side. The military measures being carried out by us are aimed exclusively against British forces getting a foothold in Greece, and not against any Balkan country, including Turkey.

II. As for instructions for conversations, in general, a reserved attitude is to be taken. In case of urgent official inquiries, it is to be pointed out, depending on circumstances, that such inquiries are to be made in Berlin. In so far as conversation cannot be avoided, an opinion in general terms is to be given. In so doing, our having reliable reports regarding larger and larger reinforcements of English troops of all kinds in Greece may be given as a plausible reason, and the Salonika operation of the last World War may be recalled. Concerning the strength of the German troops, maintenance of the present vagueness is desired for the time being. Later on we shall presumably be interested in making known the full strength of the troops and, beyond that, in stimulating exaggeration. The cue for that will be given at the proper time.

This instruction also applies, by agreement with the High Command, to the Military, Naval, and Air Attachés. Strict reserve in answering inquiries is to be imposed upon the other members of the mission.

III. Should occasion arise, please report by wire concerning the attitude of the Government, the public and the press, any inquiries by the Government there, and any *démarches* of foreign missions with the Government there.

Reich Foreign Minister

Frame 112945, serial 104

The Reich Foreign Minister to the German Ambassador in Japan (*Ott*)

Telegram

Pol. I 1650 g Rs   BERLIN, January 7, 1941.

No. 19. I request that the Japanese Foreign Minister be personally and confidentially informed that at present rather strong German troop contingents are being transferred to Rumania. The movements are carried on with the full concurrence of the Hungarian and the Rumanian Governments. These troop shipments are being carried out as a security measure for an intervention that may become necessary in Greece if English military forces gain a foothold and necessitate such intervention there.

Reich Foreign Minister

Frame 112942, serial 104

The German Ambassador in the Soviet Union (*Schulenburg*) to the German Foreign Office

Telegram

STRICTLY SECRET   Moscow, January 8, 1941—4:45 p. m.
No. 46 of January 8   Received January 8, 1941—6 p. m.

Reference your telegram of the 7th No. 36.

Numerous rumors are already circulating here concerning the sending of German troops to Rumania; the number of men in the movement is even estimated at 200,000 (two hundred thousand). Government circles here, the radio, and the Soviet press have not yet taken up the matter. Nothing is known concerning *démarches* by foreign missions with the Soviet Government.

The Soviet Government will take the strongest interest in these troop movements and will wish to know what purposes these troop concentrations serve and particularly to what degree Bulgaria and Turkey (Straits) might possibly be affected by them.

Please give me appropriate instructions or perhaps inform Herr Dekanosov there.

SCHULENBURG

Frame 112966, serial 104

The Reich Foreign Minister to the German Ambassador in the Soviet Union (Schulenburg)

Telegram

No. 57   Teletype from Fuschl No. 12 of January 10, 11:45 p. m.

Reference your telegram No. 50 of January 8.°

I request you not to broach the question of increased German troop shipments to Rumania with the Soviet Government. Should you be approached regarding the matter by Herr Molotov or some other influential person in the Soviet Government, please say that according to your information the sending of German troops was exclusively a matter of precautionary military measures against England. The English already had military contingents on Greek soil and it was to be expected that they would further increase those contingents in the immediate future. Germany would not under any circumstances tolerate England's gaining a foothold on Greek soil. Please do not go into greater detail until further notice.

RIBBENTROP

Frames 333–334, serial F 15

Secret Protocol

The German Ambassador, Count von der Schulenburg, Plenipotentiary of the Government of the German Reich, on the one hand, and the Chairman of the Council of People's Commissars of the U.S.S.R., V. M. Molotov, Plenipotentiary of the Government of the U.S.S.R., on the other hand, have agreed upon the following:

1. The Government of the German Reich renounces its claim to the strip of Lithuanian territory which is mentioned in the Secret Supplementary Protocol of September 28, 1939 [10] and which has been marked on the map attached to this Protocol;

2. The Government of the Union of Soviet Socialist Republics is prepared to compensate the Government of the German Reich for the territory mentioned in Point 1 of this Protocol by paying 7,500,000 gold dollars or 31,500,000 Reichsmarks to Germany.

The amount of 31.5 million Reichsmarks will be paid by the Government of the U.S.S.R. in the following manner: one-eighth, that is, 3,937,500 Reichsmarks, in non-ferrous metal deliveries within three months after the signing of this Protocol, the remaining seven-eighths,

° Not printed.
[10] *Ante*, p. 107.

or 27,562,500 Reichsmarks, in gold by deduction from the German gold payments which Germany is to make by February 11, 1941 in accordance with the correspondence exchanged between the Chairman of the German Economic Delegation, Dr. Schnurre, and the People's Commissar for Foreign Trade of the U.S.S.R., Herr A. I. Mikoyan, in connection with the "Agreement of January 10, 1941 concerning reciprocal deliveries in the second treaty period on the basis of the Economic Agreement between the German Reich and the Union of Soviet Socialist Republics of February 11, 1940."

3. This Protocol has been executed in two originals in the German language and two originals in the Russian language and shall become effective immediately upon signature.

Moscow, January 10, 1941.

For the Government of the German Reich:	By authority of the Government of the U.S.S.R.:
SCHULENBURG	V. MOLOTOV
(SEAL)	(SEAL)

Frames 112984–112986, serial 104

The State Secretary in the German Foreign Office (Weizsäcker) to the Reich Foreign Minister

SECRET   BERLIN, January 17, 1941.
St. S. Nr. 52

By wire by fastest means to the
Reich Foreign Minister (teletype or telephone).

The Russian Ambassador called on me this afternoon. On the basis of a memorandum which he handed me later on, he stated the following:

"According to all reports, German troops in great numbers are in Rumania and are now prepared to march into Bulgaria, having as their goal the occupation of Bulgaria, Greece, and the Straits. There can be no doubt that England will try to forestall the operations of German troops, to occupy the Straits, to start military operations against Bulgaria in alliance with Turkey, and turn Bulgaria into a theater of operations. The Soviet Government has stated repeatedly to the German Government that it considers the territory of Bulgaria and of the Straits as the security zone of the U.S.S.R. and that it cannot be indifferent to events which threaten the security interests of the U.S.S.R. In view of all this the Soviet Government regards

it as its duty to give warning that it will consider the appearance of any foreign armed forces on the territory of Bulgaria and of the Straits as a violation of the security interests of the U.S.S.R."
End of the remarks of the Ambassador.

Without taking this statement too seriously before Dekanosov, I replied that I should not like to answer him of my own accord at once, but would prefer first to inform the Reich Foreign Minister of his communication.

I then added that I should like to ask two more questions in order to understand the contents of his communication correctly, namely—

(a) From whom had the Soviet Government received the report that German troops concentrated in Rumania were aiming at the occupation of Bulgaria, Greece, and the Straits? Dekanosov replied that his Government's sources were not known to him. He referred to the fact that—as stated previously—all reports are to this effect, to which I replied—without intending to anticipate a later German statement—that it was correct that under no circumstances would we allow England to gain a foothold in *Greece* and that we were observing this matter closely. Besides, this was certainly nothing new for the Soviet Government, because this had already been stated to Herr Molotov some time ago.

(b) Why did the Soviet Government take it for granted that England, forestalling the operations of the German troops, would attempt to occupy the Straits? In this matter, too, Dekanosov referred only to his original communication. His Government did not know that anything of the sort would occur; however, it had no doubt regarding commensurate English measures if the condition mentioned, namely, the advance of German troops on Bulgaria, Greece, and the Straits, should materialize.

In conclusion, I again reserved the right to a reply to the *démarche*.

After I had made a few more remarks concerning German air successes against the British fleet in the Mediterranean, the Ambassador took his leave, hoping for an early reply.

WEIZSÄCKER

Frames 112981–112982, serial 104

The German Ambassador in the Soviet Union (Schulenburg) to the German Foreign Office

Telegram

VERY URGENT   Moscow, January 17, 1941—8 : 46 p. m.
STRICTLY SECRET   Received January 17, 1941—11 : 40 p. m.
No. 122 of January 17

For the Reich Foreign Minister.

1. Molotov asked me to call on him this afternoon and stated the following:

Since the most important economic questions in the relations between Germany and the Soviet Union had been settled by the recently concluded treaties, it would now be in order to turn to purely political issues again. The Soviet Government was surprised that it had not yet received from Germany any answer to its statement of position of November 25 (cf. telegraphic report No. 2562 [*2362*] of November 25) concerning the issues raised during the Berlin discussions, and he would appreciate it if I would bring that fact to the attention of the Government of the German Reich with the remark that the Soviet Government was counting on an early German reply.

I replied to Herr Molotov that there was not the slightest cause for any surprise, since this was a matter of issues which must first be thoroughly discussed with Italy and Japan. As soon as these deliberations had been concluded the Soviet Government would certainly be informed of our position with regard to their reply.

2. Molotov then touched upon the Balkans and in that connection stated word for word as follows:

According to all reports available here, German troops in great numbers were concentrated in Rumania and ready to march into Bulgaria with the aim of occupying Bulgaria, Greece, and the Straits. There was no doubt that England would try to forestall the operations of the German troops, to occupy the Straits, to open military operations against Bulgaria in alliance with Turkey, and turn Bulgaria into a theater of war. The Soviet Government had repeatedly called the attention of the Government of the German Reich to the fact that it considered the territory of Bulgaria and the Straits as a security zone of the U.S.S.R. and that it could therefore not remain indifferent in the face of events which menaced the security interests of the U.S.S.R. Consequently the Soviet Government regarded it as its duty to call attention to the fact that it would consider the appearance of any foreign armed forces on the territory of Bulgaria and of the Straits as a violation of the security interests of the U.S.S.R.

Molotov added that he had instructed Dekanosov to make an identical *démarche* in Berlin. In my reply I confined myself to the statements prescribed by telegraphic instructions No. 36 of January 7 and No. 57 of January 10.

SCHULENBURG

Frames 112994-112997, serial 104

The Reich Foreign Minister to the State Secretary in the German Foreign Office (Weizsäcker)

Telegram

No. 38   FUSCHL, January 21, 1941—11 : 30 p. m.

Teletype through Office of Reich Foreign Minister to State Secretary von Weizsäcker, No. 31.

1. I request that you ask the Russian Ambassador to call on you Wednesday evening and that you give him in oral form the following reply to the statement made to you on January 17. Thereupon the text of the reply is to be handed to him in the form of a memorandum.

Text of the reply:

1. The Reich Government has not received any reports that England contemplates occupying the Straits. Nor does the Reich Government believe that Turkey will permit English military forces to enter her territory. However, the Reich Government is informed that England intends and is about to gain a foothold on Greek territory.

2. The Führer pointed out repeatedly to Chairman Molotov during his visit to Berlin in November that Germany would prevent by all military means any attempt by England to gain a foothold on Greek soil.

It is the inalterable intention of the Reich Government not under any circumstances to permit English military forces to establish themselves on Greek territory, which would mean a threat to vital interests of Germany in the Balkans. It is therefore carrying out certain troop concentrations in the Balkans, which have the sole purpose of preventing the British from gaining any foothold on Greek soil.

3. Germany does not intend to occupy the Straits. She will respect the territory under Turkish sovereignty unless Turkey on her part commits a hostile act against German troops. On the other hand, however, the German Army will march through Bulgarian territory

should any military operations be carried out against Greece. The Reich Government has, of course, no intention of violating any Soviet Russian security interests nor would this by any means be the case if German troops march through Bulgaria.

4. For the action which may have to be undertaken against England in Greece, Germany is carrying on a troop concentration in the Balkans on such a scale that it will enable her to checkmate any English attempt at building up a front in those regions.

The Reich Government believes that in so doing it is also serving Soviet interests, which would be opposed to England's gaining a foothold in these regions.

5. The Reich Government—as it indicated on the occasion of the Berlin visit of Chairman Molotov—has an understanding of the Soviet interest in the Straits question and is prepared to endorse a revision of the Montreux Convention at the proper time. Germany on her part is politically not interested in the Straits question and will withdraw her troops from there after having carried out her operations in the Balkans.

6. As to the stand requested by Chairman Molotov concerning the question of continuing the political discussion begun some time ago in Berlin, the following may be stated:

The Reich Government still adheres to the ideas explained to Chairman Molotov during his presence in Berlin. The Soviet Government on the other hand made certain counterproposals at the end of November. At the present time the Reich Government is in touch with the Governments of its allies, Italy and Japan, concerning all those issues, and it hopes that after having further clarified the whole problem it will be able to resume the political discussion with the Soviet Government in the near future.

End of the reply.

2. Ambassador Schulenburg is receiving instructions from here to take corresponding action with Herr Molotov on Wednesday evening or Thursday morning.[11]

3. Furthermore, I request that, after the call of the Russian Ambassador, you hand Ambassador Alfieri a copy of the statement given to you by Herr Dekanosov on January 17, as well as a copy of our reply, for the confidential information of the Italian Government. The Duce and Count Ciano have already been informed by me here.

RIBBENTROP

---

[11] By telegram No. 129 of January 22, 1941, not printed, Ambassador Schulenburg was instructed to give an identical reply to Molotov.

Frames 112998–112999, serial 104

*Memorandum by the State Secretary in the German Foreign Office
(Weizsäcker)*

St. S. Nr. 59   BERLIN, January 22, 1941.

I received the Soviet Russian Ambassador late this afternoon and informed him orally of the reply decided upon in answer to his statement of January 17. I then handed him the text of the reply in the form of a memorandum.

I also told Dekanosov that Count Schulenburg would hand a corresponding communication to Herr Molotov either this evening or tomorrow morning.

Dekanosov then inquired—for his own information, he said—about the purport of certain expressions in the reply given to him. He wanted to find out how soon German troops might be expected to march through Bulgaria against Greece—as mentioned therein—as well as whether this decision was to be considered as definite.

I referred the Ambassador in this connection to the text of paragraphs 1 and 3 of the memorandum.

Thereupon the Ambassador repeated from his communication of the 17th instant that the Soviet Government considered the appearance of any foreign military forces on Bulgarian territory as a violation of its security interests. Our statement at the end of paragraph 3 of the memorandum was not in agreement with that view.

I replied that our view was made clear in paragraph 3 and paragraph 4 of the memorandum. We believed that our plans would actually serve Soviet interests, which are opposed to England's gaining a foothold in these regions. Moreover, I asked the Ambassador to go over the memorandum again very carefully at home. He would then surely reach the conclusion that our answer removed his anxiety.

Submitted herewith to the
Reich Foreign Minister (by teletype).

WEIZSÄCKER

Frame 113008, serial 104

The German Ambassador in the Soviet Union (Schulenburg) to the German Foreign Office

Telegram

VERY URGENT   Moscow, January 23, 1941—9:21 p. m.

SECRET   Received January 23 [24], 1941—12:25 a. m.

No. 161 of January 23

Reference your telegram No. 129 of the 22nd.[12]
Instruction carried out today.

Molotov stated that Soviet Government would examine and consider our communication, after which he would take a stand, if necessary. He understood the communication of the Government of the German Reich to mean that the transit of German troops through Bulgaria was in itself a matter that was definitely decided on, but only in the event that England should expand her military operations on Greek soil beyond their present scope.

For the rest, Molotov stated the well-known argument according to which the Soviet Government considered Bulgaria and the Straits as a security zone of the Soviet Union and that it was opposed to any spread of the war, particularly in the Black Sea, wherein it believed itself in agreement with the Government of the German Reich.

SCHULENBURG

Frame 218062, serial 426

The German Foreign Office to the German Ambassador in the Soviet Union (Schulenburg)

Telegram

No. 353 of February 21   BERLIN, February 22, 1941—6:25 a. m.

Received Moscow, February 22, 1941—11 a. m.

Confidential material. For chief of mission or his representative personally. State secret. To be decoded personally. Extremely secret. Reply by courier or secret code.

In Telegraphic Instruction No. 36 of January 7 the statement was made that, for the time being, vagueness with regard to the strength of the German forces was desirable and that at a given time word would be given for publication of the full strength of the troops. That time has now come.

---

[12] Not printed. For contents see footnote 11, *ante*, p. 272.

In Rumania there are 680,000 (six hundred eighty thousand) German troops in readiness. Among these troops there is an unusually high percentage of technical troops with the most up-to-date military equipment, especially armored units. Behind these troops there are inexhaustible reserves in Germany, including the permanent units stationed at the German-Yugoslav border.

I request the members of the mission and any available trusted persons [*Vertrauensleute*] to start, in suitable ways, to let this strength be known in an impressive manner—indicating that it is more than sufficient to meet any eventuality in the Balkans from any side whatsoever—and to do so not only in Government circles there but also in the foreign missions concerned. I leave it to your discretion not always to mention the exact figure given above. On the contrary, innuendo and circumlocution may also be used, as, for example, "almost 700,000," and the like.

RITTER

Frame 218061, serial 426

The State Secretary in the German Foreign Office (Weizsäcker) to the German Ambassador in the Soviet Union (Schulenburg)

Telegram

Multex No. 98 of   BERLIN, February 23, 1941—3 : 10 a. m.
   February 22   Received Moscow, February 23, 1941—9 : 50 a. m.

Confidential material. State Secret. Extremely secret. To be decoded only by official in charge of state secret documents. To be decoded personally. Extremely secret. Reply by courier or secret code.

Recently there have been frequent Greek assurances, intended for German ears, that, except for a number of British planes, there are no British forces in Greece and that the Greek Government has rejected and will reject British offers to send strong British forces to Greece. These assurances are apparently being made according to plan at the direction of the Greek Government directly through Greek diplomats and military attachés and indirectly through foreign governments and military attachés.

Please do not accept such assurances without rejoinder. The answer should be that the Government of the Reich had its own information regarding the numerical strength of the British troops in Greece and regarding the further intentions of the British. British Prime

Minister Churchill himself revealed the intentions of the British when he declared in the House of Commons, in the course of statements on the British military situation in North Africa on December 19, 1940: "Marshal Sir Longmore experienced the most critical moment in his preparations when he saw how big a portion of his military forces was being withdrawn in order to be sent to Greece." The Reich Government attaches more importance to these and other statements of Churchill than to the assurances of Greece, whose purpose it is easy to see through.

Confirm receipt.

WEIZSÄCKER

Frames 113086–113087, serial 104

The Reich Foreign Minister to the German Ambassador in the Soviet Union (Schulenburg)

Telegram

VERY URGENT   FUSCHL, February 27, 1941—9:50 p. m.
                    Received Berlin, February 27, 1941—10:30 p. m.
No. 144 of February 27
Transmitted to Moscow as No. 403, February 27—10:58 p. m.

For the Ambassador personally.

Please go to see Herr Molotov on Friday, February 28, toward evening and communicate to him verbally the following:

1. As the Soviet Government knows, negotiations have for some time been in progress between the Government of the Reich and the Italian Government on the one hand and the Bulgarian Government on the other, regarding the accession of Bulgaria to the Three Power Pact. These negotiations have now been concluded, and it has been agreed that Bulgaria will accede to the Three Power Pact, and the Protocol regarding this accession will be signed on March 1. The Government of the Reich is anxious to inform the Soviet Government of this in advance.

2. I would ask you to go to see Herr Molotov again on March 1, toward evening, and to tell him the following:

Reports in our possession concerning British intentions in Greece have forced the Government of the Reich to take further security measures forthwith, making necessary the shifting of German troops to Bulgarian soil. Referring to the statement made to the Soviet Government on January 23d, please add that this is a precautionary measure taken to prevent the British from gaining a firm foothold in Greece. Should Herr Molotov go into the subject in any further detail, we remind you—for your guidance—that, in the first place, these security measures are taken exclusively to prevent British entrenchment on Greek territory; secondly, that the measures are not directed at Turkey, and that we shall respect Turkish sovereignty unless Turkey commits a hostile act against us; that, thirdly, these German troop concentrations are war measures, and that the elimination of the British danger in Greece will automatically result in the withdrawal of the German troops.

Please inform me by wire how Herr Molotov receives your communications.

For your personal information, you are further informed that the Bulgarian Minister in Moscow will also make similar communications from his Government on February 28th and on March 1.

RIBBENTROP

Frame 113094, serial 104

The German Ambassador in the Soviet Union (Schulenburg) to the German Foreign Office

Telegram

VERY URGENT	Moscow, March 1, 1941—12:25 a. m.
No. 444 of February 28	Received March 1, 1941—2:10 a. m.

In reference to your telegram of the 27th, No. 403.

I called on Herr Molotov this evening and carried out instruction (1).

Molotov received my communication with obvious concern and stated that the German Reich Government had been informed of the viewpoint of the Soviet Government on November 25, 1940 (see telegraphic report of November 25, No. 2562 [*2362*]). The position of the Soviet Government in the matter was still determined by the communication of that date. Then, the future position of Bulgaria was considered within the framework of certain particular circumstances. In the meantime, events had taken a different turn. The view of the Soviet Government, on the other hand, that Bulgaria came within the security zone of the Soviet Union, remained unchanged.

Despite my objections that the accession of Bulgaria was in no way prejudicial to the interests of the Soviet Union, Molotov held to his view, stating that the accession of Bulgaria was taking place under circumstances quite different than had been anticipated, and that it was unfortunately not evident to him that events were unfolding within the framework of the Soviet Government's *démarche* of November 25.

SCHULENBURG

NOTE: Transmitted under No. 744, to special train.
Telegram Control Office March 1, 1941, 2:55 A. M.

Frames 113100–113101, serial 104

The German Ambassador in the Soviet Union (Schulenburg) to the German Foreign Office

Telegram

VERY URGENT   Moscow, March 1, 1941—10:15 p. m.
SECRET   Received March 2, 1941—2:20 a. m.
No. 453 of March 1

Reference your telegram of the 27th, No. 403.

Instruction under (2) carried out at 6:30 p. m., Moscow time, today.

Molotov, who received my communication with great gravity, stated first of all that he was informed regarding the German decision, since the Bulgarian Minister had today already apprised Herr Vishinsky. Molotov thereupon expressed his deep concern that the German Government had, in a matter of such importance to the Soviet Government, made decisions contrary to the Soviet Government's conception of the security interests of the Soviet Union. The Soviet Government had repeatedly stressed its special interest in Bulgaria to the German Government, both during the Berlin conferences and later. Consequently it could not remain indifferent in the face of Germany's last measures in Bulgaria and would have to define its attitude with regard thereto. It hoped that the German Reich Government would attach the proper significance to this attitude. Molotov in my presence drafted in his own hand a rough memorandum setting forth the position of the Soviet Government, had it copied, and handed it to me. The text of the note is as follows:

"1. It is to be regretted that despite the caution contained in the *démarche* of November 25, 1940, on the part of the Soviet Government, the German Reich Government has deemed it possible to take a course that involves injury to the security interests of the U.S.S.R. and has decided to effect the military occupation of Bulgaria.

"2. In view of the fact that the Soviet Government maintains the same basic position as in its *démarche* of November 25, the German Government must understand that it cannot count on support from the U.S.S.R. for its acts in Bulgaria."

In my reply, I confined myself to your instructions, and stressed particularly that there could be no question of an impairment of Soviet security interests.

SCHULENBURG

NOTE: Transmitted to special train under No. 771.
Telegram Control Office March 2, 1941.

Frame 24471, serial 34

Foreign Office Memorandum

STATE SECRET

Pol I M 653 g RS

General Warlimont and Naval Captain Bürkner bring up the point that for certain reasons a speedy termination of the activities of the various Russian Commissions at work on German territory in the east and their immediate despatch home is necessary. Such commissions are still on German territory in connection with the return of Lithuanian emigrants from Germany to Lithuania. The German-Russian boundary commission is also active, as well as several local sub-commissions. Of these sub-commissions some are located on Russian territory and others on German territory (and in fact south of Suwalki?). The work of these sub-commissions was to be completed by March 10th. For some reason, they have not yet begun their work. The OKW requests that everything be done to prevent this work from being begun.

The presence of Russians in this part of Germany can only be permitted up to March 25. In the northern sector strong elements of German troops are already being assembled. From the 20th of March on an even heavier massing will take place.

The question is raised in this connection as to whether the Russian consulate in Königsberg is occupied.

RITTER

BERLIN, March 13, 1941

VIII. THE SOVIET TREATIES WITH YUGOSLAVIA AND JAPAN, MARCH 25–APRIL 13, 1941

Frames 113215–113216, serial 104

The German Ambassador in the Soviet Union (Schulenburg) to the German Foreign Office

Telegram

VERY URGENT   Moscow, March 25, 1941—3 : 05 a. m.
SECRET   Received March 25, 1941—5 : 45 a. m.

No. 680 of March 24

For the Reich Foreign Minister personally.

The Japanese Foreign Minister Matsuoka, who left Moscow for Berlin this evening in accordance with his itinerary, paid a visit to the Commissar for Foreign Affairs Molotov this afternoon, accompanied by the Japanese Ambassador here. In the ensuing conversation, which lasted two hours altogether, I hear that Stalin later also took part at Matsuoka's expressed desire. Matsuoka tells me he presented to Molotov and Stalin the "fundamental problems" pending between Japan and the Soviet Union with the thought of eliminating existing differences. When Molotov and Stalin wished to reply, he asked them to withhold comment at this time, but instead to consider the subjects broached, and to continue the conversation upon his return to Moscow. He had gained a strong impression of the personality of Stalin. He would communicate to the Reich Foreign Minister personally all details of the conversation.

Since the conversation with Molotov and Stalin lasted two hours altogether, the discussion would seem, nevertheless, to have been a thorough one.

Matsuoka explained to me and the Italian Ambassador that he had for thirty years been of the opinion that relations between Japan and the Soviet Union should be good. His further pursuit of this policy, therefore, was nothing new.

Matsuoka with the greatest willingness received the chiefs of the missions here (among them also the American and French Ambassadors, whom he knew from earlier days—but not British Ambassador

Cripps), as well as representatives of the press. In all his talks, Matsuoka expressed himself very positively on Japan's attitude to the Axis, in which connection he emphasized that he had personally striven for the consummation of the Three Power Pact. With regard to his trip, he repeatedly stressed the importance of a personal meeting with Germany's great Führer, the Reich Foreign Minister, and Mussolini. In the most emphatic manner he expressed the conviction that victory was assured to Germany and Italy.

SCHULENBURG

NOTE—Transmitted to special train under No. 1085.
Telegram Control Office March 25, 8 a. m.

Frames 47400–47417, serial 67

Memorandum of the Conversation Between the Reich Foreign Minister and Japanese Foreign Minister Matsuoka in the Presence of Ambassadors Ott and Oshima at Berlin on March 27, 1941

STATE SECRET
Aufz. RAM 14/41

The Reich Foreign Minister welcomed Matsuoka cordially as a man who had shown by word and deed that he took the same attitude with regard to the problems of his country as the Führer and his co-workers had been forced to take for Germany and who, as the responsible Foreign Minister of his country, had made possible the conclusion of the Pact with Japan. The Three Power Pact was a very significant instrument for the future of the three countries and represented the basis upon which the future of the three nations could be secured in a form such as the German and Japanese patriots had always envisaged.

Continuing, the Reich Foreign Minister gave a summary of the situation as seen from the German point of view.

With regard to the military situation he pointed out that Germany today was in the final phase of its battle against England. During the past winter the Führer had made all necessary preparations, so that Germany stood completely ready today to meet England everywhere. The Führer had at his disposal at the moment perhaps the strongest military power that had ever existed in the world. Germany had 240 combat divisions, 186 of which were first-class assault divisions of young soldiers. Of these 24 were Panzer divisions, supplemented by other motorized brigades.

The Luftwaffe had grown greatly and introduced new models, so that it was a match in the future, as it had been in the past, for competition of any kind; that is, Germany was not only a match for England and America in this field, but was definitely superior to them.

The German Navy, at the outbreak of the war, had had only a relatively small number of battleships. Nevertheless, the battleships under construction had been completed, so that the last of them would shortly be put in service. In contrast to the World War, the German Navy this time did not stay in port, but from the first day of the war had been employed against the foe. Matsuoka probably gathered from the reports of the past few weeks that German large battle units had interrupted the supply lines between England and America with extraordinary success.

The number of submarines heretofore employed was very small. There had been at most 8 or 9 boats in service against the enemy at any one time. Nevertheless even these few U-boats, in conjunction with the Luftwaffe, had sunk 750,000 tons per month in January and February, and Germany could furnish accurate proof of this at any time. This number, moreover, did not include the great additional losses that England had sustained through floating and magnetic mines. At the beginning of April the number of submarines would increase eight to tenfold, so that 60 to 80 U-boats could then be continuously employed against the enemy. The Führer had pursued the tactics of at first employing only a few U-boats and using the rest to train the personnel necessary for a larger fleet, in order then to proceed to a knockout blow against the enemy with a greater number of units. Therefore the figure of tonnage sunk by the German U-boats could be expected in the future greatly to exceed what had already been accomplished. Under these circumstances, the U-boat alone could be designated as absolutely deadly.

Passing on to the subject of the military situation on the continent of Europe, the Reich Foreign Minister observed that through the overthrow of the continental countries Germany had practically no foe of any consequence other than the small British forces that remained in Greece. Germany would fight off any attempt of England to land on the Continent or entrench herself there. She would not, therefore, tolerate England's staying in Greece. From the military point of view, the Greek question was of secondary importance. The only practical significance was the fact that in the thrust toward Greece, which would probably be necessary, dominant positions in the Eastern Mediterranean would be won that would be of considerable significance for the development of further operations in these areas.

In Africa the Italians had had bad luck in recent months because the Italian troops there were not familiar with modern tank warfare and were not prepared for antitank defense, so that it was relatively easy for the British armored divisions to capture the not very important Italian positions. Any further advance of the British had been definitively blocked. The Führer had dispatched one of the most able of German officers, General Rommel, to Tripoli with sufficient German forces. The hope that General Wavell would attack had, unfortunately, not been realized. The British had come upon the Germans in some skirmishes at an outpost and had thereupon abandoned any further intention of attacking. Should they by chance attempt another attack upon Tripoli, they would court annihilating defeat. Here, too, the tables would be turned some day, and the British would disappear from North Africa, perhaps even more quickly than they had come.

In the Mediterranean area, the German Luftwaffe had been doing good work for two months and had inflicted heavy shipping losses on the British, who were holding on tenaciously. The Suez Canal had been blocked for a long time and would be blocked again after the removal of the obstacles. It was no longer any fun for the British to hold out in the Mediterranean. He (the Reich Foreign Minister) believed that even before the year's end the Mediterranean would be sealed off so effectively that the English would represent practically no further danger. Their fleet would have to protect their position in Africa.

If, then, we summed up the military situation in Europe, we would come to the conclusion that, practically, in the military sphere the Axis was completely master of the situation in the whole of continental Europe. A huge army, which was practically idle, was at Germany's command and could be employed at any time and at any place the Führer considered necessary.

The political situation was characterized by the adherence of almost the whole of the Balkans to the Three Power Pact. This morning, to be sure, news of a *putsch* and the formation of a new government had come from Belgrade, but further details were lacking. The political situation in Europe and in the whole world had also contributed to the strengthening of the Three Powers of the Pact. Germany was also still endeavoring to win over to the cause of the Three

Powers one or another of the last countries which still remained outside the Pact.   Confidentially he (the Reich Foreign Minister) could inform Matsuoka that Spain, in spirit at least, was with the Three Power Pact.   Of the two or three countries yet remaining, Sweden and Turkey were of particular interest.   He could state confidentially to Matsuoka that here, too, the attempt would be made to win these countries over to the Three Power Pact.

Certain feelers had already been put out in the direction of Turkey. Even if formally that country had an alliance with England, it was nevertheless at least not entirely impossible that Turkey would in the future move closer and closer to the Three Power Pact.

With Russia, Germany had concluded the well-known treaties. Ambassador Oshima knew how these treaties had come about.   Germany, at that time, had the desire to conclude an alliance with Japan.   In view of the situation in Japan, it had not been possible to translate this desire into fact.   On the other hand, the war clouds in Europe had become more and more threatening.   At the Führer's instruction, the Reich Foreign Minister had been prepared for the six months preceding to sign the Italo-Japanese-German alliance. This Ambassador Oshima knew.   Since the alliance was unfortunately not possible in that time, Germany, in view of the coming war, had to resolve on the pact with Russia.

Confidentially, he (the Reich Foreign Minister) could inform Matsuoka that present relations with Russia were correct, to be sure, but not very friendly.   After Molotov's visit, during which accession to the Three Power Pact was offered, Russia had made conditions that were unacceptable.   They involved the sacrifice of German interests in Finland, the granting of bases on the Dardanelles and a strong influence on conditions in the Balkans, particularly in Bulgaria.   The Führer had not concurred because he had been of the opinion that Germany could not permanently subscribe to such a Russian policy.   Germany needed the Balkan Peninsula above all for her own economy and had not been inclined to let it come under Russian domination.   For this reason she had given Rumania a guarantee.   It was this latter action, particularly, that the Russians had taken amiss.   Germany had further been obliged to enter into a closer relationship with Bulgaria in order to obtain a vantage point from which to expel the British from Greece.   Germany had had to decide on this course because this campaign would otherwise not have been possible.   This, too, the Russians had not liked at all.

Under these circumstances, relations with Russia were externally normal and correct. The Russians, however, had for some time demonstrated their unfriendliness to Germany wherever they could. The declaration made to Turkey within the last few days was an example of this. Germany felt plainly that since Sir Stafford Cripps became Ambassador to Moscow (he had recently met Eden at Ankara) ties between Russia and England were being cultivated in secret and, at times, even relatively openly. Germany was watching these proceedings carefully. He (the Reich Foreign Minister), who knew Stalin personally, did not assume that the latter was inclined toward adventure, but it was impossible to be sure. The German armies in the East were prepared at any time. Should Russia some day take a stand that could be interpreted as a threat to Germany, the Führer would crush Russia. Germany was certain that a campaign against Russia would end in the absolute victory of German arms and the total crushing of the Russian Army and the Russian State. The Führer was convinced that, in case of action against the Soviet Union, there would in a few months be no more Great Power of Russia. The Reich Foreign Minister stressed the fact, however, that he did not believe that Stalin would pursue an unwise policy. In any case, the Führer was not counting on the treaties with Russia alone, but was relying, first of all, on his Wehrmacht.

It must also not be overlooked that the Soviet Union, in spite of all protestations to the contrary, was still carrying on communistic propaganda abroad. It was attempting not only in Germany, but also in the occupied areas of France, Holland and Belgium, to continue its misleading propagandist activity. For Germany, this propaganda naturally constituted no danger. But what it had unfortunately led to in other countries, Matsuoka well knew. As an example, the Reich Foreign Minister cited the Baltic States, in which today, one year after the occupation by the Russians, the entire intelligentsia had been wiped out and really terrible conditions prevailed. Germany was on guard, and would never suffer the slightest danger to threaten Germany from Russia.

Further, there was the fact that Germany had to be protected in the rear for her final battle against England. She would, therefore, not put up with any threat from Russia if such a threat should some day be considered serious. Germany wanted to conquer England as rapidly as possible and would not let anything deter her from doing so.

In the further course of the conversation, the Reich Foreign Minister spoke of the economic and food situation. It was possible, to be sure, that certain foodstuffs were temporarily in short supply; but he could state definitely that no matter how long the war lasted, food supply difficulties would not occur in Germany. Germany had space enough to produce the necessary foods in her own territory for the duration of the war.

With regard to raw materials, there were certain bottlenecks, as evidenced, for example, by the rubber negotiations with Japan. Here too, however, it might be stated generally that a serious danger to the Reich was entirely out of the question. The Führer had accumulated such vast stockpiles of war materials that the German economy was due for a conversion. The German munitions stores were so great that for years to come not the slightest shortage would be experienced. In the next few months, therefore, a great process of conversion would take place in the economy, and the effort of the German war potential would be utilized for U-boat and airplane production. Since the German Army had practically no opponents left on the Continent with the possible exception of Russia, a high percentage of German production capacity could be used for these two arms.

In summing up, the Reich Foreign Minister declared that the war had already been definitely won for the Axis. It could, in any case, no longer be lost. It was now only a question of time until England would admit to having lost the war. When this would take place, he could of course not predict. This might be very soon, however, under certain circumstances. It would depend upon events of the next three or four months. It was highly probable, however, that England would capitulate in the course of this year.

Continuing, the Reich Foreign Minister spoke of America. There was no doubt that the British would long since have abandoned the war if Roosevelt had not always given Churchill new hope. Germany had clear and precise information from England to this effect. What Roosevelt's intention was in the long run, it was difficult to say. It was not clear whether he wished to enter the war or not. It was only certain that the aid promised England in the form of American munitions could not be conjured up from the soil. It would be a long time before this help would really be effective. But even then the question of quality would be very problematical, especially in the sphere of airplane deliveries. At the present stage of development the various models became obsolete very rapidly. From month to month, on the basis of daily experience at the front, improvements were being undertaken on German models, and it was doubtful whether a country far from the war could turn out the highest quality aircraft. What the German fliers had thus far encountered in the way of American machines, they described, at any rate, as "junk." He (the Reich Foreign Minister) therefore believed that quite a considerable time would elapse before American aid to England could make any difference. Germany was endeavoring, in any case, to end the war as soon as possible, in the interest also of its allies and friends.

The Three Power Pact had above all had the goal of frightening America into abandoning the course it had chosen and of keeping it out of the war. This goal was entirely clear and desirable. The Three Power Pact was further to serve the purpose of assuring the future collaboration of the treaty partners in the New Order that Germany and Italy wished to establish in Europe, and Japan in East Asia. The principal enemy encountered in the establishment of the New Order was England. The latter was as much the enemy of Japan as of the Axis Powers. America had to be prevented by all possible means from taking an active part in the war and from making its aid to England too effective.

In examining the possibilities that existed for further collaboration between Germany and Japan, the question had repeatedly come up in the talks with the Führer as to whether, in relation to the New Order— that is, the overthrow of England, which was necessary to the establishment of this New Order—active participation in the war on the part of Japan might not be useful. The Führer had carefully considered this question and believed that it would actually be very advantageous if Japan would decide as soon as possible to take an active part in the war upon England. Germany believed, for instance, that a quick attack upon Singapore would be a very decisive factor in the speedy overthrow of England. He (the Reich Foreign Minister) believed that from there it would be possible to work much more closely with Japan in naval and other matters. It was also certain that the capture of Singapore would be a very serious blow to England. This was of great importance, particularly in view of the rather bad morale already prevailing in the British Isles. He also believed that the capture of Singapore would perhaps be most likely to keep America out of the war, because the United States could scarcely risk sending its fleet into Japanese waters. If today, in a war against England, Japan were to succeed with one decisive stroke, such as the attack on Singapore, Roosevelt would be in a very difficult position. It would be difficult for him to take any effective action against Japan. If he did so, nevertheless, and declared war upon Japan, then he must expect that the Philippine question, for example, would be resolved in favor of Japan. This would mean a serious loss of prestige for the President, so that he would probably reflect for a long time before taking any action against Japan.

On the other hand, Japan, through the conquest of Singapore, would be in a position to operate quite differently in East Asia than formerly, since it would then command the absolutely dominant position in that part of East Asia. Germany believed, therefore, that if Japan could decide on such a move it would amount to cutting the Gordian knot in East Asia.

Summing up, the Reich Foreign Minister declared that in case Japan adopted such a course the war upon British tonnage could be waged more intensively in East Asia; America would probably be kept out of the war by Japan's bold step; and Japan could secure those positions in East Asia which, in the German view, she must eventually have for the New Order in Greater East Asia. In this connection a number of other questions would surely arise, for the discussion of which he was available at all times.

In conclusion, the Reich Foreign Minister declared that the Three Power Pact could best accomplish its true purpose—that is, to prevent the extension of the war, or, in other words, the entry of the United States into the war—if at the proper time the treaty partners made joint arrangements for the final defeat of England, over and above what had already been agreed upon. In this way the meaning of the Pact could be most effectively demonstrated by all its adherents.

At this moment the Reich Foreign Minister was summoned to the Reich Chancellery. Contrary to his original assumption that this would mean only a short absence, the discussion there lasted quite a while, so that the conversation with Matsuoka could not be continued before lunch.

Thereupon the lunch which was on the program was held in a very intimate circle, at first without the Reich Foreign Minister, who did not appear until later.

SCHMIDT

BERLIN, March 31, 1941.

Frames 47418–47444, serial 67

Memorandum of the Interview Between the Führer and the Japanese Foreign Minister, Matsuoka, in the Presence of the Reich Foreign Minister and Ambassadors Ott and Oshima, March 27, 1941

Fü/Nr. 13/41

After some words of welcome the Führer inquired how Matsuoka had found the long, tiresome journey from Japan to Germany. Matsuoka replied that he had stood the trip very well, since especially on the journey across Siberia he had been completely cut off from the outer world and had only been able to see from time to time a small Siberian provincial newspaper, in which practically no reports on current events appeared. It had been therefore much like being away on a holiday trip.

Then the Führer gave a review of the general situation. Germany had been forced into the war. She had not, however, been surprised by the war; for she had had the chance to observe for years the campaign of hate carried on by certain English, French and American circles, and was accordingly prepared for anything. In spite of this basic preparation the outbreak of war had not been one of the goals of her policy. Germany had had political claims; she had hoped, however, to be able to satisfy them by reasonable methods. In the year 1939 the previously successful methods of securing a peaceful revision of intolerable conditions had been interrupted by the resistance of Poland and the consequences which arose therefrom.

If a person considered the present situation carefully and without illusions, he would have to concede that when the war began in the year 1939, there were in existence on the side of the opposition 60 Polish, 6 Norwegian, 18 Dutch, 22 Belgian, and 138 French divisions. In addition there were 12 or 13 British divisions on the Continent. Yet in scarcely a year and a half 60 Polish divisions had been eliminated with the occupation of Poland, 6 Norwegian divisions with the occupation of Norway, 18 Dutch divisions with the occupation of Holland, and 22 Belgian divisions with the occupation of Belgium, and of the 138 French divisions there remained only 8 weak brigades. All of the English units had been routed and driven out. These were losses which could not be recouped and the position of England was no longer recoverable. Thus the war had been decided, and the Axis Powers had become the dominant combination. Resistance to their will had become impossible.

As Matsuoka knew, Germany had only at the beginning of the war set out to construct a navy. Nevertheless all of the military operations which had necessitated the use of water routes, especially those in Norway, had been carried out without successful opposition by the British. The German U-boats, as well as the surface craft (auxiliary cruisers and battleships), had, in cooperation with the Luftwaffe, caused England losses which amounted in tonnage almost to three-quarters of the English and Allied losses during the World War. At first Germany had produced few U-boats. By far the greater number of them had therefore been used to train new crews for the numerous units which were being constructed by mass production. The real U-boat warfare was just beginning in the present and coming months. England would be damaged to an extent far surpassing her present rate of losses and would no longer be able to threaten the German coasts and shipping routes in any way. Besides, Germany was tying down an increasing percentage of the English Fleet in the North Sea and in the Atlantic. The same was being done by the Italian Fleet and the German Luftwaffe in the Mediterranean.

In the air Germany had absolute supremacy, in spite of all the claims of the English to success. Matsuoka could test this assertion if he looked about in Berlin and compared present-day Berlin with present-day London. The attacks of the Luftwaffe in the coming months would actually grow much stronger. England would suffer even more severe losses in tonnage; and the effectiveness of the German blockade was demonstrated by the fact that in England, rationing was much more severe than in Germany. In the meantime the war would go on in preparation for the final stroke against England.

The Führer then took up the situation in the Mediterranean and declared that Italy had had bad luck in North Africa because the necessary antitank guns had not been available against the British armored forces. Now the danger had been eliminated with the arrival of the first Panzer division in Tripolitania, which would soon be followed by a second division. A further British advance would be impossible; on the contrary, the Axis would in a short time pass over to a counterattack.

Unfavorable weather conditions had hindered Italian operations in the Balkans. In the next few days, however, the joint advance of Germany and Italy would eliminate all difficulties there. There was no military problem since Germany had at her disposal 240 "unemployed" divisions, of which 186 were first-class combat divisions. The losses in personnel and material which had been suffered in the years

1939 and 1940 were very slight, so that in spite of the campaigns just past, Germany was stronger in every respect than in 1939.

The Führer then spoke of his conviction that England had already lost the war. It was only a matter of having the intelligence to admit it. Then would occur the collapse of the individuals and of the government which had been responsible for the insane policy of England.

In her present critical situation England was looking for any straw to grasp. She was relying principally on two hopes:

First, on American help. Germany, however, had taken such help into her calculations in advance. It could appear in tangible form only in the year 1942 at the earliest, but even then the extent of such help would bear no relation to the increased productive capacity of Germany.

The second hope of England was Russia. Both the British Empire and the United States hoped that in spite of everything they would be able to bring Russia in on the side of England. They believed that they could attain this goal, if not this year, perhaps next, and thus produce a new balance of power in Europe.

In this connection it should be noted that Germany had concluded well-known treaties with Russia, but much weightier than this was the fact that Germany had at her disposal in case of necessity some 160 to 180 divisions for defense against Russia. She therefore did not fear such a possibility in the slightest and would not hesitate a second to take the necessary steps in case of danger. He (the Führer) believed, however, that this danger would not arise.

Concerning the German war aims in Europe, the Führer said that under any circumstances British hegemony would be destroyed, British influence would be excluded from Europe, and any attempt at American interference in Europe would be beaten back. In addition, an indispensable element of the New Order on the European Continent would be the limitation of rights and duties to those who lived on the Continent, and the exclusion of all countries who wished only to interfere from the outside, especially England and America.

In the present conflict the Axis Powers were being supported spiritually, morally and, in part, materially by Japan. The Three Power Pact had through the cooperation of Japan made possible, for example, the supplying of German auxiliary cruisers in East Asia. Most important of all, it had had the effect of making America hesitate to enter the war officially. On the other hand, through her effort in the conflict, Germany had brought her Japanese partner appreciable assistance for Japan's own future.

Few situations could be envisaged which offered greater facilities for the realization of Japanese aims and larger possibility of success. England was completely engaged at sea, in the air, and on land. Increasingly powerful English forces were being pinned down in the Mediterranean. Also on the ocean more powerful units were being required for convoy service. Cruisers and destroyers were often found to be no longer sufficient, since these convoys were being attacked by the Germans with battleships. For in contrast with the World War, Germany possessed today on the long front from Narvik to the Spanish-French frontier numerous bases from which she could attack England and her approaches with naval forces. Thus England was tied down in Europe; the objective was the destruction of the British world empire.

America was confronted by three possibilities: she could arm herself, she could assist England or she could wage war on another front. If she helped England, she could not arm herself. If she abandoned England, the latter would be destroyed and America would then find herself confronting the powers of the Three Power Pact alone. In no case, however, could America wage war on another front.

Thus there could never in human imagination be a better condition for a joint effort of the Three Power Pact countries than the one which had now been produced. On the other hand it was also clear to him that in any historic act some risk had to be taken in the bargain. Seldom in history, however, had a risk been smaller than at present: while war was being fought in Europe and England was occupied there, and while America was only in the initial stages of her own armament, Japan was the strongest power in the East Asia area and Russia could not intervene, since on her western border stood one hundred and fifty German divisions. Such a moment would never return. It was unique in history. The Führer admitted that there was a certain amount of risk, but it was extraordinarily slight at a moment in which Russia and England were eliminated and America was not yet ready. If this favorable moment passed by and the European conflict ended in some fashion with a compromise, France and England after a few years would recover. America would join them as a third enemy of Japan and Japan sooner or later would be confronted with the necessity of undertaking the defense of her *Lebensraum* in a struggle against these three powers.

Even from the military point of view there had probably never in the memory of man been a situation so relatively favorable as at present, even though the military difficulties presented by a combined advance should not be underestimated.

It was especially favorable since between Japan and her allies there were no conflicts of interest. Germany, who would satisfy her own colonial claims in Africa, was as little interested in East Asia as Japan was in Europe. This was the best sort of preliminary condition for the collaboration of a Japanese East Asia and a German-Italian Europe.

Collaboration with the Anglo-Saxons, on the contrary, never represented actual cooperation, but only a playing off of one against the other. Just as England never tolerated the hegemony of one state in Europe, so in East Asia she played off Japan, China and Russia against each other, to further the interests of her own world empire. Just as had England, so would the United States conduct herself, if she inherited the world empire and set up American imperialism in place of British imperialism.

Also on personal grounds a better situation for joint action would scarcely occur again. He (the Führer) had complete confidence in himself, and the German Nation stood united behind him as it had been behind no one in its previous history. He had the necessary power of decision in critical situations, and, finally, Germany had had an unparalleled series of successes such as occurred only once in world history and was unlikely to occur again.

Next the Führer declared that his attitude toward Japan had not been adopted in the year 1941. He had always been in favor of collaboration with that country. Ambassador Oshima knew that he (the Führer) had worked resolutely for many years to that end. He was determined not to depart from that line in the future. Especially favorable for collaboration, as he had said, was the fact that there were no conflicts of interest between Japan and Germany. For, in the long run, interests were stronger than personalities and the will of a leader, and could always endanger anew the cooperation of countries in case their interests were contradictory. In the case of Germany and Japan, because of the nonexistence of such contradictions, one could make long-term plans. This had been his firm conviction since his earliest youth. The Japanese, German, and Italian peoples would achieve great successes if they drew the necessary conclusions from the present unique situation.

Matsuoka thanked the Führer for his frank presentation, which seemed to him to put the whole situation in a clearer light. He would think over once more most carefully the arguments which the Führer had advanced, although he had already deliberated at length on these subjects.

On the whole he agreed with the views expressed by the Führer. He was especially of the opinion that any action which was determined upon always carried with it a certain risk. Matsuoka declared—after referring to the reports of Ambassador Ott and the Reich Foreign Minister, through which the Führer would certainly be informed about the current situation in Japan—that he would personally set forth the situation in the frankest fashion. There were in Japan, as in other countries, certain intellectual circles which only a powerful individual could hold firmly under control. He meant by that the sort of person who would like to capture the tiger cub, but who was not prepared to go into the den and take it away from its mother. He had used this line of thought in making the same point in the presence of two princes of the Imperial Family in a conference at headquarters. It was regrettable that Japan had not yet eliminated those elements and that some of these people were even occupying influential positions. Confidentially, he could state that in the interview at headquarters, after an earnest discussion, his point of view had prevailed. Japan would take action, and in a decisive form, if she had the feeling that otherwise she would lose a chance which could only occur once in a thousand years; and in fact Japan would act without consideration of the state of her preparations, since there were always some people who claimed that preparations were insufficient. Matsuoka had also made this point with the two princes. The hesitant politicians in Japan would always delay and act partly from a pro-British or pro-American attitude.

Matsuoka declared that he had come out for the alliance long before the outbreak of the European war. He had been very active at that time to this end, but unfortunately he had had no success. After the outbreak of the European war he personally had held the opinion that Japan should first attack Singapore and bring to an end the British influence in that area and should then join the Three Power Pact, since he did not favor the idea that Japan should join the alliance without having made some contribution toward bringing about the collapse of England. While Germany had been engaged in a titanic struggle against England for a year, Japan, up to the conclusion of the alliance, had contributed nothing. He had therefore come out very strongly for the plan of an attack on Singapore, but he had not prevailed and, under the force of events, had then reversed his program and had come around to the entry into the alliance first.

He had not the slightest doubt that the South Sea problem could not be solved by Japan without the capture of Singapore. They would have to press into the tiger's den and drag out the young by force.

It was only a question of the time when Japan would attack. According to his idea the attack should come as soon as possible. Unfortunately he did not control Japan, but had to bring those who were in control around to his point of view. He would certainly be successful in this some day. But at the present moment he could under these circumstances make no pledge on behalf of the Japanese Empire that it would take action.

He would, after his interviews with the Führer and the Reich Foreign Minister, and after he had examined the situation in Europe, give his closest attention to these matters on his return. He could make no definite commitment, but he would promise that he personally would do his utmost for the ends that had been mentioned.

Matsuoka then requested urgently that the representations which he had made be treated as strictly confidential, since, if they became known in Japan, those among his Cabinet colleagues who thought differently from him would probably become alarmed and would seek to get him out of office.

In connection with his efforts to bring about the treaty of alliance he had maintained strict secrecy up to the last minute and in order to deceive his opponents he had oftentimes intentionally given the impression of having a pro-American or pro-British attitude.

Shortly before the conclusion of the treaty of alliance it had been reported to him that the British Ambassador was conducting a strong propaganda campaign among the Japanese to the effect that Japan was taking a very risky step in adhering to the Three Power Pact. The American Ambassador also had been active in the same direction. A few days after the conclusion of the treaty of alliance he had asked the American Ambassador whether the reports about these propaganda activities were correct. The latter had admitted everything and had stated as well that every Japanese whom he had met, since the adherence to the treaty of alliance had become known, had expressed the opinion that Germany would win the war. In the opinion of the American Ambassador that was false; Germany had no chance to win the war and therefore in the Ambassador's opinion it actually was a very risky step for Japan if the alliance had been concluded in the expectation of a possible German victory.

Matsuoka continued that he had answered the American Ambassador that only the good God knew who would finally win the war. He (Matsuoka) had, however, not concluded the alliance on the basis of the victory of this or the other power, but he had based his action on his vision of the New Order. He had heard with interest the statements of the Führer on the subject of the New Order and had been fully and completely convinced by them. If, however, he assumed entirely hypothetically that the fortune of war at some period would turn against Germany, he must tell the American Ambassador that in such a case Japan would come at once to the assistance of her ally.

His vision of the New Order had been set forth in the preamble to the Three Power Pact. There was at stake an ideal, which had been handed down from one generation to another from time immemorial. For him personally the realization of this ideal was his life's aim, to which up to the present day he had dedicated his fullest efforts, in order to make on his own part a slight contribution toward its realization. The Berlin–Rome–Tokyo Three Power Pact was also a contribution to such a realization. The consummation of this idea, so Matsuoka went on, would be realized under the slogan: "No conquest, no oppression, and no spoliation." This would not be understood in all quarters in Japan. If, however, Japan seemed likely to depart from this line he would be the first to attempt to prevent it.

In this connection Matsuoka referred to still another principle of the preamble to the Three Power Pact, according to which every people must assume the place they deserved. Although Japan, in the creation of the New Order, if it was necessary, would proceed by force, and although she must sometimes lead with a strong hand the peoples who would be affected by this New Order, nevertheless she had always before her the slogan which he had previously quoted: "No conquest, no oppression, no spoliation."

In the further course of the conversation, Matsuoka referred to his conference with Stalin in Moscow. As an ally he owed an explanation on that subject to the Reich Foreign Minister and he would have given it in the course of the morning's conversation, if the Reich Foreign Minister had not been called away early. Now he would give this information to the Führer.

He had first only wanted to make a courtesy call on Molotov on passing through Moscow. After some consideration, however, he had decided to instruct the Japanese Ambassador to make discreet inquiry of the Soviet Government whether the latter would be interested in an interview between Stalin and himself. However, before the

Japanese Ambassador had been able to carry out his instructions with the Soviet Government, a proposal was made by the Russian Government itself for a meeting between Stalin, Molotov and Matsuoka. He had spoken with Molotov for about 30 minutes and with Stalin for an hour, so that, taking into account the necessary translations, he had conversed with Molotov for perhaps 10 minutes and with Stalin for 25 minutes.

He had told Stalin that the Japanese were moral communists. This ideal had been handed down from father to son from time immemorial. At the same time, however, he had said that he did not believe in political and economic communism, and he rather assumed that his Japanese ancestors had much earlier given up any attempt in that direction and had turned to moral communism.

In connection with what he called moral communism, Matsuoka cited several examples from his own family. This Japanese ideal of moral communism had been overthrown by the liberalism, individualism, and egoism introduced from the West. At the moment the situation in Japan in this field was extraordinarily confused. However, there was a minority which was strong enough to fight successfully for the restoration of the "Old Ego" ["*alten Ichs*"] of the Japanese. This ideological struggle in Japan was extremely bitter. But those who were fighting for the restoration of the old ideals were convinced that they would be finally victorious. The Anglo-Saxons were basically responsible for the entry of the new philosophy which he had mentioned and, in order to restore the old traditional Japanese ideals, Japan was compelled to fight against the Anglo-Saxons, just as in China they were not fighting against the Chinese but only against Great Britain in China and capitalism in China.

Matsuoka then continued that he had discussed with Stalin his ideas about the New Order and had stated that the Anglo-Saxon represented the greatest hindrance to the establishment of this order and that Japan therefore was compelled to fight against them. He had told Stalin that the Soviets on their part also were coming out for something new and that he believed that after the collapse of the British Empire the difficulties between Japan and Russia could be eliminated. He had represented the Anglo-Saxons as the common foe of Japan, Germany, and Soviet Russia.

Stalin had arranged to give him an answer when he passed through Moscow again on his return journey to Japan; he had, however, after some reflection stated that Soviet Russia had never gotten along well with Great Britain and never would.

Matsuoka in the further course of the conversation made several remarks about the status of the Tenno. The Tenno was the State, and the life and the property of every Japanese belonged to the Tenno, that is to the State. That was, in a way, the Japanese version of the idea of the totalitarian state.

Further, Matsuoka expressed himself as marvelling over the way in which the Führer with decisiveness and power was leading the German people, who stood completely united behind him through this great period of upheaval, a period without parallel in previous history. A people found such a Führer once in a thousand years. The Japanese people had not yet found their Führer. He would, however, certainly appear in time of need and with determination take over the leadership of the people.

SCHMIDT
Minister

BERLIN, April 1, 1941.

Frames 47376–47389, serial 67

Memorandum of the Conversation Between the Reich Foreign Minister and Japanese Foreign Minister Matsuoka on March 28, 1941

Auf. RAM Nr. 18/41

The Reich Foreign Minister expressed his gratification at being able to speak with Matsuoka a second time. The Führer would have liked to define his attitude even more fully with respect to the questions under consideration, but his time had been very much taken up by developments in Yugoslavia. The details, however, were not so important. The essential thing was the question of the possibilities and prospects of a closer cooperation between Japan and Germany, that is, the transition from a passive to an active collaboration of Japan in the common cause. It was with great satisfaction that the Germans had heard of the spirit in which Matsuoka was approaching these matters. It was a question of the greatest opportunity that had ever existed for the attainment of Japanese aims, and it would be well to make use of this opportunity before it was lost. The Tripartite Pact was a most important treaty and formed a basis for relations between Japan and Germany for hundreds of years. There existed no conflicts of interest.

The situation was such that a New Order could be established only when Great Britain was completely defeated. This applied with even greater force to Japan than to Germany, who at present already dominated the European Continent and by the end of this year would also bring the Mediterranean region and Africa, to the extent that Germany was interested in them, under her domination. Germany, then, had everything that she needed. She was not striving for world domination, as Roosevelt falsely asserted. The Führer wished to end the war as soon as possible in order to devote himself again to his work of reconstruction. The goal that he had set for himself—that is, to provide the maximum security for the Reich—had, essentially, already been attained.

On the other hand, the New Order in the Greater East Asian sphere could be established only if Japan also dominated the South. For this, however, the capture of Singapore was necessary.

With reference to Russia the Reich Foreign Minister stated that the Germans did not know how matters would develop in this direction. It was possible that Russia would set out upon the wrong road, although he did not really expect this from Stalin. But one could not know. In any case Germany would immediately strike if Russia should undertake anything against Japan, and thereby keep Japan free in the rear with respect to Russia. In this way one of the misgivings of Japanese statesmen, but especially of the Japanese Army, reported by Ambassador Ott, would be eliminated with the help of the German Army. The second misgiving with reference to the English Home Fleet and the English Mediterranean Fleet, which had been voiced particularly by the Japanese Navy, he (the Reich Foreign Minister) could answer by the fact that both of these English fleets would be tied down by Germany in European and Mediterranean waters. Finally, the Japanese had also expressed concern on account of America. The United States, however, would not risk its fleet against Japan and would not send it beyond the Hawaiian Islands. A great Japanese success at Singapore would, on the contrary, strengthen American neutrality. Roosevelt would then hesitate to undertake anything rash.

Although he (the Reich Foreign Minister) fully understood the situation in Japan, which Matsuoka had illustrated by his story about the tiger and her cubs, he nevertheless had to point out again that two of the strongest countries in the world, which possessed a youthful, strong, and fearless spirit, were now offered a chance by Providence which probably occurred only once in a thousand years. Germany's great opportunity was the Führer, whose co-workers carried out his will only as his instruments. He (the Reich Foreign Minister) had repeatedly declared to the Ambassadors of England and France that they should not fall into the error of confusing present-day Germany with that of 1914–1918. Even then the Reich had held out for four years against a world of enemies; only because of its disunity and its internal weakness had it lost the war. Now, however, it was united and consequently had twice the strength—which was again increased twofold by the genius of Adolf Hitler's leadership, so that henceforth one would have to reckon with a Germany which was four times as strong as in the World War. The Ambassadors had disregarded these warnings. The predictions had, however, come true, and nothing in the world would prevent Germany and Italy from dominating the European-African Hemisphere absolutely. When under such circumstances an opportunity was offered Japan, she ought to weigh matters very carefully and not let the opportunity slip out of her hand.

When the present conflict would end, could not, of course, be predicted with certainty; he (the Reich Foreign Minister) had the feeling, however, that England might perhaps collapse sooner than was generally expected. If the English should suddenly ask for peace, it would be very desirable if Germany and Japan could establish this peace jointly.

The Reich Foreign Minister then spoke about his family traditions, which had always been pro-Japanese. Moreover, he had had an important conversation with the Führer as early as 1934 on German-Japanese collaboration. The Führer's high esteem for Japan had begun with the Russo-Japanese War. Now the most important thing was not to lose the common opportunity which presented itself in the year 1941.

Matsuoka replied that he was of the same opinion. For logical reasons, as well as from an inner feeling, he also believed that 1941 would go down in history as a fateful year. In it the greatest tragedy, the fall of the British Empire, would be consummated. The German Nation in Europe and the Japanese in the Far East were, he felt, acting almost under a divine command to break up the British Empire and establish a New Order.

Matsuoka then asked what attitude Germany would take toward the United States if England should be brought to its knees during the summer but America was not yet in the war.

The Reich Foreign Minister replied that this would depend on the attitude of the United States. The possibility of an occupation of the British Isles required, to be sure, a period of good weather, and the English would possibly try to set up a new government in the United States. But in his opinion this could not be done.

Matsuoka then made his question specific as follows: When England was crushed, the United States in his opinion would not continue to support the British Empire. Canada would simply be more or less annexed. Would Germany under these circumstances leave the United States in peace? The Reich Foreign Minister replied that Germany did not have the slightest interest in a war against the United States. Matsuoka noted this with satisfaction, remarking that one had to reckon with the Anglo-Saxons as a whole; if it should not be possible to convert America to our way of thinking, no New Order could be established. The Reich Foreign Minister replied that each would exercise dominion in its own sphere. Germany, together with Italy, would do this in the European-African sphere; the United States would have to limit itself to the American Continent; and the Far East was reserved for Japan. As far as Russia was concerned, it would be very carefully watched and would in no case be permitted any kind of subversive propaganda. In the future only the three aforesaid spheres of interest would remain as great centers of power. The British Empire would disappear.

Matsuoka replied that the only big problem still remaining would then be Russia. Japan was prepared to permit Russia an ice-free outlet to the sea by way of India or Iran, but would not tolerate the Russians on the Chinese coast. Matsuoka then asked whether the Führer had ever considered the possibility of a Russian-Japanese-German alliance. The Reich Foreign Minister denied this and said that a closer collaboration with Russia was an absolute impossibility, since the ideological bases of the army, as well as of the rest of the nation, were completely incompatible. The Soviet Union was still internationally minded while Japan and Germany thought nationally. Russia was undermining the family; Germany championed it. A union was just as impossible here as between fire and water. Stalin was very clever and had therefore concluded the pact with Germany under the circumstances then prevailing. Russia would also have joined the Tripartite Pact, but her conditions could not be met. The whole matter was now being handled in a quite dilatory manner by Germany, as he could now inform Matsuoka confidentially. Moreover, Germany was watching the Soviet Union closely, and—this Matsuoka should realize clearly—she was prepared for any eventuality. Germany would not provoke Russia; but if the policy of Stalin was not in harmony with what the Führer considered to be right, he would crush Russia. Matsuoka replied that Japan was now taking pains not to provoke Russia. Japan was waiting for the completion of the German victory in the

Balkans. Without the good offices of Germany and without her strength there was no chance for Japan to mend Russo-Japanese relations completely.

Matsuoka also spoke of the long-term trade agreement which would be concluded with Russia. He then asked the Reich Foreign Minister whether on his return trip he should remain in Moscow for a somewhat longer period in order to negotiate with the Russians on the Non-aggression Pact or the Treaty of Neutrality. He emphasized in this connection that direct acceptance of Russia into the Tripartite Pact would not be countenanced by the Japanese people. It would on the contrary call forth a unanimous cry of indignation all over Japan. The Reich Foreign Minister replied that such an adherence of Russia to the Pact was out of the question and, moreover, recommended that Matsuoka, if possible, should not bring up the above-mentioned questions in Moscow, since this probably would not altogether fit into the framework of the present situation.

In reply to a further remark by Matsuoka that the conclusion of a fishing and trade agreement would improve the feeling between Russia and Japan, the Reich Foreign Minister replied that there were no objections to the conclusion of such purely commercial agreements. Matsuoka mentioned in this connection that America was observing Japanese-Russian relations closely and was trying on her part to conclude an agreement with Russia against Japan.

Matsuoka then began to speak of Singapore again. The Japanese were not worried on account of the British Navy. But there were Japanese circles which viewed a conflict with America with great misgivings, since they assumed that this would involve a five- or ten-year war with the United States. He would readily admit that America would not risk its fleet in a war against Japan, but for that very reason these Japanese circles were worried, because under these circumstances the war would last for years. The Reich Foreign Minister replied that in his opinion Roosevelt would not let it come to war since he was well aware of the impossibility of any action against Japan. Japan, on the other hand, could occupy the Philippines and in this way deal a severe blow to Roosevelt's prestige. If Japan captured Singapore, the greater part of the world would have come under the control of the Tripartite Powers, and America would find itself in an isolated position.

Matsuoka expressed himself as personally very strongly in favor of the Reich Foreign Minister's line of reasoning. If Japan did not assume the risk connected with the capture of Singapore, he was of the opinion that it would thereby become a third-rate power. The blow would therefore have to come some day in any event. If he could succeed in keeping the United States quiet for six months, all difficulties would be overcome. A nation which continued to hesitate in a matter of such fundamental national importance thereby only showed that it lacked the most important quality, power of decision.

Berlin, March 31, 1941.

Frames 47357–47375, serial 67

Memorandum of the Conversation Between the Reich Foreign Minister and Japanese Foreign Minister Matsuoka in Berlin on March 29, 1941

Aufz. RAM 19/41

The Reich Foreign Minister referred to the earlier discussion with Matsuoka concerning the latter's impending conversations with the Russians in Moscow. He expressed the opinion that in view of the general situation it might be best not to go into things too deeply with the Russians. He did not know how the situation would develop. But one thing was certain: if Russia should ever attack Japan, Germany would strike immediately. He could give this firm assurance to Matsuoka, so that Japan could push southward toward Singapore without fear of any complications with Russia. As it was, the greater part of the German Army was on the eastern boundary of the Reich and was ready to attack at any time. He (the Reich Foreign Minister) believed, however, that Russia would not occasion any military action. But if Germany should become involved in a conflict with Russia, the Soviet Union would be finished within a few months. In that case, Japan would, of course, not have anything at all to fear, if she wanted to advance toward Singapore. So, in any case, she need not be kept from that undertaking by any fears of Russia.

Of course, we could not tell how matters would develop with Russia. It was uncertain whether or not Stalin would accentuate his present policy of unfriendliness toward Germany. He (the Reich Foreign Minister) in any event wanted to point out to Matsuoka that a conflict with Russia was always within the realm of possibility. At any rate, Matsuoka could not report to the Japanese Emperor, upon his return, that a conflict between Germany and Russia was inconceivable. On the contrary, as matters stood, such a conflict, though not probable, still would have to be designated as possible.

With regard to Russian adherence to the Three Power Pact, as had been offered to Molotov by Germany, the Reich Foreign Minister remarked that there had been no question of the direct admission of Russia into the Pact, but rather of a different grouping. As already stated, however, the Russians had set conditions for their adherence which Germany could not accept, so that matters were now in suspense.

In reply to a question interpolated by Matsuoka, whether that meant that Germany would perhaps again seek, after the lapse of some time, to get Russia to adhere to the Three Power Pact, the Reich Foreign Minister replied that an attempt of that kind would probably not be made for some time, since the conditions submitted by Russia were irreconcilable with the German view, particularly those concerning Finland and Turkey.

In reply to an inquiry by Matsuoka for further details on the Russian conditions, the Reich Foreign Minister responded that German resistance to the Soviet demands with respect to Finland was based on economic considerations, and also on sentiment. Germany had fought on the side of the Finns in the World War. Matsuoka put in here that the Finns apparently laid great stress on being considered as belonging on the German side. The Japanese Minister in Helsinki, whom he had recalled in connection with the recent shifting of diplomats, told a newspaperman at Manchuli on the trip homeward that Finland now appeared to have placed herself on Russia's side. Some time later, the Finnish Minister in Tokyo protested officially to Matsuoka against that statement and declared that Finland would never place herself on Russia's side.

The Reich Foreign Minister pointed out that the Social-Democratic governments in Finland had always been against the Führer, so that there was no reason for Germany to help them during the Russo-Finnish War. Besides, Germany had to assume an absolutely neutral position, because in the conversations with Molotov and Stalin, Finland had been designated as not lying within the German sphere of interest. But when the Finns defended themselves so valiantly against the Russians, strong feeling for them sprang up in Germany, so that it was now impossible to give up Finland, since an occupation by Russia would lead to complete destruction of the country, as was shown by the example of the Baltic States.

The second Russian condition dealt with the guarantee to Bulgaria, together with occupation of the country by Russian troops, concerning which he had already been informed in detail in the earlier conversations.

The third condition had as its subject the establishment of bases on the Dardanelles. Matsuoka was already informed on that point too. At any rate, Germany preferred the Dardanelles to remain in the hands of the Turks. Besides, she could not permit a penetration of the Russians into the Balkans. However, Russia kept trying to push forward in that direction. Thus, in connection with recent happenings in Yugoslavia, activity was now increasing partly with the aid of the Sokol organization or through direct Communist influence. At any rate, the discussions with the Russians on those conditions had not been taken up again. We had merely told the Soviet Union that Germany could not allow any new conflict in Finland or the Balkans. Since then all these questions were, as stated, in suspense, and no favorable development was to be expected.

During the further course of the conversation, the Reich Foreign Minister imparted to the Japanese Foreign Minister, in confidence, his view of the true Russian interest. The Soviet Union wanted the war to last as long as possible. It knew that it could not itself gain anything by military attacks. Therefore the exceedingly rapid defeat of France did not suit that sly politician Stalin very well. He wanted a long war that would tire out the peoples and make them ripe for Bolshevik influence. That was the true aim of Russian policy, which should never be lost sight of.

Matsuoka agreed with these ideas and cited the situation in China as an example. Chiang Kai-shek, with whom he was in personal touch, who knew him and trusted him, was greatly alarmed as to the further increase of the influence of the Red Army in China.

The Reich Foreign Minister said that it was entirely possible that the conditions previously described would lead rather rapidly to a conflict between Germany and Russia. If Germany should feel herself endangered, she would immediately attack and put an end to Bolshevism.

To a suggestion by Matsuoka, not to allow the Anti-Comintern Pact to expire, but to renew it, the Reich Foreign Minister replied that he could not take a definitive position on the matter yet, since the situation as it would appear in the autumn, at the expiration of the Pact, could not be foreseen at the present time. As a matter of principle, however, Germany's stand was always in the sense of the Anti-Comintern Pact.

When Matsuoka asked the Reich Foreign Minister to inform him in good time, before the expiration of the Anti-Comintern Pact, regarding the German stand with respect to a possible extension of the Pact, the Reich Foreign Minister rejoined that by October the situation would certainly have been clarified to such an extent that a definite stand by Germany would be possible.

Thereupon the Reich Foreign Minister spoke once more of the question of Singapore. In view of the fears expressed by Japan of possible submarine attacks from the Philippines and of the intervention of the British Mediterranean Fleet and Home Fleet, he had discussed the situation once again with Admiral Raeder. The latter had told him that the British Fleet would be so fully occupied this year in British home waters and in the Mediterranean that it could not send a single ship to the Far East. The American submarines were designated by Admiral Raeder as so poor that Japan need not concern herself about them at all.

Matsuoka at once rejoined that the Japanese Navy considered the danger from the English Navy as very slight, and was also of the opinion that in case of a clash with the American Navy it could destroy the latter without trouble. It did fear, however, that the Americans would not give battle with their fleet, and that in that way the conflict with the United States would perhaps last for five years. They were very uneasy over that in Japan.

The Reich Foreign Minister replied that America could not do anything at all against Japan in case of the capture of Singapore. For that very reason Roosevelt would perhaps think twice before deciding actually to move against Japan. For while he could not do anything against Japan, there was the probability that the Philippines would be taken by Japan; this would naturally entail great loss of prestige for the American President, since, as a result of insufficient American military preparation, he could not retaliate.

Matsuoka pointed out in this connection that he was doing everything to soothe the British with regard to Singapore. He was acting as if Japan had no designs whatsoever on this key point of England in the East. It might therefore be that in his words and acts he would assume a friendly manner toward the English. But Germany should not be misled by that. He was assuming that manner not only in order to soothe the British, but to mislead the pro-British and pro-American elements in Japan, until he should one day suddenly attack Singapore.

With regard to this, the Reich Foreign Minister stated that in his opinion the declaration of war by Japan against England should follow from an attack on Singapore.

Matsuoka remarked in this connection that his tactics were based upon the safe assumption that the whole Japanese Nation would be united at one stroke by the sudden attack on Singapore. ("Nothing succeeds like success," the Reich Foreign Minister interjected here.) He (Matsuoka) was here following the words of a famous Japanese statesman addressed to the Japanese Navy at the outbreak of the Russo-Japanese War: "Open fire, and the Nation will then be united." The Japanese had to be shaken up to rouse them. Lastly, as an Oriental he also believed in fate, which comes whether we want it or not.

As the conversation went on, it turned to the question of rubber shipments. The Reich Foreign Minister asked Matsuoka to test the practicability of shipment to Lisbon or France by one or two Japanese auxiliary cruisers.

Matsuoka agreed to this and said that immediately after the step taken by Ambassador Ott with respect to the rubber question, he had proposed having Japan provide certain amounts for Germany from her own rubber stocks and later filling up the resulting gaps with rubber from Indo-China.

In this connection the Reich Foreign Minister pointed out that traffic over the Siberian Railroad was not adequate and that, besides, 18,000 tons of French rubber from Indo-China would be delivered to Japan through the mediation of Germany. In this connection also he inquired as to the size of the auxiliary cruisers that might be available for the rubber shipments. Matsuoka, who said that he was not accurately informed, estimated the size at 10,000 tons.

In addition, referring to the discussion with Reich Minister Funk, the Reich Foreign Minister turned the conversation to future trade relations between Japan and Germany. He explained that the trade between the great economic areas of the future, that is, Europe and Africa on the one side and the Far East on the other side, would have to be developed on a relatively free basis, while the American Hemisphere, at any rate as far as the United States was concerned, would remain more to itself, as it had everything that it needed in its own territory and therefore was not to be considered for interchange with other economic areas. In South America, however, things were different. Possibilities of exchange with other economic areas actually presented themselves there.

Matsuoka replied that, for her own reconstruction and for the development of China, Japan needed cooperation with Germany. Some time before, he had given written instructions to the Japanese missions in China to grant preferred treatment to German and Italian economic interests, as had already been done in Manchukuo and North China. Japan was not in a position to develop the gigantic territories of China without the assistance of German technical skill and German enterprise. Outwardly, of course, Japan would declare the open-door policy, but in reality would grant preferential treatment to Germany and Italy.

Besides, he had to admit openly that Japanese business circles were afraid of their German competitors, whom they considered very clever, while they only smiled at British and American competition. German business circles probably took a similar stand with regard to the Japanese, and therefore complaints came from both sides. He was of the opinion, however, that the reciprocal interests could be brought into harmony, and he told Japanese businessmen that they should not be afraid of German competition, but should endeavor to grapple with the problem with equal cleverness. At any rate the Japanese Government would do everything to equalize the interests of the two sides.

Then the Reich Foreign Minister went on to speak of Matsuoka's possible trip to Vichy, which was being considered. In this connection he said that of course he left it entirely to Matsuoka to decide whether he wanted to go to Vichy or not. If he considered this trip advisable, the German Government would not have anything against it. It would by no means stand in his way if, for instance, he wanted to talk to the French about Indo-China.

Matsuoka replied that above all else the respect which he felt for old Marshal Pétain had given him the idea of going to Vichy. The Emperor, who as Crown Prince had once been a guest of Pétain, was also among the admirers of the Marshal. Besides, he (Matsuoka) would like to go to Paris, and in that case a visit to Vichy would probably be unavoidable. However, in view of the extraordinary tension between Italy and France, he hesitated a great deal to undertake this visit, and in any event he wanted to ask the Duce and Count Ciano beforehand. He was certain that in her position of power Germany would have nothing against such a visit, but he did not know if he would hurt Italian feelings by going.

Going on, Matsuoka again spoke of Japanese-Russian relations. He pointed out that he had proposed a nonaggression pact to the Russians, to which Molotov had replied with the proposal of a neutrality agreement. During his stay in Moscow he, as the one who had made the original nonaggression proposal, would be forced to take a stand in some way with respect to these matters. On that occasion he also intended to attempt to get the Russians to give up the northern half of the Sakhalin Peninsula. There were important oil deposits there, the exploitation of which was hampered in every conceivable way by the Russians. In all, Matsuoka calculated the maximum amount to be procured from these oil deposits at 2 million tons. He would propose to the Russians acquiring northern Sakhalin by purchase.

In reply to a question by the Reich Foreign Minister, as to whether the Russians would be ready to sell these regions, Matsuoka answered that it was extremely doubtful. At a hint to the same effect, Molotov had asked the Japanese Ambassador whether "that was meant for a joke." At any rate Japan was ready in return to replace the treaties of Portsmouth and Peking by other agreements and also to give up her fishing rights. In any event he would have to take up these matters and, in particular, the question of the nonaggression pact during his stay in Moscow. He asked the Reich Foreign Minister whether he should go very deeply into these questions or treat them only superficially.

The Reich Foreign Minister replied that in his opinion only a purely formal, superficial handling of these points was advisable. The question mentioned by Matsuoka with regard to Sakhalin could also be settled later. Further, if the Russians should pursue a foolish policy and force Germany to strike, he would—knowing the sentiments of the Japanese Army in China—consider it proper if that army were prevented from attacking Russia. Japan would best help the common cause if she did not allow herself to be diverted by anything from the attack on Singapore. With a common victory, the fulfillment of the wishes named above would, so to speak, fall into Japan's lap like ripe fruit.

Matsuoka went on to speak of German help in the blow against Singapore, regarding which he had received repeated assurances, and in that connection he mentioned the offer of a written promise of German help.

The Reich Foreign Minister replied that he had already discussed these things with Ambassador Oshima. He had asked him to supply maps of Singapore, so that the Führer, who certainly must be considered the greatest expert of modern times on military matters, could advise Japan as to the best method for the attack on Singapore. German aviation experts would also be available and, on the basis of experience gained in Europe, could advise the Japanese regarding the use of dive bombers against the British Fleet in Singapore from air bases nearby. The British Fleet would then be compelled to disappear from Singapore at once.

Matsuoka interjected here that Japan was less concerned about the British fleet than about the capture of the fortifications.

The Reich Foreign Minister replied that here too the Führer had developed new methods for the German attacks on strongly fortified positions, such as the Maginot Line and Fort Eben Emael, which he could place at the disposal of the Japanese.

Matsuoka replied, in this connection, that some junior naval officers who were experts on such matters and who were good friends of his were of the opinion that it would take three months for the Japanese forces to capture Singapore. As a cautious Minister of Foreign Affairs, he had doubled that time. He believed that for six months they could ward off any danger threatening from America. But if the capture of Singapore should take still longer and were perhaps protracted for as long as a year, an extremely critical situation with America would develop, which he did not yet know how to meet.

If it could somehow be avoided, he would not touch the Dutch East Indies, as he feared that in case of a Japanese attack on those regions the oil fields would be set on fire. Then they could not be brought into production again for one or two years.

The Reich Foreign Minister remarked on that point that with the capture of Singapore, Japan would also gain control of the Dutch East Indies at the same time.

Matsuoka then mentioned also that the desire for air bases in French Indo-China and Thailand had been expressed among Japanese officers. He had rejected this, however, since he was by no means willing to undertake anything that might betray Japanese intentions with regard to Singapore.

In conclusion, the Reich Foreign Minister took up once more the question of Germany's assistance to Japan. Something could perhaps be done in that field also. Japan had to understand, however, that in this war the heaviest burden was resting on Germany's shoulders. The Reich was fighting against the island of Great Britain and was tying up the British Mediterranean Fleet. Japan, on the other hand, was fighting only on the periphery. Besides, the main Russian forces were on the European side. The chivalrous Japanese Nation would surely recognize this state of affairs.

Matsuoka agreed to these ideas, in closing, and gave the assurance that Japan would always be a loyal ally, which would devote its efforts fully and entirely to the common cause and not merely in a halfhearted way.

BERLIN, March 31, 1941.

Frames 47334–47347, serial 67

Memorandum of the Interview Between the Führer and the Japanese Foreign Minister, Matsuoka, in the Presence of the Reich Foreign Minister and Minister of State Meissner at Berlin, April 4, 1941

Aufz. Füh 20/41

Matsuoka first thanked the Führer for the gifts which had been presented to him in the Führer's name, which he said he would treasure forever in an honored place as a perpetual remembrance of his stay in Berlin. At the same time he expressed his thanks for the friendly reception which he had received in Germany from the Führer, the Reich Foreign Minister, and the whole German people. As long as he lived he would never forget the sympathy which had been displayed toward him here on all sides. On his return to Japan he would exert himself with all his power to convince the Japanese people of the honored friendship and esteem in which they were held by the German people.

Next Matsuoka reported concerning his conversations with the Duce and the Pope.

With the Duce he had discussed the European situation in general and the state of the war, as well as the relationship of Italy to Germany and the future course of world development. The Duce had informed him (Matsuoka) of his views of the situation of the war in Greece, Yugoslavia, and North Africa and of the part which Italy herself had in these events. Finally the Chief of the Italian Government had spoken of Soviet Russia and America. He had said that one must have a clear notion of the importance of one's opponents. The enemy No. 1 was America, and Soviet Russia came only in second place. By these remarks the Duce had given him to understand that America as enemy No. 1 would have to be very carefully observed, but should not be provoked. On the other hand one must be thoroughly prepared for all eventualities. Matsuoka had agreed in this line of thought.

With regard to Soviet Russia the Duce had spoken only briefly and to the same effect as had the Führer and the Reich Foreign Minister. In that connection also Matsuoka had agreed with him.

As the deepest impression which he was bringing back from his conversation with the Duce, Matsuoka mentioned the sense of complete unity between Italy and Germany, whose relations, in his opinion, could never be disturbed. Both countries were at one and firmly determined not to let this position be shaken. Matsuoka had felt this previously, but his conviction after his conversation with the Duce was stronger than ever. On his return to Japan he would try to drive home this fact, especially with those Japanese who continued to believe that Italy could be persuaded by Great Britain, perhaps not to become detached from Germany completely, but at least to cease to fight with her whole heart for the common cause.

Count Ciano, with whom he was personally friendly, had informed him that he did not always completely understand the policy of the Führer, but that nevertheless he had implicit confidence in him and his decisions.

With the Pope he had had an open and friendly conversation lasting for an hour and a quarter, which was concerned in a more theoretical fashion with the present situation and the future development of civilization. They had not spoken of the war, so that it would be hardly useful to describe the conversation any further to the Führer. At his departure Matsuoka had asked the Pope whether or not the latter perceived any opportunity or chance for bringing about peace. After brief consideration the Pope had said "No," and on his part asked Matsuoka whether or not he discerned any possibilities of peace. Matsuoka had also replied in the negative. The Pope had added only that nevertheless he prayed daily for peace and he requested Matsuoka to do the same, which the latter promised to do. In addition the Pope declared that if Japan saw any possibility of peace he would be glad to give his assistance.

Matsuoka further reported that he had told the Pope that during the World War he had served in the Foreign Office in Tokyo as private secretary to the then Prime Minister, and that, in that capacity, he had sought to persuade the Prime Minister and Field Marshal Yamagata to establish communication with the Vatican for the purpose of bringing about peace. Both had been favorable in principle but they had not had the boldness to put the idea into actual operation.

Matsuoka added that he had been led to undertake these peace efforts principally in view of the personality of Cardinal Gaspari.

Further, he had sought to convince the Pope that the United States and especially the American President were prolonging the war in Europe and in China. It was not a matter of proving whether

America and her President were right or wrong. They would certainly have definite grounds for their policy. Entirely apart from the question of right or wrong, the fact would have to be recognized that they were prolonging the war in Europe and in China. In connection with China he had sought to convince the Pope that Japan was not fighting against the Chinese or China herself, but only against Bolshevism, which was threatening to spread over China and the whole Far East. It was regrettable that America and England stood on the side of Bolshevism.

The Führer here interjected that both countries had stood on the side of Bolshevism in Spain as well.

Matsuoka then advanced the request that the Führer should instruct the appropriate authorities in Germany to meet the desires of the Japanese Military Commission as fully as possible. Especially in the field of U-boat warfare, Japan required German help in the way of furnishing the latest operational experience and the newest technical improvements and discoveries. Japan would do everything in her power to avoid a war with the United States. In case his country determined on a stroke against Singapore, the Japanese Navy must, of course, also make preparations against the United States, for in such a case America might possibly come out on the side of Great Britain. Personally, he (Matsuoka) believed that the entry of the United States into the war on the side of Great Britain could be avoided. The army and navy must, however, prepare for the worst, i. e., for a war against America. They believed that such a war would last over five years and would be fought out as a guerrilla war in the Pacific Ocean and South Seas. For this reason the experience derived by Germany in her guerrilla war would be most important for Japan. It was a matter of how such a war could best be carried on and how all the technical improvements of the U-boats, down to individual parts, such as periscopes and the like, could be made useful by Japan.

Summing up, Matsuoka asked the Führer to see to it that the improvements and discoveries in the naval and military fields should be made available to the Japanese by the competent German authorities.

The Führer agreed to this and added that Germany also considered a war with the United States to be undesirable, but that it had already been included in his calculations. In Germany the viewpoint was that America's performance depended upon her transport capabilities, which in turn would be limited by the tonnage available. Germany's warfare against shipping tonnage represented an appreciable weakening not only of England but of America also. Germany had made her preparations so that no American could land in Europe. She would wage a vigorous war against America with the U-boats and the Luftwaffe, and with her greater experience, which the United States had still to achieve, would be more than a match for America, entirely apart from the fact that the German soldiers were, obviously, far superior to the Americans.

In the further course of the conversation the Führer declared that if Japan got into a conflict with the United States, Germany on her part would take the necessary steps at once. It made no difference with whom the United States first came into conflict, whether it was with Germany or with Japan. They would always be intent upon disposing of one country first, not with the idea of then coming to an agreement with the other country, but with the idea of disposing of it next. Therefore Germany would, as he had said, promptly take part in case of a conflict between Japan and America, for the strength of the allies in the Three Power Pact lay in their acting in common. Their weakness would be in allowing themselves to be defeated separately.

Matsuoka again repeated his request that the Führer should give the necessary instructions, so that the competent German authorities would make available to the Japanese the latest inventions and improvements of interest to them, for the Japanese Navy must make preparations at once for a conflict with the United States.

With regard to Japanese-American relations Matsuoka continued that in his own country he had always declared that if Japan continued in the same fashion as at present, a war with the United States sooner or later would be unavoidable. In his view this conflict might better occur sooner than later. Accordingly, so his argument had run, should not Japan decide to act with determination at the proper moment and take the risk of a war against America? Exactly by such means the war might perhaps be postponed for generations, especially if Japan secured domination in the South Seas. In Japan, however, many people refused to follow this line of thought. In those circles Matsuoka was considered to be a dangerous man with dangerous ideas. He declared, however, that if Japan proceeded further along the present course she would some day have to fight and that this might happen under more unfavorable circumstances then than at present.

The Führer replied that he had much sympathy for Matsuoka's position, since he had found himself in similar situations (the occupation of the Rhineland, and the resumption of full military independence). He had also come to the conclusion that in a period when he was still young and vigorous he should make use of favorable circumstances and take upon himself the risk of a war which was eventually unavoidable. That he had been right in taking this position had been demonstrated by events. Europe was now free. He would not hesitate a moment to reply at once to any extension of the war, whether by Russia or by America. Providence favored those who did not let perils overtake them, but who confronted them courageously.

Matsuoka replied that the United States, or rather the statesmen who were in control there, had lately undertaken a last maneuver with respect to Japan, in which they declared that America would not fight Japan on account of China or the South Pacific, on condition that Japan should permit shipments of rubber and tin from these areas to proceed unhindered to their points of destination in America. America would, however, fight Japan the moment she felt that Japan intended to enter the war with the intention of assisting in the destruction of Great Britain. With the English-oriented education which many Japanese had received, this sort of argument naturally was not without effect on the Japanese.

The Führer declared in this connection that this attitude of America meant no more than that, as long as the British Empire remained, the United States would cherish the hope of one day being able to proceed together with Great Britain against Japan, while, with a collapse of the Empire they would be completely isolated as against Japan and could accomplish nothing against her.

The Reich Foreign Minister here interjected that the Americans under any circumstances would seek to uphold the English power position in East Asia; that, however, this attitude showed how much they feared joint action on the part of Japan and Germany.

Matsuoka continued that it seemed important to him to give the Führer the true story about the actual situation in Japan. Therefore he must inform him of the regrettable circumstances that he (Matsuoka), as Japanese Foreign Minister, in Japan itself did not dare to say a word about the plans which he had set forth to the Führer and the Reich Foreign Minister. In political and financial circles it would do him much harm. He had once, previously, before he had become Japanese Foreign Minister, made the mistake of telling a close friend something about his intentions. The latter had apparently spread the matter about, so that every kind of rumor arose, which, although he always otherwise spoke the truth, as Foreign Minister he was bound energetically to contradict. Also, under these circumstances, he could not state how soon he would be able to hold a conference with the

Japanese Prime Minister or with the Emperor about the questions which had been discussed. He would first have to go into developments in Japan closely and carefully, in order to determine a favorable occasion on which to give Prince Konoye and the Emperor the true picture about his real plans. The decision would then have to follow in a few days, for otherwise the problems would be talked to pieces. If he were not able to put through his plans, it would be an indication that he lacked sufficient influence, power of persuasion and tactical ability. But if he could put them through, it would show that he had attained great influence in Japan. He personally believed that he would be able to put them through.

On his return he would admit to the Emperor, the Prime Minister, and the Navy and War Ministers, if they asked, that the matter of Singapore had been discussed. He would, however, declare that this had only been done in a hypothetical way.

In addition Matsuoka expressly requested that nothing be cabled on the subject of Singapore, since he feared that by use of telegrams something might slip out. In case of necessity, he would send a courier.

The Führer agreed and assured him that he could rely fully and completely on German discretion.

Matsuoka replied that he had confidence in German discretion, but he could not, unfortunately, say the same thing for Japan.

After some personal farewell greetings the conversation came to a close.

SCHMIDT

BERLIN, April 4, 1941.

Frames 113240–113241, serial 104

The German Ambassador in the Soviet Union (Schulenburg) to the German Foreign Office

Telegram

VERY URGENT   Moscow, April 4, 1941—10 : 28 p. m.
SECRET   Received April 5, 1941—12 : 55 a. m.
No. 796 of April 4

For the Reich Minister personally.

Molotov just summoned me to the Kremlin to inform me of the following, in accordance with the agreement to consult existing between Germany and the Soviet Union:

The Yugoslav Government had proposed to the Soviet Government the negotiation of a treaty of friendship and nonaggression, and the Soviet Government had accepted the proposal. This agreement would be signed today or tomorrow. In its decision to accede to the proposal of the Yugoslav Government, the Soviet Government had been actuated solely by the desire to preserve peace. It knew that in this desire it was in harmony with the Reich Government, which was likewise opposed to an extension of the war. The Soviet Government therefore hoped that the German Government, too, in its present relations to Yugoslavia, would do everything to maintain peace. The agreement between the Soviet Union and Yugoslavia was analogous to the Turco-Soviet Agreement of 1925, and relations of the Soviet Union to other countries were not affected by the agreement with Yugoslavia. The Soviet-Yugoslav Agreement was directed against no one and was not aimed at any other state.

I replied to Molotov that in my estimation the moment chosen by the Soviet Union for the negotiation of such a treaty had been very unfortunate, and the very signing would create an undesirable impression in the world. The policy of the Yugoslav Government was entirely unclear, and its attitude, as well as the behavior of the Yugoslav public toward Germany, was challenging.

Molotov replied that Yugoslavia had concluded a treaty with Germany regarding accession to the Three Power Pact, and the Yugoslav Envoy here, who was at the same time a member of the new Cabinet, had assured the Soviet Government that the new Yugoslav Government was observing this treaty. Under these circumstances, the Soviet Government had thought that it could, for its part, conclude an agreement with Yugoslavia that was not even as far-reaching as the German-Yugoslav Treaty.

To my objection that, to my knowledge, we had thus far received no statement from the Yugoslav Government regarding the observance of its accession to the Three Power Pact and had been given every reason to doubt its goodwill, Molotov countered with the assertion that he was convinced of the peaceful intentions of the Yugoslav Government. The latter had restored peace and order to its country and strove to create good relations with all its neighbors.

At my objection that the behavior of the new Yugoslav Government actually revealed no striving toward good relations with Germany—and despite all my efforts to obtain from Molotov the promise that the Soviet Government might reconsider the matter—Molotov repeatedly stated that the Soviet Government had reached its decision after mature deliberation. It was convinced that the step it had taken was a positive contribution to peace, which was also desired by Germany. To this Molotov added the repeated and urgent request that Germany also do all she could to preserve peace in the Balkans.

SCHULENBURG

Frames 113249–113250, serial 104

Foreign Office Memorandum

MEMORANDUM ON THE PRESENT STATUS OF SOVIET DELIVERIES OF RAW MATERIALS TO GERMANY

1) After the conclusion of the German-Soviet Commercial Agreement of January 10, 1941, there could at first be observed on the Soviet side a noticeable restraint with regard to the practical carrying out of the Soviet deliveries, which was probably attributable in part to the cooling off of political relations with the Reich. The conclusion of the individual commercial contracts also—as usual—caused great difficulties. In consequence, imports of raw materials from the U.S.S.R. remained relatively slight in January and February (17 million RM and 11 million RM; including, to be sure, as the largest and most important item, 200,000 tons of Bessarabian grain).

2) A change took place in this respect in the month of March. Deliveries in March rose by leaps and bounds, especially in grains, petroleum, manganese ore, and the nonferrous and precious metals. The grain contract, which we had struggled so hard to get, was closed in the amount of 1.4 million tons of grain, at relatively favorable prices, for delivery by September of this year. The Soviets have already made available 110,000 tons of grain on this contract and have promised firmly to deliver 170,000 to 200,000 tons of grain in April.

3) The situation as regards the German counterdeliveries is favorable in this quarter, since, in accordance with the provisions of the contracts, we only have to deliver in this quarter the balances due on the first year of the contract. It will not be possible to adhere to the later German delivery periods because of a shortage of labor and priority of the military programs.

4) Transit traffic through Siberia is proceeding favorably as usual. At our request, the Soviet Government even put a special freight train for rubber at our disposal at the Manchurian border. Negotiations are now in progress in Moscow regarding the increase in Soviet tariff rates.

To sum up, it may be said that after an initial lag Russian deliveries at the moment are quite considerable, and the Commercial Agreement of January 10th of this year is being observed on the Russian side.

SCHNURRE

BERLIN, April 5, 1941.

Frames 365281–365282, serial 1448

The Reich Foreign Minister to the German Ambassador in the Soviet Union (Schulenburg)

Telegram

VERY URGENT   BERLIN, April 6, 1941—4 : 30 a.m.
No. 703 of April 6   Received Moscow, April 6—9 : 35 a. m.

State Secret. Strictly secret. To be decoded only by the officer in charge of state secret documents. To be submitted at once to the Chief of the Mission personally. Reply by courier or secret code.

For the Ambassador personally.

Please call on Herr Molotov early Sunday morning, April 6th, and tell him that the Government of the Reich had felt itself compelled to proceed to military action in Greece and Yugoslavia. The Government of the Reich had been forced to take this step because of the arrival of British military forces on the Greek mainland in ever increasing numbers, and because of the fact that the Yugoslav Government which had come to power illegally by the *coup d'état* of March 27 had made common cause with England and Greece. The Reich Government had accurate information for several days to the effect that the Yugoslav General Staff, in conjunction with the Greek General Staff and the High Command of the British Expeditionary Army that had landed in Greece, had prepared for joint operations against Germany and Italy, which were on the verge of being carried out. Moreover, the constantly increasing number of reports on excesses against Germans in Yugoslavia had made it impossible for the Government of the Reich to remain inactive further in the face of such developments. The new Yugoslav Government had taken this course contrary to all law and reason, after Germany had for years pursued a policy of friendship with this country, which was to have reached its culmination in the recent accession to the Three Power Pact. Moreover, I would ask you in this connection to refer to the communications made

to Herr Molotov on various occasions, which you had already made to
the Soviet Government, regarding the aims and intentions of the German Government on the Balkan Peninsula: that is, that German
activity in this area is directed solely to prevent England from gaining another foothold on the Continent; that Germany has absolutely
no political or territorial interests in this area; and that German troops
would be withdrawn when their tasks in the Balkans are finished.
Please make these statements without any special emphasis, in an
objective and dispassionate manner.

Please do not on this occasion mention the communication made to
you by Molotov regarding the conclusion of a Soviet-Yugoslav Friendship Pact. Should Molotov, on his part, speak of it, then please confine yourself to the comment that you have transmitted his communication to Berlin, but have not yet received any reply.

Send telegraphic report on execution hereof.

RIBBENTROP

Frame 113266, serial 104

*The German Ambassador in the Soviet Union (Schulenburg) to the
German Foreign Office*

Telegram

VERY URGENT   Moscow, April 6, 1941—7 p. m.
No. 818 of April 6   Received April 6, 1941—10:25 p. m.

Reference your telegram of the 5th [*6th*], No. 703.

For Reich Minister personally.

Since Molotov always spends Sunday out of town, I was only able
to speak with him this afternoon at 4 o'clock. Molotov came to Moscow expressly for this purpose.

After I had made to Molotov the communications prescribed, he
repeated several times that it was extremely deplorable that an extension of the war had thus proved inevitable after all.

Molotov did not on this occasion mention the negotiation of the
Soviet-Yugoslav Pact. Therefore I, too, as instructed, did not revert
to this subject.

SCHULENBURG

Frames 84963–84964, serial 177

The German Ambassador in the Soviet Union (Schulenburg) to the German Foreign Office

Telegram

VERY URGENT   Moscow, April 9, 1941—9 : 03 p. m.
SECRET   Received April 9, 1941—11 : 05 p. m.
No. 843 of April 9

Reference my telegram No. 832 of the 7th.[13]

Japanese Foreign Minister Matsuoka will have a further conversation with Molotov this afternoon in the Kremlin. After the dinner which Molotov arranged for him this evening, Matsuoka will leave for Leningrad and spend Thursday there. Matsuoka has delayed his departure till Sunday. I have had several conversations with Matsuoka, but have not yet been able to obtain any straightforward statement from him regarding his conversations with Molotov and their concrete results. In my opinion Matsuoka went very much into detail in the conversations with Molotov, and it might well depend now essentially on the Soviet Government whether there will be any written agreements. Matsuoka promised to inform me before his departure for Toyko.

Matsuoka also related the following: At a breakfast which Steinhardt, the American Ambassador here, gave for Matsuoka by reason of his previous personal relations with him, Steinhardt tried time and again to find out from him whether a Japanese attack on America had been decided upon in Berlin. Matsuoka added that he had the impression that Steinhardt had been directly requested by Roosevelt to do this. Naturally he had replied that this was entirely out of the question.

SCHULENBURG

Frame 84967, serial 177

The German Ambassador in the Soviet Union (Schulenburg) to the German Foreign Office

Telegram

VERY URGENT   Moscow, April 10, 1041—12 : 25 a. m.
No. 851 of April 9   Received April 10, 1941—5 : 20 a. m.

This evening, shortly before his dinner with Molotov, Japanese Foreign Minister Matsuoka sent Minister Nischi, First Counselor of

---

[13] Not printed.

Embassy at the Japanese Embassy here, who was likewise invited by Molotov, to give me the following information:

Today Matsuoka had again conferred for three hours with Molotov. The result was: Matsuoka waived the original Japanese demand for a nonaggression pact and the purchase by Japan of North Sakhalin; at present it was a question of concluding a neutrality pact, to include the following main points:

1.   Friendship
2.   Respect for each other's territory
3.   Neutrality in case of war

The Soviet Government was still insisting on the abandonment of Japanese concessions in North Sakhalin as the price of a neutrality pact, while the Japanese Government was proposing that this point be settled later. Should the Soviet Government persist in this viewpoint, Matsuoka would leave here without accomplishing anything. If the Soviet Government gave in, a neutrality pact would probably be concluded.

Matsuoka is leaving for Leningrad today; upon his return Friday the decision may be made known.

SCHULENBURG

Frames 131706–131707, serial 165

The German Ambassador in the Soviet Union (Schulenburg) to the German Foreign Office

Telegram

VERY URGENT   [Moscow], April 13, 1941—6 p. m.
SECRET
No. 883 of April 13

For the Reich Foreign Minister personally.

Matsuoka has just visited me in order to make his farewell call. He stated to me that a Japanese-Soviet Neutrality Pact had been arranged at the last moment and, in all likelihood, would be signed this afternoon at 2 p. m. local time. The Soviet Government had originally insisted that Japan should at the same time give up her concession in North Sakhalin, and that this be included in an annex to the treaty. Matsuoka absolutely rejected this demand. Last evening he had a conversation with Stalin, in which Stalin, at the conclusion, had given up the demand for the elimination of the Japanese concession. Stalin declared characteristically that Herr Matsuoka was "choking him" and he made the appropriate gesture. Herr Matsuoka promised that he would do his best in Tokyo to bring the Japanese Government and Japanese public opinion around to giving up the concession. With regard to the episode, Herr Matsuoka made the following remarks:

1) In Berlin he had told the Reich Foreign Minister that in Moscow he probably would not be able to avoid discussing the question, which had been pending for a long time, of a Japanese-Soviet Nonaggression or Neutrality Pact. He would, of course, show no eagerness in the matter, but he would be compelled to do something in case the Russians were willing to agree to Japanese wishes. The Reich Foreign Minister had agreed in this point of view.

2) The forthcoming conclusion of the Pact, of course, in no way affects the Three Power Pact. My inquiry as to whether the Pact which was being concluded had any provision to this effect in it, was answered by Matsuoka in the negative, and he added that the Russians had not brought up this question, and accordingly he had not gone into it either.

3) Matsuoka emphasized that the conclusion of the Neutrality Pact was of very great importance for Japan. It would make a powerful impression on Chiang Kai-shek and would appreciably ease Japanese negotiations with him. Also it would result in an appreciable strengthening of the position of Japan as over against America and England. Matsuoka added that the American and English journalists, who had reported yesterday that his journey to Moscow had been a complete failure, would be compelled today to acknowledge that the Japanese policy had achieved a great success, which could not fail to have its effect on England and America.

SCHULENBURG

Frames 131704-131705, serial 165

The German Ambassador in the Soviet Union (Schulenburg) to the German Foreign Office

Telegram

VERY URGENT   Moscow, April 13, 1941—9 p. m.
SECRET
No. 884 of April 13

For the Reich Foreign Minister personally.

Reference my telegram of today No. 883.

1. According to a statement of Matsuoka to the Italian Ambassador at this capital, Matsuoka's assurance that he would do his best

to bring about the elimination of the Japanese concession in North Sakhalin has been confirmed in writing by a letter of Matsuoka to Molotov.

2. To a question from the Italian Ambassador to Matsuoka as to whether at the conversation between Matsuoka and Stalin the relations of the Soviet Union with the Axis had been taken up, Matsuoka answered that Stalin had told him that he was a convinced adherent of the Axis and an opponent [*Gegner*] of England and America.

3. The departure of Matsuoka was delayed for an hour and then took place with extraordinary ceremony. Apparently completely unexpectedly for both the Japanese and the Russians, both Stalin and Molotov appeared and greeted Matsuoka and the Japanese who were present in a remarkably friendly manner and wished them a pleasant journey. Then Stalin publicly asked for me, and when he found me he came up to me and threw his arm around my shoulders: "We must remain friends and you must now do everything to that end!" Somewhat later Stalin turned to the German Acting Military Attaché, Colonel Krebs, first made sure that he was a German, and then said to him: "We will remain friends with you—in any event [*auf jeden Fall*]!" Stalin doubtless brought about this greeting of Colonel Krebs and myself intentionally, and thereby he consciously attracted the general attention of the numerous persons who were present.

SCHULENBURG

IX. THE FAILURE OF EFFORTS TO PRESERVE PEACE, APRIL 15–JUNE 22, 1941

Frames 113314–113315, serial 104

The German Chargé in the Soviet Union (Tippelskirch) to the German Foreign Office

Telegram

URGENT

No. 899 of April 15

Moscow, April 15, 1941—9:34 p. m.

Received April 15, 1941—11:45 p. m.

Reference our telegram of the 7th, No. 823.[14]

The Secretary General of the Office of the Commissar for Foreign Affairs, Sobolev, summoned me to his office today and stated that, by order of Molotov, he had a communication to make on the demarcation of the section of the German-Soviet boundary from the Igorka River to the Baltic Sea. The Secretary General first went briefly into the previous negotiations, in which connection he pointed out that the Soviet proposals had been based on decisions of the Conference of Ambassadors of 1923, while the German side advocated a boundary line corresponding to the one actually existing at present. The Secretary General then declared that the Soviet Government did not wish to delay further the solution of the problem and was accordingly prepared to undertake a drawing of the boundary corresponding to its present course, in conformity with the proposals contained in the memorandum of the Embassy of March 6, 1941.[14]

The Secretary General added that all other proposals thereby lapsed; he requested that his communication be transmitted without delay to the German Government; he hoped the matter would now be brought to a speedy conclusion.

The communication made by Sobolev means the unconditional acceptance of the German demand, as postulated at the end of the memorandum composed by Minister Saucken and transmitted to Molotov through the Ambassador on March 6. Considering the pressure for the view heretofore held by Molotov in this matter, the compliant attitude of the Soviet Government seems very remarkable. Since the

---

[14] Not printed.

Soviet Government doubtless expects that its attitude will meet with proper appreciation on the part of the Germans, any delay in giving our consent would produce the greatest mistrust in the Soviet Government, as you have already rightly suspected was the case in connection with the delay in the formation of the subcommission. (See telegraphic instruction No. 456 of March 6 and telegraphic report No. 508, of March 7.)[15]

I request telegraphic instructions.

TIPPELSKIRCH

Frames 84989–84991, serial 177

The German Chargé in the Soviet Union (Tippelskirch) to the German Foreign Office

Telegram

URGENT   Moscow, April 16, 1941—12 : 37 a. m.
SECRET   Received April 16, 1941—3 : 10 a. m.
No. 902 of April 15

Reference our telegram No. 884 of the 13th.

The Japanese Ambassador, on whom I called today, told me that the conclusion of the Soviet-Japanese Neutrality Pact had created a very favorable atmosphere on the part of the Soviet Government, of which he was convinced by Molotov, who today had asked him to call immediately in order to continue the negotiations regarding a commercial treaty. The conclusion of the treaty had caused disappointment and anxiety in America, where Matsuoka's journey to Berlin and Rome had been followed with interest.

Members of the Japanese Embassy here maintain that the Pact is advantageous not only to Japan but also to the Axis, that the Soviet Union's relations with the Axis will be favorably affected by it, and that the Soviet Union is prepared to cooperate with the Axis.

Stalin's manner toward the Ambassador at the railroad station when Matsuoka left is also interpreted in the same way by the diplomatic corps here. The view is frequently expressed that Stalin had purposely brought about an opportunity to show his attitude toward Germany in the presence of the foreign diplomats and press representatives; this, in view of the persistently circulating rumors of an imminent conflict between Germany and the Soviet Union, is considered to be especially noteworthy. At the same time the

---

[15] Neither printed.

changed attitude of the Soviet Government is attributed to the effect here of the success of the German armed forces in Yugoslavia and Greece.

TIPPELSKIRCH

Marginal Note: Transmitted under No. 1196 to the special train. Telegram Control. April 16, 1941.

___

Frame 113391, serial 104

Protocol
on the outcome of conference between the plenipotentiaries of the Government of the German Reich and the Government of the Union of the Soviet Socialist Republics to inquire into the observance of the Commercial Agreement between Germany and the Union of Soviet Socialist Republics of February 11, 1940

The plenipotentiaries of the Government of the German Reich and the Government of the Union of Soviet Socialist Republics acting in pursuance of article 10 of the Commercial Agreement between Germany and the Union of the Soviet Socialist Republics of February 11, 1940, have, on the basis of their inquiry into the observance of the above-mentioned agreement as of February 11, 1941, agreed as follows:

According to Soviet calculations, the Soviet deliveries on February 11, 1941, amounted to 310.3 million Reichsmarks. The Germans will by May 11, 1941, make deliveries from Germany in at least this amount.

Two original documents executed, each in the German and Russian languages, both texts having the same validity.

Done in Berlin, April 18, 1941.

For the Government
of the German Reich
K. SCHNURRE

By authority of the
Government of the Union of the
Soviet Socialist Republics
A. KRUTIKOW

Frames 113335-113336, serial 104

The German Chargé in the Soviet Union (Tippelskirch) to the German Foreign Office

Telegram

URGENT   Moscow, April 22, 1941—12: 05 a. m.
No. 957 of April 21   Received April 22, 1941—3: 30 a. m.

The Secretary General of the Commissariat for Foreign Affairs summoned me to his office today and delivered to me a *note verbale*, in which the urgent request is again made that we take measures against continuing violations of the U.S.S.R. boundary by German planes. Violations had increased considerably of late. From March 27 to April 18, 80 such cases had occurred. The *note verbale*, to which is attached a detailed statement of the 80 cases mentioned, refers to the case of a plane that landed near Rovno on April 15th, in which were found a camera, some rolls of exposed film, and a torn topographical map of the districts of the U.S.S.R., all of which gives evidence of the purpose of the crew of this airplane.

The *note verbale* continues verbatim as follows:

"Consequently the People's Commissariat deems it necessary to remind the German Embassy of the statement that was made on March 28, 1940, by the Assistant Military Attaché of the Embassy of the U.S.S.R. in Berlin to Reich Marshal Göring, according to which the People's Commissar for Defense of the U.S.S.R. made an exception to the very strict measures for the protection of the Soviet border and gave the border troops the order not to fire on the German planes flying over Soviet territory so long as such flights do not occur frequently."

At the end, the *note verbale* again emphasizes particularly the expectation of the Commissariat for Foreign Affairs that the German Government will take all the measures necessary in order in future to prevent violation of the national boundaries of the U.S.S.R. by German planes.

The Secretary General asked me to transmit the contents to Berlin, which I promised to do.

In view of the fact that the Soviet *note verbale* refers to previous memoranda on similar border violations by German airplanes, and also reminds us of the statement of the Assistant Military Attaché, it is very likely that serious incidents are to be expected if German planes continue to fly across the Soviet border.

TIPPELSKIRCH

Frames 352987–352988, serial 1337

The High Command of the Armed Forces to the German Foreign Office

WFST/Abt. L (1 Op)   Field Headquarters, April 23, 1941.
Nr.: 00 731 a/41 g Kdos.

Secret Military Document [*Geheime Kommandosache*]
Subject: Soviet-Russian border violations.

Attention of Ambassador Ritter.

Reports coming in almost daily of further border violations by Soviet Russian planes confirm the view of the High Command of the Armed Forces transmitted to the Foreign Office by letter of March 1, to the effect that it is a matter of conscious provocation on the part of Soviet Russia.

On April 11, two 2-motor planes of the type SB 2 flew over the city of Belz at a great height. On April 11, one plane each was sighted at Malkinia and Ostrow-Mazowiki. Also on April 14, a Soviet-Russian plane was reported over Langszorgen. On April 15, several planes flew over the demarcation line in the Dynow-Lodzina area—south of Losko. On April 17 alone, eight planes were identified over German territory—four each near Deumenrode and Swiddern; on April 19, two planes over Malkinia; another at an altitude of 200 meters (!) over Ostrowice.

Besides these, a number of other planes were reported, the nationality of which, however, could not be identified with certainty because of the altitude at which they were flying. There is no doubt, however, from the direction of the flight and the evidence obtained from the German task forces stationed there, that in these cases also, border trespass flights by planes of the U.S.S.R. are involved.

The High Command of the Armed Forces now finds that the steadily mounting number of border trespass flights can only be regarded as the deliberate employment of the air force of the U.S.S.R. over the sovereign territory of the Reich. Since more German units had to be brought up for security reasons because the forces on the other side of the German eastern border were strengthened, we have to reckon with increased danger of grave border incidents.

The orders of the High Command of the Armed Forces for the exercise of the utmost restraint nevertheless continue in force.

The Chief of the High Command of the Armed Forces
By order: JODL

Frame 218002, serial 426

The Naval Attaché of the German Embassy in the Soviet Union
(Baumbach) to the Naval High Command

[Telegram]

No. 34112/110 of April 24   April 24, [1941.]

For the Navy.

1. Rumors current here speak of alleged danger of war between Germany and the Soviet Union and are being fed by travelers passing through from Germany.

2. According to the Counselor of the Italian Embassy, the British Ambassador predicts June 22 as the day of the outbreak of war.

3. May 20th is set by others.

4. I am endeavoring to counteract the rumors, which are manifestly absurd.

Naval Attaché

———————————

Frames 314–320, serial F 15

Conversation of the Führer With the Ambassador Count von der Schulenburg, on April 28, 1941, From 5:15 p.m. to 5:45 p.m.

STATE SECRET

The Führer commenced with the question whether I would be back in Moscow by May 1, which I answered in the affirmative since I wanted to be present at the review.

The Führer then mentioned that I had been present in Moscow during the visit of Matsuoka, and asked what was the opinion of the Russians of the Russo-Japanese agreement. I replied that the Russians had been very pleased at concluding it, even though they had to make concessions.

The Führer thereupon asked me what devil had possessed the Russians to conclude the Friendship Pact with Yugoslavia. I expressed the opinion that it was solely a matter of the declaration of Russian interests in the Balkans. Russia had done something each time that we undertook anything in the Balkans. Then, too, we had probably been obligated by the consultative pact to consult the Russians. Russia, to be sure, had no special interest in Yugoslavia, but certainly had in the Balkans, in principle. The Führer said that upon conclusion of the Russo-Yugoslav Friendship Pact he had had the feeling that Russia had wanted to frighten us off. I denied this and repeated that the Russians had only intended to serve notice of their interest, but had nevertheless behaved correctly by informing us of their intention.

The Führer then said that it was not yet clear who had pulled the strings in the overthrow of the Yugoslav Government. England or Russia? In his opinion it had been the British, while the Balkan peoples all had the impression that Russia had been behind it. I replied that, as seen from Moscow, there was nothing to support the theory that Russia had had a finger in the pie. As an example, I cited the lack of success of the Yugoslav Minister in Moscow, Gavrilovitch, whose attempts to interest the Soviet Union in the Yugoslav cause were abortive until the last moment. The Yugoslav-Russian agreement had only become a reality when Yugoslavia seized the initiative after the Putsch and sent officers to request the agreement. Russia had then concluded the agreement on the principle that an instrument of peace was involved. Now, Russia was very apprehensive at the rumors predicting a German attack on Russia. The Führer insisted that the Russians had been the first to move, since they had concentrated needlessly large numbers of divisions in the Baltic States. I replied that this was a matter of the well-known Russian urge for 300 percent security. If for any reason we sent *one* German division, they would send 10 for the same purpose in order to be completely safe. I could not believe that Russia would ever attack Germany. The Führer said that he had been forewarned by events in Serbia. What had happened there was to him an example of the political unreliability of states.

The Führer went on at some length about the nations misled by England, particularly about the development of its political endeavors in Yugoslavia. England had hoped for a Yugoslav-Greek-Turko-Russian front in the southeast and had striven for this broad grouping of powers in memory of the Salonika front in the World War. He regretted exceedingly that—because of these efforts of England—he had now been forced to move against poor little Greece also. It had been repugnant to him to have to strike down, against his natural impulses, this small, plucky nation. The Yugoslav *coup d'état* had come suddenly out of the blue. When the news of it was brought to him on the morning of the 27th, he thought it was a joke. When one had gone through that sort of thing one was bound to be suspicious. Nations today allowed hatred and perhaps also financial interests to determine their policy rather than good sense and logic, and so it had happened that as a result of the promises and the lies of the British, one after another, the Poles, to whom he had offered the most favorable terms; France, which had not wanted the war at all; Holland and Belgium; Norway, and now Greece and Yugoslavia had plunged to disaster. It might be said that the masses could not help it, but he dealt not with the peoples but with the governments. And Greece had decidedly not been neutral! Its press had been impudent. Greece had always been sympathetic to England and had, above all, placed its shipping and its submarine bases at the disposal of England. Turkey, too, had very nearly taken the same road. He did not, it was true, believe that Russia could be bought to attack Germany, but strong instincts of hatred had survived, nevertheless, and, above all, Russian determination to approach closer to Finland and the Dardanelles was unchanged, as Molotov had allowed clearly to be seen on his visit. When he considered all this, he was obliged to be careful.

I pointed out that Cripps had not succeeded until 6 days after the conclusion of the Russo-Yugoslav Treaty in even speaking to Molotov's deputy, Vishinsky. I further reminded him that Stalin had told Matsuoka he was committed to the Axis and could not collaborate with England and France, as well as of the scene at the railroad station, which Stalin had purposely brought about in order to demonstrate publicly his intention to collaborate with the Axis. In 1939 England and France had taken all conceivable means to win Russia over to their side, and if Stalin had not been able to decide in favor of England and France at a time when England and France were both still strong, I believed that he would certainly not make such a decision today, when France was destroyed and England badly battered. On the contrary, I was convinced that Stalin was prepared to make even further concessions to us. It had already been intimated to our economic negotiators that (if we applied in due time) Russia could supply us up to 5 million tons of grain next year. Citing figures, the Führer said he thought that Russian deliveries were limited by transportation conditions. I pointed out that a more thorough utilization of Russian ports would obviate the difficulties of transportation.

The Führer then took leave of me.

The original of the enclosed memorandum with two carbon copies was sent to Vienna today at 3 p. m. via air courier.

Respectfully submitted to the State Secretary, for his information.

ADEMANN

BERLIN, April 29, 1941.

Frames 311–312, serial F 15

*Memorandum by the State Secretary in the German Foreign Office
(Weizsäcker)*

Teletype

BERLIN, April 28, 1941.

To the Reich Foreign Minister.

Concerning Count Schulenburg's memorandum on German-Russian relations:

I can summarize in one sentence my views on a German-Russian conflict: If every Russian city reduced to ashes were as valuable to us as a sunken British warship, I should advocate the German-Russian war for this summer; but I believe that we would be victors over Russia only in a military sense, and would, on the other hand, lose in an economic sense.

It might perhaps be considered an alluring prospect to give the Communist system its death blow and it might also be said that it was inherent in the logic of things to muster the Eurasian continent against Anglo-Saxondom and its following. But the sole decisive factor is whether this project will hasten the fall of England.

We must distinguish between two possibilities:

a) England is close to collapse: if we accept this [assumption], we shall encourage England by taking on a new opponent ["We shall" is deleted, but the words written in above are illegible.] Russia is no potential ally of the English. England can expect nothing good from Russia. Hope in Russia is not postponing England's collapse. [In handwriting:] With Russia we do not destroy any English hopes.

b) If we do not believe in the imminent collapse of England, then the thought might suggest itself that by the use of force, we must feed ourselves from Soviet territory. I take it as a matter of course that we shall advance victoriously to Moscow and beyond that. I doubt very much, however, whether we shall be able to turn to account what we have won in the face of the well-known passive resistance of the Slavs. I do not see in the Russian State any effective opposition capable of succeeding the Communist system and uniting with us and being of service to us. We would therefore probably have to reckon with a continuation of the Stalin system in Eastern Russia and in Siberia and with a renewed outbreak of hostilities in the spring of 1942. The window to the Pacific Ocean would remain shut.

A German attack on Russia would only give the British new moral strength. It would be interpreted there as German uncertainty as to the success of our fight against England. We would thereby not only be admitting that the war was going to last a long time yet, but we might actually prolong it in this way, instead of shortening it.

WEIZSÄCKER

This position is drafted in very brief form, since the Reich Foreign Minister wanted it within the shortest possible time. Weizsäcker.

Frame 365359, serial 1448

The German Ambassador in the Soviet Union (Schulenburg) to the German Foreign Office

Tgb. Nr. A/g/229/41   MOSCOW, May 2, 1941.

SECRET

Subject: Rumors of German-Russian military showdown.

Reference instruction Pol. V 1495g of April 16, 1941.[16]

I and all the higher officials of my Embassy have always combated rumors of an imminent German-Russian military show-down, since it is natural that rumors of that kind constitute a great hazard for the continued peaceful development of German-Soviet relations. Please bear in mind, however, that attempts to counteract these rumors here in Moscow must necessarily remain ineffectual if such rumors incessantly reach here from Germany, and if every traveler who comes to Moscow or travels through Moscow not only brings these rumors along, but can even confirm them by citing facts.

COUNT VON DER SCHULENBURG

Frames 218003–218004, serial 426

The German Foreign Office to the German Ambassador in the Soviet Union (Schulenburg)

Telegram

No. 878 of May 3   BERLIN, May 4, 1941—5 : 45 a. m.
                          Received Moscow, May 4, 1941—10 a. m.

Secret. To be decoded only by the officer in charge of State Secret documents. Reply via courier or secret code. For Military Attaché. Secret Military document No. 602/41 G. Kdos. Att Abt O Qu 4, for Herr Osten, Military Attaché, Moscow . . . OKW Wf St/ Abt. L, advises on May 3 under No. 952/41g Kdos., as follows: Re: Telegram Naval Attaché of April 24, No. 34112/110.[17]

---

[16] Not printed.
[17] *Ante*, p. 330.

Instruction on No. 1: The same war rumors are current here as in Russia so we suspect a renewed attempt on the part of England to poison the wells. Reports that are without any foundation—as, for example, stories about extensive map making (the Ukraine) in Prague, or about the landing of more than 12,000 German soldiers in Finland—confirm these suspicions. Moreover, currency is given to such rumors by substantial Russian troop concentrations near the border, especially since they are without military justification, since on the German side, only such forces are posted at the border as are absolutely necessary as rear cover for the Balkan operations.

On No. 4: The quashing of rumors by the German officials there is very desirable, in which connection use can be made in suitable form of the fact that German troop transports are being carried out from east to west, which in the first half of May will reach considerable proportions (added only for personal information: (8 divisions). General Staff of the Army, Attaché Division T. No. 602/41 G. Kdos.

KRAMARZ

Frames 113418–113419, serial 105

The German Ambassador in the Soviet Union (Schulenburg) to the German Foreign Office

Telegram

VERY URGENT   Moscow, May 7, 1941—2:02 p. m.
SECRET   Received May 7, 1941—3:10 p. m.
No. 1092 of May 7

Stalin has taken over the chairmanship of the Council of People's Commissars in place of Molotov and thereby has become head of the Government of the Soviet Union. Molotov received the rank of Deputy Chairman of the Council of People's Commissars and will remain People's Commissar for Foreign Affairs. This change is being explained by the pressure of work on Molotov, but it actually means a considerable abridgment of his former authority. The reason for it may be sought in the recent mistakes in foreign policy which led to a cooling off of the cordiality of German-Soviet relations, for the creation and preservation of which Stalin had consciously striven, while Molotov's own initiative often expended itself in an obstinate defense of individual issues.

In his new capacity as Chairman of the Council of People's Commissars, that is, as Prime Minister of the Soviet Union, Stalin assumes responsibility for all acts of the Government, in both the domestic and foreign fields. This will put an end to the unnatural situation wherein the position of the recognized and undisputed leader of the peoples of the Soviet Union was nowhere established in the Constitution. The centralization of all the powers in the hands of Stalin means a consolidation of governmental authority in the U.S.S.R. and a further advancement of the position of Stalin, who obviously felt that, in a situation which he considered serious, he personally had to assume full responsibility for the fate of the Soviet Union. I am convinced that Stalin will use his new position in order to take part personally in the maintenance and development of good relations between the Soviets and Germany.

SCHULENBURG

Frames 365383-365388, serial 1448

The German Ambassador in the Soviet Union (Schulenburg) to the German Foreign Office

Tgb. Nr. Ag/259/41   Moscow, May 12, 1941.

SECRET

Subject : Appointment of Stalin as Chairman of the Council of People's Commissars.

With reference to telegram No. 1092 of May 7 and also to Nos. 1113 of May 8, 1124 of May 10, 1115 of May 9, 1120 of May 9, and 1137 of May 12.[18]

The present political position of the Soviet Union is illustrated by the appointment of Stalin as Chairman of the Council of People's Commissars. Stalin's decision to take over this office, which V. I. Lenin was the first to fill after the Bolshevist Revolution, gains especial significance from the fact that Stalin had previously avoided taking a government post. Stalin won his position of power in party and state solely by his personal authority and by the aid of men devoted to him. No problems of domestic or foreign policy had heretofore been able to induce Stalin to abandon this characteristic attitude. Even when the Stalin constitution, his personal work, went into effect, he had apparently deliberately refrained from occupying the highest government post by allowing himself to be elected chairman of the presidium of the Supreme Soviets.

The reasons that now caused Stalin to make this decision cannot be ascertained, for example, by direct questioning of competent Soviet officials, because of the peculiar conditions here. The new French

---

[18] Nos. 1113, 1115, 1120, 1124, and 1137 not printed.

Ambassador, who was ignorant of this situation, attempted to do so nevertheless, and asked this question on the occasion of his initial visits to First Deputy Foreign Commissar Vishinsky, Secretary General of the Commissariat for Foreign Affairs Sobolev, and Division Chief Kusnetzov. The three gentlemen interrogated expressed themselves spontaneously and unanimously to the effect that the appointment of Stalin to the chairmanship of the Council of People's Commissars was the greatest historical event in the Soviet Union since its inception. Asked as to the reasons for this appointment, the three gentlemen declared after brief hesitation that the appointment of Stalin had been occasioned by the all too heavy burden carried by Molotov. When the disparity between cause and effect was pointed out to them, the gentlemen consulted could make no further reply.

There can be no doubt that the assumption of the chairmanship of the Council of People's Commissars by Joseph Stalin constitutes an event of extraordinary importance. That this event was brought about by problems of domestic policy, as was first asserted here, especially among correspondents of the foreign press, I do not consider correct. I do not know of any problem that could have been raised as a result of domestic conditions in the Soviet Union of such importance as to necessitate such a step on Stalin's part. It can rather be stated with great certainty that if Stalin decided to take over the highest government office, it was done for reasons of foreign policy. In order to clarify the specific circumstances that must have influenced Stalin's decision, one must refer to some occurrences that took place in the days previous. It was generally noticed that at the great review of May 1 the Soviet Ambassador to Berlin, Dekanosov, stood directly next to Stalin, on his right, on the Government reviewing stand. This prominence given to Dekanosov must be regarded as a special mark of confidence on the part of Stalin. Also, a remarkably large number of generals and admirals of the Red Army and the Red Fleet participated in the review and the large reception in the Kremlin that followed. Finally, on May 5, the graduation exercises of the War Academy were the occasion of a rather large ceremony, at which Stalin made an address of some 40 minutes' duration. Since the appointment of Stalin was announced by the Kremlin on May 6, the obvious assumption is that the conversations with the Soviet Ambassador to Germany and the mingling with representatives of the staff of generals precipitated Stalin's decision to take over the Chairmanship of the Council of People's Commissars. No other reason for this action could have applied than a revaluation of the international situation on the basis of the magnitude and rapidity of German military successes in Yugoslavia and Greece and the realization that this makes necessary a departure from the former diplomacy of the Soviet Government that had led to an estrangement with Germany. Probably, also, conflicting opinions that were noted among the party politicians and high-ranking military men, confirmed Stalin in the decision to take the helm himself from now on.

If one reviews the pronouncements and decrees that have been promulgated since Stalin's assumption of office, insofar as they enter into consideration, one can state that the point of the matter was undoubtedly missed by the version originally circulated by foreign correspondents, especially by the Japanese Domei agency, to the effect that the appointment of Stalin legalizes an existing condition and that everything otherwise remains the same. The pronouncements and decrees in question are all in the realm of foreign policy. The matters involved are:

1. The Tass denial of alleged strong concentrations of military forces on the western border of the Soviet Union, etc.
2. The decree regarding the restoration of diplomatic ranks (Ambassador, Minister, Chargé).
3. The decision regarding the closing of the Embassies of Belgium, Norway, and Yugoslavia, and
4. The government decision regarding the opening up of diplomatic relations between the Soviet Union and Iraq.

These manifestations of the intention of the Stalin government are calculated in the first place, while safeguarding its own interests, to relieve the tension between the Soviet Union and Germany and to create a better atmosphere for the future. We must bear in mind particularly that Stalin personally has always advocated a friendly relationship between Germany and the Soviet Union.

It is self-evident that in the diplomatic corps here there is a great amount of guess-work being done as to what could have induced Stalin at this time to take over a government office created by the constitution. It is remarkable that groups representing the most divergent opinion agree in the presumption that Stalin is pursuing a policy of *rapprochement* with Germany and the Axis.

In my opinion, it may be assumed with certainty that Stalin has set himself a foreign policy goal of overwhelming importance for the Soviet Union, which he hopes to attain by his personal efforts. I firmly believe that, in an international situation which he considers serious, Stalin has set himself the goal of preserving the Soviet Union from a conflict with Germany.

COUNT VON DER SCHULENBURG

Frame 113434, serial 105

The German Consul at Harbin (Ponschab) to the German Foreign Office

Telegram

URGENT   HARBIN, May 13, 1941—12:50 a. m.
SECRET   Received May 13, 1941—10:30 a. m.
No. 39 of May 13

Reference my telegram No. 37 of the 11th.[19]
Circular instructions from Moscow of May 9:

Although German-Russion negotiations are proceeding normally, it has become imperative for the Soviets, in view of Germany's dictatorial attitude, to warn Germany that the Soviets are prepared to protect their interests, if (this group missing in the original telegram) they are violated. Under the circumstances it is very important to learn the attitude of all other countries in the event of a German-Russian conflict. It is necessary to proceed with the greatest caution. A survey of the situation and prompt report are requested.

PONSCHAB

Frames 24524–24527, serial 34

Foreign Office Memorandum

Ha Pol 294/41 g RS
STATE SECRET

SECOND MEMORANDUM ON THE STATUS OF GERMAN-SOVIET TRADE RELATIONS*

1) The discussions concluded a few days ago with Krutikov, First Deputy People's Commissar for Foreign Trade of the U.S.S.R., were conducted in a notably constructive spirit by Krutikov. It was therefore possible to settle satisfactorily difficult points in the Trade Agreement of January 10, 1941, such as delivery of oil seed, nonferrous metals, petroleum, and transit of raw rubber from East Asia through the territory of the U.S.S.R. Despite his constructive attitude, Kruti-

---

[19] Not printed.
* My first memorandum on the same subject, of April 5, is attached. [Footnote in the original. For this memorandum, see *ante*, p. 318.]

kov's stand when defending Russian interests was firm. He showed no extreme willingness to give way which might have been construed as weakness.

2) Difficulties arose, as in the past, regarding the execution of German delivery commitments to the U.S.S.R., especially in the field of armaments. We shall not be able to adhere to the more distant delivery dates. However, the nonfulfillment of German commitments will only make itself felt after August 1941, since until then Russia is obligated to make deliveries in advance. Difficulties arose especially with respect to the execution of certain contracts covering supplies for the air force, as the Reich Ministry for Air will not release the aircraft promised and already sold. Krutikov brought up these questions, without too great insistence, however. Construction of the cruiser L in Leningrad is proceeding according to plan, with German supplies coming in as scheduled. Approximately seventy German engineers and fitters are working on the construction of the cruiser in Leningrad under the direction of Admiral Feige.

3) The status of Soviet raw material deliveries still presents a favorable picture. Of the most important items of raw materials, the following deliveries were made in April:

Grain	208, 000 tons
Petroleum	90, 000 tons
Cotton	8, 300 tons
Nonferrous metals	6, 340 tons; copper, tin, and nickel.

With regard to manganese ore and phosphates, deliveries suffered from the lack of tonnage and transportation difficulties in the Southeast area.

The transit route through Siberia is still operating. The shipments of raw materials from East Asia, particularly of raw rubber, that reach Germany by this route, continue to be substantial (raw rubber during the month of April, 2,000 tons by special trains, 2,000 by regular Siberian trains).

Total deliveries in the current year amount to:

Grain	632, 000 tons
Petroleum	232, 000 tons
Cotton	23, 500 tons
Manganese ore	50, 000 tons
Phosphates	67, 000 tons
Platinum	900 kilograms

4) Great difficulties are created by the countless rumors of an imminent German-Russian conflict. Official sources are in large measure

responsible for the persistence of these rumors. These rumors are causing grave anxiety to German industry, which is eager to withdraw from its engagements with Russia and in some cases already refuses to dispatch to·Moscow the personnel needed for the execution of the contracts.

5) I am under the impression that we could make economic demands on Moscow which would even go beyond the scope of the treaty of January 10, 1941, demands designed to secure German food and raw-material requirements beyond the extent now contracted for. The quantities of raw materials now contracted for are being delivered punctually by the Russians, despite the heavy burden this imposes on them, which, especially with regard to grain, is a notable performance, since the total quantity of grain to be delivered under the agreement of April 10 of this year and the Belgian and Norwegian agreements, amounts to over 3 million tons up to August 1, 1942.

6) For the end of May or beginning of June, the Trade Agreement of January 10, 1941, provides for new negotiations in Moscow regarding settlement of balances. Such negotiations would, however, only make sense if they were used to present specific German demands. If this is not to be the case, I intend to procrastinate with regard to the date of the negotiations.

SCHNURRE

BERLIN, May 15, 1941.

Frame 217951, serial 426

The German Foreign Office to the German Ambassador in the Soviet Union (Schulenburg)

Telegram

No. 938 of May 14   BERLIN, May 15, 1941—6 : 27 p. m.
                        Received Moscow, May 15, 1941—10 : 30 p. m.

Confidential material. Secret. To be decoded only by officials authorized to handle confidential material. Reply via courier or secret code.

In reference to telegraphic report No. 957 of April 21, and written report No. A: 1408 of April 22, 1941.[20]

Please inform the Commissariat for Foreign Affairs that the seventy-one cases mentioned of border violations by Germans are being investigated. The investigation will require some time as the

---

[20] Latter not printed.

air force units and crews concerned will have to be interrogated individually. Please effect the early release by the Soviet Government of the plane that made the emergency landing near Rovno on April 15.

RITTER

Frame 217944, serial 426

The German Minister in Sweden (Wied) to the German Foreign Office

Telegram

Pol. I M 3378 g   STOCKHOLM, [May 16, 1941.]
No. 534 of May 16

I have learned that the Soviet Russian Minister here, Frau Kollontay, said recently that at no time in Russian history have there been stronger troop contingents assembled on Russia's western border than now.

WIED

Frame 113436, serial 105

Memorandum by the State Secretary in the German Foreign Office (Weizsäcker)

St. S. Nr. 340   BERLIN, May 17, 1941.

Ambassador Oshima asked me today in the course of a conversation on Japanese-American negotiations whether an "easing of tension" had occurred in German-Russian relations. I replied that German-Russian relations were unchanged. We were observing Russia carefully. Russian concentration at our border was a matter of common knowledge. That we had also sent German troops to the East in reply, was natural. We had not exactly liked everything the Russians had been doing in the last few months. I would not, however, call it a state of "tension."

In the diplomatic corps, the subject of Russia is much discussed. I recently told the Swedish Minister, in reply to a direct question, that developments between Germany and Russia depended on Stalin's conduct.

WEIZSÄCKER

Frame 217949, serial 426

The German Ambassador in the Soviet Union (Schulenburg) to the German Foreign Office

Telegram

No. 1193 of May 18   Moscow, May 17, 1941.

Reference your telegram No. 938 of May 14.

The case of the German plane that made the emergency landing near Rovno, with which the liaison staff of the Red Army and the Commissariat for Foreign Affairs are already occupied, was also brought up today with Secretary General Sobolev, with the request for early release of the airplane. At the same time, the communication ordered by you regarding the investigation of border violations by the Germans was made. S [obolev] countered that the Soviet Government awaited the German reply, and referred gravely to the fact that border violations by German planes were continuing and were still frequent.

SCHULENBURG

Frames 24480–24482, serial 34

The German Foreign Office to the German Ambassador in the Soviet Union (Schulenburg)

Telegram

BERLIN, May 24, 1941.

Reference your telegram No. 1192 of May 17.[21]

I. By Sobolev's reply, our wishes regarding the final demarcation of the boundary from the Igorka River to the Baltic Sea have been satisfactorily met. Since, however, the settlement of our claims under the treaty of January 10, 1941, has been protracted for months due to no fault of ours, both Minister von Saucken and Departmental Counselor Conrad had to be employed at other urgent tasks and are therefore not available at this time. We are trying to release them as soon as possible in order that they may resume their work in the Central Boundary Commission and we will shortly make a proposal for another date.

Since, under the circumstances, Assistant Wieber would have to remain idle there for ome time, while he is urgently needed here, please arrange for his return.

[21] Not printed.

II. The instrument of ratification for the treaty of January 10, 1941, has been executed by the Führer. Kindly notify the Soviet Government so that preparations for the exchange of documents can be made.

WOERMANN

Note for the Office of the Reich Foreign Minister, Fuschl

Berlin, May 24, 1941.

The intent of the attached telegram to Moscow is a further effort to treat in a dilatory manner the matter of the boundary commission, since otherwise the next step would be a survey of the boundary by a Mixed Commission.

On the other hand, Soviet wishes are deferred to, in that we have now declared ourselves prepared to exchange instruments of ratification for the boundary treaty of January 10, 1941.

WOERMANN

Frame 113450, serial 105

The German Ambassador in the Soviet Union (Schulenburg) to the German Foreign Office

Telegram

URGENT   Moscow, May 24, 1941—3:45 p. m.
SECRET   Received May 24, 1941—6:15 p. m.
No. 1223 of May 24

Reference my telegram No. 1092 of the 7th.

On May 22 I called on Molotov to discuss with him current negotiations on cultural questions, release of prisoners, etc. Molotov received me in the same study that he had formerly, surrounded by his usual staff in the Kremlin. He was as amiable, self-assured and well-informed as ever. The only difference was the name-plate at the entrance, bearing the new inscription "Molotov, Deputy Chairman, Council of People's Commissars." There was nothing to indicate that his position with Stalin was shaken or that his influence as People's Commissar for Foreign Affairs had suffered any diminution.

This and other observations made here since Stalin took over the supreme power of the state, show that the two strongest men in the Soviet Union—Stalin and Molotov—hold positions which are decisive for the foreign policy of the Soviet Union. That this foreign policy is, above all, directed at the avoidance of a conflict with Germany, is proved by the attitude taken by the Soviet Government during the last few weeks, the tone of the Soviet press, which treats all the events which concern Germany in an unobjectionable manner, and the observance of the trade agreements concluded with Germany.

SCHULENBURG

Frames 113497–113499, serial 105

The German Ambassador in the Soviet Union (Schulenburg) to the German Foreign Office

Telegram

No. 1368 of June 13   Moscow, June 14, 1941—1:30 a. m.
                                       Received June 14, 1941—8 a. m.

People's Commissar Molotov has just given me the following text of a Tass despatch which will be broadcast tonight and published in the papers tomorrow:

Even before the return of the English Ambassador Cripps to London, but especially after his return, there have been widespread rumors of "an impending war between the U.S.S.R. and Germany" in the English and foreign press. These rumors allege:

1. That Germany supposedly has made various territorial and economic demands on the U.S.S.R. and that at present negotiations are impending between Germany and the U.S.S.R. for the conclusion of a new and closer agreement between them;

2. That the Soviet Union is supposed to have declined these demands and that as a result Germany has begun to concentrate her troops on the frontier of the Soviet Union in order to attack the Soviet Union;

3. That on its side the Soviet Union is supposed to have begun intensive preparations for war with Germany and to have concentrated its troops on the German border.

Despite the obvious absurdity of these rumors, responsible circles in Moscow have thought it necessary, in view of the persistent spread of these rumors, to authorize Tass to state that these rumors are a clumsy propaganda maneuver of the forces arrayed against the Soviet Union and Germany, which are interested in a spread and intensification of the war.

Tass declares that:

1. Germany has addressed no demands to the Soviet Union and has asked for no new closer agreement, and that therefore negotiations cannot be taking place;

2. According to the evidence in the possession of the Soviet Union, both Germany and the Soviet Union are fulfilling to the letter the

terms of the Soviet-German Nonaggression Pact, so that in the opinion of Soviet circles the rumors of the intention of Germany to break the Pact and to launch an attack against the Soviet Union are completely without foundation, while the recent movements of German troops which have completed their operations in the Balkans, to the eastern and northern parts of Germany, must be explained by other motives which have no connection with Soviet-German relations;

3. The Soviet Union, in accordance with its peace policy, has fulfilled and intends to fulfill the terms of the Soviet-German Nonaggression Pact; as a result, all the rumors according to which the Soviet Union is preparing for a war with Germany are false and provocative;

4. The summer calling-up of the reserves of the Red Army which is now taking place and the impending maneuvers mean nothing but a training of the reservists and a check on the operations of the railroad system, which as is known takes place every year; consequently, it appears at least nonsensical to interpret these measures of the Red Army as an action hostile to Germany.

SCHULENBURG

Frame 103716, serial 93

The Reich Foreign Minister to the German Minister in Hungary (Erdmannsdorff)

Telegram

STATE SECRET   VENICE, June 15, 1941—9:40 p. m.
No. 552 of June 15   Received Berlin, June 15, 1941—10:15 p. m.
Transmitted to Budapest under No. 1021

For the Minister personally.
Please inform the Hungarian Minister President as follows:

In view of the heavy concentration of Russian troops at the German eastern border, the Führer will probably be compelled, by the beginning of July at the latest, to clarify German-Russian relations and in this connection to make certain demands. Since it is difficult to foretell the outcome of these negotiations, the German Government considers it necessary for Hungary to take steps to secure its frontiers.

The above order is of a strictly confidential nature. Please also mention this fact to the Hungarian Minister President.

RIBBENTROP

Frames 113558–113562, serial 105

The Reich Foreign Minister to the German Ambassador in the Soviet Union (Schulenburg)

Telegram

VERY URGENT   BERLIN, June 21, 1941.

STATE SECRET

By radio

For the Ambassador personally.

1) Upon receipt of this telegram, all of the cipher material still there is to be destroyed. The radio set is to be put out of commission.

2) Please inform Herr Molotov at once that you have an urgent communication to make to him and would therefore like to call on him immediately. Then please make the following declaration to him.

"The Soviet Ambassador in Berlin is receiving at this hour from the Reich Minister for Foreign Affairs a memorandum giving in detail the facts which are briefly summarized as follows:

"I. In 1939 the Government of the Reich, putting aside grave objections arising out of the contradiction between National Socialism and Bolshevism, undertook to arrive at an understanding with Soviet Russia. Under the treaties of August 23 and September 28, 1939, the Government of the Reich effected a general reorientation of its policy toward the U.S.S.R. and thenceforth adopted a cordial attitude toward the Soviet Union. This policy of goodwill brought the Soviet Union great advantages in the field of foreign policy.

"The Government of the Reich therefore felt entitled to assume that thenceforth both nations, while respecting each other's regime and not interfering in the internal affairs of the other partner, would arrive at good, lasting, neighborly relations. Unfortunately it soon became evident that the Government of the Reich had been entirely mistaken in this assumption.

"II. Soon after the conclusion of the German-Russian treaties, the Comintern resumed its subversive activity against Germany, with the official Soviet-Russian representatives giving assistance. Sabotage, terrorism, and espionage in preparation for war were demonstrably carried out on a large scale. In all the countries bordering on Germany and in the territories occupied by German troops, anti-German feeling was aroused and the German attempt to set up a stable order in Europe was combatted. Yugoslavia was gladly offered arms against Germany by the Soviet Russian Chief of Staff, as proved by documents found in Belgrade. The declarations made by the U.S.S.R. on conclusion of the treaties with Germany, regarding her intention to collaborate with Germany, thus stood revealed as deliberate misrepresentation and deceit and the conclusion of the treaties themselves as a tactical maneuver for obtaining arrangements favorable to Russia. The guiding principle remained the weakening of the non-Bolshevist countries in order the more easily to demoralize them and, at a given time, to crush them.

"III. In the diplomatic and military fields it became obvious that the U.S.S.R.—contrary to the declaration made at the conclusion of the treaties that she did not wish to Bolshevize and annex the countries falling within her sphere of influence—was intent on pushing her military might westward wherever it seemed possible and on carrying Bolshevism further into Europe. The action of the U.S.S.R. against the Baltic States, Finland, and Rumania, where Soviet claims even extended to Bucovina, showed this clearly. The occupation and Bolshevization by the Soviet Union of the sphere of influence granted to her clearly violated the Moscow agreements, even though the Government of the Reich for the time being accepted the facts.

"IV. When Germany, by the Vienna Award of August 30, 1940, settled the crisis in Southeastern Europe resulting from the action of the U.S.S.R. against Rumania, the Soviet Union protested and turned to making intensive military preparations in every field. Germany's renewed effort to achieve an understanding, as reflected in the exchange of letters between the Reich Foreign Minister and Herr Stalin and in the invitation to Herr Molotov to come to Berlin, brought demands from the Soviet Union which Germany could not accept, such as the guarantee of Bulgaria by the U.S.S.R., the establishment of a base for Soviet Russian land and naval forces at the Straits, and the complete abandonment of Finland. Subsequently, the policy of the U.S.S.R. directed against Germany became more and more obvious. The warning addressed to Germany regarding occupation of Bulgaria and the declaration made to Bulgaria after the entry of German troops, which was of a definitely hostile nature, were as significant in this connection as was the promise to protect the rear of Turkey in the event of a Turkish entry into the war in the Balkans, given in March 1941.

"V. With the conclusion of the Soviet-Yugoslav Treaty of Friendship of April 5 last, which was intended to stiffen the spines of the Yugoslav plotters, the U.S.S.R. joined the common Anglo-Yugoslav-Greek front against Germany. At the same time she tried *rapprochement* with Rumania, in order to induce that country to detach itself from Germany. It was only the rapid German victories that caused the failure of the Anglo-Russian plan for an attack against the German troops in Rumania and Bulgaria.

"VI. This policy was accompanied by a steadily growing concentration of all available Russian forces on a long front from the Baltic Sea to the Black Sea, against which countermeasures were taken by Germany only later. Since the beginning of the year this has been a steadily growing menace to the territory of the Reich. Reports received in the last few days eliminated the last remaining doubts as to the aggressive character of this Russian concentration and completed the picture of an extremely tense military situation. In addition to this, there are the reports from England regarding the negotiations of Ambassador Cripps for still closer political and military collaboration between England and the Soviet Union.

"To sum up, the Government of the Reich declares, therefore, that the Soviet Government, contrary to the obligations it assumed,
1) has not only continued, but even intensified its attempts to undermine Germany and Europe;
2) has adopted a more and more anti-German foreign policy;
3) has concentrated all its forces in readiness at the German border. Thereby the Soviet Government has broken its treaties with Germany and is about to attack Germany from the rear, in its struggle for life. The Führer has therefore ordered the German Armed Forces to oppose this threat with all the means at their disposal."

End of declaration.

Please do not enter into any discussion of this communication. It is incumbent upon the Government of Soviet Russia to safeguard the security of the Embassy personnel.

RIBBENTROP

Frames 038–031, serial F 20

Letter From Hitler to Mussolini

June 21, 1941.

DUCE!

I am writing this letter to you at a moment when months of anxious deliberation and continuous nerve-racking waiting are ending in the hardest decision of my life. I believe—after seeing the latest Russian situation map and after appraisal of numerous other reports—that I cannot take the responsibility for waiting longer, and above all, I believe that there is no other way of obviating this danger—unless it be further waiting, which, however, would necessarily lead to disaster in this or the next year at the latest.

The situation: England has lost this war. With the right of the drowning person, she grasps at every straw which, in her imagination might serve as a sheet anchor. Nevertheless, some of her hopes are naturally not without a certain logic. England has thus far always conducted her wars with help from the Continent. The destruction of France—in fact, the elimination of all west-European positions—is directing the glances of the British warmongers continually to the place from which they tried to start the war: to Soviet Russia.

Both countries, Soviet-Russia and England, are equally interested in a Europe fallen into ruin, rendered prostrate by a long war. Behind these two countries stands the North American Union goading them on and watchfully waiting. Since the liquidation of Poland, there is evident in Soviet-Russia a consistent trend, which, even if cleverly and cautiously, is nevertheless reverting firmly to the old

Bolshevist tendency to expansion of the Soviet State. The prolongation of the war necessary for this purpose is to be achieved by tying up German forces in the East, so that—particularly in the air—the German Command can no longer vouch for a large-scale attack in the West. I declared to you only recently, Duce, that it was precisely the success of the experiment in Crete that demonstrated how necessary it is to make use of every single airplane in the much greater project against England. It may well happen that in this decisive battle we would win with a superiority of only a few squadrons. I shall not hesitate a moment to undertake such a responsibility if, aside from all other conditions, I at least possess the one certainty that I will not then suddenly be attacked or even threatened from the East. The concentration of Russian forces—I had General Jodl submit the most recent map to your Attaché here, General Maras—is tremendous. Really, all available Russian forces are at our border. Moreover, since the approach of warm weather, work has been proceeding on numerous defenses. If circumstances should give me cause to employ the German air force against England, there is danger that Russia will then begin its strategy of extortion in the South and North, to which I would have to yield in silence, simply from a feeling of air inferiority. It would, above all, not then be possible for me, without adequate support from an air force, to attack the Russian fortifications with the divisions stationed in the East. If I do not wish to expose myself to this danger, then perhaps the whole year of 1941 will go by without any change in the general situation. On the contrary. England will be all the less ready for peace for it will be able to pin its hopes on the Russian partner. Indeed, this hope must naturally even grow with the progress in preparedness of the Russian armed forces. And behind this is the mass delivery of war material from America which they hope to get in 1942.

Aside from this, Duce, it is not even certain whether we shall have this time, for with so gigantic a concentration of forces on both sides—for I also, was compelled to place more and more armored units on the eastern border, and also to call Finland's and Rumania's attention to the danger—there is the possibility that the shooting will start spontaneously at any moment. A withdrawal on my part would, however, entail a serious loss of prestige for us. This would be particularly unpleasant in its possible effect on Japan. I have, therefore, after constantly racking my brains, finally reached the decision to cut the noose before it can be drawn tight. I believe,

Duce, that I am hereby rendering probably the best possible service to our joint conduct of the war this year. For my over-all view is now as follows:

1) *France* is, as ever, not to be trusted. Absolute surety that North Africa will not suddenly desert does not exist.

2) *North Africa* itself, insofar as your colonies, Duce, are concerned, is probably out of danger until fall. I assume that the British, in their last attack, wanted to relieve Tobruk. I do not believe they will soon be in a position to repeat this.

3) *Spain* is irresolute and—I am afraid—will take sides only when the outcome of the war is decided.

4) In *Syria*, French resistance can hardly be maintained permanently either with or without our help.

5) An attack on *Egypt* before autumn is out of the question altogether. I consider it necessary, however, taking into account the whole situation, to give thought to the development of an operational unit in Tripoli itself which can, if necessary, also be launched against the West. Of course, Duce, the strictest silence must be maintained with regard to these ideas, for otherwise we cannot expect France to continue to grant permission to use its ports for the transportation of arms and munitions.

6) Whether or not *America* enters the war is a matter of indifference, inasmuch as she supports our opponent with all the power she is able to mobilize.

7) The situation in England itself is bad; the provision of food and raw materials is growing steadily more difficult. The martial spirit to make war, after all, lives only on hopes. These hopes are based solely on two assumptions: Russia and America. We have no chance of eliminating America. But it does lie in our power to exclude Russia. The elimination of Russia means, at the same time, a tremendous relief for Japan in East Asia, and thereby the possibility of a much stronger threat to American activities through Japanese intervention.

I have decided under these circumstances, as I already mentioned, to put an end to the hypocritical performance in the Kremlin. I assume, that is to say, I am convinced, that Finland, and likewise Rumania, will forthwith take part in this conflict, which will ultimately free Europe, for the future also, of a great danger. General Maras informed us that you, Duce, wish also to make available at least one corps. If you have that intention, Duce—which I naturally accept with a heart filled with gratitude—the time for carrying it out will still be sufficiently long, for in this immense theater of war the troops cannot be assembled at all points at the same time anyway. You, Duce, can give the decisive aid, however, by strengthening your forces in North Africa, also, if possible, looking from Tripoli toward the West, by proceeding further to build up a group which, though it be small at first, can march into France in case of a French violation of the treaty; and finally, by carrying the air war and, so far as it is possible, the submarine war, in intensified degree, into the Mediterranean.

So far as the security of the territories in the West is concerned, from Norway to and including France, we are strong enough there— so far as army troops are concerned—to meet any eventuality with lightning speed. So far as the air war on England is concerned, we shall, for a time, remain on the defensive,—but this does not mean that we might be incapable of countering British attacks on Germany; on the contrary, we shall, if necessary, be in a position to start ruthless bombing attacks on British home territory. Our fighter defense, too, will be adequate. It consists of the best squadrons that we have.

As far as the war in the East is concerned, Duce, it will surely be difficult, but I do not entertain a second's doubt as to its great success. I hope, above all, that it will then be possible for us to secure a common food-supply base in the Ukraine for some time to come, which will furnish us such additional supplies as we may need in the future. I may state at this point, however, that, as far as we can tell now, this year's German harvest promises to be a very good one. It is conceivable that Russia will try to destroy the Rumanian oil region. We have built up a defense that will—or so I think—prevent the worst. Moreover, it is the duty of our armies to eliminate this threat as rapidly as possible.

If I waited until this moment, Duce, to send you this information, it is because the final decision itself will not be made until 7 o'clock to-night. I earnestly beg you, therefore, to refrain, above all, from making any explanation to your Ambassador at Moscow, for there is no absolute guarantee that our coded reports cannot be decoded. I, too, shall wait until the last moment to have my own Ambassador informed of the decisions reached.

The material that I now contemplate publishing gradually, is so exhaustive that the world will have more occasion to wonder at our forbearance than at our decision, except for that part of the world which opposes us on principle and for which, therefore, arguments are of no use.

Whatever may now come, Duce, our situation cannot become worse as a result of this step; it can only improve. Even if I should be obliged at the end of this year to leave 60 or 70 divisions in Russia, that is only a fraction of the forces that I am now continually using on the eastern front. Should England nevertheless not draw any conclusions from the hard facts that present themselves, then we can, with our rear secured, apply ourselves with increased strength to the dispatching of our opponent. I can promise you, Duce, that what lies in our German power, will be done.

Any desires, suggestions, and assistance of which you, Duce, wish to inform me in the contingency before us, I would request that you either communicate to me personally or have them agreed upon directly by our military authorities.

In conclusion, let me say one more thing, Duce. Since I struggled through to this decision, I again feel spiritually free. The partnership with the Soviet Union, in spite of the complete sincerity of the efforts to bring about a final conciliation, was nevertheless often very irksome to me, for in some way or other it seemed to me to be a break with my whole origin, my concepts, and my former obligations. I am happy now to be relieved of these mental agonies.

With hearty and comradely greetings,

Your
[ADOLF HITLER]

Frames 24545–24548, serial 34

Memorandum by the State Secretary in the German Foreign Office (Weizsäcker)

St. S. Pol. No. 411
BERLIN, June 21, 1941.

MEMORANDUM

The Russian Ambassador, who had wanted to call on the Reich Foreign Minister today and had been referred to me instead, called on me this evening at 9 : 30 p. m. and handed me the attached *note verbale*.

This note refers to a complaint of the Russian Government of April 21 of this year, regarding 80 cases of flights of German aircraft over Soviet territory in the spring of this year. In the meanwhile, says the note, 180 more flights of this kind had taken place, against which the Soviet Border Patrol had each time filed a protest with the German representatives at the border. Moreover, the flights had assumed a systematic and intentional character.

In conclusion, the *note verbale* expresses confidence that the German Government will take steps to put an end to these border violations.

I replied to the Soviet Ambassador as follows: Since I was not acquainted with the details and in particular was not conversant with the protests allegedly filed at the border between the local authorities, I would have to refer the *note verbale* to the competent offices. I did not wish to anticipate the German reply. I should like to say only this much in advance, namely, that I, on the contrary, had been informed of wholesale border violations by Soviet aircraft over German territory; it was therefore the German and not the Russian Government that had cause for complaint.

When Herr Dekanosov tried to prolong the conversation somewhat, I told him that since I had an entirely different opinion than he and had to await the opinion of my Government, it would be better not to go more deeply into the matter just now. The reply would be forthcoming later.

The Ambassador agreed to the procedure and left me.

As a German interpreter for Russian could not be located at the time, I had Minister von Grundherr attend the conversation as a witness.

Submitted herewith to the Reich Foreign Minister.

VON WEIZSÄCKER

[Enclosure]

The Soviet Embassy in Germany to the German Foreign Office

No. 013166

NOTE VERBALE

By order of the Soviet Government, the Embassy of the Union of Soviet Socialist Republics in Germany has the honor to make the following statement to the German Government:

The People's Commissariat for Foreign Affairs of the U.S.S.R. by *note verbale* of April 21 [22] informed the German Embassy in Moscow of the violations of the border of the Union of Soviet Socialist Republics by German aircraft, which in the period from March 27 to April 18 of this year amounted to 80 cases registered by the Soviet Border Guard. A reply to the foregoing note has not yet been received from the German Government. On the contrary, the Soviet Government must state that violations of the Soviet boundary by German aircraft during the last two months, namely, from April 19 of this year up to and including June 19 of this year, have not only not ceased, but are increasing and have assumed a systematic character, attaining the number of 180 in this period, regarding each of which a protest was made

---

[22] For contents, see telegram No. 957 of April 21 from the German Chargé in the Soviet Union, *ante*, p. 328.

by the Soviet Border Guard to the German representatives at the border. The systematic nature of these flights and the fact that in several cases German aircraft penetrated 100 to 150 kilometers and more into the U.S.S.R. preclude the possibility that these violations of the border of the U.S.S.R. by German aircraft could have been accidental.

In drawing the attention of the German Government to this situation, the Soviet Government expects the German Government to take measures toward putting an end to the violations of the Soviet border by German aircraft.

BERLIN, June 21, 1941.

Frame 113550, serial 105

The German Ambassador in the Soviet Union (Schulenburg) to the German Foreign Office

Telegram

VERY URGENT   Moscow, June 22, 1941—1:17 a. m.
SECRET   Received June 22, 1941—2:30 a. m.
No. 1424 of June 21

Molotov summoned me to his office this evening at 9:30 p. m. After he had mentioned the alleged repeated border violations by German aircraft, with the remark that Dekanosov had been instructed to call on the Reich Foreign Minister in this matter, Molotov stated as follows:

There were a number of indications that the German Government was dissatisfied with the Soviet Government. Rumors were even current that a war was impending between Germany and the Soviet Union. They found sustenance in the fact that there was no reaction whatsoever on the part of Germany to the Tass report of June 13; that it was not even published in Germany. The Soviet Government was unable to understand the reasons for Germany's dissatisfaction. If the Yugoslav question had at the time given rise to such dissatisfaction, he—Molotov—believed that, by means of his earlier communications, he had cleared up this question, which, moreover, was a thing of the past. He would appreciate it if I could tell him what had brought about the present situation in German-Soviet Russian relations.

I replied that I could not answer his question, as I lacked the pertinent information; that I would, however, transmit his communication to Berlin.

SCHULENBURG

Frames 47072–47075, serial 67

Memorandum of the Conversation Between the Reich Foreign Minister and Soviet Russian Ambassador Dekanosov in the Foreign Office at 4 a. m. on June 22, [1941]

Aufz. RAM 37/41

The Reich Foreign Minister began the conversation with the remark that the hostile attitude of the Soviet Government toward Germany and the serious threat that Germany saw in the Russian concentration on the eastern border of Germany, had forced the Reich to military countermeasures. Dekanosov would find a detailed statement of the reasons for the German attitude in the memorandum, which the Reich Foreign Minister then handed him.[23] The Reich Foreign Minister added that he regretted very much this development in German-Russian relations as he in particular had made every attempt to bring about better relations between the two countries. It had, however, unfortunately transpired that the ideological conflict between the two countries had become stronger than common sense, upon which he, the Reich Foreign Minister, had pinned his hopes. He had nothing further, the Reich Foreign Minister said in conclusion to add to his remarks.

Dekanosov replied that he had asked for an interview with the Reich Foreign Minister because, in the name of the Soviet Government, he wanted to pose a few questions that, in his opinion, required clarification.

The Reich Foreign Minister thereupon replied that he had nothing to add to what he had already stated. He had hoped that the two countries would contrive a sensible relationship with each other. He had been deceived in this great hope for reasons that were explained in detail in the memorandum just delivered. The hostile policy of the Soviet Government toward Germany, which had reached its climax in the conclusion of a pact with Yugoslavia at the very time of the German-Yugoslav conflict, had been evident for a year. At a moment when Germany was engaged in a life-and-death struggle, the attitude of Soviet-Russia, particularly the concentration of the Russian military forces at the Soviet border, had presented so serious a threat to

---

[23] Not printed here.

the Reich that the Führer had to decide to take military counter-measures. The policy of compromise between the two countries had therefore been unsuccessful. This was, however, by no means the fault of the Reich Government, which had carried out the German-Russian treaty in detail, but was attributable rather to a hostile atti-tude of Soviet Russia toward Germany, that had existed for some time. Under the pressure of a serious threat of a political and mili-tary nature which was emanating from Soviet Russia Germany had since this morning taken the appropriate countermeasures in the military sphere. The Reich Foreign Minister regretted not to be able to add anything to these remarks, especially since he himself had had to conclude that, in spite of earnest efforts, he had not succeeded in creating sensible relations between the two countries.

Dekanosov replied briefly that, for his part too, he exceedingly re-gretted this development, which was based on a completely erroneous conception on the part of the German Government, and, in view of this situation, he had nothing further to say except that the status of the Russian Embassy would now be arranged with the competent German authorities.

He thereupon took leave of the Reich Foreign Minister.

MINISTER SCHMIDT

BERLIN, June 22, 1941.

NOTE ON FILES

The documents selected for inclusion in this publication have been taken from the special file of the Reich Foreign Minister, from the regular files of the German Foreign Office, and from the files of the German Embassy in Moscow which were returned to Germany in 1941 shortly before the outbreak of war between Germany and the Soviet Union.

Those from the special file of the Reich Foreign Minister are copies which were separated out from the regular Foreign Office files for the use of the personal office of the Reich Foreign Minister.

Those from the regular files of the German Foreign Office include papers from the files of the Bureau of the Reich Foreign Minister; of the State Secretary; of the Under State Secretary; of the political divisions (*Pol*), especially those of *Pol V*, dealing with the Soviet Union; of Dr. Ritter, the commercial specialist of the Foreign Office; and of Dr. Paul Schmidt, who acted at conferences as interpreter for Hitler and the Reich Foreign Minister.

The documents from the Moscow Embassy files include personal papers of the Ambassador Count von der Schulenburg, the secret political reports of the Embassy, the Embassy's general files on relations of Germany with the Soviet Union, and numerous other files, many of them containing material concerning German foreign policy sent by the Foreign Office to the Embassy for its information.

The documents of the Foreign Office and the Embassy were bound into volumes by the Germans. These volumes have been filmed and the documents published in this collection are identified in each case by the film serial number and the frame numbers on the film, which are printed in the upper left-hand corner of each document. The following list, showing the film serial number and the description of the German file, permits ready identification of the exact location in the German Foreign Office archives of the copy used for this publication.

Film Serial Numbers	*German File*
F 1–F 20	Special file of the Reich Foreign Minister.
34	
(frames 23886–24248)	S t a t e Secretary: Russia—July–December 1939.

Film Serial Numbers	*German File*
34 (frames 23181/1–23885 and 24249–24884)	Under State Secretary (Political Affairs) : Soviet Union.
66	Files of Dr. Paul Schmidt, volumes 1 and 2.
67	Files of Dr. Paul Schmidt, volumes 3, 4, and 5.
93	State Secretary: Hungary, volume 4.
103	State Secretary: Russia, volumes 1 and 2.
104	State Secretary: Russia, volumes 3 and 4.
105	State Secretary: Russia, volume 5.
127	Moscow Embassy: *Pol 2 Nr. 1*, volumes 1–3—Political relations between the Soviet Union and Germany.
147	Bureau of Reich Foreign Minister: Poland Conflict.
155	*Pol VIII, Japan 2*, volume 5—Political relations between Japan and Germany.
165	Moscow Embassy: *Pol g*, volumes 3 and 4—Secret Political Papers.
177	State Secretary: Japan, volume 3.
270	Moscow Embassy: *Pol g*, volume 1—Secret Political Papers.
273	*Pol V, Russland 2 Nr. 3 Molotow*—Visit of the Chairman of the Council of People's Commissars and Foreign Commissar Molotov to Berlin in November 1940.
276	Moscow Embassy: Personal files of Ambassador Count von der Schulenburg, Political, volume 1.
292	Moscow Embassy: *Sonderakte–Geheim–Politik*—Special secret political file.
354	Moscow Embassy: *Sonderakte–SD Pol 2. Krieg*, volume 2—Special file, Political relations between Germany and other countries. War.
357	Moscow Embassy: *Sonderakte–SD Pol 2. Krieg*, volume 3—Special file, Political relations between Germany and other countries. War.

Film Serial Numbers	German File
380	Moscow Embassy: *Pol 2 Nr. 3 Balk*, volume 3—Political relations of the Soviet Union with the Balkan States.
384	*Pol V–Russland 2*, volume 3—Political relations of Russia with Germany.
388	*Pol V–Russland 2*, volume 2—Political relations of Russia with Germany.
407	Under State Secretary (Political Affairs): Incidents in relations between Lithuania, Latvia and Estonia, and the Soviet Union.
426	Moscow Embassy: *Pol Mil. g*, volume 1—Military affairs (secret).
432	Moscow Embassy: *Pol 2 Nr. 3 Balt*, volume 2—Political relations of the Soviet Union with the Baltic States.
439	State Secretary: Correspondence on political affairs, volume 6.
459	State Secretary: Differences between Rumania and Russia.
472	State Secretary: Correspondence with German diplomatic representatives abroad, volume 6.
485	State Secretary: Memoranda of diplomatic visits, volume 6.
495	State Secretary: Memoranda of diplomatic visits, volume 7.
506	State Secretary: Memoranda of diplomatic visits, volume 8.
644	Political Division: Treaties, Soviet Union, 1939–1941.
695	Moscow Embassy: *Pol 2 Nr. 1*, volume 1—Political relations between the Soviet Union and Germany. Supplementary to serial 127.
838	Under State Secretary Hencke: Personal, Moscow 1939–1940.
1228	Political Division: *Pol geheim, Russland*, volume 7—Political affairs, Russia, Secret file.
1337	Files of Dr. Megerle: *Megerle 2, 8*—Reports from OKW to Reich Government on Soviet Russian aggression against Germany.
1369	Files of Ambassador Ritter: Moscow, volume 1.

Film Serial Numbers	*German File*
1379	Moscow Embassy: *Pol 2 Nr. 1*, volume 3—Political relations between the Soviet Union and Germany. Supplementary to serial 127.
1448	Moscow Embassy: *Pol g*, volume 4—Secret Political Papers. Supplementary to serial 165.

○

90 0707626 X

**This book is to be returned on or before
the last date stamped below.**

-6. FEB. 1998

27. FEB. 1998

CANCELLED

-6 NOV 2000

**PLYMOUTH POLYTECHNIC
LEARNING RESOURCES CENTRE**

Telephone
Ply. 21312
Ext. 219

Telex
45423

A book may be renewed by telephone or by personal visit
if it is not required by another reader.
CHARGES WILL BE MADE FOR OVERDUE BOOKS.